EMIL HOLUB's *Travels*
north of the Zambezi
1885–6

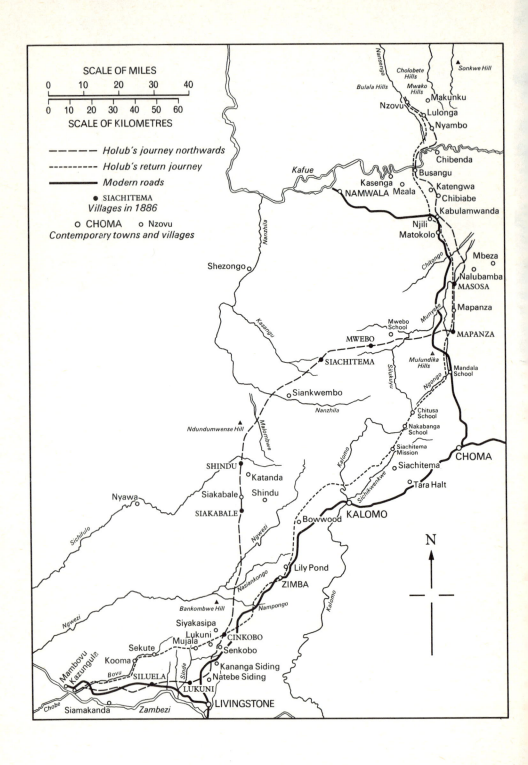

SCALE OF MILES

0   10   20   30   40

SCALE OF KILOMETRES

0 10 20 30 40 50 60

– – – – – *Holub's journey northwards*

- - - - - - *Holub's return journey*

────── *Modern roads*

● SIACHITEMA
Villages in 1886

○ CHOMA   ○ Nzovu
Contemporary towns and villages

Nansenga
Cholobete Hills
▲ Sonkwe Hill
Bulala Hills
Mwako Hills
Nzovu
● Makunku
● Lulonga
● Nyambo

Kafue
● Chibenda
Busangu
Kasenga
● Maala
NAMWALA
● Katengwa
● Chibiabe
Kabulamwanda

Nanzhila

Njili
Matokolo

Chitongo
● Mbeza
● Nalubamba
MASOSA

Shezongo

Kasangu
Mwebo School
Munyeke
● Mapanza
MAPANZA

MWEBO
● SIACHITEMA

Mulundika Hills
Mandala School

Silukuyu
● Siankwembo
Nanzhila
Ngongo
Chitusa School
Nakabanga School

Malombwe
Ndundumwense Hill ▲

Kalomo
Siachitema Mission
● Siachitema
CHOMA

SHINDU
● Katanda
Shindu
Siakabale
SIAKABALE

Sichikwenkwe
● Tara Halt

Nyawa

Ngwezi
Bowwood
KALOMO

Sichifulo

N

Ngwezi
Lily Pond
ZIMBA

Nasiankongo
Bankombwe Hill ▲
Nampongo
Kalomo

Ngwezi
Siyakasipa
Lukuni
Mujala
CINKOBO
Sekute
Kooma
Senkobo
Kananga Siding
Mambovu
Kazungula
Bovu
SILUELA
Sinde
Natebe Siding
LUKUNI
Chobe
Siamakanda
Zambezi
LIVINGSTONE

LIST OF ILLUSTRATIONS

FRONTISPIECE

Map of Emil Holub's route prepared by Ladislav Holy

Emil Holub's sketches are reproduced by courtesy of the Naprstek Museum of
African, American and Asian cultures, Prague

INTRODUCTION

THIS BOOK IS THE SECOND VOLUME of Holub's travelogue first published in 1890 in German under the title *Von der Capstadt ins Land der Maschukulumbe*. It is Holub's personal record of his journey north of the Zambezi into the Ila country beyond the Kafue River which led for its most part through the outer provinces of the Lozi kingdom ruled not directly by the Lozi but by local chiefs who were responsible mainly for forwarding tribute to Lozi kings. It was conducted at the time of one of the most turbulent periods of the Barotse history with more civil strife than at any other period.

Lozi king Sipopa, who ascended the throne after his successful rebellion against the Kololo rule in Barotseland in 1864, was killed in 1876 and Mwanawina II was appointed king. There was a rebellion against him in 1878 and Mwanawina fled to the east trying in vain to regain the throne. Lubosi, the son of Sipopa's brother, later known as Lewanika, became the king. In 1884 Lewanika was attacked by chiefs led by Mataa who attempted to kill him. He escaped and took refuge with the Mashi in the south while Akufuna Tatila ascended the throne with Mataa as his *ngambela*. In October 1885 when Holub was already in Panda-ma-Tenga, Lewanika, supported by the people of the south of the Zambezi valley, regained the throne in a fight against Mataa and Sikufule, the chief at Lukwakwa who aspired for the throne himself. After regaining the throne Lewanika took revenge on the relatives and supporters of Mataa. Malusiane of Sesheke was attacked in December 1885; he escaped and fled to the Tonga chief Siachitema, whom Holub visited shortly afterwards. Holub himself witnessed Lewanika's revenge against Leswane, a chief or headman responsible for the ford in Kazungula who also sided with Mataa in the rebellion against Lewanika.

Crossing the Zambezi, Holub thus entered the area of great political uncertainty. Moreover, many Toka chiefs[1] through whose territories he travelled had a tendency to regard the Lozi rather as enemies than lords, irrespective of which king was ruling over Barotseland at the moment. Holub had quickly acquired certain insights into the situation and sometimes managed to play the various political forces off one against another in his quest for porters. The fact that he was never able to understand fully all the various political forces at play was at the same time the main reason why his journey ended differently from what he had intended. Holub's story gives a vivid impression of the political and inter-tribal relationships north of the Zambezi at the end of the nineteenth century, shortly before this area was open to systematic European penetration. This story is told by a man who was at that time certainly not a novice to African travels.

Emil Holub was born on 7 October 1847 in Holice, in what is now Czechoslovakia, as a son of a physician. Already during his high school years he was interested in natural history, archaeology and geography. He was greatly influenced by David Livingstone's books of travels and following Livingstone's example he decided to study medicine, considering a medical career to be the best preparation for his intended African travels. He studied at the Charles University in Prague from 1866 to 1872 and immediately after graduation he started to prepare himself for the departure to South Africa. He mentions three main motives which led to his decision: first of all, he wanted Austrians, or specifically Czechs, also to take part in the exploration of Africa as well as the British, French, German and Portuguese; second, he wanted to assemble a large natural-historical and ethnographic collection and build an African museum in Prague; and last, he wanted to find in Africa a suitable new land for Czech emigrants.

Holub left Prague for Africa on 18 May 1872, being financially supported by Vojta Naprsteck, founder of the ethnological museum in Prague.[2] On the 26 May he boarded a boat in Southampton and on 1 July he landed in Cape Town whence he proceeded further to Port Elisabeth. After a short stay he left through Fauresmith for the diamond fields near Kimberley and settled down in Dutoitspan where he started to practise medicine with the intention of financing his future travels in Africa from the proceeds. He undertook his first journey at the beginning of 1873; its main purpose was to get experience in travelling in Africa. He made a trip to Taung and the present Schweizer-Reneke in the Harts valley and he travelled in the Vaal valley through Christiana and Bloemhof to Potchefstroom, from which place he visited stalactitic caves and Wonderfontein, west of the present Johannesburg. At the end of 1873 he set off on another journey from Dutoitspan. Through Taung and Molepole he travelled to Shoshong which he reached in January 1874. From there he returned through Marice valley and Dwars Berg via Zeerust and Potchefstroom back to Dutoitspan.

Holub practised medicine throughout the whole of the next year to earn enough money to be able to finance his major expedition to the Zambezi which he started on 2 March 1875. Through Christiana and Zeerust he again travelled to Shoshong and from there through Makarikari Salt Pan to Panda-ma-Tenga which he reached on 31 July.

Panda-ma-Tenga, on the present Botswana–Rhodesia border, thirty-seven miles south of the Zambezi, was at that time a small settlement on a rocky hill at the headwater stream of the Matetsi river. It had permanent water and was a starting point for European traders, hunters and travellers going to the Zambezi valley and the Victoria Falls. One could reach Panda-ma-Tenga from the south in ox wagons travelling on more or less regular roads; travellers heading for the Zambezi left their wagons here because of the tsetse fly beyond. For many years after 1871, Panda-ma-Tenga was the headquarters of the trader George Westbeech and his long-time partner George Blockley.[3]

Holub met Blockley upon his arrival at Panda-ma-Tenga. He learned from him that Westbeech, who was at that time absent, had heard of Holub's arrival from a missionary in Shoshong and that he had reported it to the Lozi king Sipopa in Sesheke who had willingly granted Holub permission to pay him a visit. Holub grasped this opportunity and together with Blockley, who had already spent several months in Sesheke, set off on 3 August 1875. On 9 August they reached the Chobe mouth and ten days later they were in Sesheke where Holub met Sipopa. Through Blockley acting as an interpreter he discussed with Sipopa his future travel plans. Sipopa tried to discourage him from travelling by boat upstream on the Zambezi and recommended instead a foot journey to the Lake Bangweulu. Seeing that he had to rely on the help of an interpreter, he advised him to learn an African language. However, Holub, who apart from Czech and German, spoke limited English, succeeded in picking up only a few Lozi words.

On 30 August Holub left Sesheke for Panda-ma-Tenga to prepare himself for his journey north along the Zambezi to its source. In Panda-ma-Tenga he met Westbeech and his wife, who together with five other traders planned a trip to the Victoria Falls. Holub joined their party and visited the Falls on 7 September. On 24 September the party was back in Panda-ma-Tenga and at the beginning of October Holub was again in Sesheke together with Blockley and Westbeech. He stayed there continuously for almost three months and on 1 December started his eagerly awaited boat journey up-stream on the Zambezi. He only reached Ngambwe rapids, however, fourteen miles north of Katima

Mulilo. After wrecking a dugout canoe containing his medical chest and collected specimens and after he had fallen seriously ill, he returned to Seskeke on 9 December. He hoped
to convalesce and resume his travels, but as his condition did not improve, he followed
Westbeech's advice and after a month went south. He stayed for over a month in Shoshong and for almost three months in Zeerust practising medicine to earn money to finance his travels. On 26 November 1876 he returned to Kimberley after twenty-seven
months of travelling.

In January 1877, Holub exhibited his collection in Kimberley, hoping to raise funds
through this action to enable him to return to Europe. The exhibition, however, appeared
to be a financial loss and Holub was once again facing serious financial difficulties. He
again resumed his medical practice, interrupted by occasional exploratory and hunting
expeditions. In December 1878 he started his journey back to Cape Town. He interrupted
it to stay for six months in Cradock practising medicine, and eventually on 5 August 1879
he left Cape Town, arriving in Prague on 18 October.

He brought with him 30,900 ethnographic and natural-historical specimens. The most
important part of his travels was his more than four months' stay in Seskeke devoted to
systematic ethnographic investigations and observations. While still in Kimberley, he
wrote up the result of his ethnographic research conducted in Seskeke in the form of a
short monograph which was published by the Geographical Society in Vienna in 1879
under the title *A Cultural Sketch of the Marutse-Mambunda Empire*. It remained the most important of all Holub's scholarly writings. It is not only the first ethnographic account of
the Barotse, but one of the earliest of all ethnographic monographs.

Holub devoted his stay in Europe to lecturing about his experiences in Africa and to
writing a book of travels and several articles dealing primarily with ethnography and
ornithology of Africa south of the Zambezi.[4] During his four years' stay in Europe he was
busily preparing himself for his second Africa expedition. His ultimate plan was to cross
the African continent from the south to the north, starting again in Cape Town. From
there he wanted to reach the Zambezi, explore Barotseland and particularly the area between the Zambezi and Kafue rivers. The expedition should then have proceeded to Lake
Bangweulu and followed the course of the Congo River. Holub wanted then to explore
the course of the Uele River and eventually reach Egypt through Darfur. He estimated
that he would need three years to accomplish his plans.

The expedition was planned on a big scale. From seven hundred applicants Holub
selected six men to accompany him to Africa: Josef Spilar, Antonin Haluska, Oswald
Söllner, Karl Bukacz, Ignaz Leeb and Fekete Janos. All six were ex-servicemen and skilled
artisans. The first two were Czechs, the other three Austrians and the last a Hungarian. By
having all the major nationalities of the Austrian–Hungarian empire represented, the
expedition became a true Austrian–Hungarian undertaking, which enabled Holub to gain
better financial support for it than if he had had to rely on limited financial resources in
Bohemia alone. The last member of the expedition was Rosa Hof, a daughter of the Inspector of the exhibition buildings in the Prater of Vienna, whom Holub married in 1883,
two weeks before departing for his second African journey.

The expedition left Prague in November 1883; Holub and his party boarded a boat in
Hamburg on 22 November and after a month landed in Cape Town. They set out on a
journey to the north travelling through Colesberg, Fauresmith, Jagersfontein, Bloshof,
Christiana, Bloemhof, Lichtenburg and Zeerust to Shoshong, which they reached at the
end of July 1884. On the way north from Shoshong at Matlamanyane Pans, Holub met
with the first serious accident: several of his draught oxen died after having grazed on

some poisonous plant. He was, however, able to resume his journey and the expedition reached Panda-ma-Tenga on 26 September 1885. From there they travelled first to the Victoria Falls, which they reached on 15 October. On 7 November they were back in Panda-ma-Tenga, all except Mrs Holub suffering from heavy attacks of malaria. Holub was busy with preparations for the journey north of the Zambezi. On 1 February he started another short journey from Panda-ma-Tenga to the Lesuma valley and the Chobe mouth where he wanted to complete his natural-historical collections which were to be sent south before the final departure of the expedition north across the Zambezi. During this journey, Bukacz, Spiral and Haluska fell seriously ill. Spiral never recovered from the serious attacks of malaria and died in the Lesuma valley on 23 March 1886. The others returned to Panda-ma-Tenga on 3 April. Karl Bukacz first recovered, but then he suddenly and unexpectedly died on 9 May. Haluska's condition remained serious and Holub decided to send him back to Europe with his collections. On 24 May two of Holub's big ox-wagons fully loaded with collected specimens left Panda-ma-Tenga for the south with Haluska in charge of the transport. As Westbeech was sending his own wagons to the Lesuma valley, Holub used this opportunity and sent with them most of his luggage in the company of Oswald Söllner.[5]

Apart from Holub himself and his wife, the members of his trans-African expedition were reduced to three other Europeans: Söllner, Fekete and Leeb. Holub had twenty African servants, each willing to accompany him for three years for the payment of a rifle. The three most important of them were Jonas, a Toka whom Holub considered to be his best interpreter, and Boy and Mapani, his Kalanga interpreters.

I turn now briefly to the book itself. As all explorers of his time, Holub had no one specialised interest. The range of his interests covering ethnography and all fields of natural history is well reflected in his narrative. To bring out his inaccuracies in these many differing fields would require editing his text page by page. As the book is being published for its value as a primary historical source, this is not necessary. Not to overload the publication with notes, no attempt was made to evaluate Holub's natural-historical observations; his ethnographic observations are commented on only when they seem to be obviously wrong. The names of people and places in the book are given in Holub's German transcription; very often place-prefixes of Bantu languages are treated by Holub as an inherent part of the name, and the spelling of many names which Holub learned from his guides and interpreters is sothoized. It seems that some places, especially rivers and streams, are no longer known under the names attributed to them by Holub. Wherever it is possible, modern names and modern spellings of Holub's names are given in the glossary. Since apart from a few Lozi words, Holub did not know any African language, most of his vernacular expressions are extremely inaccurate in spelling and sometimes only vaguely resemble the actual words they are supposed to stand for. Relying completely on his interpreters and on his own limited knowledge of Lozi, Holub puts Lozi words into mouths of people who could not possibly have spoken anything else but Tonga or Ila.

The highlights of Holub's narrative are his stay in the Ila country and the Ila attack on his camp at Lulonga which, I think, deserve a short comment. Holub was not the only European who had bad experiences with the Ila. In 1888 Selous had virtually the same experience as Holub had two years earlier,[6] and as late as 1903 Rawson had an armed engagement with the Ila.[7] On the other hand, the first missionaries who settled among the Ila in the early nineties encountered no difficulties.[8]

It is impossible not to agree with Smith and Dale who conclude that Holub displayed a lack of courage and tact in dealing with the Ila, that he was over-suspicious at times, often led astray by his interpreters and that if he had been more tactful with the people, had understood them better and had shown a bolder front, he would have had a milder adventure.[9]

From his own narrative Holub appears as a rather arrogant man, not too patient in any of his dealings with the Africans and always suspicious of them. His own evidence clearly reveals how considerably his impatient and suspicious attitude towards the Africans and his arrogance increased after he had crossed the southern border of the Ila country. Holub came to the Ila clearly prejudiced towards them as enemies. He had his preconceptions confirmed by imputing motives which he could not possibly have known into the actions of the Ila. He had them equally confirmed by overhearing and claiming to understand people talking in a language which he did not know. He persuaded himself that the Ila were hostile towards him. In most of his initial encounters with them his own narrative shows that they were not aggressive. Instead of with open hostility, he was received with wariness and suspicion, justifiable in the light of Ila experience with Arab slave traders, the only 'white men' they had met so far. The fact that Holub travelled with Lewanika's permission could not improve the situation; only four years before Holub's arrival, the Ila were raided by the Lozi. Mutual understanding of each other's intentions never rose above this level of suspicion. Holub, more than the Ila, was responsible for the situation. He never tried to explain to them why he came or to persuade them practically of his good intentions.

While travelling in Toka and Tonga areas, Holub met chiefs formally and distributed presents to them. He made no attempt to behave in the same way among the Ila, who were his enemies long before he actually met them. Several events which he records himself could not possibly have improved his tense relations with them: he shot a dog of the Ila; he used as firewood poles obviously lent and not sold to him by the Ila for construction of his own camp; he poured carbolic acid over the naked feet of the Ila sitting at his fire, etc. When in spite of all that he managed to march through nine-tenths of the Ila territory, one can hardly avoid the feeling that he would have passed safely through the Ila country if he had behaved less arrogantly and more diplomatically and if he had at least adopted the same approach towards the Ila as towards their southern neighbours.

In the last three chapters of his book, which have been omitted from this edition, Holub describes his return journey from Panda-ma-Tenga to Cape Town and back to Prague. He was again facing severe financial difficulties and intended to start practising medicine in Shoshong to earn money for his journey back to Europe and for the transport of his collections. While in Shoshong he received the good news that the Czech committee established for his support was sending the first instalment of the proceeds from a public collection which enabled him to pay his debts. Later he received another subvention which enabled him to return to Europe.

Back home, Holub immediately started writing his second book of travels, published several articles in different popular magazines and journals and engaged in intensive lecturing not only in Austria but also in Germany, England and France. At the same time he was preparing a big exhibition of his collections which was opened in May 1891 in the Prater of Vienna and a year later transferred to Prague. Although both exhibitions were visited by almost four hundred thousand people, they were still a financial loss for Holub. Holub's original plan to establish an African museum in Prague did not materialise for many reasons, and his collection eventually ended up scattered in the museums in Vienna, Prague, Budapest, Lisbon, Madrid, Rome, Paris, Leningrad, Belgrade, Bucharest, Athens, Brussels, Munich, Stuttgart and Jena. Apart from that, Holub made generous donations to almost six hundred schools. He negotiated for a display of his collections in Chicago, but his attempts failed as he was not able to meet the cost of transport and could not find anybody willing to subsidise him. After all attempts to move his collections to America failed, in 1894 he was at least invited to give lectures in Chicago, New York, Omaha, Milwaukee and St Paul.

Holub spent the last seven years of his life in Vienna suffering from malaria and sciatica, disappointed about the failure of his plans and bitter about what he thought was a complete lack of comprehension and understanding for his work and efforts in the public as well as the scientific circles of Austria. He never resumed his medical practice and made his living only by writing and lecturing. He died in poverty on 21 February, 1902.[10]

Livingstone, 1972   LADISLAV HOLY

I

Departure for
the trip north of the Zambezi
From Panda-ma-Tenka
to Gazungula

BEFORE I LEAVE PANDA-MA-TENKA where the mission station was abandoned in 1885[1] and the trading post was given up after Westbech's death in 1888,[2] I consider it necessary to make a few comments about the problem of the African slave trade which today has become of new importance, at least as it concerns the Zambezi area. The British Government has already spent millions for the suppression of slavery, yet nevertheless it has not been able to date to crush this traffic in human beings—not even along the coasts! Neither will the very recent action of Britain and Germany reach this goal. The sums which are reportedly spent for this purpose are at most sufficient to undermine the transportation by ship along the coasts. One should not think that slavery and trade in human beings are the rule only among Moslem tribes. On the contrary, almost all African tribes for as long as we have knowledge about them have had the institution of slavery.

I shall return to this subject later on and want to mention only two occasions upon which we have personally become acquainted with this damnable slave trade on the Zambezi.

One of the coloureds had a black female servant about sixteen years old whom he had bought from the slave trader R. He had granted her freedom since she was employed by him as a nanny without salary. In return she was treated like one of his own children. Unfortunately, as might have been expected, she had not received a good education from the slave trader and her main fault was that she stole regularly. My wife liked to play with the child, who had been entrusted to her care. Thus unsuspecting we had allowed her to visit our hut. The reader therefore will understand my surprise when I tell him that one day the wives of the coloureds Ma-Tom and Clara appeared with necklaces of golden glass beads around their necks. Except for us nobody else in Panda-ma-Tenka had such glass beads. Upon investigation it was not difficult to find out that Hanna had used the visit to our house with the child for stealing. Hanna was lacking a few fingertips on both her hands. She had been mutilated terribly by her former boss. He had perpetrated this cruelty upon her as a kind of punishment although at that point she had been stealing out of hunger. How this happened is frightening, but it is so typical for black slave traders that I will tell this incident briefly.

On a fortnight's journey by foot from the home town of the slave trader R. to Panda-ma-Tenka the whole party suffered from great hunger. The party consisted of the slave trader, his wife, female slaves and male slaves as porters—the latter having even to carry their boss and his wife. Slave traders strangely enough do not hunt on such trips. Even though they engage excellent elephant hunters (also Africans) they use them only for hunting elephants and rather content themselves on their trading excursions with the poorest type of food. The slaves whom they take along as porters and as items for sale as a rule are very poor hunters. These people mostly have such bad rifles that in general good fortune in hunting cannot be anticipated. Slave trader R.'s party merely set small traps every night around the camp, which was always pitched near some water. As a rule, however, only mice or rats were caught in these traps. Apart from the millet bought from the Africans these animals made up the normal food. It so happened that the slave trader wanted to save the millet for a few days; he gave his servants merely the mice and rats they caught. Unfortunately, however, during this time so few were caught that only the adults—as is usually the case in such a situation—got the animals whereas the younger ones did not get anything and had to put up with their empty stomachs as best as they could. This, however, was mainly the fault of Madame.

The rats caught during the night proved to be so extraordinarily fat that Madame was tempted to claim the best parts of the catch for herself. In an unguarded moment Hanna, driven by hunger, stole a few of the fat rats. She quickly fried them over a small coal fire and ate them. When later that day the millet gruel mixed with the fried rats was served to Madame, who was resting in a hammock, a shrill cry came from her protruding lips. Half of the rats were missing! 'Who did this? Who was so bold to dare to do this?' Immediately the boss appeared. It was not difficult to find the thief and the inhuman punishment was carried out on the spot. The poor girl was dragged to the fire and her hands were stuck into it until some of her fingertips were charred. They subsequently fell off. This mutilated girl Hanna was later sold in Panda-ma-Tenka for one musket.

Europeans do not stay long in the central Zambezi area before Zambezi Africans, in particular Wanke's Makalaka, Matoka, Maschupia and Marutse offer not only young children, but also young men and women for sale. The asking prices are objects worth one woollen blanket or at most a rifle. The poor victims whom they offer for sale are either children of slaves from the above-mentioned tribes or children from tribes with whom they barter living with them. I have known cases where these children were bought but where the buyer then granted these poor creatures their freedom. Of course, these freed slaves then have to stay on the southern banks of the Zambezi, for were they to return to the northern banks their former masters or their chiefs would immediately claim them as their possession. In general the Zambezi is the southern border of slavery in the black continent. Up to there British law reaches and inflicts a penalty of fourteen years in prison for such an offence. This law should contain another clause, i.e. wherever the Europeans are too weak to free the slaves, either by arms or by diplomatic negotiations, they be empowered to buy slaves and set them free immediately. This, however, is at present impossible as according to the letter of the law such a humanitarian would risk a law suit or imprisonment for fourteen years if he bought slaves. At this point I cannot help but appeal to the rich philanthropical society in London which would find a wide field for humanitarian deeds along the Zambezi. It would not be hard for those rich gentlemen who are members of this society to give £5,000 sterling (60,000 guilders) annually in order to free hundreds and hundreds of miserable creatures from slavery. This action of emancipation, however, should be undertaken very cleverly; only those children should be bought who are offered to someone for the exchange of material goods. Children for sale should not be requested specifically, otherwise children would become highly sought-after articles and slave hunts would be the consequences. Philanthropy exercised in the wrong way would overnight make 'human flesh' a highly desirable commodity. This should be prevented in order to avoid even more insufferable misery than that which exists presently along the Zambezi.

At one point on my journey a young boy was given to me as a present. I freed him immediately. Jonas, as this promising youngster was called, shortly afterwards took advantage of my generosity and disappeared forever. Before he was given to me he had changed hands twelve times by sale and resale. Everywhere he was used, so to speak, as a beast of burden. The kind of treatment he got from me he had never before enjoyed in his life. He ate the same food as we Europeans and on the journey he only had to carry his blanket and one of my rifles. I had even allowed him to use the rifle for hunting whenever he liked to do so on our trip. My porters called him the 'master' and my servants called him 'the child of the white man'. And yet he could not bear our company and preferred a free, but uncertain future. This is characteristic of the nature of the inferior negro.

I want to end this short report about one of the saddest aspects of the conditions along the Zambezi with the description of another deplorable scene which we witnessed in Panda-ma-Tenka. Since this episode has already been related by my wife in the magazine *Viennese Fashion* of 1 January 1888 I will let my wife tell it:

'Bana, Bana, niaja lisa m'uschemani a mee' (Men, O men, no, leave my child), the poor woman was crying in broken words. Tears were choking her voice so that she hardly could get the words between her lips. 'Men, O men, have pity. I am willing to carry the heavy load of *mabele* and *niama* [a kind of sorghum and meat] as I did until this morning. I will gather for you many baskets full of *mohamami* and *mobula* [two edible fruits of the Zambezi woods] without fatigue. I will pound the grain for your *bochobe* and the *butschuala* [polenta and the usual sorghum (*mabele*) beer]. I am even ready to starve. I am willing to do anything and everything, but leave me my child, my poor child.' And even more closely she hugged and pressed her nearly eighteen-month-old boy to her naked breast. The little boy cried bitterly. The woman fell down on her knees, bent forward, and tried to protect her child with her back facing the aggressors.

This is the fate of a female slave on the central Zambezi. This sad scene took place at

Panda-ma-Tenka, the trading post on the Matetse River, in the open space between the
little huts of the settlement built on poles and the huts of the elephant hunters. A group of
merciless men shouted and screamed at the woman. All of them were Makalaka subject to
the nineteen-year-old chief Wanke[3] who, as mentioned earlier, had fled across the Zambezi when many years ago he was harassed by the warlike Matabele. There he had
founded a small empire mostly of Makalaka refugees. These Makalaka come occasionally
to Panda-ma-Tenka in order to exchange grain, corn, the well-known Matoka dwarf
goats, as well as tobacco for cotton material, glass beads, and ammunition. Yet sometimes
they even offer human beings for sale.

That very day a group of these Makalaka had arrived accompanied by a few women
and female slaves. One of those, a woman of about thirty years, obviously exhausted by
hard work and having nobody at home with whom she could have left her baby, was that
poor woman whose child they tried to tear away in order to sell it. And, indeed, it was
torn away from her, she was pushed back, beaten with a whip, and the child was sold. A
coloured man from the south, who happened to be in Panda-ma-Tenka for a visit, bought
it. A cotton blanket, a miserable rag hardly worth a Dutch guilder, was given in return for
the child. It was lucky that the coloured man only bought the child out of pity. A few
weeks later he took him back south. Since in the town where he lives slaves are no longer
allowed, he treats the boy like his own child and trains him to become a shepherd. Yet
before he left Panda-ma-Tenka several weeks passed, as has already been mentioned. The
man was absent from Panda-ma-Tenka during that time and had entrusted the child to a
black woman. This was a bad time which this poor creature had, when he had to stay with
this Matoka woman. He got very little food, but he received beatings in abundance. Every
day we saw the naked child several times crawling in the cooled ashes around the fire-
places in order to warm himself and to protect himself from the mosquitoes by a covering
of ashes. Very often we tried to act as an intermediary, but any intervention on our part resulted in even worse treatment of the child.

Finally on 24 May we left Panda-ma-Tenka in a wagon which was lent to me
by Mr Westbech and which was driven by a coloured named 'Speedy'. For a
stretch of the way we travelled together with Blockley[4] who had been called to
Panda-ma-Tenka at Westbech's request in order to work there as supervisor of
the huts.

Blockley, who came riding after us on horseback, had encountered a pair of
leopards on the way without, however, being able to take a good shot. While
riding along between the first and the second stop of the journey where the hilly
country ends and the Gaschuma laterite ridge, densely overgrown with bush,
begins, he noticed a conspicuous movement in the dense high grass on his left. He
immediately stopped his horse and stood up in his stirrups. At the very moment
that his eyes were searching the top of the grass, which suddenly had become
motionless, the heads of two leopards squatting closely together rose out of the
grass, also in order to look around. Blockley grabbed his rifle immediately, yet
the heads of the two carnivores dropped down quickly and the movement of the
grass indicated that they had taken to flight once again. Because of the high grass
and since he considered them two dangerous enemies Blockley did not think it
advisable to dare to pursue the animals.

Even though I got the fever very soon on this trip to the Leschumo valley,[5] I walked the whole way on foot except for four English miles. I did this deliberately in order to train myself for the long march which was to come. Because of my continuous sickness I only had been able to make short trips during the last months so that—as one would say in Vienna—I had literally forgotten how to walk. On our trip we had to suffer much from the lack of water as for a distance of over fifty kilometres no water could be found and the track was very exhausting for the draught oxen because of the deep sand.

Early on 27 May we arrived in the Leschumo valley and were pleasantly surprised to find Oswald looking very well. As the reader might remember we had sent him out in advance with Westbech's wagon.[6] He came to meet us and seemed to be feeling very well. I found the goods entrusted to him in excellent condition. For our future porters he had even obtained three sacks of millet by exchange. I stayed in the Leschumo valley until 1 June. Then we were to leave for the mouth of the Tschobe. True as usual to the slogan of our travels—i.e. the greatest possible advantage while on African soil for our expedition—we succeeded during this short time in increasing our Africana collection, this time mostly with tools of the natives. Particularly interesting seemed some of the beautiful Mankoja bows, which are very much desired on the Zambezi, and huge wooden bowls for meat made by the Mabunda tribe as well as spears, pole-axes and little wooden stools. I had ordered some of my future porters to come from Mambowa[7] to show them the loads they were supposed to carry. To my surprise they did not agree with several details. After lengthy debates I finally decided to rearrange the loads according to their liking, so that later on our expedition the porters would not cause delays by unnecessary complaints. This work took us almost two days and two nights. Mr Blockley agreed to keep the boxes which we had filled with the newly collected items; he promised to send them south at the next occasion. At the same time Coillard's[8] wagon, which had been sent to Pretoria in January, came back from the south. It was laden with goods and Coillard's inspector even brought a horse, a female donkey and some Angora goats. The missionary wanted to acclimatise the latter to the Marutse area in order to establish a more friendly relationship with the Marutse. The long trip and the change in food, however, did not seem to agree with the animals; only a small part of the original herd could be brought to the Zambezi and after a few days this part, too, was reduced to very few animals, and even these were sick so that there seemed to be no prospect for improving the breeds of goats and sheep along the Zambezi. The characteristic symptom of their disease was extensive catarrhal inflammation of their intestines.

On the night of 1/2 June we left in order to bring the largest part of my equipment and luggage by wagon to the mouth of the Tschobe river, i.e. to this side of the banks of the Zambezi, which is called Gazungula after a shady Gazungula tree growing right on the river bank.[9] We intended to stay there until our crossing of the Zambezi. Near the tree was the place where the Panda-ma-Tenka firm was planning to establish itself after Blockley had been forced to leave the Leschumo valley.[10] As mentioned before we found it necessary to pass through this area during the night. Since the tsetse fly is very dangerous there during hot daytime this district can be crossed only at night. If indeed the tsetse fly is the dangerous creature which in certain African areas kills our domestic animals by poisonous stings, as one usually assumes, then it is no protection, in my opinion, to one passing at night through these densely wooded, tsetse fly-infested laterite ridges which as a rule intersect our course. Admittedly this dangerous insect sleeps on the branches during the night, but the path is so narrow and the trees so close to it that one cannot pass without the animals and the wagon hitting the branches and thus shaking down the tsetse flies, carrying them along and thus spreading them. I found that at the time of my first visit the tsetse fly area on the stretch from Panda-ma-Tenka to the mouth of the Tschobe reached from the Snowman Pan (twelve English miles from the Leschumo station) up to the mouth of the Tschobe. Since then the tsetse fly has slowly been destroyed by periodic forest fires in this area except for one laterite ridge near the intersection of the Leschumo and the Zambezi valleys.

Since, however, a wagon passes through this area only twice or at most three times a year, there had been no opportunity to spread this poisonous fly extensively and it remained restricted to a narrow stretch of wood. When, however, in 1885 the missionary Coillard repeatedly drove from the Leschumo to the Zambezi in order to shift his post to Schescheke[11] and when, furthermore, the trading post was moved from Panda-ma-Tenka to Gazungula in 1886, and thus this area was crossed often by wagon and draught animals, the spread of the fly into the Leschumo valley was facilitated. I had already expressed this fear during my first visit this time to the Leschumo valley (in February 1886). I was glad when I could finally leave and when I had brought my draught animals safely back to Panda-ma-Tenka from the Leschumo valley. Indeed, it was high time for this, for when later Mr Westbech and Rev Coillard travelled back and forth between the Leschumo valley and the Zambezi more often, so many flies were spread into the first valley that the insect was able to settle there and soon the consequences became obvious. The draught animals of other travellers who came up into the Leschumo valley from the south turned ill with the symptoms of the tsetse poison and died, except for two animals. This much is certain. This dangerous insect which will cause great difficulties in the colonisation of southern Africa, withdraws from civilisation and disappears. The Leschumo valley, from our mission station onward until it enters the Zambezi valley, is slightly hilly. It is only several hundred metres wide, covered with high grass, and park-like woods, and is bordered on both sides by the high laterite ridges. At the end of the Leschumo valley a spur of the left laterite ridge stretches towards the right one. This heavily wooded spur was supposed to be the remaining tsetse area, whereas the flat part, covered with grass, bush and shrubs was supposed to be free from tsetse flies from the spurs up to the Tschobe and the Zambezi rivers. I never believed this and I think that those who spread this rumour did not believe it themselves in the beginning. For why did Mr Westbech and Mr Coillard always drive their draught animals back the same night to the Leschumo valley when they had brought goods to Gazungula during the night? Slowly, however, they forgot about this precaution and in spite of my advice Coillard left his draught animals in Gazungula since Mr Westbech's assurance that 'there were no tsetse flies in Gazungula' seemed to carry greater weight than mine.

Still in Panda-ma-Tenka I informed Mr Westbech that I planned to have my ninety-six loads carried by porters to the Zambezi. Yet my friend did not want to hear anything of this sort. He said that if his wagon could bring me from here into the Leschumo valley his oxen also could continue this trip up to the Zambezi. There would be no danger for them at the tsetse ridge.

Thus we arrived with all our things at the Zambezi. Under the aforementioned Gazungula tree we found a large Masarwa family. Near one fire the men and boys were sitting; near another one, on this side of the tree, the women with their babies and the girls. They were refugees from the nearby Bamangwato land. King Khama[12] had sent people out into the northern parts of his land in order to look for the Masarwa and Madenassana people who were living there in a very dispersed way, and to gather them and to assign to them certain areas for settlement.

On 2 June we began with the crossing of the Zambezi and by 3 June at 10 a.m. we had brought everything across the river. However, because of the strong south-east winds, this would not have been possible even within a week if we had had to rely on those miserable Maschupia canoes cut out of one tree trunk. How inefficient those canoes are can be proved by the fact that these canoes on those two days made only five trips for me and each time could only take the loads of two porters (about fifty kilogrammes) and that I had to pay 10 m of calico for these five trips. The natives cannot use these canoes at all on the broad, choppy river if there is a strong wind blowing, since the canoes can turn over rather easily and the shipwrecked persons are then in great danger for their lives because of the numerous crocodiles. Only early in the morning and late in the evening were the winds relatively weak; at other times a strong south-east wind was blowing every day so that the natives would not have dared to make the trip under any conditions.

In this difficult situation the iron boat which had been sold to Westbech, but had been lent to us for this trip, was of great value. With my help Fekete[13] carried out the transportation of our equipment, and in spite of the rough wind we took a load of ten to twelve porters each time and in addition one member of our crew. As soon as we had let our iron boat into the water curious onlookers appeared from everywhere. For them the pontoon from the royal imperial navy arsenal in Klosterneuburg was the same as the first steamboat had been for the people near the European rivers sixty years ago: they were strange monsters beyond their comprehension. What they could not understand at all was the fact that the *makoa* (boat) was able to carry such a heavy load so fast and in such a strong wind.

Livingstone, Bains,[14] the missionary Coillard and the elephant hunter Selouts[15] had brought boats to the Zambezi made out of wood, metal and sailcloth, yet had not been able to use them efficiently in this river. The success which we had on the first attempt with our iron pontoon, consisting of three parts, had never been seen before by the natives along the Zambezi. No European boat had ever before been admired by them to such an extent.

The economic advantage of such a large vehicle which could be used in any weather was unfortunately not understood by the natives. They only applauded the spectacle, clapping their hands enthusiastically, yet they had not learned anything. They had no idea what they missed. In addition to the safety and the quick trip with the boat I also saved at least sixty guilders which I would have had to pay in the form of calico to the natives (at the Zambezi) as a ferry fee.

Thus I stood with my companions and everything I could call mine on the much sought-after northern bank of the huge Zambezi. Blockley and his wife had followed us, too, to the north bank and would have liked to accompany us for several days march if Blockley's obligation had not required him to take up his job in Panda-ma-Tenka. We parted with heavy hearts, in particular Mrs Blockley. She had come to like my wife very much and knew that she might perhaps never again establish such an intimate relationship with a white friend during her entire stay in Africa. I understood the tears of that poor woman: her sobbing was a sign of renunciation for the sake of the man whom she had followed into the wilderness of the Zambezi.

Shortly before Mrs Blockley's departure Mr Westbech arrived unexpectedly in our camp together with Mr Weyr[16] and the king's son Lytia[17] with his entourage. Westbech's arrival was very advantageous for me in solving the difficult question of the porters.[18]

Mr Westbech had not only come to the Zambezi in order to give Lytia a friendly escort, but he had another reason—namely, business.[19] Luanika, the King of the Marutse,[20] had sent him a message saying that he wanted to buy a large quantity of goods from him and that for this purpose he had sent Liomba, a chief who held a position similar to trade minister, to the mouth of the Tschobe.[21] Liomba was a commoner who on the return of the king had suddenly risen to become the holder of the third highest position in the country. Before the expulsion of the king he had been merely a normal royal vassal. He remained, however, faithful when everybody else deserted the king and he even fled with him to the swamps along the central part of the Tschobe river which were inhabited by the Bamaschi. After some time he left the king in order to influence Khama in Schoschong on behalf of his master's cause and, as wicked tongues maintained, in order to find a more pleasant refuge than the Tschobe swamps. He knew perfectly well how to play the role of a poor exiled person. King Khama gave him a very friendly welcome. Liomba even succeeded in interesting the Europeans living in Schoschong as well as the chiefs of the Bamangwato in his cause and his financial situation, for he had no money at all because of his expulsion. Thus he did not lack anything during his exile and he received many presents, especially from those Europeans who intended to travel to the Zambezi. On the one hand, he was able to give good information about the Zambezi and on the other, it was certain that he would rise to high honours if Luanika ever was to ascend the throne again, and then he would be a very useful spokesman for every traveller.

Liomba also used the period of his stay in order to get some information about the relationship to the Bamangwato of the few English traders living in Schoschong and in particular about their mutual exchange of goods as well as about the prices of most of their objects of trade in order to get acquainted with the value of 'money'. He got so much experience in this respect that the reports he gave to Luanika after his ascension to the throne filled the king with such a respect for his knowledge in economics that he appointed him to the abovementioned high position. In addition he was ordered to make all the purchases for the royal household as well as to purchase all arms for the empire on the king's account, as the king had previously done himself.

When Westbech arrived at the Zambezi, Liomba and his escort, too, had arrived and had pitched camp on an island densely overgrown with shrubs and reed which was in the Zambezi near the northern bank. Thus, I, too, had the opportunity very soon to get to know him. I must admit that I found him to be an extremely clever yet cautious man and a reliable official who looked after the interests of his ruler very well. In any case he was more experienced in the field entrusted to him than Mr Westbech and Mr Wa[22] who realised all too soon that Liomba had learned more from the whites than they would have wished. In addition Liomba was honest and open and in this respect also different from most of the Marutse. Yet he had the same general fault as all the natives along the central Zambezi: 'Beg from each and every European'. Even in this respect, however, he was a laudable exception as he did not beg for everything he happened to see but he asked directly for the particular object he needed at that moment. If you did not have it he did not bother you any longer. Thus Liomba appeared to be quite a tolerable person and I owe him much for his help in finding my porters. The other representatives of Makumba[23] would have fleeced me much more if their fear for Liomba and his reports to the king had not prevented them from doing so.

Yet my other European friends there did not like this representative of the king at all, and in fact his offers of exchange were clearly unacceptable in the actual market conditions on the central Zambezi. He and his king had become trading aristocrats who knew trading better than anything else. With the inevitable invectives against 'those white traders' Liomba had told his king about the great difference between the prices which they had to pay at the Zambezi and those which prevailed in Schoschong. The king had given orders to Liomba to exchange goods only on the basis of the Schoschong prices. The two black businessmen, however, had forgotten to account for the freight cost for the 700 km from Schoschong to the Zambezi. They had overlooked as well that for any skipper the stretch between Schoschong and the Zambezi was the most difficult and expensive section between the southern coast and the Zambezi. The king, however, had some doubts that Westbech would accept their unusually low bids, but the answer he got from Liomba was: 'Those from the south bring oxen, skins and wagons to exchange; we, however, bring ivory.' In addition the king had still another reason to give Liomba full power. For years Portuguese traders had come to him from Benguela as well as the two brothers Lorenz and Mr MacDonald[24] from Walfish Bay to whom he owed considerable sums, just as he did to West-bech, for goods they had delivered to him. He now intended to take revenge on those demanding creditors by using the ivory—i.e. 'the gold of the country' which had been hunted in the meantime for new purchases from other trad-ers—instead for paying his debts. Mr Westbech had occasionally exhorted him to pay but without any success. Luanika took this demand just as ungraciously as some European debtors. In fact he felt so offended that he said: 'I should pay? I, who have done so much good for Westbech! Did I not allow him to trade within my empire? Did I not allow him to hunt elephants in my territory? Did I not re-ceive him hospitably on his frequent visits and did I not give the orders that my people should feed him in those villages through which he passed on his boat trips? Look here'—and Luanika began to count with his fingers—'I have given to him and his retinue forty-seven oxen as a present. How can he now ask for payment for that *mosiri* [gunpowder], that *marumo* [lead] and those *koto* [percussion caps]?' Westbech did not get any money and once more had to give him some ammuni-tion on credit just when we were staying in the Leschumo valley.

Westbech, who by the way had returned the King's presents ten times over through presents to him, his wives and his children, swallowed this insult, hoping to make up for the loss in his next trading encounter. This type of forbearance oc-casionally occurs also in Europe. Of course, Westbech would have liked to know how much ivory Liomba had brought along for trade; Liomba on the other hand consciously wanted to conceal this since he had only a little over 1,500 pounds of ivory. He was well aware that the Englishman would not make an exceptional offer for such a relatively small amount of ivory and that he certainly would not accept the Schoschong rate.

In order that the Englishman, who was much more liked by the Maschupia than Liomba with his Marutse, did not realise the true story, Liomba had established residence on the island and the ivory which had been brought there by boats was buried in the sand immediately after unloading. The black businessman with his ministerial portfolio was an equal match for the old white trader. Very soon my friend Mr Westbech complained about the bad deal he had to make with Liomba in order not to lose the ivory he had brought. He said it was the worst deal he ever had made in his fifteen years on the central Zambezi. Unfortunately, during the days of negotiations some Maschupia arrived on Coillard's wagon which was returning from the south. They had worked in Schoschong and could confirm Liomba's claims that the prices in Schoschong were indeed lower. Coillard's wagon was supposed to cross the Zambezi and to penetrate into Barotse which had only once before been reached by a wagon. By this means Rev Coillard planned to avoid the tedious question of the porters.[25]

II

From Gazungula to Mo-Rukumi

DURING MY STAY ON THE NORTHERN BANK I had a good chance to observe the exhausting efforts of Rev. Coillard to transport across the river merely those goods which had been brought from the south by wagon. Then imagine the continuation of the journey! Indeed, the King had ordered the forest cleared for him in certain places; however, it was most certain that Coillard would lose all his draught animals from the tsetse fly. Since porters are much more reliable in the interior of the kingdom than at the eastern border where I had to use them, I believe this method of transportation would have been a lot cheaper for the clergyman and the journey would have been completed much faster than he was able to do by the means of the transport used in the south.

I had to stay twelve days at the Zambezi and during this period the missionary was able to bring only one third of the freight plus the draught animals across the river. Because of the strong wind the natives were only able to make a couple of trips across in the morning and in the evening with their tiny boats. I had sold my pontoon to Mr Westbech, but he was not willing to lend it without payment. Furthermore, the natives worked for Coillard only very reluctantly, and if Liomba had not prompted them to work, Rev. Coillard would have had to stay at the mouth of the Tschobe for a long time before everything had been brought to the northern bank.

As Coillard had come personally this time I had the chance to get to know his energetic and admirable character. Yet with a little bit more generosity towards the natives, without yielding to arrogant demands, he would have achieved his goals more easily. As it was, however, we heard constantly the same line from the chiefs, as well as from the workers, about his 'tight fist'. By means of the iron pontoon those two wagon loads could have been transported across the river within six or seven days. The river was at this place about 1200 meters wide, according to my estimate.

Mr Coillard was so kind as to give us a loaf of bread, which we appreciated very much. For nobody can imagine how delicious it was for us to taste some bread again. Even though we had goats and sheep enough for slaughtering we had only polenta and millet for bread. Mr Coillard pointed out to my wife all the great dangers she inevitably would have to face if she were to accompany me further north. With my consent he invited her to go with him to Schescheke and to wait for me with his family. My wife immediately refused this offer even though we appreciated Rev. Coillard's kind-heartedness. Yet we were determined to share our fate. But whenever Coillard saw my wife he repeated: 'A woman, a weak creature should not dare such a thing! A trip to those wild tribes who are feared by all the natives living around us who are themselves pretty dangerous!' And the clergyman shook his head over and over again and repeated that 'this should not happen'.

He denied that Westbech had helped him with his missionary tasks (although Westbech argued to the contrary). He told me that he had become the successor to the Jesuit missionaries in Barotse, i.e. that he had obtained for his missionary stations the two places which Luanika had assigned to the Jesuits and that he was planning to go immediately to Barotse, i.e. still during the winter before the great floods of the late summer could make such a journey impossible. Like anyone who knew Luanika only for a short period of time, Coillard praised the king—except for his cruelty, about which he told hair-raising stories. I would be very surprised if Coillard today would still have the same positive opinion about this tyrant. The ambitious missionary would, however, be in quite a safe position if at some time Marancian, the chief who was expelled from Schescheke[1] were to ascend the throne in Marutseland, since Marancian had favoured Coillard for a long time.

In this way we talked politics in the evenings. During the day, however, from sunrise to sundown, we were busy with the crossing of the Zambezi and with tedious negotiations with the chiefs for porters. I had the greatest difficulties with the transportation of the two donkeys, and Coillard with the transport of his draught animals. The animal was pushed forcibly into the water and had to swim beside the boat. One man rowed in the rear of the boat and a second knelt in the front trying to keep the head of the ox above water by means of a leather strap tied around his horns, or in the case of the donkey by means of his halter. This always caused quite an excitement and was extremely exhausting job, for only very few animals understand what one wants from them. Usually they kick violently in all directions or they try to jump into the boat with their front legs and thus they endanger the lives of those sitting in the boat. The tribes along the river take for such crossings only their biggest boats in order to keep a certain balance with the stubborn and intractable animals. On the northern bank we camped in the harvested field of Luschuane, the superintendent of the Gazungula crossing whose sad death is already known to the reader.[2] We lived in two old reed huts. This was my camp and my first residence on the north bank of the central Zambezi. I had to stay here until I had gathered all my porters. Apart from the astronomical determination of our location and some meteorological observations it was impossible to carry out any other scientific work, since all my time was taken up by the negotiations with the chiefs to get the porters and by making an inventory of the contents of all the pieces of our luggage.

Already during my first visit to the central Zambezi in 1875 and 1876 I had realised how difficult a trip north of the Zambezi would be if one had to rely on porters from the Zambezi tribes. Yet I had no idea of the mountains of difficulties I
would encounter when I attempted the trip in reality. All troubles had the same
root: always and everywhere Sepopo, the almighty ruler on the Zambezi whose
orders frightened all his subjects and were immediately obeyed, was absent.
During my first stay at the Zambezi this 'Peter the Great' of the Negro rulers was
still alive.[3] He had not only great power and was strict and at times cruel but he
was also open to new ideas and most of the time kept his word, and thus was a support for all whites. After Sepopo's death the conditions all over the empire became much looser. The authority of the Marutse in the eastern provinces had
become illusory and my trip went through exactly these provinces. Furthermore,
the state of morals had declined sharply during the civil wars after Sepopo's
death—all the more since the indulgence of some Europeans had made the natives
bold and insolent.

These conditions alone made it rather difficult for me to get together a caravan
of porters. In addition to this my trip was going to the much feared Maschukulumbe tribes. While I could have easily hired 300 porters within three weeks for a
trip to the south, it was unbelievably difficult to get hold of only 100 porters and
then only to the border of the Marutse lands. In Sepopo's time the Maschukulumbe lived on good terms with the Marutse and the tribes subject to them.[4] But
after Luanika's invasion into their territory,[5] there was the greatest hostility between the two peoples. The Maschukulumbe had only limited contact with a few
of the Matoka tribes who were nominally subject to the Marutse, but who in fact,
were rather hostile to them. In brief, the conditions along the central Zambezi had
become worse in every respect and especially the authority of the white man was
undermined. His prestige was not only broken but during our travels there every
European coming from the south was regarded with great mistrust and was
treated as a spy of the much feared Matabele who had in recent years taken possession of a strip of the East Bamangwato land between the big salt pans and the
Zambezi and thus had come closer to the Marutse.

The question of the porters was hell for us even before we had advanced a single
kilometre and I had a vague idea of what I would have to expect. Yet all these
troubles could not reverse my decision to penetrate into the black continent by a
new way and to lift the veil a bit further.

I cannot however, deny that at the bottom of my heart I often envied those
explorers who were able to travel in Central Africa with reliable Zanzibaris as
their porters. In particular I envied the great Stanley who had sufficient financial
means to hire a small army of Zanzibaris which spared him the whole problem of
the porters. Not only can he travel fast, but he is also almost in the position of a
ruling sovereign with respect to those petty black rulers with whom poorer travellers have to negotiate sometimes as long as a whole week in order to obtain
maybe fifty porters from them.

The great Arab trading network in north and east Africa will probably also change much along these lines. I will reserve closer consideration of these questions until the end of the book. Here I only want to compare the porters from Zanzibar with those from the Zambezi countries as the situation was in 1886.

Until recently, that is until the beginning of the present catastrophe at the east coast, the Zanzibaris were by far the best porters in Africa. They are thoroughly trained by their long contact with the white man, they have their fixed rates which they observe strictly, they are well disciplined, yet always cheerful, and they go wherever you want them to go without being afraid. The people from the Zambezi carried loads which were on the average 10 kg lighter than those the Zanzibaris carried which, if you have 100 porters, is a considerable loss for a traveller along the Zambezi. The reliability of the Zanzibaris has become proverbial. Travellers would have their caravan travel for days in advance and they were sure to meet them at a set place with everything in perfect order. The contrary holds for the Zambezi tribes. Among 100 porters there were hardly five reliable and honest men so that all had to be watched closely. Only occasionally fear of their chiefs (i.e. if a certain chief really was respected) prevented them from open theft and even robbery. An exception to this thieving attitude was found only among those porters who were hired for a trip to the south and this only because they were punished very hard by Khama, the Bamangwato king as well as by Lo Bengula, the Matabele king[6] if they were caught at theft. Many chiefs on the northern bank of the Zambezi, however, through whose territory we had to travel, do not mete out justice to a stranger. On the contrary, they try to exploit him as much as possible either by simply robbing him as do all Maschukulumbe rulers or by squeezing out of him so many so-called testimonial gifts that he might as well be robbed. What then can we expect from porters whom we have to take from those tribes? In addition another major difficulty for any traveller at the Zambezi is the fact that the people at the Zambezi, in contrast to the Zanzibaris, do not allow themselves to be hired as porters for an extensive trip to the north. This reluctance dates from Livingstone's time.

Many natives had gone with Livingstone from Barotse to the west coast, but only a few of them returned home. They told such miserable tales about the hardships they had endured that their stories lived on as oral tradition in Marutse land and served as a deterrent against anybody daring a similar trip. But for people from the Zambezi the land to which they would never go was that of the Maschukulumbe, to which, of course, I wanted to go. Because of this insurmountable fear I had to change my porters ten times over a stretch of about 500 km. The explorer travelling with Zanzibaris pays his porters in cash when he arrives at his destination. He only takes along as many goods for exchange as he needs for buying food and as presents for the chiefs. I, however, had to pay the porters whom I hired at the central Zambezi—and to whom the value of money was yet unknown—with calico, glass beads and similar objects—and this over and over again. Thus I needed a huge amount of these goods and therefore many more porters than would have otherwise been necessary. In order to get porters I had to give much larger presents to the individual chiefs than, for example, Stanley who had only to pay for the guides, i.e. for one or two men for an easy job. Yet I was not spared from paying this fee as well. Although my porters knew the way well which I had to go, I was forced, willy-nilly, to take at least one subchief and usually two, as so-called guides. When I refused to take them, arguing that because of the large number of porters no guide was necessary, I got the answer that I would need these men as supervisors because of the obstinacy of the porters. In the beginning I believed this and did not mind paying for this police protection. Soon I found out that these subchiefs whom they had assigned to me had no control over the porters whatsoever, that the porters even occasionally attacked them, and that I had been cheated. These guides, or puppet-chiefs, as I used to call them, were, however, entitled to substantially higher pay than the porters. Thus expenses increase considerably for a journey north of the Zambezi if one undertakes it with native porters, even though food is generally inexpensive in these areas. How different this would be if one could travel with armed porters as on the Congo!

With regard to the problem—which arose, in particular, because of Stanley's success—of whether it is better to travel in Africa with a strong armed force or only with a small unarmed escort—I would like to state the following principles. Both ways are right, yet each only in certain areas. Where the negroes are still living in heavenly innocence or recognise the authority of the white man completely one simply needs no armed escort. Where the negroes out of their own initiative or under the influence of the Arabs have States with a military organisation and modern armed forces it is plainly dangerous to travel with an armed escort since this protection does not create fear but only invites an easy fight. Therefore it would be stupid to invade the Mahdi empire with about 500 armed men or even the empire of Uganda or that of the Matabele or Damara who themselves have thousands of guns at their disposal.

For all trips, however, from the Zambezi up to the southern border of the Mahdi empire in the north I believe that the protection of armed men like those led by Cameron or Stanley is necessary, if one at all wants to realise one's plans. In fact almost all travellers in central Africa until recently were able to arm their porters partly and could use them in an emergency as soldiers. Along the central Zambezi, however, one unfortunately could not establish such an escort. One could not dare to arm the porters hired there if one intended to keep one's guns and did not want to be the first one to be shot. Slowly I had gathered twenty men from the south and from the Zambezi area who were bound by a contract to accompany me not as porters but as servants up to the coast. Only three out of those twenty, namely Boy, Mapani and Jonas (who was given to me by Blockley as a present) I could entrust with a gun. Never could I lend a gun to my porters because otherwise they would have disappeared with it during the night or perhaps even on our march during daytime since we had mostly to walk through woods or through dense and high grass similar to our reed grass. In our camps the spare guns had to be put between our sleeping places because otherwise the porters would have stolen them. What a difference between my porters and Stanley's, Cameron's, and other explorers' armed porters! Those travellers could rely completely on their porters and they could pass the nights in peaceful slumber under their protection. We, however, had to keep our eyes on the horde day and night if we wanted to secure our belongings and later even our lives.

The attitude of our porters became worse from day to day. The porters among the Matoka who were partially subject to Luanika, the King of the Marutse, occasionally shrank back from excesses out of fear of Makumba, the governor of the Maschupia in Mambowa who favoured me. The free Matoka behaved much worse—even though the villages which we visited had never been visited before by a European. The worst, however, we experienced among the Maschuku-lumbe. The Matoka only went along with us for three days. If they had to march for four to six days they revolted even if they had contracted themselves for the whole distance. The Maschukulumbe porters, however, (and thus it became worse from day to day on our journey to the north) were not willing to 'sleep out', i.e. they refused to stay away from their home villages overnight. Every night the whole troup of hired porters returned home and every day I had to hire new porters from village to village.

I have had to keep the kind reader rather long with this porter problem since it not only required fantastic sacrifices of time and money, but it also became the reason for the catastrophe which later befell my expedition.

I had not yet left my camp in Gazungula when I realised that we had fallen into the hands of hostile porters and chiefs. There was only one hope, i.e. to find better conditions further north. It was only this hope which spurred us to start. To follow a definite direction straight to the north for my intended journey was not possible at all. As the Arabs cross the Sahara by going from one oasis to the next because of the water, my caravan had to move zigzag from one village to the next without considering whether this way agreed with my compass, but because only there could I get porters for the next day. Among the worst experiences of this journey north of the Zambezi were the negotiations for new porters and the payment of the old ones. You cannot imagine what we had to suffer and to endure. A single mistake in such an hour, a sign of weakness or yielding, perhaps as a consequence of an attempted intimidation, would certainly have caused a catastrophe in which we all except for my wife would very possibly have been killed.

Often we were pushed into a dense crowd so that in case of an attack we would not have been able to fire a single shot in our defence. Everything depended, of course, on whether or not the chiefs or the village headmen wanted to give us porters, because I could not force them to do so. All these petty rulers competed in trying to exploit me. They all agreed in one thing, i.e. that their men were never allowed to go any further than to the border with the next chief; their demands kept becoming more and more insolent. Already the second chief put forward such great demands for porters that I could not have met them if I did not want to ruin the whole expedition from the very beginning. In this emergency, when I already thought that my journey would have to come to a premature end only a few kilometres north of the river, I was helped by my medical profession, that good luck charm on all my African journeys. The physician is—as I have already mentioned several times—a wizard among all these tribes and without wanting it I had acquired the reputation of a sought-after wizard and that helped where everything else failed. But I shall talk about this later in more detail in a more suitable place.

I was told about all this at the Zambezi and I was advised to return home. But the more the worries about this journey north of the Zambezi increased the firmer was our decision not to give in but to succeed to Livingstone's and Serpa Pinto's inheritance.

Finally in the beginning of June we got under way. The two new servants, Monohela and Simunday, whom I had sent east to the Matoka Chief Matakala[7], returned on 7 June to Gazungula with thirty-three porters. Since Makumba's representative, who was supposed to give me ninety men, only came up with thirty, I again had to wait and could not start on 8 June. I decided to send the thirty-three porters of Matakala ahead under the control of Fekete and Oswald. I then intended to follow myself with the rest as soon as I had hired the necessary number of porters. I sent with this advance guard the two black servants, Simunday and January. My friend Westbech was so kind as to help me settle the payment of these men for their three days services as porters. Two metres of calico (the value of which at the Zambezi was 1 fl 20 kr) plus food for this period were agreed upon for each man. On 8 May I had succeeded in hiring two more Makalaka and one Matoka as servants for the entire journey. One of them I called 'Braggart' and the second one 'Kabrniak',[8] but I did not change the name 'Siroko' of the Matoka.

I complained about my troubles to Liomba, i.e. that I had only thirty porters instead of the ninety who were agreed upon, and Liomba drew Lytia's attention to the way that the king's orders had not been fulfilled. Lytia, who was just about to leave for Mambowa in order to participate in a drinking-bout which Makumba's wives were giving in his honour, promised his help and deplored the fact that Makumba was absent. Because of Lytia's and Liomba's support twenty more porters arrived and the rest I got as an exchange for presents to the chiefs of several villages which were scattered in the laterite hills. The Gazungula porters, however, even at the start when they were picking out their loads, made much more fuss than Matakala's men. Even though my loads were very well prepared for carrying the porters found a lot which was wrong with them. They had objections to this and to that so that it was quite an effort finally to get them moving. Most of them cut 1·5m sticks for themselves to which they tied the packages with bark in order to handle them more easily while walking.

Because of all these difficulties I did not get around to collecting any material in Gazungula. Yet I succeeded during my stay there in obtaining from the natives through exchange various objects which filled about two boxes. I gave them to Westbech to keep them for me and to send them south if any opportunity arose. For hunting we had hardly any time either. Every night we heard hyenas in the immediate vicinity and we also found kudu tracks near the Zambezi, yet we were so exhausted from our daily labours that—even when success seemed most certain—we did not think of sacrificing a night for such a hunting expedition.

Before leaving Gazungula I still have to mention a man who, because of his peculiar character, was more feared than esteemed and very well known in the whole central Zambezi area. This was Sinjandu, the ferryman of Gazungula.[9] The murdered Luschuane had had the title of a ferryman, yet he actually was only the supervisor at this place. He had to see that nobody crossed the Zambezi from the south without the permission of the King or of Makumba. The actual ferryman, however, was Sinjandu, an old unassuming little man who was feared very much. I was told that he was held in great respect at the river, yet I considered this report to be a joke. Yet very soon, before I left Gazungula, I came to realise that it was true. While in a drunken condition, Afrika,[10] the elephant hunter who is already known to the reader, had given Lytia out of the few animals which were still left from his beautiful herd a small young black ox for slaughtering. The ox was standing at the southern bank of the river and Sinjandu was supposed to take it across in the usual fashion. There was a strong south-easterly blowing and it would have been extremely dangerous even to dare an attempt. Nobody, however, between Victoria Falls and distant Barotse knows better than this weak old ferryman the malice of the Zambezi waves if agitated by a storm. Since the Zambezi, except for a few short twists in its central course, mostly flows quite straight for miles the east and west winds can agitate the deep waters so much that even European boats have to use the utmost caution and the primitive boats of the natives cannot get across at all. Sinjandu, well aware of this, answered: "No, I do not go." Lytia's servants urged him in vain to go, he did not even answer to their requests any longer. So they brought the court councillor, an old chief, who kindly requested him to go, but without any better success. Then there appeared the other subchiefs, among them those black characters who had kept begging us in Panda-ma-Tenka, and those who had committed that horrible murder.[11] As usual, they used high-sounding phrases and tried to tell Sinjandu that he actually was not a Marutse but a slave who had to obey. Still the man did not answer a word. He sat motionless on the ground. His indifference finally upset those who were trying to persuade him so much that they started shouting. But then the unexpected happened. Sinjandu suddenly jumped up and a torrent of invectives came out of his mouth. What the old chief, the court councillor, had been unable to do the old ferryman achieved. He made the voices of his attackers inaudible by his shouting and forced them to be still. 'Who else but me has taken you across back and forth? I should be afraid of you? Kill me, you screaming raven, try it! I have nothing in my old hands and your arms are armed with spears. Come on, you cowards! Ha, ha, ha. I am not going to risk my old life for one stupid ox even if he belongs to Lytia, the King's son. Never!' This was the way in which the old man was arguing and everybody around became quiet; not even Lytia, who had appeared in the meantime, dared to say a word. Nobody in the Marutse kingdom, unless he had been sentenced to death, would have dared to talk to a group of people so close to Luanika in such a way or to deny them anything. In our hearts we could not help but hail this old man and even the Maschupia around sneaked down to the river in order to giggle there undisturbed.

It was only the next day, when the wind had stopped, that Sinjandu took the little ox across. What protected Sinjandu so that he could oppose the courtiers in this fashion? The crocodiles did! Living for years at the river Sinjandu had every now and then thrown tasty bits and scraps to the crocodiles swimming by. Thus the animals were used to coming close when they heard Sinjandu at the river bank. The Zambezi tribes, however, feared crocodiles more than any other wild animals. Whatever primitive races and men fear they respect as well, and all the more anybody who seems to be close to the forces of nature. For fear of the crocodiles not a hair of Sinjandu's head was allowed to be hurt, since the crocodiles had respect for him. It was impossible for me to gain Sinjandu's confidence since I had done him too much harm, as he claimed, by bringing the iron boat which resisted the wind and could easily be manoeuvred. Thus I had partly destroyed his reputation since I had crossed the river several times per day in spite of the wind and with such a heavy load. He remained reserved and grumbled at us. In particular he was cross with my wife since she was in charge of the distribution of the food for our expedition north of the Zambezi and had paid the old man for his work, but had not given him any extra presents. We had also taken across the Zambezi our dogs, a few goats, the three donkeys, and the tame baboon. The latter especially was a lot of fun for all of us and the natives enjoyed it thoroughly when he teased them continuously. They expressed their astonishment and surprise by shouting loudly or making funny gestures, in particular when Pit felt cold or when it became evening and he grabbed a sack and pulled it over his head and body in order to hide or to warm himself. When the natives were standing around him in a big crowd he all of a sudden jumped right among them so that they rushed away screaming and many fell down. I shall return to this animal later for zoological observation. After a lot of effort we finally succeeded in leaving Gazungula on 10 June at about 1 p.m. and we followed the servants who had left two days before. From the very beginning I tried to establish some military discipline within the caravan. My wife with Leeb,[12] Jonas and Kabrniak led the train, Boy and the rest of the servants walked in the middle of the sixty porters as supervisors, while I followed in the rear in order to prevent the porters from escaping or from sitting down, as well as to defend the rear-guard from any possible attacks. As none of the natives knew how to drive donkeys, I had to do the job of donkey driver as well.

It is indeed hard to describe what I had to go through that afternoon. Completely exhausted and so tired that I was not even able to speak any longer I finally arrived after sundown at the first camp of our journey north of the Zambezi. I was the very last one, together with the sick Muschemani who suffered from syphilis.

Not knowing that I would still need them, I had sent my pack saddles south. Thus I had to make do with my riding saddle and that of my wife. I had made another saddle out of straps for the third mule, or rather for the female donkey I had bought from Rev. Coillard for £5 (60 fl). I loaded the animals with one and a half porter loads, i.e. each with 45 kg of glass beads in small sacks. But only James, the mule I had bought from the hunter, Afrika, for a pair of boots and a few yards of calico, carried what I had put on his back. The others were stubborn and tried to buck until the loads slipped down under their bellies and were dragging behind, hanging from the straps. In addition, each mule ran in a different direction. Only with great effort was I able to catch them again. In the end I was perspiring profusely and was hardly able to catch up with these animals. The strength of Muschemani, the sick black, was soon exhausted. He merely staggered behind us and even lost my big umbrella which was supposed to protect me as well from the sun on this journey. I cursed these bad mules but each time I was glad when I had caught one of them again in order to put his load on his back for the nth time. These mules on strike did not glorify my journey north of the Zambezi as allegedly the striking sailors glorified Columbus' expedition; however, they did not discourage me either. On the contrary each step further into this virgin land seemed to inspire me with new hopes. The first day's march was about eight kilometres and ended at the right bank of the Silamba stream[13] north-east of our point of departure. I regretted that our route went so much to the east, but I had to give in since the porters had not been granted to me for the most direct trip to chief Sietsetema.[14] Instead they were ordered to take the longest zigzag tour possible and I had to be glad that we could at all follow a somewhat northerly course. The path went through a depression overgrown with high grass and reeds parallel to a wooded ridge on the left. We crossed the spur of the ridge after five kilometres and came into the valley of the Silamba stream which flows into the Zambezi two kilometres further south. In the bottom of the valley is a channel called Ki-Mona (the man). It is silted and dry at the end of the valley, but near the first spur of the wooded hill towards the east it is still broad and deep. I do not know whether the Silamba flows into this channel as I arrived after dark and left at daybreak. I had to follow the porters as fast as possible since they were not willing to extend their three-day march. Between the main river and the old channel, which is full of fish, crocodiles and hippos and alive with birds in the dense reeds on its banks, there is a small sandy elevation mostly covered with mimosa trees. On this elevation is located the town of the Maschupia chief Makala, who is well esteemed in general and in particular by Luanika. The surrounding plain is partly cultivated. The most interesting point of that journey was the spot where we crossed the laterite ridge. Below the broad Ki-Mona lagoon with its dark blue water began. This journey offered many interesting things for zoologists and botanists. A four weeks stay would have been extremely rewarding for the study of the mammals alone. In spite of the disturbances caused by the mules, which could be heard and seen from a great distance, I saw three to five herds of Orbeki antelopes and black-tailed antelopes, both species being splendid and elegant reddish brown and yellow-brown little animals. In addition, I saw reedbuck bigger than our deer, I saw hippos and baboons, I heard hyenas and grey jackals and I saw fresh tracks of the latter two from the night before. I also saw tracks of leopards, caracals and genet cats, of kudus, pukus and striped gnus. Two different types of partridge near the river, always in twos or in tens, as well as rather large numbers of guinea-fowl, medium-sized bustards and fish eagles could be seen quite often. Yet I was so occupied with my noble job as donkey driver that it would have been senseless to kill any game. Since I and the sick Muschemani were the last ones and I had to carry the load of the mules which they continually threw off and Muschemani had to carry my equipment, who would have carried the kill? The wooded ridge to the left was part of the high plateau stretching to the Maschupia—Inguisi river which flows south-westerly until Mambowa and then into the Zambezi. The Maschupia call the Makumba rapids at Mambowa 'Kalata', the next rapids between those and the ferry at the mouth of the Tschobe 'Sanza' and the one in the south which we could hear very closely from our first camp 'Nampe'. On our journey I noticed many mimosa and mopani trees full of thorns; the soil was humus and brackish clay in the valley and laterite in the woods.

Instead of the chief who had been given to me as a guide I found in the camp two different guides, Monoisah and Mangwato, equally 'nice gentlemen' as their predecessors. The camp-site was located on the lower Silamba, which is a stream covered with high reeds. At the time of our expedition it consisted only of deep pools full of fish and sometimes inhabited by crocodiles. It lay about 970 metres above sea level.

Early in the morning (of 11 June) our second day's journey began. We rested at noon on the left bank of a deep brook, the Silamba, after a trip of 8 km. Our resting place was situated 1,002 m above sea level and north-east of our last camp. The route went up through the Silamba valley, first on its right bank, then on its left bank. In the beginning this journey was not too hard. Yet already by 9 o'clock the heat was very great even though this time I had two more blacks helping us to drive the stubborn mules who were not yet used to their loads. Slopes of laterite ridges are characteristic of the Silamba valley. In the south, on the left bank, they stretch down to the Zambezi and in its broad valley there were impenetrable thickets of mimosa trees and bushes as if the rather flat wooded plateaux were armed against would-be intruders against their open sides. In the third kilometre where the valley bent we heard lion roaring at short intervals which terribly frightened James who had been bought from Afrika whereas the female donkey trotted on undisturbed. The second mule which Rev. Coillard had given to my wife as a present was unworried by the impending danger and began to nibble on grass and flowers. His relaxedness surprised us more than James' nervousness. I understood why the female donkey, coming from the south, was not impressed by the lion's roar. Yet Coillard's mule had already gone through some quite bad experience in this respect. On his way from Mambowa to Schescheke (when Coillard was moving there) two companion mules were torn from beside him by a pride of lions and were devoured. We saw for the first time on this trip the most beautiful hartebeest, the Kakatombe hartebeest, yet we could not get close enough to these magnificent creatures to shoot one of them. The bird life seemed to be very rich in the valley, especially on the shady wooded slopes where they were very well protected by the thorny bushes. The reeds around the pools were also full of birds. When I arrived at our resting place by a small tree under which our tablecloth was spread, I found some of our porters in the nearby pool fishing in a completely new style. The men waded up to their chests in the water and pushed their harpoon lances slantwise in front of them into the water—in fact, they literally threw them and in a short time they had speared nine catfish even though the very same pool had been fished twice already with similar success by the first group of porters under the control of Fekete and Oswald on their way back and forth. The catfish when chased seem to dig themselves into the mud and thus the weapon hits them more certainly than if they were to swim. With respect to the porters I did not have too many complaints on those first days' journey. The only thing I did not like even during those first days was their reluctance to stay overnight in the places I chose. Admittedly 8 km was not a long journey but, on the one hand, it was quite hard labour for me to drive the mules before I had trained Muschemani and two other attendants for this noble job and, on the other hand, we had slowly to get used to walking. For we had to carry our guns and ammunition ourselves as well as our barometers, thermometers and chronometers because of the barely sufficient number of porters. And finally the noon rest place was a place which promised fresh meat and the skin of a kakatombe antelope. This skin had to be cured very quickly in order to be sent to Blockley with the porters going back to Panda-ma-Tenka. Already on our second day's journey the porters gave away their tactics. If they had been paid a flat fee for a certain distance, for example, for a trip that required a three day journey, i.e. a distance of fifty to sixty kilometres, then they tried to walk this distance very fast—if possible in two days. They followed, however, the opposite tactics if they were paid per day's journey. If, for instance, the distance could be covered easily in two days they tried to stretch it over three days. This comprehension of the tariffs reminded me slightly of the European hackney coachman; later, however, it became worse. If the distance was 90 km, i.e.five to six days' journey, I could be sure that they would throw down the bundles on only the third day and would refuse to go any further even if a fee had been agreed upon for the entire distance. Our third day's journey went through the Silamba valley and then right into a side valley which we entered from the north. It contained, like all these valleys, a depression. The ground of the valley was sand, clay, crumbling clay and humus out of which the termites had built conic hills 3 m high which had underground structures of corresponding depth.

We continued our journey in the afternoon until the evening when after eleven kilometres we reached a harvested corn field of Mokanda's village[15] at 1,002 m above sea level. Towards evening the journey was slightly more interesting than early in the morning but the ground was so hard and so hot that our feet became sore.

To my great mortification the course which we followed was directly to the east. Had we had Zanzibaris as porters we would have gone straight to the northeast to chief Sakasipa.[16] Like this, however, we were forced to take the course to the east to Matakala's residence and only from there could we go more to the north in order to reach Sakasipa's. This way which we were forced to take ran almost parallel to the Zambezi. During the first kilometres we passed a pool of stagnant rainwater on the right called *kilinda* and one on the left, called *kaunga-unga* which previously were both fed by a spring. In their vicinity had existed some villages which were abandoned after the water ran dry. Abandoned also was the old village Mo-Goma (a snuffbox) about four kilometres to the right in the bush along the laterite hill. Instead, after ten kilometres, we passed the new Mo-Goma village,[17] situated like most Maschupia and Matoka villages high up in the wooded laterite hills and about one to two kilometres away from the nearest water source. On the northern bank of the central Zambezi it happens quite frequently that a village is shifted after the soil, which is never fertilised, has been exhausted by farming. The village is shifted for a rather short distance, up to at most ten kilometres, and then as a rule has the same name or more often is called after its chief, for example, Mokanda's village.

We passed literally through a labyrinth of huts dispersed across the slope of the wooded laterite hill and finally reached the place where Fekete's porters had already established their camps. Here we met two more Makalaka who had come from the north in order to be hired. They were called Sealand (a true giant who turned out later to be quite a coward) and Chimborasso (the black sheep of our bodyguard). The women were still busy everywhere in the fields harvesting the pumpkins so that many of the little huts in the fields, in which they live in the summer when working, were occupied. A real emigration from the village to the rather distant huts takes place when the fields are being worked in the summer. If the tribe is well-to-do and if the area is full of wild animals the huts are enclosed by a fence of high and strong palisades taken from wood which has just been cleared to make a field. Even though it was in the middle of the winter the harvested fields were full of blooming plants especially along the ridges. They were mostly from the family of the cynarcea of which a dark blooming centaurea and a purple conyca were particularly attractive.

Here we encountered the kindest people of our whole expedition north of the Zambezi. The women who were living all around us in their huts in the fields flocked around us, in particular to gaze at my wife. The men of the village might have already seen Europeans when visiting Gazungula and Panda-ma-Tenka, and some of them might even have seen Mrs Westbech and Mrs Coillard. The women, however, who had never been south of the Zambezi had seen neither European men nor women. This was the reason for their curiosity which, however, was mostly concentrated on my wife. These women, who, because of the mingling of the Matoka and the Maschupia, had the most beautiful faces among all negro women we saw on our trip, came up to my wife, kneeling down in front of her and clapping their hands. They gave her the title 'Morena mosari' (princess) and gave her presents. These were bowls full of corn, millet, beans and peanuts. The men brought us beer, and some of it even for my black servants. It goes without saying that all these people had to be given gifts in return since this is implied in the concept of a present on the central Zambezi. Thus they got glass beads—chief Mokanda, however, a 'sitsiba'. This is a two metre piece of cloth just enough for the customary small leather or grass skirt.

That evening I bought food for my porters, i.e. beans and millet, and early the next morning we left the place. I knew that we were to go to a chief called 'Matakala'. Since I had heard of him in the Zambezi area neither in 1875 and 1876 nor during the last eight months, and since I had not heard anything about him during my three weeks' stay at Victoria Falls, I was certain that he was living very far from the Zambezi. You can imagine my surprise when we were told during our journey of 12 June that we would get to Matakala on the next day. Yet I was even more surprised that we maintained all the time an easterly direction and that we were still so close to the Zambezi that, when the path turned at some point, I was able from our high wooded laterite hill, to recognise the river shining like a silver band in the south, although we had left it four days ago.

I had been told in Gazungula that at first I had to go towards the east—I have already mentioned why this was necessary—but I thought that Matakala's residence was at least forty kilometres north of the Zambezi. This, indeed, was a great disappointment. Now everything was completely clear to me, even before I ever

1   *The Matoka (Toka) women of Mokanda's (Siamakanda) village bring presents to Mrs Holub*

reached the chief. It did not seem as if Matakala would be a very promising friend and patron for us. This was proved by the message he had given to our servant Simundaj whom we had sent to him during our stay in Gazungula in order to hire porters for me. Simundaj went there to find out whether he could hire porters. His fellow-countrymen were immediately willing to do this in order to earn something. Yet Matakala had the recruiter caught and asked him for my presents. 'You will get them when my master arrives', Simundaj replied. Yet this answer was obviously not satisfactory for Matakala and he took Simundaj's pole-axe as security until he received my presents. And he gave the servant the following message for me: 'Tell your master that, if the Marutse King Luanika wants to give him porters and has ordered them for him, he himself should herd the "Batu" [people, porters] together with a stick, i.e. by force. If however, I, should give them voluntarily, your master will have to pay me for them. My people are not allowed to go with him unless I give them permission.' Yet his men (thirty-three of them) came anyway. Simundaj, however, did not get his axe back until I bought it back with presents after my arrival at Matakala's.

The two journeys we made on 12 June were 11 and 5 km long respectively. The two places were 1,065 and 1,046 m above sea level. At noon we arrived at the first place, the lower course of the Kamakuni stream and in the evening we arrived at the village of the subchief Seruera,[18] situated among fields. On our journey in the morning we first marched alongside the deeply indented hilly and rocky slopes of the Zambezi laterite mountain range formed by trachyte boulders and slag. We then crossed two temporarily dry tributaries flowing into the Silamba on our left and entered a huge laterite hill range more than six kilometres wide overgrown with numerous trees such as *mohamane, mororo, mochuluchulu* etc. which were laden with tasty fruits.

The march was very exhausting as is usually the case in such forests with loose ground. Because of these long journeys on foot to which she was not accustomed my wife's feet had become sore and she tried to ride one of the three mules. We chose the strongest and most able one for her. This was Jacob. Since he was on principle against such an employment he tried in the beginning to get rid of his rider through all kinds of possible and impossible jumps. When all this did not help he ran with his load against the trees on the left and right hand side of the road. Thus my wife was forced to jump down if she did not want to have her limbs broken. Under his previous load of glass beads, however, Jacob trotted on quietly and seriously as if nothing had ever excited him. Thus, Mrs Holub's ride north of the Zambezi ended after a dangerous experiment of one half hour.

The afternoon march went through the valley of the Ketschwe stream which flows south into the Zambezi. Then it went again up a laterite ridge and we came into Seruera's village situated in the midst of large fields. It gave us a picture of the life of southern Matoka families in their 'summer residence'. Within the palisade fence the maize cobs were hanging from poles and trees. Two eleven to twelve-year old girls dressed in little leather skirts only reaching to their knees were taking the maize cobs down and throwing them on a place on the ground which had been stamped flat. Then naked little boys or six to eight-year-old little girls in short skirts of leather straps beat the cobs with sticks in order to thrash out the corn. Two female slaves and subwives of the owner of the farm, also naked except for the short little skirts, were threshing the maize which was slightly soaked in water. With a peculiar rapid and jerking movement of their bodies they swayed their long and heavy clubs rhythmically. In the meantime the head wife was sitting on a mat separating the fully-threshed from the half-threshed maize in order to throw the latter once again back into the mortar. She did not seem to exhaust herself very much since she was here the mistress and enjoyed the special graces of her master and husband as his momentarily favourite wife. Perhaps she will be in favour with him for years, perhaps only for a few months, yet the poor creature knows how to use this time well. And yet these women, unless they are slaves, get better treatment than the women of the Makalaka, the Matabele and those Betschuana tribes among whom the plough has not yet been introduced. The men of this village were busy chopping and clearing the bush to enlarge the fields. Two men cut off the thick branches in the top of the big trees. Others cut down the dead trees and bushes completely. The strong thick branches they then carry to the edges of the piece of land chosen for the field, and here they build a low fence against antelopes. The young boys pile the dry bushwood on the laterite ground and around the trees, the branches of which have just been cut off. A few days later they burn these piles of wood in order to use the ashes as fertiliser as well as to speed the process of decay of the truncated trees by burning them. It has become evening by now and the housewife keeps a moderate fire going to her left near the hut where in a shallow hollow two pots, each sitting on three stones, are simmering and bubbling. Millet is boiling in one pot and dried sliced pumpkin in the other. This is for the big meal of the day which these tribes eat in the evening. The men of these Zambezi tribes help the women much more with their fieldwork than the men of southern tribes. Yet during the times when there is not much fieldwork they go hunting or put up their fish nets and weirs in the Zambezi and in its lagoons and tributaries. The central and northern Betschuana, especially the Bakwena and the two Bamangwato tribes as a rule hunt for five or six months which is not the case with the Zambezi tribes who usually only go hunting for several hours or days. If these Matoka hear that no Matabele are in the area and that Europeans have arrived from the south in Panda-ma-Tenka or in Gazungula they rush there with baskets full of fruits on their carrying poles. This is always very welcome for the arriving stranger. Or they bring containers made out of pumpkin or so-called calabashes filled with thirty to forty kilograms of millet, maize, beans or groundnuts. They walk very fast, lifting the carrying pole resting on their left shoulder with a stick which is resting on their right shoulder in order to lighten the load. This shorter stick serves also as a weapon in addition to the two spears which they carry in their hands and which they also use as knives in order to cut the grass for their camp site in the evening and to dig holes into the ground to stick branches in for the fence around the camp. They ask for calico and glass beads for the objects they bring to exchange. As soon as the exchange is made they force the cloth into the calabashes and hurry home happily to their people where they tell all they have seen in great detail and at great length. This trade is really well organized and the Matoka like it very much. Often the actual tradesman is accompanied by his brothers as porters who then ask the same in return from him. Many, however, have slaves who have to do the carrying. The Victoria Falls are considered by the natives as the best trading area. Often they bring the cheap cloths they get there further north to the Matoka in order to exchange them for cheap grain with at least 100 per cent profit. If a European does not know the peculiar characteristics of the individual tribes he is generally cheated and robbed considerably. For his calico has a rather high monetary value at the Zambezi, i.e. at least sixty kreuzer, and even the cheapest rejects obtain this price.

When we got up in our camp early in the morning of 13 June we were very surprised to see a white smoke column in the south-south-east which was identified by our porters as the spray of the Victoria Falls. Matakala's village thus was very close to them. Yet during my three weeks' stay at this wonder of nature I did not hear anything about this village. After a march of several hours we arrived at noon on 13 June in Mo-Rukumi[19], Matakala's residence. This village was to the north-east of Seruera's village. Our camp was situated 998 m above sea level and the whole trip had been 16 km. Mo-Rukumi again consists of several villages, usually named after their chiefs, scattered through the bush along a huge laterite ridge. The residence of the Paramount chief, however, with about twenty huts, is located in the valley on the little Kikinde stream. On our journey we crossed three laterite ridges which became increasingly wider the further north we went. On the first one (only 4 km wide) we passed abandoned huts in the fields and fallow soil. In the bush itself we saw many *mosauri* trees. From there we came into the valley of the Derefe stream where I detected conglomerates of swamp ore and brown clay iron ore. In the bush on the second laterite ridge we found the *biscuit fruit* tree and the *mohamane* tree and in a clearing a type of protea.

This laterite ridge was more than five kilometres long and sloped in the east towards the valley of the Katumba stream.[20] Both valleys narrowed into a gorge towards the Zambezi valley. One could see clearly that from these basin-like depressions here in the laterite ranges the breakthrough to the Zambezi valley had taken place, whereas now those depressions only form the valleys of the upper and the central course of the above-mentioned two streams. In the Katumba valley I spotted a small herd of gnus and tried to stalk them from the dried out stream bed. The others were following behind, among them a servant to whom I had entrusted a rifle. Without looking at me he walked directly up to the animals and thus scared them away so that I could not make even a single shot. Coming out of the stream bed I climbed a nearby small hill, where I sat down for a while since I was seized by fever on this day's march and was only able to drag myself on with great effort. Soon my wife and Leeb were sitting next to me and we watched a rather funny scene which made us laugh heartily. Ever since Gazungula Pit, our tame baboon, had run along completely freely among the dogs, which he liked to tease a great deal, in particular Witstock, Leeb's dog. While I had walked ahead to stalk the gnus he lost sight of me and ran into the bush where he could not find us. I was already about to follow him into the bush when he appeared between the trees, stood up, and looked around in order to spot us. Then he ran a few steps, stopped again, barked loudly, and expressed great fear in his gestures and shrieks. Yet he did not see us and I did not allow my people to call him in order to see what he would do. I had just given this order when Pit rapidly climbed a nearby *mopani* tree and looked around, without, however, being able to spot us since we were sitting in the high grass. So I could not help but walk up to him and the animal was overjoyed. He ran up to me, chattered with his teeth, clasped my knees and then jumped up several times looking in the direction from which he had come, growled angrily as if something had misled him and was responsible for his misfortune.

From the last laterite ridge we overlooked the Ki-sinde valley which is two to three kilometres wide. From this distance we saw already the grass roofs of the royal residence built along the edge of the woods at the foot of a kopje across the valley. We first walked through one of those dangerous grass walls, which we subsequently found so often and which caused us some quite serious trouble. These are grass thickets about two metres high. Then we came to a clearing. These clearings turned out to be tobacco fields, mostly located in the shade of huge blue mimosa trees. Near one of those fields a beautiful fan palm towered high over the bushes, and this place, which was also marked by subdivided tobacco fields, was pointed out to us as the venerated burial place of the last chief. After a half hour march through the valley we arrived at the Sinde stream which is a clear burbling little stream 1·5 m wide and about forty centimetres deep. In several of its deeper pools, however, crocodiles can be found frequently. Soon after we had crossed the river we came to the camp of our advance guard, led by Oswald and Fekete, which had arrived the previous day. They had pitched camp under a big mimosa tree. Well-prepared goat meat was awaiting us for a welcome. We enjoyed it immensely and when we had stretched out, relaxed and comfortable, we exchanged our experiences on the trip. 'Everything went well,' Fekete and Oswald reported. 'We had a rather pleasant journey, good fishing in the Silamba and the 2 m of cloth were accepted willingly as payment by the porters. We repaired a rifle for the king and he gave us a goat in return. The king hopes for a present not less than a rifle, otherwise he would not be able to give us porters.' These words confirmed what I had feared and yet I could not give away even a single gun. And even if I had had one to spare I would not have been able to give it away since I had to promise formally to the Marutse King Luanika neither to give a single rifle under any circumstances to the Matoka, Makalaka, Mankoja etc. who owed tribute to him, nor to his enemies the Maschukulumbe. Only under these conditions had he allowed me to pass through his country. This promise as well as the thought that I might perhaps have to return to the Marutse once again determined me not to accede to King Matakala's demands. As soon as we had eaten we grabbed a particular bundle containing Leuzendorf linen, a special wide sort of linen with red stripes which literally cannot be worn out, and we began to cut from it over fifty sitsibas (two-metre-long skirts) in order to pay our porters immediately. I was very surprised that only a few porters were present; all the others had gone to the king's residence. Immediately I suspected something bad and unfortunately I was again right this time. I immediately called my own men together and told them not to leave our loads under any circumstances. Then I told my white companions that the porters had gone to Matakala to ask him for a share of the booty and to squeeze out of me at least double the payment that they had agreed upon at the Zambezi. My native people refused to believe this and even Oswald laughed saying that those people were 'good'. He had already paid some of them and had even given them the cheap quality cloth, whereas I was willing to give them the first rate linen. Yet I maintained my assertion and the following half hour proved that I was completely right.

From the village came a line of about fifty men, and behind them walked my Maschupia porters, all walking in an orderly fashion in single file. From the wooded laterite ridge to the right (to the east) came another group with women and children. On the whole there might have been 300 people who thought it proper to appear for the official visit. Matakala's area might have a total of 3,800 to 4,000 inhabitants and it stretches down to Victoria Falls. He is subject to the Marutse yet has the title 'king'. In his empire are only two Marutse subchiefs, so to speak, as representatives of Luanika. They live in the immediate vicinity of Victoria Falls; one of them is the political official, the second one the so-called watchman of the boats. He has the same function as Luschuane had in Gazungula. Without his consent no foreign black coming from the north may cross the Zambezi, and no European coming from the south. It is also the obligation of the first official to report immediately to the distant Marutse court any movement of the Matabele in the south of Albertsland.[21] Apart from a more nominal than actual subjection which requires merely an annual present as a tribute, Matakala is really absolutely sovereign in his kingdom. His government is despotic even though it is not as bad as that of Luanika over the Marutse, and that of Lobengula over the Matabele. In my earlier book I have already reported about the manners and customs of the Matoka who were previously living in Albertsland on the southern bank of the Zambezi. Now I was personally going to meet Matakala who previously had caused me so many troubles and difficulties. He soon appeared in the open space before us and sat down on a wooden stool which was brought after him. The accompanying crowd, among which we detected a few hatchet-faced old men as his counsellors, squatted down on the ground close behind and next to him. To his right our porters sat down with their leaders Mangwato and Monaisak in the front, while the Matoka women and children and those who came later sat down in the rear at a little distance.

I greeted the king through my interpreters Boy and Mopani. The king returned my greetings and then told me that I should pay my porters. I replied 'The payment upon which they have agreed in Gazungula before their chiefs is already prepared for them' and I pointed to a big pile of pieces of calico cloth which formed a loosely stacked little mountain 2 m long. My men then stepped forward handing them out to the porters. They began however, to laugh, clutching their loads closer to them. Matakala told me I had to give to each of the porters 'two sit-sibas, i.e. instead of the agreed 2 m, 4 m of cloth'. 'No, I shall not do so! English-men when they need porters give only two yards which is less than 2 m. I anyway give them more and I even provided the porters with food which Englishmen do not do.' At this point all my Maschupia porters started shouting. They jumped up, waving their sticks and threatening with their spears. And among each other they shouted 'No, we will not accept such a miserable payment.' Matakala's people laughed and agreed with them while the king remained calm and called one of his servants to give him an order. The main thing was not to lose nerve in the face of such turmoil. I remained calm, indeed, studying the features of the king. Matakala was a young man of hardly twenty years of age. Passion, however, had already traced deep furrows in his face. He had a restless eye and he was unable to look openly into our faces. This disclosed, more than anything else, his wicked and per-fidious character. He was clad in a short woollen shirt and a cloth skirt; his people wore short and filthy cloth skirts and the even poorer ones leather skirts, all of a disgusting brownish colour.

The porters showed by angry words and threatening gestures that they would not give back the loads they carried. In the midst of this turmoil the servant whom Matakala had sent away returned with a two-year-old boy. He was a charming little child and Matakala's favourite son. He stared at us with great curiosity since we were the first white men he had seen. I gave my wife a sign and she took a little hand mirror and two little wooden whistles which we always carried along in a box for possible presents, and gave them to the child. I saw the effect of this in Matakala's features and tried to use it at once. I called on my servants as witnesses and I shouted at Monaisak and Mangwato that I as physician and *Naka* (magician) would call them liars if they would not admit that only two metres of cloth and not more were agreed upon in Gazungula as payment. Monaisak kept quiet and would not look me in the eye; neither would his companion. Immediately I tried to use this moment. 'No, I shall never give two sitsibas, yet'—and I turned to Matakala—'since the men did a good job I will still give each of them this much in addition'—and I showed a 20 cm stick of wood—'but I will not give any-thing more. If they want more they should try to take it by force.' The porters became silent. Matakala talked to Monaisak and Mangwato in a low voice. Both got up and began to talk to their people. These gentlemen who shortly before tried to threaten me gave in and were satisfied with the new payment which I had indicated—except for five who were Matakala's tribesmen whom Westbech had already pointed out to me as scoundrels in Gazungula. Yet I had had to hire them in that emergency. A new roll of linen was taken out and new sitsibas were measured, cut and distributed. The two guides got double payment and when later on they came secretly and asked more for their 'good service.' Monaisak got some more trinkets but Mangwato did not get anything more. The five shady characters did not accept the payment. I finally threw it in front of them, picked up our loads from the ground and carried them into our camp. This camp consisted of two enclosures formed by thorny bushes around which our servants had been sitting so that nothing got stolen while all of us were negotiating with Matakala and our porters.

2 *(Toka) Matoka chief (Mudukula) Matakala*

Since all the rest of the porters immediately turned around to go home the five recalcitrants were forced to accept their payment as well, because otherwise Matakala would simply have taken away their pieces of cloth. I gave the king a few trinkets and promised my exchange visit for the afternoon in order to bring the actual presents and to negotiate about the next porters. We could breathe somewhat freely again, but this event had made it clear to me how difficult it would be to get porters. In a minute the scene had changed immediately with the swiftness of primitive people. It was an atmosphere of love and friendship. Women, children and men came up to us to sell us milk and even butter, goats and bread. Only the Matoka in the very south and then again those in the very north, i.e. Mapanza's people,[22] have a few head of cattle, otherwise there are no cattle in the country since the tsetse flies are too dangerous for them.

Except for the Marutse and the Maschupia I found that among those tribes I know only the Matoka make butter; and they alone make bread. For this they take *mausa* meal pounded in the wooden mortars and mix it with a sweetish fruit in order to thicken it. Then they work the dough with their hands into firm balls. These are formed, boiled, and eaten after they have become cool. For twelve of these rolls which are about as big as a fist people ask just as much as for one dwarf goat, that is, they ask for one sitsiba. After the men had been paid we grabbed those loads which contained presents and I selected the following pieces: for Matakala a Belgian bayonet, a bar of lead, two brass poles about a finger thick and 1 m long, thin copperwire, a pipe, a trooper's helmet, a blanket, a pair of black trousers with two broad red stripes down the sides, a few sitsibas of cheap cloth, 2 lb of big, blue glass beads and a box of costume jewellery, from the Pforzheim theatre company, which Westbech had given to me. For his head wife I selected a skirt of *cosmanos* upholstery material and for the children some toys. Boy carried the standard before us; my wife and I plus two natives armed with guns followed. The huts of the residence were scattered and there was no fence around them. We were led into a small hut, the only one which seemed surrounded by a palisade fence close to its cylindrical wall. Inside the hut the young chief was lying in a half reclining position on a low hard bed of straight branches. Without a word he accepted our presents and I realised how much he was disappointed by the fact that the gun was missing. Yet he did not mention it. He offered us beer which a female servant brought and put on the floor between us and the chief. He drank first from it in order to show us that the drink was not poisoned, then the well-known ladles made out of long stemmed gourds called *mokopes* were brought and we sipped the liquid called *butschuala* which is made of fermented millet and looks like thin beer but with a not unpleasant taste. After we had exchanged some greetings I immediately brought up my request for porters. The king answered negatively using all kinds of excuses. He would not have enough people, they were out hunting, they were far away fishing and similar phrases. I did not press any further since I realised that I had to apply a similar policy.

We left. A newly filled pot—or rather a beautifully burnt clay container of approximately seven litres' capacity—was carried after us. We had hardly returned to the camp and were sitting on the grass to eat our supper when representatives of the king showed up. Mopani translated what they were saying: 'You have bought a present for the king's wife—this is for his current favourite.' My wife got curious. What? This fellow has several wives? The messengers continued: 'Now the other seven complain about this.' My wife thought she had misunderstood and made Mopani to ask them once more. But the messengers began to tell the names of all these beauties and they counted them on their fingers, starting with the small finger of their left hand moving towards the right and then continuing to count from the thumb of the right hand until they in fact got it up to eight wives for this rather insignificant man. My wife was extremely upset and decidedly against any present for these women. 'Why does he take them?' she said, looking at me reproachfully. 'Well, my dear, it is not my fault that Matakala is so rich in wives,' I replied, 'and you know it is very dangerous to have women as your enemies'—she gave me a very cross look—'and thus I think we shall give some presents to the other seven as well. Just remember, I must get porters, we cannot get stuck here for ever.'

My wife personally selected seven more short skirts. The female readers of this book will understand completely that this time she did not take the solid upholstery material but rather the contrary. The messengers left, but they were back again in the evening. The king now asked for a rifle. He sent his messengers in the evening so that if I should give him one none of his subjects should be able to see it and possibly report it to the Marutse. I did not give him the rifle yet I sent him instead 0·25 of coarse gunpowder even though I really did not like to do so. It was the first and the last time on this expedition north of the Zambezi that I gave gunpowder to natives whom I did not know personally. This then was the end of our diplomatic relations on the first day.

Except for the howling of hyenas and the call of a lonely leopard roaming on the other side of the Ki-Sinde stream, nothing disturbed the night's rest. We got up early to prepare for the astronomical determination of our location and in order to pick out the objects for exchange needed for the day. In spite of my exhaustion from the past days I had not slept very well since the question of the porters worried me terribly.

Very early in the morning little boys and girls came with milk; then at eight o'clock His Highness appeared—this time dressed in a different coloured shirt which many months before might have been white. The headman whispered a report to me that He, the great man, had not slept a wink all night as he was so anguished with my hard-heartedness about the rifle. 'I have only as many as I need myself,' I said, 'and you know that I am going to the Maschukulumbe.' 'Oh, no, Sir, do not go there, they shall kill you all.' 'Yet I have to go there and from what you said just now we shall be needing our guns there very much.' The king got up, discontented, and walked away. As soon as he got up one of his attendants grabbed the beautifully carved wooden stool and followed His Highness. But after about twenty steps the latter stopped and immediately the true attendant put the stool down behind him. Yet Matakala turned around and came back again. He began a long speech talking about ingratitude, about the first thirty-three porters whom he had sent to me at Gazungula, about how he had helped me the day before when the Maschupia porters of Makumba had given me a hard time. I had my interpreter tell him the following in a very casual way: that I had already given presents and that I had sent through Monaisak yesterday a letter to Monari Westbech telling Liomba, the representative of the Marutse king, in what an unruly way the porters had behaved. Matakala pricked up his ears and showed an ugly smile. 'That may be'—he said—'go ahead and report about me also to the Marutse, our suppressors. In this country I am the king and you shall not get any porters. What do you do then? Then everything is mine, everything you have.' 'Mopani,' I shouted at the interpreter, 'tell Matakala that I cannot give him a rifle and that my things are not in his possession. I would rather pile them all up and set them on fire than let him take them by force.' At that Matakala became very furious and his people displayed a rather menacing mood. My people had already reached for their rifles and our few black men seemed to start polishing their spears, but at that point an unexpected figure appeared on the scene. The person who arrived was a young, rather stout black of medium height wearing a top hat. He was Mokuri, the subchief from Victoria Falls and Matakala's nephew. I had given him this hat in October 1885, but I had not bought the millet and the beans which several of his slaves had brought to me for purchase.[23] Thus he had left me rather cross. But when he appeared now, he did not remember anything about this incident. Even though it was early in the morning he was rather high—as often happened with him—from drinking too much *butschuala*, and so he was in a very gay mood. He behaved rather familiarly and before Matakala's eyes he collapsed the old hat. When he pressed the hat down on his knee for the first time Matakala bent down to marvel at the miracle of the *hutsi* (the word for straw hats, since the natives only wear straw hats which they make themselves). At that moment Mokuri let the spring snap and the poor king jumped up in a fright which his little son enjoyed very much. Now Matakala tried himself to make the mechanism work and caused terrific amusement for everybody around—expressed by a Homeric roar of laughter. This laughter, however, caused a bad coughing fit in Matakala. The cough sounded hoarse and ugly and when coughing he distorted his face with vehement pain. Immediately I addressed the king through Jonas, my valet, saying: 'Sir, you are ill.' Matakala looked up with surprise. Yet before he could say a word, Mokuri told him that I was a great physician and that I had cured several porters who were ill. All of a sudden Matakala's countenance became more cheerful, a big grin appeared on his face. '*Naga, Naga*,' he said in a low voice, '*Naga* help me.' I at once began to describe to him the symptoms of his disease and he nodded his head without saying a word. None of the Matoka doctors had ever explained it to him like this. Once he had placed his confidence in me I began to examine his sick chest by listening and tapping. I found a severe chronic bronchial catarrh from which he must have already suffered for quite some time, as an emphysema-type dilatation of the lungs had developed. Immediately I gave him medicine, three jars (morphia with digitalis at intervals with aqua laurocerasi and some specamanha syrup) per day, in order to soothe the coughing and I promised him the real medicine for later, when I had seen the effect of these three jars. Matakala felt better after the first jar and he asked for all the medicine. 'No, sir, I cannot give it to you now.'—'I shall give you two goats.'—'No, thank you.'—'Then a sheep, just think, a sheep.'—'No, thank you.'—'Do you want young boys?'—'No, but porters.'—'Porters?'—'Yes, indeed. Listen, Morena, you will give me *kamuso* [tomorrow] when the *letsatsi qua* [the sun is there], eighty-nine men as porters'—the number of my loads had decreased because of the payment to the porters and the presents. Furthermore I had added to ten loads 2 lb each—'and I will go with them to the next chief.'—and I pointed to the north. 'Having arrived there I will give your men this medicine to take it back to you.' Matakala seemed stupefied by my argument and finally agreed without objections. Later that day in addition a sheep was brought to me as a present anyway, for which I immediately gave him some colourful pieces of cloth as presents in exchange so that one could not say that I owed him anything. In the evening he again sent some of his closest and most reliable men to me. He obviously seemed to regret his promise. His original plans 'to squeeze as much out of me as possible' had not been realised and thus these courtiers came to me with an old musket and asked me 'to exchange' the king's *monati tlobolo* (beautiful rifle) against a breech-loading rifle. They could not get me to do it even when they came back once more and wanted to add one more sheep to the exchange price.

While all these political negotiations were going on, our camp was the object of the greatest curiosity on the part of the natives. Their eagerness for fraternisation and friendship went so far that my servants were invited by the female servants of the king for a cancan in the evening. Some of my servants promised to come while others refused, for most of these female slaves had husbands, given to them by the king, who worked in fields in the nearby bush. If these temporary 'widows' are caught, doing such a dance, the guilty males get a good beating, unless they have been invited to the dance by the husbands and have previously paid them the usual handful of blue glass beads or a tablespoon of small white glass beads as compensation. Then it is all right. Oh well, every country has its own customs! Three of my servants asked me for glass beads and I gave them to them. In the evening that dance really took place right in front of the king's huts and with loud shouting and the sound of castanets. We Europeans, however, stayed in the camp and it is needless to say that we watched our belongings particularly well. Early in the morning the natives sitting around a fire were talking about the events of the night and Siroko's name especially was mentioned very often. As this caught my attention I asked for him and found out that Siroko was missing. 'Okai Siroko?' (where is Siroko?). They started laughing and then I learned that he got beaten up during the dance and that he was down at the river pouring cold water over his painful back. That was the end of the little dance.

About the dance itself we learned the following: men and boys form a circle and, clapping their hands, they sing a monotonous song. Seventeen women and girls showed up who one by one assumed a position among the clapping men. One of the men jumps into the empty centre of the circle, bending forward and backward and jumping hither and thither, until a woman or a girl whom he pleases jumps into the circle as well and then both start an obscene dance with gestures and jumps. When they are tired they move back to their former position and another man takes the dance up again and so on.

That day I hired a new servant, a subject of Matakala called Monohela who soon proved to be very useful and became one of my best men. The first of the porters I required came early but most of them only later in the morning so that it was not possible to set out finally on our journey before eleven.

The scattered settlements which comprised Matakala's town along the laterite ridge have special district names according to the headmen, who are Matakala's subchiefs. Often they are so far apart that one has to walk for hours between one settlement and the next. They are all located far away from water and in the middle of the fields. This dispersion of their settlements is advantageous for the Matoka since they do not have to walk for hours to their fields as the Betschuana tribes have to do. Furthermore, this arrangement is useful in strategical respects. It is impossible for their enemies, whether they are the Marutse or the Matabele whom they fear even more, to use their otherwise favourite tactics of setting the whole town on fire during the night and plundering it. I shall illustrate by sketches some of the villages and kraals, partly surrounded by palisades, partly unenclosed, which we saw. Individual kraals were always enclosed, villages, however, seldom. Fewer measures for personal security seem to be taken where several homes are located close together. Yet this also depends on the nature of the subchiefs—whether they are alert or lazy men. I will not dispute that rather large Matoka villages also exist, i.e. a type of town, but I did not find any. Instead I saw many towns broken up into single kraals and villages. These settlements, which often lie from hundreds of metres up to several kilometres apart, and which are regarded by us Europeans always as individual settlements, number 5–150 inhabitants each. The average number should be forty-five to sixty people per village and five to twelve per individual kraal.

Among the new porters whom I hired at Matakala's was an old acquaintance. He was a Matoka called Jonas, one of our best servants in Panda-ma-Tenka who had been in our service for quite some time. Later, however, he had gone home. It was a great pleasure to see this good man among all these tramps. Yet it was sad that Jonas did not let himself be hired as a servant but was only willing to come with us to the next chief. To our surprise we found out that he was Matakala's closest relative. If the latter were to die before his little son reached maturity Jonas would become chief of the southern Matoka along the Ki-Sinde stream, since he had greater claims to the 'throne' than the drunkard Mokuri who is already known to the reader. Even though he was a prince, if only a very poor one, he worked like any normal Matoka since his father had not left him anything. He preferred to go into the service of Europeans if such by any chance came to Panda-ma-Tenka or to the Falls. Yet he never engaged himself for a long period of time since Matakala's weak state of health did not exclude his early death and Jonas wanted to be relatively near in that case. Jonas had the most beautiful Bantu head I have seen on all my trips through Africa. And his beautiful face, which had not even become defaced by the *lubeko* (the spoon-like instrument for cleaning the nose which deforms it), was especially lively because of his eyes which were the most beautiful pair of dark eyes I ever saw. In addition Jonas was self-disciplined, honest, faithful, diligent and even though he owned a mirror he was not vain. Before we left Matakala I fixed the payment of the porters for the two and a half days' work they had to do. I ripped off a piece of cloth of 2 m plus and gave it to the king when we left, but before our departure he had to lift it up high and to show it to all the porters present. Then I ripped off a second piece of cloth of equal length and gave it to the first guide Lutschobe whom Matakala had assigned us. He was to take this piece of cloth along and to keep it in order to cut the sitsibas to the right length in the end for the payment.

Of all the long journeys we had to make on the Zambezi from one chief to the next, this journey promised to come closest to what I wished. For when I asked where chief Sakasipa lived, whom I had to visit first according to the message of the Marutse king Luanika, the guide pointed towards north-north-east. When we were just about to leave a group of Matoka men appeared and brought two sheep and two rams. Among these men were those five rebellious porters who refused to take their share when I paid the Makumba porters. Now they wanted to barter and to let themselves be hired again as porters. I refused to take them and called them bad names which they deserved. This caused great amusement among my porters. We left and moved ahead rapidly. I was, however, overjoyed that I had found ways to hire porters among the Matoka.

Thus we left this place, which could have become our grave, newly encouraged, with happy faces and in the best of moods which nobody would have thought possible twenty-four hours before. We began again to trust our good fortune and we marched ahead vigorously towards the unknown north.

III

The Matoka tribes
From Mo-Rukumi to
Mo-Sinkobo

WE COVERED THE MARCH FROM CHIEF MATAKALA to Sakasipa, i.e. from the residence of Mo-Rukumi to Ki-(Mo-)Sinkobo in three successive day journeys. The
first journey of about twelve kilometres took us straight north to the slope of the
large laterite ridge where the settlement Mo-Rukumi is located. Our camp for the
night to the north-east of Mo-Rukumi was 1,123 m above sea level. The second
journey ended after nine kilometres on the upper course of the Kabonda stream
which is a tributary of the Ki-Sinde. The third march of 15 km led in the same
northern direction up to the top of a laterite ridge where Sakasipa's residence Mo-
Sinkobo is situated at 1,254 m above sea level.

Matakala's whole area as well as the Maschupia province through which we
passed belong to a system of laterite ridges between which there are shallow valleys traversed by little streams which never dry out. The laterite ridges as well as
the valleys are well watered and therefore fertile.

Sakasipa's area in its southern part consists of a huge laterite ridge. Its northern
part consists of wooded hills which are partly the central course of the abovementioned stream. In the far north towards the Luenge river there are again laterite
ridges. Before I describe our first day's journey I should like to give a general ethnographic description of the Matoka since at Mo-Rukumi we had reached the first
Matoka settlement which is worth mention. In comparison with the Marutse, the
dominating tribe living in the large bend of the Zambezi, the cultural level of the
Matoka is much lower than that even of the Maschupia, of the Mabunda, of the
Mankoja [Mankoë] and of other tribes within the Marutse empire. Everything is
more primitive in this tribe, the customs are simpler and they are much poorer.
They are poorer because, on the one hand, their rulers, the Marutse, squeeze
everything out of them and because, on the other hand, they can only raise cattle
in a very small area because of the tsetse fly. The Matoka are divided into a host of
small sub-tribes. The most influential tribes of these are tribes in the south which,
however, are less interesting for an ethnographer. They trade more actively, have
more agriculture and are better off than the tribes in the central and northern

areas. The smallest principalities are found in the northern parts; this is among the independent and, as I might say, 'real' Matoka. The southern tribes have often lost their customs and their particular way of life since they have adopted the way of life of the Maschupia and/or the Marutse, and the tribes in the east have adopted the way of life of the Makalaka who moved into this area. Thus these Matoka lost many of their virtues and have gained a lot of vices. As servants to Europeans they are less suitable than their northern fellow tribesmen.

While the Matoka in the north are pure blooded and have a completely black complexion, the southern tribes vary from dark brown to almost black. One tribe, i.e. that of Sakasipa, even has brown people since in a war against the brown Makololo they captured many women. The pure Matoka have longer hair and they mostly wear their kinky frizzled hair hanging down. Their hair is an unmistakable sign of their pure race. The southern tribes have much shorter hair in comparison.

The northern Matoka take special care of their hair, that is of their thick frizzles. Their hair is their pride and they nurse it with greater diligence than their own children. The southern tribes who have greater wants to satisfy which have developed from their contact with the Marutse and the Europeans, have less leisure to play around with their hair and consequently they neglect it. The thick frizzles of these Matoka of more mixed ancestry become shorter from generation to generation and finally their hair is as short as that of the pure Betschuana. Thus, the characteristics of many tribes are changing and some features which many a traveller lists as the characteristic signs of a tribe are nothing other than the varying results of the mingling of neighbouring tribes. During this process the bodies as well as the customs lose their original features and assimilate with each other.

The northern Matoka speak only pure Setoka; in the south this is already mixed with Sekalaka and Serotse words. The language of Sakasipa's sub-tribe is even contaminated by Sesuto words, so that it is not difficult to converse with this tribe if one comes from the south. The pure Matoka use a long form of greeting; the southern Matoka, however, use the Sekololo and also Sesuto greeting *ki-atumela* and the person greeted answers with the Marutse word *schangwe-schangwe*.

The wealthiest tribe of all is that of Matakala. It lives closest to civilisation, has the most active trade, can sell its grain very well, is able to raise cattle, and finally its men can easily take service with the Europeans who happen to visit Panda-ma-Tenka and the Falls as well as with the coloured people who live there (and who are mostly elephant hunters).

Already the housing of the pure Matoka shows their low culture. Following the primitive habitation of the true bushmen when they were independent and the primitive housing of their descendants—the Masarwa—come the huts of the Matoka. Their type of hut is similar to the low Betschuana hut. Among the approximately sixty villages which I visited only five were comparatively well built. The huts are roomier than those of the Betschuana but the walls—except for a few huts of the chiefs—are very much lower. They are only 1·3–1·5 m high. The roof, however, is large and literally reaches down to the ground. Yet neither

are the walls as well built as those of the Betschuana tribes nor is the roof as beautifully built as that of the Marutse. The walls are roughly plastered with a mortar of
clay mud, but as a rule this is only smeared into the gaps between the individual
poles of which the wall consists. Even this is done so poorly that the plaster soon
peels off and falls down so that the wind and the rats can enter freely even the huts
of the most influential Matoka chiefs. The grass on the roof, especially on the
upper half of it towards the peak, is very loose since it is supposed to let the smoke
through and thus it looks brownish even from quite a distance. The Betschuana
use a straight tree trunk to support the peak of their conical roof as do the Marutse,
if they build huts of the Betschuana type. Yet the Matoka often use four or more
poles merely to support the miserable roof. They put them up in the interior of
their huts without arranging them in a symmetrical order.

The entrance of the Matoka huts, however, is generally better protected than
that of the Betschuana. The latter, if they do not yet use European doors which by
now are fairly common, have mostly mats made out of small branches or reeds.
The Matoka, however, make the opening with a double frame of poles as thick as
an arm. In this frame they insert a slab made out of branches or they pile up poles.
This device for closing fits the huts very well and also locks the entrance to the
yard. In many kraals one finds scaffolds for storing containers and baskets; in some
I even saw stands for storing weapons, i.e. the assegais and the shoulder yokes.

I have already mentioned on several occasions the arrangement of the Matoka
kraals, their enclosures which can be found here and there and their fields. In general, the field dwellings of some of the Matoka tribes, i.e. those huts in which they
live only during the time they work in the fields, are built and fortified in a better
fashion, since wild animals appear more often here than in the little villages which
have been inhabited for decades and are more heavily populated. Much more
solidly built than their dwellings are the grain storage containers of the Matoka.
They have different shapes among the various sub-tribes, each characteristic of the
individual sub-tribe. I will leave a detailed description for the discussion of the
sketches which I made at various places. In general, I only want to mention here
that these African silos are small cylindrical or rectangular huts which strike you
from a distance by the fact that they are built on poles and thus stand, so to speak,
in the air. They are made out of hewn pegs, dry branches, reeds, maize stalks and
wicker. Sometimes they are smeared with a light-coloured sand plaster from the
outside or from both sides. They can hold up to 4,000 kg of grain. A fence made
out of thorny bushes is put around them and some wooden rattles or little turtle
shells and clappers are hung on to the bushes in order to keep thieves and wild animals away.

When I compare these grain containers with those of the Betschuana and
Marutse, the grain containers of the Matoka are rather inferior. Although they are
larger they are less practical. The most practical ones are those of the Marutse.
They hold 50 to 150 lbs of grain, are mostly cylindrical, and are very well built.
They have in addition to the main upper opening through which they are filled a
second small and oval shaped opening at the lower end of the cone through which

they are emptied by the mere pressure of the grain. This second opening is covered with a clay or wooden cover which has a little piece of wood as a knob so that it can be pushed out more easily. Except for those round huts described above some of the Matoka tribes still have miserable grass and reeds huts in which sometimes women and children, and sometimes the slaves, live. Their shape can be best compared with a huge nightcap. In the immediate neighbourhood of the small Matoka villages big hyena and lion traps can often be found. I will speak about them later.

Many kraals are decorated with hunter's trophies such as animal skulls or antelope horns similar to those one finds among the Maschupia and the Marutse. The Matoka men work relatively hard in the fields and faithfully help their dear spouses who in return reward them with lots of home-brewed millet beer. For field work the man uses a rectangular hoe as wide as a hand which is a much desired and expensive trading object in the area within the large bend of the Zambezi. For fourteen of these hoes one can buy a woman.

The laterite ridges which preserve the moisture as well as the streams and rivers which flow through the central area of the Matoka lands guarantee a much richer and safer harvest than that in the Betschuana areas.

They grow mostly two types of large millet, called *mabele*; a small cereal called *mausa* or *rosa*; a type of small grained maize; two types of beans; *maschoschwani* —ground nuts; yam-roots, called *manza* there; two types of pumpkin; and much tobacco.

For their tobacco fields the Matoka use mostly ant-hills of very large size or the ruined sites of abandoned villages and houses. Occasionally they build primitive watch huts on poles by these fields. Similar scaffolds, yet without a hut on top, are often found in the maize fields or in palisaded kraals in the vicinity of which many lions live. From them the inhabitants can easily keep watch.

The central and northern Matoka mostly till the valleys and slopes of the laterite ridges and only very rarely the heights. It is striking that they never use the flowing streams to water their fields. The same neglect of precious water could also be observed among the Betschuana before they learned the method of irrigation from the Europeans. The Matoka will very probably benefit from their streams only in the same way. Only in one instance did I see a ditch designed to catch the rainwater and to lead it to a pond of reeds from which drinking water was taken because there were no streams nearby. Yet the ditch was constructed in the wrong way. Instead of digging it above the village which was situated on a wooded slope they had dug it below the village so that with any big rainfall all the dirt of the village was washed into the reservoir of drinking water.

The bush in which most Matoka villages are situated yields many valued products of the vegetable kingdom, i.e. numerous tasty fruits, the most important of which are the strychnia fruits called *mo-chuluchulu* and *mo-schuku* fruits. Other fruits worth mention are the *mo-neko* (manego) which grows in the bush. It yields pure sugar in a slimy form. *Mo-neko* grows on shrubs and little trees, has woolly leaves and belongs to the genus mallow. The *mosauri* is a beautifully strong leguminous tree. It has brown seeds in thin red sugar-containing pods. We soaked the seeds overnight in water; in the morning the loosened pods were swee-tened with honey and we obtained a rather tasty drink quite refreshing in the hot weather. The *mobulu* fruits if dried and pressed are a very tasty and sweet refresh-ment on long journeys. The bulbs of various plants are also eaten but only after their resinous skin is peeled off.

Because of the tsetse fly most Matoka raise only dwarf goats or small fat-tailed sheep; some of the northern Matoka also raise a larger mostly black thin-legged sheep of the same kind. Furthermore, they have dwarf chickens and dogs which have degenerated under the influence of the tsetse fly; in particular, a central Afri-can greyhound degenerated into a housedog. I am quite astonished that people have not yet tried to tame one or another type of wild animal—for example eland, zebra, wild pig, genet cat, guinea-fowl, etc. These animals would be com-pletely suitable for domestication. Among the dwarf goats there is one rather at-tractive type similar to a gazelle as well as a rather degenerated dwarf species originating from the west coast.

As a rule a Matoka has anything from five to twenty goats and some, in ad-dition, two to five sheep. Among the numerous tribes of southern Africa un-doubtedly the Makalaka, living in the western part of the Matebele land, are the filthiest. After them come the Masarwa, a few Hottentot tribes, and then the Matoka follow immediately as the dirtiest in southern Africa. Mercy upon him who has to spend some time in close contact with a large group of Matoka, who must—as we had to do—walk in a group of Matoka beginning to sweat from carrying heavy loads, and who has to stand that terrible smell! About the good and bad aspects of the character of the tribes in the south and in the north I have talked already, yet I have to repeat here that the central tribes in this respect should be considered as the best ones. There is no doubt that the tribes furthest to the south are the worst. After them come the ones furthest north who have some con-tact with the Maschukulumbe. With respect to bravery and courage I should think most of the Matoka tribes possess these qualities. Many a Marutse ruler took refuge with the Matoka when he was expelled from his country and was searching for support to regain his throne. The Matoka have less courage and bravery, how-ever, when dealing with wild animals. Like all Zambezi tribes they have great veneration for their dead chiefs, especially for those who were murdered or died in a battle against their enemies. Their women get better treatment than the Bets-chuana women, yet it is still worse than that of the Marutse women. The Matoka have many slaves although they are not rich themselves. Their slaves are either children of former slaves or the children of neighbouring tribes whom those tribes themselves sell to the Matoka.

I have already discussed this subject and I want only to add that people some-times came up to us in order to sell us millet and other cereals, baskets full of wild fruit, plugs of tobacco, or their handicrafts. When we had bought everything from them they often offered to sell us the boys who had carried their loads.

Since the climate of the areas north of the Zambezi, which are much closer to the equator, is warmer and much more even than that in the Betschuana areas, these people do not have to worry about their winter clothes. A simple short shirt cut out of superficially-cured skins is sufficient for winter and summer.

As comfortable as this paradise-like original way of dressing may be, especially for the husbands, it militates against the development of any crafts related to the making of clothing. How completely different is the situation on the high plateaux of South Africa where the rapid change of temperature and the cold during the winter are very noticeable. Thus the Betschuana tribes are forced to make good leather and fur coats. For the sake of survival in the cold they have become true masters of the tailor's trade. This is one of the many examples of how primitive peoples are trained by their needs and thus develop their culture.

In curing furs and sewing them with animal ligaments the Marutse, of all trans-Zambezi tribes, come closest to the Betschuana, and our Matoka again are much inferior to the Marutse in this respect. Their little skirts, no matter whether they are made out of smooth or rough-cured skins, are very primitive. Often the tail of the little wild animal, ranging from the small mongoose to the grey jackal, is still hanging from the fur. One skin forms the front part and a second one the rear of the little skirt. They are worn by means of a waist belt. If they have any type of decoration at all they have many holes the size of a bean cut in a row along the margin. These, however, are only noticeable in smooth-haired furs. Other but rarely used pieces of clothing are small coats cut like a Spanish cape out of duiker, oribi, kabunda or goat fur. They are somewhat similar to the Betschuana coats, yet only somewhat. The Betschuana coats are beautifully made out of the skins of small antelopes, klipspringers, hares and carnivores, and the Marutse coats are skilfully made out of cow hide reaching down to the ankle. The short Matoka coats, however, are only made out of one fur of the beautiful Kakatombe hartebeest or, among the northern Matoka, out of the furs of the lechwe and puku antelopes; the furs are only slightly cut to shape. The women wear little aprons and skirts mostly made out of goat and sheep skins but normally without any decoration as is common among the Betschuana and Makalaka. Neither are they made so skilfully as the little skirts of the Marutse women which usually are also made out of cow hide, and are worn with the hair side out. Little girls wear fringes of leather straps of twelve to fifteen centimetres long around their waists instead of aprons but they are not nearly as long as those of the Betschuana and not even as long as the aprons of the Masarwa which reach down to their knees. At times these aprons of fringes go all around the hips like a wreath.

The belts are made of leguan, or antelope skins. Among men little sitsiba skirts of cloth are already quite common as well as calico sheets of about two metres in length and one and a half metres in width. Some, in particular the southern Matoka, wear little hats of grass and bark fibre or of palm leaves. Sometimes on a long march they wear sandals of gnu, eland or zebra skin. In terms of decorating their bodies the men decorate most of all their hair; the women, however, their arms, their neck and their breasts. Particularly rich is the hair decoration of the southern Matoka even though of a rather original and

for us somewhat unaesthetical form. The hair is never cleaned; instead, however, all kinds of things are rubbed into it and it is decorated with lots of trinkets.
The usual ornaments are beetles; very tender horns of antelopes; blown-up gall
bladders of various animals; claws of carnivorous animals and birds; tortoise scales
or whole shells of young tortoises; scales of armarylles; small tails of hares; little
bones of various animals (mostly metacarpels); little bags of leguan skin; teeth;
little wooden pegs and pins with or without burnt-in ornaments; red seeds of
leguminous plants arranged in little balls and glued by means of wax to strychnia
fruit shells; colourful feathers of roller-birds, long-tailed shrikes, parrots and several types of white heron; furthermore, empty cartridge cases, glass beads, little
brass plates, etc. All these so-called decorative and beautifying objects are tied to
their curly hair by means of grass threads. More frequently than all other Zambezi
tribes the Matoka wear coloured wooden combs in their hair, in particular the
northern Matoka who groom their hair more than those in the south. A very original decoration consists of strips of the manes of roan antelopes, water antelopes,
striped gnus and zebras. They arrange them in a way similar to the Masarwa custom, as a ring, and put them on their heads. One should not, however, forget to
mention that the Matoka of all peoples of Africa have the most useful decoration
of their heads, i.e. the giant weevil which they implant alive in their thick hair in
order to keep it clean.

I did not believe my eyes when I saw this hunting weevil for the first time in
their hair. The South African weevil (i.e. the *brachycerus apterus*) is the most beautiful and biggest one of all. This magnificent insect is mostly found under the leaves
of an amaryllis which grows on the ground. There it is well hidden during daytime. Only in darkness does it hunt for its food. Its basic colour is a rusty to dark
black-brown. Its capuchin-like hood is marked with beautiful round red spots. In
some places, especially in grassy clearings, it leaves its safe hiding place after rain.
At that time we were able to catch many of these animals.

This beautiful beetle is much desired among the Matoka and the neighbouring
Makalaka. It is caught by them and the tips of the legs are cut off so that it can
move only very little. Some of the Matoka tribes partly shave their heads, others
rub them with some oily substance. In other sister tribes only the women rub
themselves periodically with the oil obtained from groundnuts which they mix
with some ochre or reddish bark. This makes them somewhat lighter and—as
they think—more beautiful. These women look as if one has dipped them into
reddish melted butter and they are a more than disgusting sight.

Vanity exists among the Matoka just as among all peoples on earth. Yet a rather
tyrannic law opposes the general development of vanity. Only the wives of chiefs
wear necklaces and around their breasts strings of large glass beads and strong
brass or copper wire. They also wear bracelets of the same metals or of ivory. The
average woman might possess some of this too, yet they never wear it since the
first chief would legally be able to take it away from them. Wealth thus has to be
hidden just as in the Orient.

The tobacco pipe plays a very important role in the life of the Matoka. Like the people in the Orient they are addicted smokers and they, too, smoke tobacco produced from hemp. Excellent tobacco can be grown in their soil and these countries along the Zambezi could become first-rate tobacco countries if a rational agriculture were to be introduced. Since they have not yet learnt to know 'Fire water' and its pleasures, smoking, which the Matoka very probably learnt from the Portuguese, is for them more or less the epitome of all narcotic stimulation of their nerves. They have a surprising skill in making highly artistic tobacco pipes and dagga pipes (i.e. water hemp pipes).

The bowls of the pipes are made of burnt clay and have carved animal heads such as wild pigs, gnus, buffaloes, roan antelopes, water antelopes, oxen, goats, lions, etc. The smoke is sucked up by a reed. Some of these pipes have a sort of a pike attached to their bowls by which they can be stuck into the ground like the old Heidelberg pipes. Then they can just suck at the end of the reed. The pipe is lit with coal. To handle the coal the tribes use little fire tongs made by the Matotele. The tobacco is kept in skin pouches which they fix to their belts just like our fellow countrymen. They always take along their pipes on a trip as well as while working in the fields, carrying them in their hands together with a spear.

They smoke at any time of the day and when a Matoka in his state of *dolce far niente* smokes his pipe, who on earth could be happier than he? Smoking, however, is a sacrosanct affair among the Zambezi tribes as among the American Indians. While they are smoking all quarrel and strife is suspended and when they invite strange and unknown visitors to smoke with them this is a sign of friendliness (like the pipe of peace).

The tools the Matoka make such as awls, knives, nose cleaners etc. are rather poorly made even though they are good enough for their purposes. In the old settlements of these tribes on the southern bank of the central Zambezi I found smelting hearths for iron ore. Decades ago they must have worked as smelters themselves and may have satisfied their own needs. Now this is no longer done. The best metal workers in the Marutse empire are the Matotele and the Mangete who are sister tribes of the Marutse. They also make for the Matoka the previously mentioned hoes, the spears, the pole-axes, and other iron tools, the quality and form of which is remarkable. After the Zulus they are probably the best native iron workers in southern Africa.

All other necessary essentials of the Matoka are as primitive as the huts and the clothing. This holds as well for those weapons which they make themselves. But of all their arms they make only rather poor dagger-type knives, sticks with knobs, and shields. They take not a little pride in their shields. On first sight they look very similar to the protective shields of the Marutse and to the so-called large shields of the Matabele, yet they are much narrower and of poorer quality. Those tribes only use the strongest cow hides, mostly black, but also piebald skins. Yet the Matoka, lacking cattle, have to take the skins of the striped gnus and of the eland which are much less strong and do not give the desired protection to fighting men. I have a lot of Matoka weapons in my collection of arms.

The Matoka already possess quite a number of rifles which they have earned as servants of elephant hunters in Panda-ma-Tenka and of the tradesmen in Schos-chong. On the average they have to serve two years for each rifle. Since they are less thrifty with their ammunition than, for instance, the Indians of North America and waste it at random, particularly at first, these weapons are for months a useless decoration and thus the game is largely protected. In general, the Matoka are poor hunters with their own weapons as well as with the rifle. The taunting remark of the Makalaka and the Marutse, 'The Matoka has meat only if the lion leaves him some', is thus justified. Most of their game the Matoka catch with their primitive traps, especially small carnivorous animals, gazelles and rodents.

Of the musical instruments of the Matoka large elongated drums of fifty to seventy centimetres length are quite original. They are either similar to the tube drums of the Marutse which they beat with their fingers or they are so-called rubbing drums. The latter type is a wooden tube of fifty to sixty centimetres length and ten to twenty centimetres width. It is covered on one end with a drumskin with a hole in the middle. A stick reaches into the cavity of the drum and is fixed with a cross stick below and above the hole. One ties a piece of moistened baobab bark fibre around one's hand and rubs the stick up and down rapidly. This makes a deep droning double tone. The first drum is called *Mo-Rupa* and the second one is called *Namarva* or *Wupu-Wupu* (because of the sound). The Makalaka, however, call it *Wuruma*. They are very hard to get, yet I have a particularly beautiful specimen in my collection which was a present from Mr Blockley.

I also want to mention those characteristic longish bottle-shaped clabashes which are hollowed, have numerous holes, and are filled with pea-shaped seeds or little stones. These calabashes are a type of musical instrument which the women in particular shake violently when they dance and thus get rhythm into their movement.

In boat building the Matoka did not get any further than the single dugout tree like our inhabitants of the Alps use. They make their canoes just as the Marutse out of a burnt-out tree trunk, yet one does not find as big and as beautiful canoes among the Matoka as among the Marutse. For the Marutse would take them away immediately. They are afraid to have such large canoes, which can carry between seven and fourteen people, in the possession of the Matoka along their river banks and so close to Victoria Falls. Otherwise strangers and especially the Matabele could use them to cross the Zambezi. Thus here as also elsewhere politics prevent the development of the art of shipbuilding.

With respect to other wood carving the Matoka are also not very skilled. How artistically carved are the head rests of the Maschona tribes and their neighbours along the east coast. How beautiful are the head rests, as well as the stools, of the Mabunda, Mankoja and the Marutse if one compares them with the little boat-shaped wooden stools and wooden blocks of the Matoka which may be quite original, but are very poorly made. These domestic utensils are decorated with quite unattractive burnt-in ornamentation. I presume I need not tell the reader that these certainly rather hard rests are not actually for the head but for the neck. The head rest is used by these peoples in order not to destroy their hair-styles so that they do not need to set their hair for months except for keeping it clean with the weevil.

One of the best developed crafts of the Matoka is their pottery, even though it is not as artistic as that of the Marutse. For their pottery they use only special types of clay which often have to be obtained from far away. The men's task is to get the raw material and to make the furnaces (actually these are pits) while the women make the pots. Their products are not nearly as fire-resistant as those of the Marutse which are also distinguished by a much greater variety of forms.

While the baskets and the wooden pots and bowls made by the Matoka are hardly worth mentioning I would, however, like to point out that they do some cotton weaving even though its quality is much lower than that of other tribes. The cotton grows wild, mostly on the laterite ridges.

Soon after we left Matakala's town Mo-Rukumi two servants of the chief came running after us and brought a fat-tailed sheep as a present. Already the day before Matakala had sent back the bayonet I had given him together with a sheep. This had been not at all an act of subtle thoughtfulness from a patient but rather that of a king making his last attempt to obtain a rifle. As even this had not done the trick, the first sheep had disappeared the same evening from our small goat herd. The little sheep he now sent through his servants was meant to be a substitute for the one which had disappeared. Since I had not sent back the bayonet it was only a very meagre little sheep, not comparable with the present of the day before.

The first journey (of about twelve kilometres) went across the laterite ridge of the town Mo-Rukumi and through the Ki-Indabile villages.[1] We met a chief who was a subject of Matakala and was just about to go and pay him a visit. He had a subchief and armed slaves with him. Two slave boys were carrying very heavy containers with grain and beer. Immediately he made his people stop and offered us some beer. We took a *makopa* full (a ladle made out of a pumpkin shell which holds about one third of a litre) and we gave him a few glass beads in return. On this march we again had much amusement from our tame baboon Pit. He amused the porters in particular by the way in which he teased the dogs, so much so that the men became very cheerful and began to hum some tunes and later on were even chanting refrains in their loud and rough way. Since Pit, however, also chased women and children as soon as he spotted them in the wood, my wife had to take the baboon on the leash whenever we passed houses. Sir and Leeb took the lead, I inspected the porters up and down the line and Fekete and Oswald were the last ones in the file. When we came to a village I went to the head of the caravan. The mules who were now only carrying our food still made some trouble every now and then.

We reached the end point of this day's journey and we began to establish camp. The porters had barely delivered all their loads, which we had counted and put in a storage place prepared by our small bodyguard, and the grass for our sleeping place had hardly been collected when several Matoka, attracted by the noise, appeared with beer to sell. We had not yet fetched any water and since Pit appeared to be very thirsty I gave him a cup full of this rather cool drink. With great pleasure he took the cup as usual with both hands, held it to his lips, sat up on his hind legs, and drank and drank until he had swallowed down more than half a litre. Then, however, one could see the consequences very rapidly. Pit was totally drunk and his gay intoxication kept us amused until long after midnight. At one time he got up on his head but he could not possibly keep his balance. The next moment he had turned over and was lying there like a log, growling and grunting and constantly showing his teeth, but in a good-natured way which was meant to be laughter. Then he teased the porters who were laughing aloud and they let him do what he wanted. In spite of his drunken mind Pit picked out some of the most stupid ones as his victims. They were teased by their companions as 'Pit's recognised relatives'. Even though they were angry they could not help but laugh with all the others. From one of them Pit took away his little leather coat and before he knew it it was hanging in one of the low trees around—as Pit was no longer able to climb high trees in his condition. He pulled the little skirts off others and he turned over the pots of still others which fortunately were empty. In brief he played all kinds of tricks until he fell into a long sleep from which he must have woken with the usual hangover, for from that day on Pit did not want to see any *butchuala* any more, no matter how thirsty he was. With genuine disgust he threw any cup away even if it only smelled of beer.

On 16 June we made a journey of only 9 km; we crossed the lower course of the Kabonda stream and then a laterite ridge. Soon afterwards we heard the deep hollow double tone of the *Wupu-Wupu* drum and after six kilometres we got into the village of a subchief of Matakala, called Kakalemba. My plan was to reach Sakasipa that day. But already at Kakalemba's the porters refused to go any further since they were promised a lot of beer if they could get me to stay there. Boy and the other servants did their best to persuade me to stay. Yet all their rational arguments could not move me. After a short rest I had pointed out to me the next water course and I then called for departure.

The fact that the porters refused to march on had a deeper reason than just their desire for Kakalemba's beer. They knew that we could get to Sakasipa that same day, yet they were afraid of being paid for only two days. This is why they tried to squeeze out a three-day journey. Three kilometres further on we arrived at the upper course of the Kabonda stream and we established our camp for the night near the deep pond of the stream. I intended to stay here somewhat longer and perhaps to get a few things for my collection. The chief Kakalemba and almost all his people came running after us, yet even now I did not take his beer, I did not give him the slightest present for his suite of honour but rather gave his subchiefs and those who had led us to the water a larger present than I perhaps normally might have done. Then he started to quarrel with these men, yet his subjects shouted their lord down. I enjoyed the beautiful afternoon and had just decided to go for a walk in the magnificent woods nearby when I was hit by a sudden fever attack which kept me on my grass bed until midnight and caused me terrible pains. While I was lying there I observed all of a sudden that one of the porters was undergoing a very strange metamorphosis in his costume which reminded me of a Greek Dionysian festival. He had taken off his short fur skirt and in a surprisingly short time had made a type of short petticoat out of green branches and had wound green leaves around his arms, legs and head. Decorated like this he began a very funny dance while his companions shrieked loudly. Because of my terrible headache I denied them this fun and thus the dancer to whom I had not paid any attention went into the village together with Kakalemba's people in order to continue his dance there and to get beer and millet as a reward. Early the next morning he returned to the camp rich with presents.

That afternoon five young men came to our camp, travelling from chief Sietsetema to Panda-ma-Tenka in order to find work. They were very tired and hungry. I took them in very warmly and gave them beer, millet gruel and meat and two of them who were sick (one with a catarrh in his eyes and the other with wounds on his feet) even got some medicine. All of this was so surprising for these men that after a short conversation with Boy and Mopani they sent their leader called Maruma to me to ask me whether I could hire them as servants for my entire expedition and shortly thereafter the contract was made with Maruma, Pikanini, Goritani, Kondongo and Twisted Mouth as I named him.

On 17 June we left very early in the morning following the Kabonda stream and then crossed the upper course of the Ki-Sinde stream from the banks of which we had to start climbing another laterite ridge. On its crest we walked for some kilometres. When the path turned more or less on the highest part of the ridge we found ourselves right before Mo-Sinkobo, the residence of Sakasipa.[2] Again it consisted of several separate villages of which we had already passed a few. In the south-west about 400 m away from the town we were assigned a camp site in the shade of a low but thick strychnos tree. My people immediately began to cut off branches and to get grass in order to make a kind of fence. The Ki-Sinde stream which we had passed on our fourteen kilometre journey (after 9 km) and at the banks of which I had detected limonite conglomerates, was the border between Matakala's and Sakasipa's territory.

Immediately we had arrived and even before I ordered a meal cooked I asked the porters to come and get their payment. Their guide brought the piece of cloth which was supposed to be the measure as was mentioned earlier. And I measured the necessary sitsibas in front of his eyes. This job was done very quickly yet the porters whom I had called did not move. The old story of Mo-Rukumi was repeated again in Mo-Sinkobo. They refused to accept the payment which was agreed upon; they shouted, screamed, threatened and called upon Sakasipa for help against us. Sakasipa was not at home, yet one of his subchiefs advised the porters to accept what I offered them saying that 'it was very decent pay for the short trip from Matakala to here'. Yet the porters, even though they were now shouting less loudly, remained stubborn and refused to accept my payment. Under these circumstances I did not pay any attention to them for the time being. I left the pieces of calico cloth which I had cut off lying beside me and I began to dig the hole in the ground for our cooking pots. Soon my servants began to start the cooking preparations. My bodyguard collected logs of wood from nearby and others brought thorny branches in order to make the fence around our camp even thicker.

During my work I watched the porters constantly and as soon as I realised that one part of them had decided to accept the payment and tried secretly to persuade their companions to do the same I decided to end this situation quickly. I ordered my servants to get out my medicine chest and had Mopani tell the porters that their hearts were evil and that I would not take their behaviour seriously. Then I got out of my medicine chest a bottle of alcohol and poured some on a plate. I then called one of my servants with a loud voice to bring *molelo* (fire) in order to light the *meci* (water). As soon as the alcohol started to burn some of my servants shouted *Batu bona, bona molelo mo meci* (look here, fellows, this is fire in the water!) and all the porters as well as Sakasipa's people stared at the burning 'water' with stupefication. The loud shouting of the various groups together stopped all of a sudden and one could see an almost frightened surprise on the faces of the people. Those who stood called those who were further away to come close for every-body wanted to see the burning water. I did not pay any attention to the whole thing. My assumption that this event would greatly impress these superstitious people had immediately become true. There were no longer any objections and soon one porter after the other appeared to exchange the little slip of paper given to him in Mo-Rukumi for his 2 m of calico. I gave our former servant Jonas double the payment since he had been eager when all these difficulties arose to explain to his unsatisfied fellow men how wrong they were. Then I handed out the medicine promised to Matakala and the whole group left.

In the evening Sakasipa's head wife came into our camp. She brought us two pots full of beer and told us that Sakasipa would come personally the next morn-ing. 'You see,' she said, 'today is the anniversary of the death of the father of the king who was killed several years ago by the Marutse. He was a brave and cour-ageous king and we venerate his memory highly and every year five days are dedicated to the memory of this great man. Only because of you memorial cere-monies will not last that long this year and our master will return tomorrow to visit you. Morena had just gone today as usual into the wood to the tomb of his *Ra* [father] in order to give to the deceased the usual ceremonial honours. The chiefs and subchiefs of the tribe have gathered to pray and to talk to him all day long; they tell the great deceased man all their grievances and in this way they show him their high esteem and great respect. For five days beer is poured on his grave and they always wait until the deceased has drunk the beer [until the content of the pot has been sucked up by the ground] when they pour the thirsty man fresh beer again. When the mourning men come home in the evening they refresh them-selves with meat and beer and there is also dancing going on which you can attend tomorrow if you wish.'[3]

We gave the queen generous presents and then we continued talking for a long time about the events of the day sitting around the evening fire in Mo-Sinkobo.

As I had determined Mo-Rukumi astronomically so I did with Mo-Sinkobo (I determined its latitude and made two determinations of time). The latter town, that is to say the villages of which it consists, is situated in vast fields which are partly cultivated and partly lying fallow. The large laterite slope on which the town is situated, as well as many other villages which are strung out for miles, slowly becomes flat towards the north. At some places, however, it goes down rather steeply towards the hilly middleland of the Matoka area which is traversed by small rivers and streams. In this Matoka area, that is in the northern part of the above-mentioned laterite slope, are found all the sources of the rivers and watercourses of the eastern part of the large Zambezi bend running from the mouth of the Luenge in the east up to the Matschila river in the west. Yet the hilly northern country, still more fertile and richer in water, sends its numerous little rivers and streams as a rule into the northern or north-eastern direction to the Luenge.[4]

3 *Matoka (Toka) chief (Siyakasipa) Sakasipa*

In the morning after our arrival Sakasipa really did come to our camp. He was of stately appearance, he was tall, brown with an aquiline nose and longer and better groomed thick hair than is normally found among the southern Matoka. He was wearing European clothing and on his chest he was wearing the talisman *impande*, in the miraculous power of which not only the peoples of this area but also all the peoples towards the north even beyond the Maschukulumbe tribe believe. They shun no effort or sacrifice in order to obtain this talisman. Such an *impande* is a white round disc-like chalk shell of a marine animal as smooth and shiny as china. They wear it pierced and with a string around their necks and they believe that it protects them against all kinds of evils, diseases, misfortunes, persecutions by wild animals and enemies, and even against the bullet of the white man. Undoubtedly this *impande* is the most valuable talisman among the Zambezi tribes. We were attacked and persecuted later many times because we were believed to have a lot of these *impandes* along with us. They thought we refused to sell them since in their belief they made people immune to the effect of our bullets. These articles as well as the cowrie shells (*Cypraea moneta L*) are imported by the Portuguese. In addition to Sakasipa his wives and some of his children were wearing such *impandes* around their necks. The king was accompanied by all his people who happened to be in the town and I noticed that a lot of these half-naked creatures who had squatted down around us had many wounds, especially on their feet, which they had probably come by in the bush or in the poorly cleared fields. No medical attention had been paid to these wounds, yet they were easily curable abscesses. Immediately I had Leeb prepare a weak iodine solution and then I cauterised those parts of the wounds which appeared to be full of putrid pus and then I applied the previously mentioned black plaster which had given us excellent service. I intend to plead to our medical faculty for its introduction into the Austrian –Hungarian pharmacies because of its excellent healing effect on suppurating abscesses.

Then I gave Sakasipa presents similar to those I had given to Matakala with which he was just as unsatisfied as any other chief, and he asked at least for twenty times more. However, one could talk with him about it more easily than with Matakala, the king of Mo-Rukumi. In principle Sakasipa promised me porters, yet he wanted me to take along three guides. I refused, saying that one guide was perfectly sufficient and that these subchiefs as guides were more annoying than useful and would not be respected by the porters at all. All I wanted from these so-called guides who did not have to guide anybody since every porter knew the way, was to get to know through them the topography of the area through which we passed. I was thus looking for men who knew the names of all places.

Sakasipa sent us that same day five huge pots full of beer which contained at least forty litres of this intoxicating beverage which is so much desired by the natives in the north of southern Africa. In addition Sakasipa gave us so much corn and beans as presents that I did not have to buy any food for my many porters for the planned stretch of way from Sakasipa to Sietsetema, that is for a period of eight days. The natives brought goats, chicken, flour and other things for sale and we paid for one goat just as much as for five chickens, that is one sitsiba equalling 2 m of calico or 0·25 kg of the smallest glass beads.

In the afternoon Sakasipa left again for his father's tomb in order to tell him—as he said—about our arrival as well as about the presents we had brought and in order to offer the deceased over and over again some *butchuala* (beer) to drink. In the evening Sakasipa returned with his people shrieking loudly. Most of the men and the women had painted one, and some both, sides of their faces with chalk, which was an ugly sight. The whole crowd, including ourselves, then went from our camp to the king's huts. The largest part of Mo-Sinkobo consists of the royal residence. The residence itself consists of a medium-sized courtyard enclosed by high poles. In it, leaning against the poles of the wall, are several huts of the king. Around this enclosure the unfenced huts of his wives and servants are situated. Some hundred steps to the side the huge grain containers and corn storage huts of the king are located in a cleared place surrounded by thorny bushes.

Upon their arrival at home the whole crowd made a big circle; Sakasipa's wives brought a huge pot of beer and stationed themselves here and there between the circle and the wall of poles. Sakasipa, who, like his loyal subjects, was somewhat gay from the memorial ceremonies, first went up to his favourite wife, the same one who had visited us the day before. She gave him a fresh drink of beer with a large *mokope* (ladle). Then, already rather drunk, he took her by her hand. She, however, grabbed a big pear-shaped hollow pumpkin shell filled with hard dried seeds. Then both stepped into the circle and while the spectators were singing and clapping their hands to keep the beat the two performed a leaping dance which ended with a dance of the woman around the man in which she was shaking the rattling pumpkin shell back and forth with rapid movements. Then she returned to her pot of beer and other men out of the circle, mostly dignitaries, came up to her to drink. In the meantime the king had approached another of his wives, had drunk her beer and then the same dancing and drinking scene followed.

After Sakasipa had honoured several of his wives in this way he left the enclosed area together with all his followers and they all sat down in groups outside the enclosure around big beer containers and the actual big drinking of the evening began.

We, too, were invited to sit down and after he had explained to us that his head wife had just left in order to get some *sitscho* (food) for us, he introduced us to one of his relatives who actually was his uncle whom he, however, called 'father' and who had a long white beard, much to our surprise. The woman soon returned with the beer and put it in front of us as a special honour. When the king sat down with us I tried to use his gay mood well and I talked about the continuation of our trip and asked him for porters. I had hoped that in his drunken mood we would be able to finish and solve this difficult problem in a few words, counting on the effect of alcohol which loosens tongues and hearts. Yet completely unexpectedly my royal drinking companion was all of a sudden so sober and rational that he called two of his subchiefs to participate in our discussion.

Sakasipa refused to give us porters to Sietsetema. The town of this chief is in the north-east of Mo-Sinkobo while the direction Sakasipa suggested to me and very strongly advised me to take went to the north-west. Then I would have had to go back very far to the east in order to reach Sietsetema. 'No, Morena,' I said, 'I do not want to take a detour.' Yet all my objections were in vain; it was decided by the chief and his advisers that we should only reach our aim via the village Ki-Schindu[5] and that he would give us porters only in this direction. 'How far is it to Ki-Schindu?' 'Half the way to Sietsetema.' 'But has Ki-Schindu enough inhabitants so that I can get a sufficient number of porters there?' 'Very probably not.' 'King Luanika, however, ordered that you should give me porters to Sietsetema.' 'King Luanika is living far from here. It is easy to give orders from such a distance. Our porters, however, do not go as far as Sietsetema. He is living too far away, they need even five days to get to Ki-Schindu.' I realised that I had to give in with respect to Ki-Schindu and the following day, on 17 June, I asked for porters to that village. Sakasipa then sent messengers out to all the villages on his laterite slope in order to get enough men together. More came than I needed. Since the porters refused to go further than Ki-Schindu I told them that I would proceed as is customary along the central Zambezi, that is, that I would not provide their food. The hired Zambezi porter who offers his services to the traveller for at most three to six days takes his calabash along filled with three or four kilogrammes of millet. Every fourth or fifth man carries a water container and a cooking pot on his head instead of the millet. If they feed themselves in this way the men eat only once a day—and this in the evening. In spite of my original threats I could not bring myself to make my porters march ten to fifteen kilometres per day with this meagre food and I even promised them before we left to give them food—on the condition, however, that each man would have to carry this food in addition to his load for those five days. Since I had hired three new servants, as already mentioned, near the Kabonda stream I could save in total nine normal porters so that I had to hire only fifty-two men from Sakasipa as porters.

By the way, Sakasipa was not at all interested in getting rid of us very soon; on the contrary he tried everything possible to persuade us to stay longer. On 19 and 20 June he went with his men *gulube* (wild pig) hunting in order to provide us with fresh wild pig meat, yet he did not have any luck.

A group of men of Matakala had also followed us. They had nothing to do at home and thus followed us speculating that we might by some chance need more porters and would then have to pay them very well. They wanted now to be hired from Sakasipa to Sietsetema, yet Sakasipa's people objected to this. They instigated their king so much against these people that he jumped up in the middle of a discussion in our camp, rushed up to this group squatting around us, and threatened them with his hippo-leather sjambok. However, none of these men moved a muscle and the angry ruler did not dare to hit them. I chose out of this group five men with trustworthy faces and promised them their loads as porters. Sakasipa's people annoyed us so much in our small camp that we could hardly move in it any longer. Finally, I had to ask the king to make his subjects move out of our camp. But again this time the royal influence was so weak that neither his commands nor his threats had any success. Only with his stick did Sakasipa make a few men move out of our camp. The honourable reader can hardly imagine what great efforts we had to make from dawn to 11 o'clock at night to secure our various pieces of baggage, our weapons hanging in the tree and our cooking utensils, from the thievish tricks of these natives.

Before we left Mokuri, Matakala's relative, the owner of the collapsible top hat and subchief in the Victoria Falls area whom I have already mentioned twice before, appeared once more to try for the last time to beg for a woollen blanket. For this purpose he had brought along a goat as a present. Yet I rewarded his thoughtfulness only with one sitsiba of calico.

Since Mokuri was very drunk this time also, he did not seem to mind this lack of success very much and had soon fallen asleep in the middle of our camp. We called his people and they lifted him up and placed him under the nearest strychnos tree where he lay until the evening. This unpleasant reunion was followed by a very pleasant one. Namely, that very day one of my old servants from my earlier expedition to Africa visited me. He was Tschukuru who had always behaved very well. He brought a hollow pumpkin filled with ground-nuts as a present and showed me his wife who had the most pleasant face I had ever seen on a Matoka woman.

In spite of my objections I had to take along the three subchiefs, Simutuli, Sipanga and Mopiti as so-called 'guides'. The fact that I had healed some sick children of Sakasipa's had impressed him very much in my favour. Yet I regretted very much in my further travels that he had so little power over his men. They not only did not obey his orders later but even acted against them and began an open revolt against me. The actual and essential reason for this outrage was probably the insolent behaviour of Matakala's men upon their payment—a scene which my newest porters had watched. The Matakala, however, had been so insolent as a consequence of the impertinent and upsetting behaviour of the Maschupia of Gazungula and Matakala's support for them. Thus, this poisonous breath, that is to say the disastrous opposition of the first porters, propagated itself northwards into the nest of the hornet, i.e. into the country of the Maschukulumbe, just like 'the bad deed which incessantly has to give birth to more evil'. This time also the payment of the porters was agreed to be one sitsiba which I had measured 20 cm longer than I had paid Matakala's people and thus we left Mo-Sinkobo without any further obstacles. Sakasipa even announced that he would escort me personally.

From Mo-Sinkobo to
Mo-Monquembo

SAKASIPA REALLY DID ESCORT US for a short distance beyond his residence and then he left us to our future fate.

The first journey from Sakasipa on the way to Ki-Schindu northwards ended at a water hole, Njama. Our way led us first towards north-north-east up to a village, and from there on northwards. After ten kilometres we crossed several low depressions grown over with high grass through which the valley of the Namasumbi stream goes. Then we came again to a wooded laterite ridge and we proceeded north-westward to Njama, situated at the foot of this laterite ridge in the Matoka hills. From the crest of this laterite ridge we saw in the west, about twelve kilometres away, the chain of hills called Namponga.[1] That day we marched for 15 km. Our camp was situated 1,139 m above sea level and I determined its location astronomically. It was here that I hired the three aforementioned Matoka as servants. Their names were Maruma, Stoffel (who had served earlier with a Dutch elephant hunter on the southern bank of the Zambezi) and Sibungu. The name of the latter, however, I changed to 'Tschimborasso'.

On our way across the first laterite ridge we crossed many different traces of wild animals and we also found a lot of animal traps, which I wish to describe in more detail as follows: on both sides of a large number of footpaths at a distance of two to three metres little resilient straight saplings were dug into the ground. On their pointed tops were fastened grass or bark strings two or three metres long, very well made and strong as a lead pencil. In the path itself was an oval opening usually 30 cm long, 20 cm wide and 20 cm deep, covered with dusty pieces of bark so that the place looked like the rest of the ground. Then the little sapling was bent, the string which was tied to a loop in its end was pulled tight and introduced into the opening. Thus the loop was spread out and in a very primitive way, by means of a little twig: it was placed around a little wooden stick which had a notch on top and was stuck into the ground. Then the string was caught in a little trap stick. The opening afterwards was covered with those pieces of bark. Gazelles, large rodents, genet cats, jackals, etc. are caught when by chance they step on the pieces of bark, break through and then are caught with one leg in the loop and pulled high up by the string. Soon I was to realise how effective these traps are since twice one of my mules got caught in such a trap and was not able to free himself without my help. For small carnivorous animals, especially for jackals, the Matoka built little pitfalls—like our poachers, i.e. like the so-called maxes in which the neck of the animal is caught in a loop if it is trying to get the bait.

In this way the Matoka get the skins they need for their little skirts. In contrast to these traps the hyena traps, which I found near some of the kraals which we passed on our way, are much more impressive. Seventy to eighty centimetres apart from each other two parallel rows of poles, more than one metre high, are pounded into the ground. Between them a board is suspended in a slanted position. Its shorter end is touching the ground at the rear end of the alley formed by the two rows of poles. The other end of the board sticks up high supported by a stick resting on a trap board. Thus the board forms a kind of a railroad gate. This gate is weighted down with stones and falls down like a heavy block if one tries to loosen the carcass fixed on the trap board as a bait. The trap board, too, is resting on a hole partly filled with stones (see plate 4). Even though this trap cannot kill all hyenas and leopards, the animals as a rule are wounded so seriously that they are found defenceless in the vicinity of the trap and can be killed easily. These traps are usually set up in the outskirts of settlements and villages.

For this completely original invention of the natives, too, a comparable phenomenon can be found among European traps. In our pheasant preserves wing-shaped wooden fences lead from both sides into similar falling traps for polecats and martens.

After thirteen kilometres we found villages and fields next to which the fallow areas were covered with such a lush vegetation of *composites, malvaceae* (mallows) and *gramineae* (grasses) that we hardly could work our way through. Near these villages we crossed the already mentioned low Namasumbi stream where we saw a herd of eland antelopes for the first time on this expedition. Unfortunately I had to leave it to the quick 'Boy' as well as to Mopani, Kabrniak and Muschemani to stalk them and to try to provide us with fresh meat. I and my wife, as well as Leeb, would have liked to try our hunting luck this time too, as one gains great respect among the porters if one has success. But we could not leave these porters, that is, the first thirty-five of them whom we had to watch. Thus we had to stay behind as watchmen as we were afraid that some of them might otherwise disappear with our packages.

It was a real delight to arrive at the Njama pond and at the slope of the wide valleys of the central bed of the western Inquisi. For the first time since we had left the Zambezi we enjoyed an open view all around us. On our long journey our view had always been limited by the low trees of the rather monotonous bush of the laterite ridges. From the area of *melaphyre* we had come into the area of mica slate and gneiss stones. Towards the north-east and the north-west some insignificant, yet wooded, ranges of hills and individual flat or cone-shaped hilltops delimited the horizon. At their feet lay fertile valleys, not yet touched by man's industry.

Immediately upon arrival the porters began to make a fence from *mopani* branches for our camp as Sakasipa had instructed them to do. Yet unfortunately this fiery zeal cooled down very quickly, and soon my servants were the only ones working. When I called on the three subchiefs, asking them why their men obeyed the orders of the king so poorly, they said: 'Master, the men say that they should be paid an additional fee for their help with the camp.' 'Well, I do feed them in addition.' 'This they do not count.' During these negotiations Boy came up to me asking me to lend him my carbine or Fekete's rifle since he 'wanted to go and hunt for eland antelopes'. I was about to deny this to him saying, 'Look it is impossible for you to go alone and the others have to make the fence.' But he answered quite correctly, 'I do not need our people. These lazy porters will run along immediately as soon as they realise that they can snatch a juicy piece of

4   *A hyena trap of the Matoka (Toka)*

venison.' I gave him the rifle and he shouted to those men hanging around '*Hela, Batu, njama, r'camaja chat-schuma*' (Hey, men, meat. We're going hunting). These words had a truly magic effect and Boy and the subchiefs had to ward off the men who came rushing up so that not all of them went along. Boy selected ten of the strongest men and the group marched off. Hardly two hours had passed. I was just recording the meteorological readings of the week before when my wife, who was strolling in front of the camp with her butterfly net in the high grass, called me to tell me that Boy was returning. I jumped up and welcomed Boy who had tied an eland tail as a trophy to his rifle. As is the custom he came up to me with the well known greeting '*Kia-Tumela*' and sat down quietly. Only after I had addressed him he began to tell the hunting episode with full details—how he had spotted a herd of eland, how he had stalked them, and how being hidden in a rocky dried-out stream bed he had penetrated right into the middle of the herd, and how he had selected the fattest bull and had shot him down with two bullets. Immediately I gave Boy a sitsiba as a present. The next morning I sent Oswald out with ten more porters to get all the rest of the meat. How I would have loved to cure the skin and take it along, yet this was out of the question since unfortunately it had been damaged by Boy and thus had become useless for my purposes. Around 10 o'clock the men whom I had sent out returned and brought beautiful meat which was only slightly too fat. I knew that there was no fatter deer in southern Africa than the eland; thus I realised when I dissected it that our specimen was only moderately fat and yet the pericardium (fatty covering around his heart) weighed more than three kilogrammes and the perirenal fat (around each of the kidneys) more than one kilogramme. We filled several pumpkin containers with the melted fat. We stayed here also for 22 June so that I gained enough time to make one more determination of the location.

Yet north of the Zambezi staying or not staying was no longer simply a matter of my decision as it had been south of the river. I first had to ask my porters. This time they stayed since there was meat. In other cases when I wanted to stay on in order to make a determination I had to give each of them an extra present. They said they wanted to march fast (sic) in order to earn their sitsiba quickly. On 22 June my wife and Oswald suffered a severe attack of fever and I a light one. And on the same day the vertical sphere of my universal instrument was damaged by one of the porters when I left the instrument for a moment during one of the determination processes in order to give my wife medicine. Since the damage caused a constant deviation I hope that this error has not affected my subsequent calculations.

During that night Oswald came down with an attack of dysentry which got worse in the morning. I had to leave him for several hours under Fekete's care. I left two servants with Fekete, ten porters and a mule, and since Oswald was unable to ride (he had always been only a pedestrian) he had to be carried by the porters for the larger stretch of our march on 23 June. They in turn gave their loads to some Matoka who were living near Njama and had visited us there. I paid them with glass beads for this one-day journey.

I was seriously worried about Oswald that day and was very happy when he caught up with us in the evening of 24 June feeling better. Apart from Oswald several porters, too, got sick. The disease very probably had its cause in the fact that they had eaten too much of that fat meat and that they had drunk too much of the Njama water instead of *butschuala* or cold and bitter tea. First I gave them a light laxative and then chlorodyne at intervals of five to six hours. The result was excellent. The journey of 23 June was 18 km; during the first five kilometres we followed a course to the north and for the rest of the journey a north-easterly course with many insignificant twists.

This was the first journey through the rolling Matoka country and it was much more interesting than the entire trip through the laterite ridges. We crossed eleven side valleys and numerous water holes. We crossed the Nampongo stream in the fifth kilometre, the Dongafa in the seventh, the Sinjika in the tenth, the Mokuruani and the Kapani in the fifteenth, the Manscha and the Kurunda in the seventeenth, and in the nineteenth kilometre we crossed the Inquisi river and the Tschi-N'kosia stream flowing into it.[2] All these streams flow westwards and many have fresh clear water all year round in contrast to the streams of the southern high plateaux, since they flow in a rocky bed mostly cut deep into the ground. During the rainy season they very probably have an enormous amount of water and many of them could form long ponds full of fish if they were dammed. The western Inquisi, on which we camped overnight, had only a small amount of water, yet it flows all year round and even crocodiles live in its deeper sections. These saurians as well as two kinds of otters eat such a great quantity of fish, especially during the winter when the water is low, that it is amazing that fish can still be found at all in these streams.

The banks of the Inquisi are scarcely inhabited by men, but rather thickly populated by animals. On the entire way I found chlorite slate which on the Nampongo stream has a slope of fifty degrees stretching from north to east and which has a slope of sixty degrees northwards on the Kapani stream stretching from north to north-east. This chlorite slate is interspersed occasionally by narrow veins of rose-quartz which sometimes, however, are as wide as one metre, and by reefs which probably contain gold. I determined the sea level on the Sinjika, the Mokuruani and the Inquisi stream.

On our further march we passed through a generally lovely rolling countryside. The valleys and hills in some places were thickly grown with bushes and trees of which *mopani* trees, fan palms, grass trees, a type of aloe and euphorbiaceae dominated. We even found fresh traces of lion, hyena, grysbock, impala and eland, kakatombe hartebeest, and a herd of elephants.

Since we were still rather weak and exhausted because of the fever attacks from the day before, we twice made a half-hour rest on this march which I used to determine the sea level. Rather tired we reached the Inquisi at 4 o'clock in the afternoon and waded through it a few metres above the place where the Tschi-N'kosia stream flows into it. Unfortunately I only realised too late that we could have crossed the river with dry feet a little further down where many rocks were lying in the water. As usual I chose our camp site also that day and was eager for relaxation. Yet it was meant to happen otherwise. My servants had just begun to work on an enclosure when the porters started shouting loudly and Simutuli, one of the guides, began to speak as the headman on behalf of the complaining porters. The rumour I had already heard the day before at the Njama pond was now confirmed. Simutuli said: 'We left our huts three days ago. Even Matakala's men and the men from Mambowa did not go with you for longer than three days and therefore we refuse to carry your loads any longer for only a single sitsiba. If you still want us to go with you for two to three more days to Ki-Schindu you have to give us another sitsiba for that stretch.' 'Oh, well,' I answered, 'I saw very well yesterday how this poison entered your heart. You did not carry my loads for three days but only for two, for the day in between you only gorged yourselves with the eland meat. Did you not promise your chief to carry my stuff for one sitsiba as far as Ki-Schindu? No, I won't pay more. You will have to carry on.' I ordered my servants to start preparing the meal and the camp. I let the porters yell and grabbed my rifle and left for a few hours to hunt for animals since I was no longer tired because of this uproar. I returned only late at night and found the porters sitting quietly around their pots and enjoying their eland meat spiced with stewed beans. When we left this place early the next morning I ordered two of my servants to wait for Oswald with medicine and food on the Inquisi. He arrived at that place with Fekete and his porters shortly after our departure.

Our journey of 24 June was again 18 km long in a north-north-east direction and our camp site was the village Ki-Assa. We crossed many valleys and streams. In contrast to the area we had passed through the day before, this area sloped towards the south-east and all the streams flowed to the Inquisi and to the Tschi-N'kosia stream. We crossed the Njunjani and the Karsibabatunja stream in the first kilometre, two streams in the eighth, the Usanga stream and another stream in the ninth, the Tschi N'kosia stream in the tenth, the Lo-Lente stream in the twelfth, the Mokau stream in the thirteenth, a stream in the seventeenth and the Mo-Shabati stream in the eighteenth kilometre.[3]

In all these streams was some water. Orographically this stretch of land through which we passed was first hilly country with two large longitudinal valleys, one in the west and an even larger one in the east where all the above-mentioned streams seem to come together. In the second half of our journey the country was a high plateau grown over with high grass which is dangerous to pass because of its buffalo herds. It contained the Tschani springs which are noteworthy because they carry water all year round. To these springs led such wide, deep and well-trodden buffalo trails (not paths) that I read them wrongly on first sight and thought that the Matoka of Ki-Assa, who are living close by, raised cattle which they would drive every day to the water. The march through the high grass and on the rocky heights following one another like steps was so exhausting that we were forced to rest several times. The view was very beautiful with the three valleys and the mighty palm trees reaching up every now and then out of a clearing, and the baobab trees growing together in small groups. This sight would have been full of interesting motifs for a painter. The clearings were often several kilo-metres long and overgrown with huge grass and when this was waving in the wind it created in our minds the memory of our waving cornfields. Sadly we thought of our home and of our distant friends. Here also were growing the so-called *masuku* trees (with magnolia leaves) with numerous tasty fruits which were, however, not yet ripe at that time. These trees form a zone which stretches as far as the laterite hills of the Luenge and maybe even beyond the Luenge. Twice on this trip we determined the altitude—once in the sixth kilometre and the second time at the Tschani springs and finally in the evening and in the morning at our camp site of Ki-Assa. On our trip we saw zebras, gnu herds and impalas, and we saw the fresh trails of a black rhino and of a big elephant herd which had moved westward only the night before.

Ki-Assa consisted only of three kraals lying in the midst of a bare maizefield. The field borders two copses, otherwise it is surrounded with a thicket of high grass which is a real grass wall and makes a crackling noise of dryness in the winter. Two hours after our arrival Fekete and Oswald arrived with those ser-vants we had left with them and I was happy to convince myself that Oswald was better. He had felt so well, indeed, that he had been able from early morning on to walk the whole way from the Inquisi and even from a few kilometres before the river.

Ki-Assa belongs to a Matoka chief residing further to the west whose name the inhabitants of the village would not tell me.[4] They complained a lot about wild animals and were forced because of these wild ruminants to dry their unripe grain on scaffolds. The ears of their beautiful big millet were piled up neatly and with great effort on the slanted plane of a scaffold resting on four high poles. This looked as attractive as it proved to be practical.

When I was about to leave early the next morning our three guides as well as the porters told us that as they had now carried our goods for three days, they would not move from this place and should get their full payment as if they had carried our load for five full days as far as the Ki-Shindu village. The men's behav-iour was much worse than the first time and to make things even worse a small group of men arrived just then at our camp from Mo-Sinkobo in order to look for work as porters. I realised that the whole mutiny was a preconcerted plan of Sakasipa's people and that I must not give in under any condition. If I yielded, the newly-hired men might have carried our loads perhaps only for one day's journey and not any further. 'If you refuse to go,' I told them, 'well, then I go.' And I ordered my servants to pick up their luggage and to follow me. I called Fekete and Oswald not to stay behind as usual but to follow us and leave the porters if they were to stay.

I started out followed by my wife, Leeb and five servants as well as by three porters. It was a grey day; we passed through a valley with rather deep water holes of the Muembwa with green grass growing all around them. This was very inviting for a swim, yet our serious situation did not allow us to realise such an en-joyable idea. Soon we passed through a thick *masuku* forest absolutely filled with trails of various animals of buffalo, kakatombe antelope, gnu and zebra. Then after seven kilometres we reached a village called Amare⁵ which consisted only of a few huts. We came just in time to prevent the attack by a band of monkeys on a pumpkin field. The monkeys on guard had spotted us from a high tree and thus a successful shot was impossible. I made a sketch of the Amare village (*not included in the present edition*). Amare was situated at the tail end of a narrow field surrounded on all sides by lion grass. We stopped here and since it was cold that morning we made two fires for our half-naked blacks. Here I waited in peace for our porters for I was absolutely certain that they would give in and stick to their contract and follow us for fear of my supposed witchcraft. In front of the blacks who were with me I had to pretend to be relaxed and self-assured since one porter tells the next one everything and my temporary uncertainty would have been exploited by all future generations of porters. And, indeed, one hour after our arrival my dear porters showed up protesting and threatening me. They threw their packages down and refused to go any further. 'Oh, you will go,' I shouted at them, 'You will follow me. I shall, however, go to Ki-Schindu. From Ki-Schindu there are direct paths as you well know to Schescheke and to Mambowa, the residences of the two idunas of the Eastern Marutse empire. As soon as I arrive there, I shall send messengers to both places in order to voice my complaints about you directly before Luanika through the two chiefs.' 'Ha, ha, ha, you may well do so, we are not afraid.' I turned around to leave, yet not all my servants—only a few plus those three porters—followed me. The others stayed behind, intimidated by the porters.

Through the calmness of the southern African wilderness which I had entered I could still hear for a long time the loud protesting, shouting and screaming of the mutinous hirelings. A few kilometres further on we stopped for half an hour since Boy wanted to go deer stalking and asked us to wait for him. When we were just about to leave Fekete came with four of my servants reporting that none of the porters was willing to move and that Oswald on his own responsibility had stayed with the porters, laughing at them while they were screaming. Therefore, he said, they were beginning to fear him and this all the more since I had shown no signs of being alarmed about my possessions. They were saying to each other that I very probably had already prepared my *malemo* (spell) to hurt them if they were to pinch anything. Fekete finished his report as follows: 'They will be coming for certain, yet hardly today for they are already gathering wood to prepare their camp for the night.'

During our journey one of my servants who had stayed behind all of a sudden came rushing after me. He was already shouting from a distance that one of the porters whom I knew as one of the main ringleaders, had taken his load, a bag of glass beads, by force after he had caught up with him in the woods. 'You coward slave,' I shouted at him, 'why did you not follow me?' I ordered him to follow our train. But now a few words about the journey of that day; in the meantime the blacks will probably catch up with us.

On the journey of 25 June we covered 20 km. The first 7 km went north-west,

west, then strictly north to our camp for the night. In the ninth kilometre we crossed a stream, in the tenth and eleventh kilometres two streams in each kilometre, and in the sixteenth kilometre another one (called Wuamba), all flowing to the west. We also passed through many valleys. The entire country sloped towards the west into a long valley which seemed to be limited by a wooded laterite ridge. On our march, mostly in the northern parts, we saw many kakatombe-hartebeest as well as fresh tracks of lions, warthogs and elephants. Also, we could see very thickly grown euphorbia trees, 8·5 m high. The second time we stopped for a rest was in the sixteenth kilometre on the Wuamba stream. We secured our camp with strong branches since we did not trust the Matoka in this area. While my men were busy constructing this camp I was planning to go on a hunting trip. I saw some kakatombe hartebeests, yet I felt a revival of my fever and therefore had to return quickly. Yet I sent Fekete to follow the animals. I was particularly keen on securing a kakatombe skin since these hartebeests are found nowhere south of the Zambezi except for the Maschona country which I did not visit. Consequently my collection was still lacking a sample of this skin. One kilometre from our camp the servant who accompanied Fekete spotted five kakatombe in the high grass. Fekete's first shot was a failure. The animals fled, but stopped in the middle of a nearby clearing in the valley and Fekete shot a second time. '*Retabile, retabile*' (It's wounded, it's wounded), his companion shouted, and waved his spear. The chap had obviously heard the bullet 'hit'. The hartebeest sank down on its front legs and before it was able to get up again the quick black had pierced its breast with his spear.

Hearing the two shots I pulled myself together, got up, and looked for Fekete. Soon I was able to congratulate him upon his shot. Now my men had to leave their work as I sent all of them except for Leeb and Boy to skin the animal as quickly as possible and to bring it to our camp.

The kakatombe hartebeests have on and behind both shoulders a black spot which the blacks consider to be the natural colouring of their skin. I became convinced to the contrary. As no other type of the big antelopes, these animals have the habit of very often turning only their heads instead of their whole bodies in order to look behind them. Their big glands under their eyes excrete a large quantity of an oily fluid which stains these particular parts of their shoulders. Dirt is caught on these spots. Since these antelopes like to rub themselves against trees and since the trees in many of the woods are covered with black soot because of the numerous fires, parts of their breasts become so dark, in particular during the winter, that these animals seem to have large black spots on their breasts. Seen from a distance their exact nature cannot be determined. My servants who had grown up in kakatombe country refused to believe that these were stains of dirt. Only after I gave them some soap and asked them to try to wash it off were they finally convinced.

The kakatombe hartebeests have a peculiar habit. They look out from the top of the anthills, which are huge in this area. From there they look all around. One of the animals always takes on this chore. This vigilance and special curiosity which is innate to this antelope more than to others, just as is the case with some species of birds, for instance the shrikes, is the reason that the kakatombe antelope is constantly looking back with one side of his face resting against his shoulder. This, of course, indicates a particular flexibility in his cervical vertebrae. The young antelopes do not resemble the old ones at all, particularly with respect to the shape of their heads. They have one peculiar feature—that is, they leave the herd in time of danger and flee in the direction indicated by the old ones. Whereas the old ones, in order to mislead the enemy, first run back and forth before they finally follow in the indicated direction.

Even though we were very tired we had the impression that we had to be especially cautious that night, all the more since our camp was not sufficiently entrenched because of the hunting episode just mentioned. I believe that the streams which we crossed on 25 June flow into a left tributary of the Madschila or themselves form a tributary which flows directly into the Madschila.[6]

The area through which we passed that day was beautiful. It was fertile and seemed to be extremely suitable for colonisation had it not been for the fever. The tsetse fly obstacle could probably be eliminated if one were to apply the necessary precautions several years before the actual attempt to colonise this area.

My companions were hoping that the porters would catch up with us that night. I did not have such utopian hopes, yet I was sure that they would catch up with us by Ki-Schindu. On 26 June we started out very early and after a very exhausting and dangerous trip we arrived that afternoon at Ki-Schindu. This march of a few kilometres was dangerous because for long stretches it went through giant grass more than two metres high which according to the tracks we found was densely populated, not only with buck and antelopes, but also with buffalo and lion. After 3 km we crossed the important Go-Tschoma stream into which flow several tributaries from that grassland. It was notable that the water of these streams and the sometimes swampy tributaries had a thick milky-white colouring which did not, however, change its taste.

The country dropped towards the west and south-west into that long valley which we had seen on our left during our journey of the day before. We crossed another seven streams before we reached the high ground and the breezy Mopani woods and before we left the dangerous grasslands through which there was no real path.

If those three porters out of the mutinous crowd had not followed us we would not have found our way. The people of Ki-Schindu hardly ever go to Sakasipa or to Amare and Ki-Assa. Only very few go there during the year and wherever possible they avoid the grassland because of its dangers. We, too, were fully aware of these dangers and used extreme precautions.

We walked slowly one behind the other. In front went two blacks without any load. With their short spears they separated the reeds and pressed them apart as much as possible. Then we stepped firmly on the half broken reeds with our boots in order to break them down completely and to make a path for the others. We were holding our guns at the ready: every forty to fifty metres we stopped and listened to hear whether anything moved in the grass. If something was moving we stood still and if the noise was not heard again we threw little stones in the direction from which the noise came in order to force the enemy to disclose himself. Usually those animals who alarmed us were small rodents, guinea fowls and genet cats scurrying by. Fortunately we were spared attacks from dangerous animals, but we only felt completely safe when we left the high grass thicket behind us and had reached the northern border of the thin wood. The march had exhausted us and so we enjoyed a rest on the hill.

When we marched on we came to a branch off our path which we were told went north to a village. It was called Mo-Longa by one of our porters, the two others called it Karanda (very probably Ki-Randa).[7] Our course up to now was almost northward, from here on it became north-north-western until Ki-Schindu. The march along the valley of the Mo-Romenonghe stream was very interesting. Its whitewashed bed (out of mica slate) was full of marvellous naturally cut bowls, basins, holes and lodes very probably washed out by the erosion of the grinding sand and stones during the rainy season. Elsewhere I had only found this phenomenon in sandstone—for instance on the Luala. Here and there, where the layers of the mica slate were harder, islets and banks perpendicular to the river remained. This day's journey was 18 km whereas the whole trip from Sakasipa to Ki-Schindu was 91·5 km and showed in geological terms nothing but mica slate. We passed a few abandoned hunting huts; Boy told me that he had once before accompanied some of Blockley's hunters up to this area. These hunters of Blockley's were probably responsible to a large extent for the decline of the trade. He had obviously trusted the Zambezi blacks too much by taking them into his service as elephant hunters. On the one hand, they did not exert themselves much on the hunting expeditions which became more and more difficult. They preferred to stay in their huts and to live well off the provisions which they had brought. On the other hand, they simply robbed their masters. Of twenty servants barely six or nine captured any tusks, which did not even cover one fourth of the expenses for the hunting season. In addition, many of the servants did not hand all the ivory to him. Westbech knew much better how to manage these things. Westbech had much stricter control over his hunters by one very simple device. His hunters were the coloureds from Panda-ma-Tenka who were mentioned before. Blacks from the Zambezi were assigned to them as servants. Both parties trusted each other so little that each of them would immediately have reported any misappropriation of ivory.

Boy told me now when we passed one of these deserted hunting huts that he, too, had lived there for quite some time with Blockley's people and had lived well. 'Nearly every other day we had fresh buffalo meat. The people of Ki-Schindu came out to us and brought us flour, pumpkins, and beer and we gave them in return much meat and all buffalo skins.' Ninety per cent of these hunters hired by Blockley thus were miserable cheats and thieves. After such a confession I lost much of my previous good opinion about Boy.

Ki-Schindu lies, as I said, in a broad well-irrigated valley, the river of which flows into the Mo-Romenonghe. The huts of the inhabitants were lying at the northern wooded edge of the valley. I stopped near them and chose our camp site. Everybody began his work immediately for the preparation of the camp. Half the Africans rushed out into the valley in order to cut grass with their spears for our sleeping places, the others went to fetch branches and brushwood whereas we Europeans took over axes and bayonets and began to cut young trees in order to make a solid fence. Thus all of us were working except for my wife and Pit who were on guard. My wife was holding my Werndl carbine in her hand. She was surrounded by three dogs, Daisy, Sidamojo and Witstock and was looking out into the distance, while Pit, our extremely cautious baboon, was watching the near vicinity, standing again and again on his hind legs and being the best guard of us all. The smallest noise, any movement in the grass, was immediately noticed by him. If the cause was a grasshopper, a loud humming giant horse beetle, a guinea-fowl or a small harmless mammal, he was quickly content and continued with his job, i.e. to watch out and to search for beetles, spiders, berries and seeds. If, however, the cause of the noise was some bigger wild animal—cattle, stray dogs, snakes, etc.—he became very nervous. He began to growl and to bark, showed his teeth and ran up to my wife in order to get her, or at least the dogs', attention. Pit was good—very good. He followed me, was faithful and vigilant and a source of infinite fun especially when he rebuked our merry little tyrant Daisy. We were only too ready to forgive him all his many playful and funny games. The mental abilities and qualities of this baboon were for me a continuous subject of inter-esting studies.

The camp was ready, it was getting dark, our fires were already burning. Still there was no visit from the village even though the loud shouting of the villagers proved that they had noticed our arrival. Since we had only kakatombe meat, our flour and corn being left behind with the mutinous porters, I sent two well-armed servants into the village in order to get some of the people to come. They gave them flour and groundnuts and promised to come the next morning. They also gave Boy some pertinent information about the real reasons for the mutiny of our porters. The porters did not dare to get near to the outlying areas of the village since they had pillaged this village in a very perfidious fashion about a year before when they were pursuing Marancian, the chief of Schescheke. Since they had lacked the courage to attack the village openly they had hidden in the woods and had only sneaked into the village when almost all the inhabitants were out work-ing in the fields. They took what they could carry along, set the huts on fire, and violated the women whom they had met by chance in some of the millet fields on their retreat. They never boasted of these deeds, for not even their chief Sakasipa knew anything about them. This is why he had ordered his men to carry my things up to Ki-Schindu which otherwise he would never have done. On our way those porters who had been involved in this attack had confessed this story, out of fear, to their leader Simutuli. He chose as a way out the smaller evil, i.e. to let me pay for it. He agreed that the porters would mutiny on the Inquisi and then again in Ki-Assa in order to get home and to escape safely. This information caused quite a shock among my people, especially to my wife, and the blacks were sure that the porters would never come to us and that we could bid goodbye to our belongings. I had a different idea. Since the natives of the Zambezi and in particular the Matoka are very superstitious I was quite sure that the porters would follow us to Ki-Schindu as otherwise they would suffer from pangs of bad conscience. Luanika's influence and power reached as far as Sakasipa. Luanika certainly would have the thieves killed, but neither as an act of justice nor with the honourable intention of giving me my stolen property back. Oh no! He would kill them merely out of anger that they had stolen things on their way to him which either his men might have earned or which he could have received as presents from me. Luanika would have sent a company to Mo-Sinkobo in order to kill the thieves and to fetch the stolen objects as well as some head of cattle (goats, sheep) in addition, as a special punishment. This is the way blacks think and act.

Furthermore I could count on the effect which my profession as physician, i.e. 'magician', would have. It was sufficient to say that my '*malemo*' would take care that all my things would be brought back to me and even by the mutinous porters themselves. The natives were unable to escape this fear. Of course, this psychological spell was only effective as long as the people took some medicine from me —that is, as long as they recognised me as a witchdoctor and were in great awe of me.

I took the kind reception of my messengers in the village as a good omen for our relations with the inhabitants. This prognosis later proved to be quite right. Ki-Schindu belongs to a chief called Schindu[8] who lives with Sietsetema and is said to recognise him as king. To me, however, this seemed to be more like a friendship than a lord–subject relationship.

Early the next morning after our arrival the Matoka came to our camp and brought so much grain that in two hours time I had all that I needed for ninety people over the next week in exchange for yellow glass beads. When I asked how many porters Schindu could give me, his representative answered sixteen to eighteen men. Indeed, this was good news. I continued to ask how many days it would take me to get to Sietsetema. Four days, was the answer. When I then offered the men a normal sitsiba as payment they all shouted 'too small, too little'. Yet I was neither able nor willing to give more since otherwise I would not have progressed very far with our supply and since one sitsiba was a perfectly adequate payment in this area.

Thus I dared to wait and indeed, on 30 June, when we were about to leave, the Ki-Schindu people came—even more than eighteen. They literally fought for the bundles which they were now very ready to carry for only one sitsiba. Meanwhile in the afternoon of 29 June that which I had so firmly expected happened. The mutineers came sneaking up to us without much ado. They brought our bundles and sat down at a little distance. The three headmen came up to greet me but I did not respond to them. I only had that servant come to me whose bundle one of the porters had taken away in Amare. I told him to show me the man who had done this. This poor person suffered from partial chorea (St Vitus' dance), in particular in his lower face muscles and in those around his mouth. If this young Matoka of about eighteen years was excited by something his mouth began to make terrible grimaces and, constantly jerking, it protruded like a trunk. Because of my harsh grilling this poor fellow became so nervous that when he stood before me his mouth and his thick lips began to shake so much that I had to press my own lips tightly together in order not to burst out laughing. My wife, however, hid her face quickly in the pillow on her bed while Leeb, Boy and Mopani who happened to be present ran away because they were unable to hold back their Homeric laughter any longer. All this, of course, did not agree very well with the role of judge which I had to play. I got up and shouted loudly to the porters: '*Okai Moloj*' (the wicked witch, i.e. the worst name one can call a bad person). And lo, all looked at the same spot where just then a porter got up with a bundle. It was the very bundle of glass beads which had been taken away from the stutterer. The man came up to me, knelt in front of me and clapping his hands he put the bundle in front of my feet. 'Master, here is the bundle.' 'All right,' I said, 'so you had to carry two.' The man asked for my forgiveness and the three headmen too came forward and tried to excuse themselves. 'Your turn will be soon, *ba-pila* [just wait], but I have to tell you, Moloj, that you have to die for your deed. Not through me but through Luanika since I sent him yesterday a message with my *lungalo* [letter, book, paper] and some Matoka took it along.' (This was a trick since I had no opportunity to send a message to Luanika.) Then I left the evildoers and walked out of the camp in order to demonstrate that I no longer wanted to have anything to do with them. I returned only after they had left the actual camp and were squatting around outside the camp waiting to see what would happen. This moral victory had to be exploited at once. Thus taking advantage of the momentary mood I ordered my people to take the sitsibas which already had been cut and to call upon the porters to come and get their payment. For the first and last time during this expedition, north of the Zambezi, it happened that the natives accepted their payment without grumbling and even gratefully. These people had become so intimidated that they all would have gone with me to Sietsetema for only one additional sitsiba. But at this point the abovementioned perfidious attack became an obstacle. Since Sakasipa's people were in the majority this time, the people of Ki-Schindu did not dare to do anything against them to take revenge but they did not allow the porters into the village and threatened them with Sietsetema. The effect of this threat was that all those who had been involved in this perfidious deed turned around to go home and were glad to escape safely. Half the porters who were innocent promised to continue carrying for me. I hired them since at this time I still needed fifty-eight more porters. The kakatombe skin and other items which I had collected—mostly handicrafts of the blacks—I packed up well and gave them to the two servants, January and Piccanini, who refused to go further north. They were returning to the south and thus I gave them these light bundles to take to Mr Westbech in Gazungula who was supposed to send them home via Schoschong if an opportunity arose, together with other things I was still intending to send him.

My people looked at me with amazement when I even paid these porters. They did not believe that any of these objects would ever arrive. The first guide who was related to Sakasipa was ill. The day before two porters had been fighting with each other for water on their trip and when the guide had tried to separate them he was hit with a pole-axe, right over his eye. The wound looked rather serious and I tried to ease his pains as best I could and gave him some medicine for the journey. Probably the dirtiest of all the dirt-covered Matoka were the people of Ki-Schindu, and among them, especially, the promising male youths up to twelve years of age. Every day these youngsters visited us their bodies were covered with a grey coating of ashes and soil which came off easily. In the morning and in the evening they rolled themselves in piles of ashes in order to protect themselves with this coating against the cold at night and against mosquito bites during the day time. This, too, is a type of cosmetic.

Here for the first time we tried *mokanda*, the weak sweetish beer made out of maize. The poorer natives who do not have that much millet to prepare a *butshuala* or even the strong *matimbe* have to be content with this maize beer and even like it. Here for the first time, too, we saw the claws of birds of prey and the tusks of warthogs being used as jewellery arranged in a type of necklace. The inhabitants of Ki-Schindu obviously regarded their rifles as a kind of indispensable decoration, for they were constantly lugging around their heavy muskets even though they had no ammunition. Of course, they were carrying them, too, whenever they honoured us by their visits. Before we left, Boy came to me and asked me to give a hearing and forgiveness to the main ringleader who had instigated the porters first on the Inquisi and in the end had taken the bundle of glass beads away from 'jerk-mouth'. Boy believed that he was a friend of Marancian's and that he surely would be killed if only the slightest news about his deeds were to reach Schescheke. Boy claimed also that he was no Matoka but a Marutse and that he had already earned three sitsibas, as he had been carrying loads for me ever since Mambowa. From Boy's words I guessed more than he probably knew himself. This man simply wanted to get to Marancian. Playing the unsuspicious role of one of my porters, he used the opportunity of my trip to make a journey which otherwise would have cost him his neck. His behaviour as a rebel was only a pretext. He wanted to impress me and prove himself as a man who could lead the porters by the nose and with whom I had to reckon and therefore keep on good terms. For a black he was very shrewd, yet in me he found his master. I lent him an ear and he asked me to be allowed to continue carrying a load for me up to Sietsetema for only his keep and without any pay whatsoever. I accepted his services in return for his keep plus a sitsiba. And after having sent Boy away I said to this man before letting him go, '*Wuena Mulekan a Marancian*' (You are Marancian's faithful friend). He jumped up with a sudden expression of fear in his face and his carriage, 'How can you say this, master?' he asked. 'Be quiet, my *malemo* [medicine, charms] have told me so, but I am not going to tell anybody. At Sietsetema's you probably will leave us and go your own way'—and I pointed westwards—'and you will then go to your chief. Be quiet, you can go with us but do not reveal yourself to the others. Look how they are staring at us, I won't say anything and I shall forgive you.' The man began to have confidence in me and I did not have cause to regret this conversation. On the contrary, I owed this man much on our journey to Sietsetema.

On 30 June we started out from Ki-Schindu and we were able to make a journey of 16 km that day which was very interesting. Our route led through wooded hilly country and in some parts it was full of interesting sights. I carried out altitude measurements on the hill near the Ki-Schindu village and in the ninth kilometre near the little village Tschi-(ki)Akuruba. I found formations of weather-worn gneiss, which added much to the bizzare structure of some of the stream banks. In the fourth kilometre we crossed the Mo-Kongo stream and in the fifth a second stream as well as the Gu-Njati river whose gneiss boulders, dense reeds, and elephant grass presented a magnificent and wildly romantic panorama. We crossed six more streams which rushed to the west to flow into the Gu-Njati which itself is probably a tributary of the Madschila. In the bush we found the big-gest ant-hills yet seen; they were true 'tumuli' with a diameter of ten to thirty metres. We saw several herds of five to twenty kakatombe hartebeest. On all the paths over which we came we found numerous traps for small mammals of the kind I have already described. The chief of Akuruba gave us some *mokanda* as refreshment and several of the village youth wanted to join our expedition—yet on an unacceptable condition: that I would not go to the much feared Maschuku-lumbe but north-westwards to the Mankoya. Even more they would have pre-ferred to go south, because then they could have offered their services to someone else after I had dismissed them and thus could have earned a rifle quite easily. Our camp site was north-east of Ki-Schindu on the northern bank of the Tschi-Rufumpe stream. The banks of this stream had been badly uprooted by warthogs. Soon after our arrival I started out eastwards and Leeb westwards, also ac-companied by a native, in order to hunt for fresh meat. In the meantime the others were supposed to set up the camp in the usual way. Yet only too soon I was forced to return quickly. For from the east a terrible danger to the camp had arisen and we rushed back to prevent it if possible. I had not yet walked far along the stream bank, accompanied by a black and little Daisy and was intending to hunt for warthogs in the reed thicket when a rumbling noise in the east caught my attention. I stopped and listened. My servant, too, had noticed it and almost simultaneously we shouted '*Molelo, hakagala*' (fire is near). Indeed, not very far away a bush fire was raging which the wind blew towards us. The noise in-creased instantly, indeed as fast as I can write this the roar and crackling became clearer and nearer and soon one could see the smoke which was rolling closer from the east over the treetops. A few minutes later it had already formed a thick low hanging cloud over us moving east and south-westwards. 'Back, immedi-ately back, Siroko,' I shouted, 'so that we can still reach the camp before the fire.' And now a race for life began with the raging, wind-fanned fire. When we had covered half the stretch gasping and panting, a deep narrow water course, half overgrown with grass, suddenly opened up in front of us. This rain hole, which was a hiding place for wild animals, forced us to slow down. We climbed down the slope with care and up the other side and entered the edge of the bush. The burnt black reeds were already falling on us like a thick rain. Looking back we saw the fire already covering the whole breadth of the bush. It was following us like an inevitable fate—a red and yellow mass often leaping up to the treetops and belching light grey smoke clouds towards the sky. We ran as fast as our feet could carry us and finally we saw our camp. Thank God they were already working on preventive measures and my wife shouted a relieved greeting to me from the distance. 'Oh, how glad I am that you are coming.' Initially the blacks had not thought that the fire would really come near. My baggage would have been lost if my wife had not intervened and when words could not persuade them had finally beaten the blacks with a whip in order to make them work.

Rapidly the fire came closer and we all worked so hard that in a few minutes we were dripping with sweat. My wife had read the situation correctly; it was necessary to cut down the grass quickly around the camp and thus to create a fire belt around it. Since the actual cutting of the high grass would have taken too long we burnt the grass down in a five-metre-wide patch around us. Like the American Indians do in bushfires we tried to defeat the fire by fire.

At a short distance from the actual camp we set fire to the grass but we kept its force down by beating it with heavy broad branches as soon as the strip of approximately five metres was burnt. Thus we succeeded in a relatively short time in creating a barren safety zone around our camp. When the wind then really drove the bushfire near to us the blazing flames and the choking smoke surrounded us indeed from all sides. Yet the fire could not jump over the burnt out belt of black soil. It moved on and our camp with all that was hidden in it was safe.

In front of us the sea of flames was raging, as we found out later, for a width of 3 km from north-east to south-west. It was a frighteningly beautiful sight. The burning waves of high grass looked like fiery masses of lava flowing in even waves fast approaching the woods. So great was the crackling, murmuring, roaring, and crashing from this blazing mass that one could hardly understand what the person next to one was saying. To the right and to the left of our camp in the middle of that fiery mass were two of those huge ant-hills which I mentioned earlier. Each of them was about seven metres high and wide, covered with thick trees, high grass, and huge dry tree mallows. This dry vegetation was linked by liana vines with the green treetops. The fire had hardly reached these hills when the flames greedily licked at the trees. In a few minutes hills and trees were transformed into huge fire columns from which the wind blew sparks towards our post. We had to extinguish them quickly with the green *mopani* branches.

It was raining grasshoppers and butterflies on to our oasis as if the dry grass on which we were standing were a flower garden full of honey. Small and big animals ran away from the sea of flames to save their lives. Small rodents, lizards, and snakes who did not happen to be near some hole or in the vicinity of their lairs were caught by the fire and burnt. Black clouds which were hanging lower and lower indicated which course the fire took far away from us. Luckily, we had survived one of those violent bushfires as they occur quite frequently in those prairie areas. If the wind is strong they do not harm the woods through which they pass since there is no time for the heavy trunks to catch fire. But if it were calm and the fire had more time to burn on one and the same spot and to catch the dry underbrush it would do a lot more damage. As it is, however, such a fire is usually extinguished in the woods since there are many large, almost barren, spots or places with very short grass because of the shade from the trees, and over these the fire rages quickly without finding much fuel.

Only after the danger was over we realised how great it had been. What would have happened if the fire had jumped across the barrier, and had caught our boxes filled with cartridges or our barter goods? And what would have happened if some of us had received serious burns and had become unable to march on? These were the frightening thoughts of the restless night which we spent after the fire. As great as the feverish excitement had been earlier, so strong was the subsequent reaction of paralysing exhaustion. We were sitting there exhausted as after a serious illness and needed days to recover fully. We were helped to recuperate by the beautiful and interesting area through which we passed the following day on 1 July and which was one of the most instructive and most interesting journeys of our expedition north of the Zambezi. Our camp for the night was situated on the Moko-mo-Prosi stream north-east of our last camp site. On this journey we crossed several times the valley of the Ki-Angamargua stream which we only left behind us after travelling 11 km. There were huge ant-hills, some as large as 100 m², on both sides of the narrow path through the burnt-out bush. We found them as long as we were in that valley. Mica slate and gneiss formed interesting hill crests similar to those of granite near Schoschong, yet they were not quite as high.

From the ninth kilometre on the terrain dropped towards the north-west, then we crossed numerous ranges of hills which were all wooded and seemed to descend into a large depression. We crossed several streams and in the thirteenth kilometre we reached the Navieti river, the crossing of which was very difficult and took a long time because of its steep vertical banks of mica slate. I tried to make a sketch (*not included*) of this scene. The river was much deeper, yet I had to draw it as much shallower and more open in order to show how we crossed it.

It took a very long time before all our porters had passed this spot. We rested for a little while on the opposite bank and waited for both the whole train of porters, since some had stayed behind on the hard and stony path, and for Boy and his companion who tried hard to hunt for some buck. We had spotted some kaka-tombe and striped gnus and for the first time since we had left the Zambezi we also found the beautiful Harris antelopes. Before we even reached the Navieti we had an interlude which began tragically yet ended rather amusingly. All of a sudden we met a group of Matoka coming towards us. They did not look at all friendly. As soon as they saw us they lay down on the side of the path and remained there like logs without greeting us. They were twenty men looking quite fantastic with their heads decorated with bunches of white heron feathers. Beside them were lying their arms, i.e. fighting axes, throwing spears, and hand spears, shields and staves. This group caused extreme nervousness for our genius Boy. Hardly had we passed these people when he came running up to me whispering in a low voice: 'Baas, these are people who go around to kill whomever they encounter on hunting or trading expeditions. They have young boys with them whom they sell to us, the Makalaka or to the Matoka living on the river, as well as to the Mambari⁹ and to the Maschukulumbe.'

I could not help but smile and so did my wife and Leeb who followed me closely. We mocked Boy's great trepidation. 'Well, master, you laugh, but it is really true.' Boy stared at me and displayed such a miserable expression on his face that this man, who otherwise was so strong and brave in the face of every wild animal, all of a sudden looked like a frightened old woman.

'They are Matoka, Boy, are they not?' 'Yes, Baas.' 'Well, as far as I know them, every Matoka steals unless you watch them closely every single minute. And these are just like all the others.' Yet I grasped Boy's fear that these honourable twenty chaps might practise an even 'higher craft' than mere stealing. I agreed to stop at the next wooded slope and wait until all our porters had caught up with us. On that particular day we happened to have many who were slow in following. Before all our porters had come down the hill, a few men of the Matoka group came up to us unarmed and expressed their surprise that we had passed them without hearing the great news. I did not answer but asked Boy whether these people had already greeted us. When Boy reminded them they greeted us immediately and then they began such a rapid flow of words that one hardly could hear one's own words. They said that they had come from Sietsetema, that he was well except for a wound on his foot, that they were on their way home and were living at some place in the bush. Finally they suggested that I should give them the usual presents. Since I refused to do so they were satisfied with five empty cartridges which they seemed to welcome greatly as snuff boxes.

During this conversation I was looking out for our porters and when I saw the last one coming with Oswald I realised that our tame baboon was missing. I looked around to see whether he perhaps was lying exhausted in the shade near us. '*En, en tshen.*' We suddenly heard a noise from the other side of the clearing where the rest of the supposed robber barons were still squatting in the same place. All of a sudden they were literally overrun by Pit who had stayed somewhat behind. Pit knew and loved the twenty blacks whom I had hired as servants on a long-term basis and had travelled with us for weeks and fed and patted him often. Yet he hated all the porters with a passion, just as I did. He had recognised at once that those blacks so fancifully decorated with white feathers were strangers and he obviously had quickly decided to play them a nasty trick. As usual he approached them without making any noise. Suddenly he jumped on the back of the man who was sitting furthest away. Frightened because he was attacked from the rear he jumped up. Yet in so doing he fell on the two men next to him while Pit had already attacked the fourth one and in dashing off had scratched the calf of one of the boys sitting at the other end who had jumped off in order to run away. All of this was done in one moment so that we only heard the loud shrieks and saw a crowd of people striking out violently and falling on top of each other in a confused heap. A little further away we soon recognised the wailing boy lying on the ground and screaming as if a rhino had pierced him with his horn. Nothing could be seen or heard of Pit. Where was he? Already near us? And what did the brave robbers among us do—the robbers of whom Boy had been so afraid? They tried to escape. One of them even had grabbed Mapani's spear to arm himself against Pit. I called the baboon. He allowed himself to be caught and was given a maize cob. Yet as soon as he noticed the Matoka with their white feather bushes who were making their retreat, Pit tried to free himself and to run after them in order to leave these heroes a souvenir from his teeth. Yet I held him back. After I had finally gathered all the porters we left in good spirits, our hero Pit in our midst.

In the sixteenth kilometre our path led through a narrow pass and shortly thereafter we saw a plain stretching west and north-westwards below us. In the eighteenth kilometre we passed the deep valley of the Matso stream and on its slope we passed through a deserted village where we entered Sietsetema's actual territory. In the bottom of the valley I shot two vervet monkeys. To my surprise and distress at the same time, they were the same type which lives in the south. Their area of distribution thus seems to reach from the sea coast in the south up here to the north. For 4 km we marched through the huge plain which is limited in the north and north-west by a range of wooded hills. ·

Since we still felt extremely tired, as a consequence of the excitement of the day before and of our long journey, we intended to pitch our camp for the night earlier than usual. Unfortunately, however, we could not find any water, not even in the small valleys through which we passed. Thus we had to continue our march in spite of our fatigue. I regretted this forced continuation of our journey even more since the banks of one of these dried-out little streams showed the most beautiful display of plants which I had hitherto seen during the winter season on the high plateau of southern Africa. The most beautiful decoration of these stream banks were acacia trees of medium height whose branches were laden with gorgeous deep pink and light crimson flower clusters. They could be seen from afar and created a marvellous and attractive sight among the green of the other trees. The bush, out of whose fruits the Matoka make their snuff boxes, was also in bloom. And on the whole the bushes and plants along the banks which had been safe from fire for years were full of everything alive and blooming as at home at the beginning of the summer. Before we left the plain in order to reach a sandy and hilly wood via a low ridge, the heights of which were crowned with high fan palms full of ripe fruits, we saw several herds of small reddish antelopes as big as duiker gazelles and two big zebra herds. Yet we were far too tired to try our hunting luck. But we had hardly chosen our camp site on the Mokomo-Rosi stream when the numerous tracks of wild animals tempted Boy to go deer stalking with some of the porters. To our pleasant surprise he killed a striped gnu and a kakatombe bull and seriously wounded a male zebra. On this journey I had skins prepared only in very exceptional cases since it was too difficult to transport them. Thus this time also I gave the gnu meat to the porters and the skin I gave to my servant to make sandals. I kept only the kakatombe skin.

On 2 July we made only 10 km. This slowdown of our journey I had to blame on my own generosity with the gnu meat. We had to start later since my porters were still busy cutting up the meat and we had to march more slowly since their load now had become twice as heavy. Thus we could not get on as fast as usual but were forced to rest more frequently. We followed the stream for a while, then turned right again into a very high sea of grass with brushwood and scrub growing in between. We reached a deep cut like a stream bed with hills on both sides and with truly magnificent and literally impenetrable vegetation along the banks. During the summer there should be glorious subtropical flora, a delight for any botanist. Broad buffalo tracks (one can no longer call them paths) disclosed to us who was ruling there and advised us to exercise the necessary caution while we were walking through the thick reeds in order not to fall victim to a sudden attack of the buffaloes.

An hour later we had passed the dangerous spot and were ascending a sparsely wooded laterite ridge, the slope of which descended to the cut which we just had passed through. I went first, accompanied by my wife and Leeb who ever since Bukacz' death was bravely carrying the chronometer on a leather strap.

The numerous animal tracks persuaded me to try my hunting luck; perhaps I could obtain a rare skin. In any case, I wanted to get more supplies of fresh meat. I told my wife to continue leading the file and I intended to hunt together with Leeb in a semi-circle through the wooded valley and then later meet up with them again. In the middle of the valley was a huge, densely overgrown ant-hill. Using this as a cover we were able to sneak up to some grazing hartebeests among which was as usual a gnu. At the foot of the hill I left my cartridge pouch, my hunting knife, my water bottle and my black hat. Then I crept up, took my post behind a tree, and aimed at the nearest animal standing about 120 m away from me. At that moment another animal came up to it and thus covered it with his body. I therefore was forced to shoot at this second animal since it was in a better position for me. I would have liked to listen to and study these completely unaware animals. Yet because of this passion of mine it had often happened that we had not a single bite of fresh meat even when near the fattest animals.

At this point I also had the desire to gain one or two of these rare specimens for my collection. I hit the animal, but it got up again and the bull and lord of the herd came up to it without realising that I was so close. Quickly I aimed at him, yet alas, what bad hunting luck! The cartridge failed and the herd fled up the valley. The wounded animal was limping and followed the others with great effort. Another shot at the bull failed again. I realised that many of my cartridges must have been spoiled. The fleeing animals ran in the same direction which I had to take, and alas, all of a sudden I saw my wife in front of me. Not far from her was lying the female animal which I had hit with my first shot and which had now collapsed. We stopped and waited until the first servants arrived in order to skin the dead animal and to take along the meat which was to be distributed among them.

Since I wanted to prepare and cure the skin that very day and have it dried by the next morning I decided to make an exception and to rest earlier this day and to go along as far as Kandantzowa i.e. only a few kilometres further. When we were dissecting the animal we found that it was highly pregnant and the not yet fully-developed foetus substantially enriched my collection, which consisted already of two males and one female.

On our further journey we came to a park-like plain full of *mopani* trees. Towards the north it was bordered by a range of wooded hills. At the foot of these hills I found five zebras and I succeeded in shooting one with my Werndl rifle from a distance of 250 m. Unfortunately my shot had not killed it so that it escaped anyway. Little Daisy pursued it with bravery yet he did not accomplish anything beyond making us wait uneasily for his return for about an hour and we were lucky that he found our track at all.

My hunting luck on this journey was not very good even though I shot well and had met a lot of game. A great deal of our failures, however, must be assigned to our rifles. These rifles, the kind with the small solid bullets called Kropatschek, Werndl, Winchester and Schulhof, were indeed excellent for our self-defence against blacks in attacks at close quarters as well as against wild animals, yet they were not very effective when hunting for game, especially when one had to shoot from a great distance. Little Steenbok gazelles were still running away with our bullet wounds. The little Winchester bullet might very well disable a human, but it does not harm game so much from that distance unless the animals are shot right through the brain, the heart or the spine. They could escape successfully into the impenetrable thorn, wood or reed thickets and thus were lost for the hunter. In those southern African areas the best bullets for hunting are those which are long and flattened on one side and are partly hollow. They get compressed when they hit bones and create large wounds in the body and thus kill the animal because of the great loss of blood or because of an extensive destruction even of some of the lesser organs.

I was often asked why I did not shoot with dum-dum bullets which certainly would give the best guarantee to get the game once it was hit. I can only say to this that I do not like to shoot with these bullets. And just as I do not like it, neither do the best and most famous elephant and lion hunters of South Africa. The hollow bullet kills just as certainly as the dum-dum bullet but does not destroy the body to the same degree as the dum-dum. This is very important for the scientist and thus, for example, for me too. And it is more sportsmanlike if I may say so. The dum-dum bullet lulls the hunter much too easily into a false self-confidence so that finally he no longer pays attention and loses his accuracy of fire. This is what I was most afraid of for my staff who often were also very enthusiastic about the dum-dum bullet. I never allowed a dum-dum cartridge to be used, not even when we hunted for rhinos, buffaloes, hippos and elephants, not to speak of the really big carnivores. This I learned from the 'Afrikaners' and I have become that much of a hunter that I do not regard the hunt as being a massacre but rather a battle and I want to be victorious openly in this battle without being protected by the infallible technology of a chemical compound.

This is said as my excuse also to all my readers who have thought to themselves often and maybe also just now while reading this last hunting adventure: 'Why does this Holub take so very many pot-shots? He should use those dum-dum bullets instead if he is such a poor shot.'

While talking about the results of our hunt we were descending, or rather climbing down, the slope. The descent was very steep and laborious; however we were rewarded by the view of a beautiful broad valley covered with the well-known elephant grass in the middle of which there was a dark blue pond surrounded by green reeds. On the water surface a host of light blue water lilies were waving in the breeze and into the pond a slowly moving little stream was flowing. For us this wonderful view of the valley was not only a beautiful scene of nature but it was truly delightful and heartwarming.

Years ago this valley had been inhabited by hundreds of elephants and therefore it is called elephant valley by the natives. A few weeks before our arrival the unfortunate Mr Thomas[10] had hunted there. We found his 'skerm' (camp) still on the slope in the bush. Sietsetema's town which is 18 km away was the furthest point he had reached on his expedition from Matabeleland coming from the south-east. While he was staying in the Kandantzora valley he heard about the approach of Luanika's troops in pursuit of Marancian and he thought it best to retreat towards the south-east. Immediately after we had entered the valley we had an adventurous experience which could have had very bad consequences for us. When we were trying to establish our camp we were looking for a place which was not overgrown with grass. Yet we could not find one and we decided to make one by burning down the high grass as we had already done many times on our journey. We selected a spot with rather short grass in the vicinity of the water and laid the fire. I could not help but think of Schiller's verses 'Salutary is the fire's power' and I was just citing 'Yet beware if it is unleashed'. At that moment I realised that the high bush-grass growing around this spot had caught fire and it threatened to become a terrific fire. In the next second we rushed to the shrubs growing on the ant-hill near which we were standing and ripped off branches full of leaves. And there we were, all of us thrashing the crackling flames even though the fire was licking up at our hands and eyebrows. Thanks to the fact that the winds were all calm we succeeded in mastering the flames. It would have been a terrible thought for me that I had been the cause of a big bushfire, especially since I had my people observe extreme caution whenever we made a camp fire.

The distance which we were able to cover this day was only about ten kilometres. As rock formation I found sand in elevated places, whereas laterite, as mineral debris of mica slate (lying in a north-north-east direction at an incline of forty-five degrees) was deposited over firm humus.

Our camp in the Kandantzowa valley was in a north-eastern direction with respect to our last camp site on the Mokomo-Rosi stream. In this camp we did not experience anything noteworthy. Some of Sietsetema's people who passed our camp in the evening told us that we would reach Sietsetema's town easily the following day and that we would surely find the chief there. The distance which we had to cover was 18 km and Sietsetema's homestead was in a north-eastern direction from our camp.

We started out early in the morning. We passed through a valley and a hilly area which towards the north lead to the Sianquimbi valley. We rested several times and met a few women and two young men, one of whom was introduced to us as a lion killer. It had been only a short time ago that he had done this heroic deed, when with only two spears he had killed a lion who had been eating his nearby prey. The young man looked weak, rather than strong, and yet he had succeeded in the kill.

Even though there are woods on the sandy or rocky ridges in the vicinity, Sietsetema had preferred to establish his residence in the plain of the Sianquimbi valley overgrown with high grass. He, too, has taken over the system of dispersed kraals, which is characteristic of the Matoka, in order not to be surprised and destroyed by the enemy. Yet the location of this settlement seemed to me even more dangerous. Already in Ki-Schindu, Ki-Assa and Amare we had found the kraals no longer situated in the woods. Instead, the huts and the surrounding large or small fields were located amidst those high grass thickets and thus were continuously exposed to the danger of total destruction in the event of fires which break out often in the high grass thickets from May to September.

The plain of the valley in which Sietsetema's town Mo-Monguembo (also called Mo-Kalubanda)[11] is situated in one big field of humus which during the rainy season is transformed into a bottomless swamp. The fever then should be terrible in this area.

The first kraal which we found on our way, or rather along the maze of innumerable paths through which our people from Ki-Schindu guided us, was the residence of chief Schindu. He was a guest of Sietsetema's and chief of the Schindu village. In one of the kraals (consisting of two miserable huts in a small cut-over maize field closely surrounded by the grass thicket) I saw white and grey domestic pigeons, completely tame. It was the first time since I had left the Transvaal border that I found these birds but the people refused to tell me how these pigeons got there. The only explanation for the occurrence of these birds in this area which I can find is that they had been obtained from the Portuguese and had been brought here from the east. A trading station exists on an island near the mouth of the Luenge river and the pigeons might have come from there. In any case their existence in this area was quite interesting.

Soon we saw Sietsetema's kraal. It consisted of eight huts built on some meadowland in the shade of a few big mimosa trees and in the middle of a grass thicket. For us it was an important event each time we entered a so-called royal residence and each time it made our blood flow faster. What were we to experience here and in what state would we leave this place again which meant nothing to all of the educated world but which at the moment meant all to us? Under a roof supported only by poles we found a few men smoking their dagga pipes. They were the immediate court council of the most powerful of the Matoka chiefs, the last one in the north-east who plays tribute to Luanika, the Marutse king. I established our camp under a tree and it was not long before Sietsetema appeared in our midst. He was a tall strong old man, naked except for some strings of glass beads around his loins and a miserable black woollen blanket over his shoulders. Sietsetema's name was well known on the Zambezi, and Blockley, who had heard much about him, had only good things to tell. Yet I had heard a contradictory opinion from a rather dubious source which was suspect to me from the very beginning—namely from the coloured called 'Afrika' whom I have already mentioned several times. Sietsetema was once visited by this coloured man who was hunting for Westbech in this area north of the Zambezi. Afrika was well waited on by Sietsetema, yet he got so drunk that he was madly hitting out around himself with his walking stick, scolding everybody and finally saying that he wanted to beat up Sietsetema as well. His servants pulled their raging master aside quickly so that they would not all be killed together by their furious Matoka host.

I personally was very kindly welcomed by Sietsetema. I gave him a few presents and he immediately sent out for maize, goats and other things as compensation for what he had received from me. He also promised to get porters for me and I rewarded his willingness to help me, which was otherwise very rare, by volunteering to treat a bad wound on his right leg which he had not been able to get healed for two years. I treated the wound with 'lapis' and to his great satisfaction the infection was gone by the third morning. I soon became very familiar with Sietsetema. In one of our conversations he pointed to an empty hut in the middle of his kraal and said: 'There they were both lying asleep and I gave them food and drink.' 'Who, Morena? Who were these two?' 'Who else but Monari [Mr Thomas] and Marancian. First one and then the other left when the troop of the Marutse and the southern Matoka pursuing them came closer. Monari was afraid for his ebony and Marancian thought that he was not safe. The leaders of those sent after them told me I should know where Marancian was. I said "No! I satisfied his hunger yet I did not dog his footsteps." I realised that these pursuers were actually afraid of Marancian and were only looking for an excuse to end their pursuit right here and to return home. Marancian had soon found out all this and one day my herdsmen, who were living in the north, came and told me that Marancian offered his pursuers *kia-tumela* [welcome greeting] and that soon he would come himself in order to welcome them properly in this area. At that point nothing could keep these cowards any longer and before the day was over they had left.'

When Sietsetema left our camp I called the porters in order to pay them. All of a sudden the situation changed completely. We had to go through a similar scene to that at Matakala—only we were more fortunate for, on the one hand, Sietsetema did not support the porters and, on the other hand, the poor devil who had taken away the bundle from my servant 'jerkmouth' between Amare and Ki-Schindu had persuaded the porters successfully so that they now finally accepted the pay which had been agreed upon before. They were satisfied with the grey Holleschowitz calico, but only after a lot of shouting for about two hours. Yet so that we could sing the old song 'It would otherwise have been too perfect' on the first day of our stay pitiless fate again had another evil prepared for us. Namely, I made two observations which caused considerable worry for us all. I realised that some of my best servants, Boy, Mapani and a few others, had suddenly undergone a change. They were talking surprisingly much with Sietsetema's people about the Maschukulumbe and the more they talked the more afraid and changed they became.

Boy prepared a sleeping place for himself at some distance and not, as usual, immediately near our camp. He had secret conversations with all the servants whom he asked to come to him. Therefore I sent some of my people out deliberately to get this or that for me. I pretended to be very sleepy and I flung myself on the pile of grass which they had fetched for the camp. I had been lying there only for a short while when they began to talk in a less inhibited way. My suspicion proved to be completely correct. Boy reported such terrible things about the Maschukulumbe that some of the listening servants—and they were mostly Makalaka—exclaimed in great fear. Boy concluded his long speech with the resolution to desert us on the spot and not to accompany us to the end of our expedition as they had agreed initially. 'We shall ask for our pay and this the *Njaka* will have to give to us.' 'But then we won't get any rifles' suggested Kabrnik. 'Well perhaps we won't get these arms but we shall claim blankets and sitsibas', answered Boy. I had heard enough. Indeed, it was true after all that our servants planned to desert us at the border of the Maschukulumbe. In the meantime, Mapani had risen, come closer and pretended to look for something. When he believed that I was fast asleep he sneaked into our camp. I caught him just as he had one hand in Leeb's cartridge pouch and was reaching out with the other one to a plate on which were the glass beads which I wanted to exchange.

My wife was not a little surprised when I told her the news that those servants whom we considered as our main support in all situations throughout our whole expedition planned to desert us and that the honourable Mapani, in whom we had had so much confidence, was an inveterate thief who very probably had stolen things from us more than once.

The next morning I called all my servants together and told them in a very relaxed way that I had realised from my *malemo* (medicine) that they were planning secretly to desert us and that Boy had persuaded them to do so. They felt very ashamed to admit their fear of the Maschukulumbe. And Boy, their insiduous confident and conspirator, looked long for an excuse until he finally said, 'Well, master, we planned to leave you since you had promised us to give us a sitsiba every now and then so that we can buy *butschuala* [beer] but you did not stick to your word.' 'Did I not buy you a pot full of beer in every village where we stayed overnight and every day when we stayed for several days?' Then even Boy had to keep silent.

I had preferred to buy the beer for them myself, since the servants often tried secretly to get the women's favour with sitsibas and I then had to hear the complaints from the male population that my twenty native servants were true robbers. At Sietsetema's I had no need to be afraid of this since he was such a strict master and ruler that my servants lost all desire for amorous adventures. They knew that a mere flirtation would have brought the *slepe* (fighting axe) over the neck of the would-be lover.

The first thing Sietsetema's people told my men was the story of the two unfaithful wives of the king and of their frightening punishment. Since this story is going around like a legend from one to the next in Sietsetema's country I shall tell it briefly. Seduced by some Matoka, who were passing through, two of the king's wives escaped many years ago. Of course, they were his youngest and favourite wives. They eloped to the north into the neighbouring independent areas of some small Matoka princes. Here they had the misfortune that their seducers soon had to leave the country. Thus they had no protection. The Matoka prince of this area used this opportunity to ingratiate himself with the rather powerful Sietsetema. He had the escaped women tied and brought them back to their husband. Sietsetema smiled when he saw them 'Well, you come back home' he said 'into the huts which you left. But you do not return voluntarily and with remorse, but you were forced to come since you are tied. And I should forgive you? Never. Even if you promised not to run away again, you would do it anyway. Since you fill me with disgust you must die.' One can see the man did not believe in women's vows and the otherwise so good-natured Sietsetema turned out to be a true Nero in love matters. His smile changed into a bloodthirsty grin. At a sign from him the two women were grabbed and their feet were tied. Then a few strong men with whom Sietsetema had already planned everything beforehand held the two women upside down with their faces to the ground. Sietsetema, armed with a small rather dull-bladed fighting axe, took his post between the two victims who were screaming on the ground. He began to hit the necks of the two women alternately striking out to the right and to the left until he had separated their heads from their trunks. About forty strokes were necessary to cut each head from its trunk.

Through this cruelty Sietsetema had secured the faithfulness of his other wives for ever, and nobody heard that the desire for amorous adventures had ever again brought any Matoka to this court. However, Sietsetema had become the horror for all women in the country.

Yet with regard to me Sietsetema behaved as the most decent, kindest, and most helpful person. I must regard him as the best of all the Matoka chiefs whom I got to know. To my own and his pleasure his old shin wound looked much better after it had been cleaned out several times on the first day. The old man tried to do all he could to show me his gratitude. The most valuable things he could offer me were valuable reports about the neighbouring territories. He told me many really interesting things. But the final refrain of each report was that I should not go to the much-feared Maschukulumbe. At least, I should stay with him longer than only three days. He would give me some ivory and would supply me with beer day and night. And when Boy told him that I collected animals he said that I should now give up the idea of the Maschukulumbe altogether. He offered to give me many people to go hunting with me, for all those animals which existed in the great Marutse empire also lived in his area. In short, he did everything possible to keep me with him. Of course, I did not change my decision but his words made a terrific impression on my frightened servants. They heard only horrifying and hair-raising tales about the Maschukulumbe. If, however, we had stayed there a well-filled beer pitcher was certain for them every day. They could enjoy it without any danger and exhaustion. How could they be undecided about what they would like to do? Certainly they did all they could to persuade me to stay on.

Sietsetema let me know that in the north where I wanted to go directly there were many small independent Matoka chiefs. The same would hold for the east where no chief would have enough men to supply me with porters.[12] Therefore he gave me the advice to go either north-east or north-westwards where two great princes were residing: in the north-east Mo-Panza[13] and in the north-west Siasonga.[14] He, Sietsetema, could give me porters at three day's notice. He would need that much time to call them together from all the surrounding kraals. These porters would go with me either to Mo-Panza or to Siasonga according to what I would decide to do.

I realised that Sietsetema was right in what he was saying and I asked him which of the two princes had contact with the Maschukulumbe. He named Mo-Panza and that suited me well since I had already heard on the Zambezi that Siasonga was a treacherous individual. The way Sietsetema described Mo-Panza to me he appeared to be exactly the man who could help my purposes best of all since he had the most intimate relations with the Maschukulumbe of all Matoka princes. Sietsetema even advised me to ask Mo-Panza for porters to go directly to the Luenge if I really refused to give up the idea of going to the Maschukulumbe. Sietsetema did not stop warning us. As if he wanted to rid himself of any responsibility for our inevitable misfortune he continued to tell new evil tricks and crimes of the Maschukulumbe. 'Only four days ago'—and the speaker indicated the number by showing me four fingers of his left hand—'we got the news about their newest attack on the Matoka. One of the smaller chiefs living there'—and Sietsetema pointed to the north—'had disturbed the Maschukulumbe several times and since they tolerated it he had stolen a few head of cattle from them. For this he had to suffer. They attacked him and killed him alone without taking anything but their cattle. The wives of the murdered chief fled to Mo-Panza who graciously included them in the number of his own wives only out of "pity" since these poor females had become orphaned although they had brought along all their possessions. Mo-Panza claimed the area which bordered on his territory in return for the protection he had given these women.'

These and other things the upright Sietsetema told me. Yet everything was in vain. My plans remained unchangeable; 'We have to go north.'

The thing which surprised me most of all these reports was to hear over and over again that the Maschukulumbe were also living on this side of the Luenge. According to all that we had heard previously Mo-Panza should have been living right on the river and now I found out that I had to pass first through three different Maschukulumbe chieftaincies in order to reach the Luenge. We were told, however, that south of the Luenge the Maschukulumbe were wedged in between the Mankoja, whom they had pushed back across the river at the time when they had come from the north—that is from the great lakes—and had moved south to conquer new territory. At that point they had extended their empire south across the river. Now, we were told, they were on good terms with the northern Mankoja tribes and traded with them. They bought tobacco and grain, fish traps, and household utensils from them and gave them in return lechwe, puku, and antelope skins as well as cattle. Yet they had only very little contact with the southern Mankoja since they were subjects to the Marutse and they regarded them as Marutse spies.[15] The Maschukulumbe were subdivided into numerous tribes who 'for our benefit', as my old princely reporter remarked, were ruled each by their own chief. Their territories were no larger than the small territories of the Matoka chiefs. Because of this weakness they might not become dangerous for us either.

Before we left this place we still had the opportunity to see an example of the brutality and oppression of the Marutse from which all their subject tribes have to suffer. The last morning before our departure we heard to our great surprise a little bell and we saw some of the Matoka women with their children coming up in single file, the smallest child being the last one in the line. The man who led them had a rather crude little iron bell hanging from the back of his belt which rang pretty loudly with each step he made. These Matoka had brought their tribute to Schescheke to the Marutse chief living closest to them, who acted as the representative of king Luanika. When the Marutse chief heard that they came from Sietsetema, the leader (i.e. the man with the little bell) was asked whether he had seen the fugitive Marancian in his home country. 'No, not with my eyes.' 'You are lying, you son of a bitch', was the answer shouted at him. And before he could even defend himself so many cane strokes rained on him that he was knocked unconscious, fell to the ground, and was left lying there like a dead man. In the evening when the Marutse had retreated for their beer-drinking bout into their huts, the friends of this maltreated individual sneaked near and carried him away. They brought him to the river and they succeeded in getting their still half-conscious comrade back to life by splashing him with water. Then they carried him to a rather remote wood thicket where he had to stay for a full day until he had recovered to the point that he could start his trip back with his people. I understood very well why all the tribes north of the Zambezi agreed so much in this one thing, i.e. in their hatred of the Marutse.

In Sietsetema's kraal, too, our baboon made numerous friends. The king fed him personally and so did his wives and children and, of course, the first dignitaries of the province could not stay back behind them and brought some quite nice titbits for him. A few times Pit visited the royal kraal, which we realised immediately because of the loud shouts. Pit teased every woman by pulling her little leather skirt or he caught the children, yet without doing them any harm.

His greatest fun, however, was to climb the two to four-metre-high scaffolds which stood here and there around the huts and upon which were maize cobs, pumpkins and gourds filled with fruits. These scaffolds served as storage places to which the termites did not climb so easily. Pit created quite a mess on these scaffolds, but people were not even upset about him when he threw down many of their gourds. Yet this he actually did only if he was detected by the owner of the storehouse and was chased away by him. The natives had a lot of fun when Pit all of a sudden attacked a dog who was not expecting anything. Pit sneaked up to him quietly from the rear, literally inaudibly, and then he jumped up, grabbed the mutt by the end of his tail and after he had pulled him violently and quickly, he then let him go and fled immediately to one of the nearby trees or to the roof of a hut.

What struck me about the so-called court of Sietsetema was the lack of a council of elders. Elsewhere I had found around every chief five to ten old men. They were advisers upon all kinds of foolish activities and stupid tricks. They had already caused a lot of mischief as representatives of the most flagrant superstition; as witchdoctors they brought relief only to very few people. This chief, however, had only young men around him as court advisers and they were very sound drinkers. Thus Sietsetema had the *butschuala* beer flowing from 9 o'clock in the morning until late at night, perhaps in order to test their political abilities. The chief's wives made their people brew new beer almost every day and furthermore beer was brought continuously to the court from all over the country as a kind of goods tax on the subjects.

In the morning before we left Sietsetema's kraal the heir to the throne introduced himself to us. He was a man of about thirty-five years and wanted to dance in our honour. On his head he wore the skull of a big toucan (hornbill) which is found in these areas. It was painted horizontally with white and red stripes and was fixed to his head by means of a strap. He wore still other feather decorations in his curly hair, including the shell of a young turtle. In short, he had decorated his head rather fantastically. Around his loins he had the skin of a cheetah tucked into his belt in front and at the back. Around his waist and around his calves he wore rattles made out of fruit shells and tied together with bark fibre. His dance was a sort of jumping from one foot to the other and only very fast half turns with his rump constituted some distinct movements. In his father's presence the young man did not behave like a privileged prince but rather like a normal subject: he did not utter a sound and gave brief answers, usually without looking up, only when asked by Sietsetema.

Soon after his dance a violent whirlwind moved across Sietsetema's kraal, damaging the poorly-roofed huts quite badly. At first it seemed as if all gaiety was over, but it took only a few hours and the damage was repaired. In a little while almost a hundred people had come together to mend the damage, not only women as among the Betschuana but also men and young boys. In some Matoka tribes the stronger sex helps the women regularly with the cultivation of the fields as well as with hut building.

In order to pay back some of the friendship we had received and in order to

make my servants more willing to travel on since we had prevented them only
with difficulty from deserting us, I organised prize-fighting on the last evening.
The winner was rewarded with a sitsiba and for the losers I bought some beer to
comfort their self-respect which had been hurt by the blows they had received. As
is the custom north of the Zambezi, the two combatants kneel or squat down
opposite each other at a distance of about one and a quarter metres. Each of them is
armed with a stick of a length of 1·3 or 1·5 m in each hand. All four sticks must be
of equal length. They use either one or the other stick as an attacking or a defence
weapon. Of course, this striking out and warding off in all directions is very en-
joyable, at least according to the idea of the black audience. And everybody was
very grateful that I had arranged such farewell festivities, especially since I was not
thrifty with the necessary drinks going with it.

My servants as well as a few villagers participated in the competition, and See-
land, Mapani and 'Braggart' won the prizes. The fight with these long sticks is
among various people of the Bantu tribes usually the first military exercise which
the older men try to teach the boys even at a very tender age. Except in a few
Kaffir tribes, among which the long stick is used as an offensive and defensive
weapon even in mature age, the growing youth slowly gives up this weapon and
gets used to the Kiri (cudgel) and the assegai. As defence weapons they then use a
shield made out of strong animal skin.

Finally the hour to say farewell had come and we had to leave. As I mentioned
earlier, of all Marutse and Matoka chiefs whom I had met on this journey Sietsetema was without doubt the most pleasant. He really was a good hearted man so
that we indeed felt rather touched when we departed. We still remember him
warmly and gratefully and I for my part hope that his kraals remained undamaged
during last year's plundering invasion by the Matabele.[16]

Shortly before we left a few porters, who had already carried our loads from
Ki-Schindu onward, asked whether I would accept their further services and
when I allowed this they brought a cross-eyed young man to me. He was dressed
in a sweater and was said to be Sakasipa's brother who had followed me ever since
Mo-Sinkobo together with five companions merely, as I was told, to earn a sitsiba
by carrying loads for me. I did not like his features, yet unwisely enough I was
persuaded to accept him and his companions. How much I would have to regret
my misplaced good-heartedness only two days later!

V

From Mo-Monquembo
to Mo-Ponde

AT 7 O'CLOCK IN THE MORNING ON 7 JULY we left Sietsetema's kraal Mo-Monquembo and followed a north-eastern course. We made 25·3 km that day and in the evening we camped in the Ki-Bondo village. For the rest of my life I shall probably not forget this day's journey and that night's camp. I myself as well as my wife and Leeb suffered the whole day from attacks of fever. In addition, we did not pass a single water course during the whole day's journey, which was quite exceptional. The sun was beating down even though it was in the middle of the winter. It was so hot that walking became more and more a real agony and we had to rest all too often.

First we passed through a rather monotonous plain. It was overgrown with high grass, at places it was burnt and at other places it was either densely or sparsely wooded. In the north it was bordered by dense shrubs and bushes. In the seventh kilometre we turned sharply east and when we reached the edge of the wood we found some deserted villages. Among the ruins of one of these villages I saw a palm tree which from the distance I thought to be the well-known Makuluani fan palm. When we came closer it turned out to be indeed a fan palm, yet of a kind which was so far unknown to me. The striking feature of this palm tree is its trunk which leads me to label this species as bottle-shaped. Since I lost in Galulonga my original sketches, the measurements, and the fruits I collected. I could draw a sketch (*not included*) and give a description of this tree only on the basis of my memory. The bottle-shaped trunk is very thick, up to one metre above the ground. Then it becomes slightly thinner towards the middle, yet swells up suddenly to the same thickness as near the ground. Then, however, it very abruptly becomes very thin at the top half—so much so that the trunk does not look very dissimilar from a huge English ale bottle. The tree top has fewer long-stemmed leaves than the common false fan palm found in South Africa, yet it is much denser. The fruits are not round but egg-shaped, bigger than a fist and slightly flattened on one of the long sides, or they are clearly heart-shaped. They are ripe in August and September and are densely covered with a greenish yellow type of wool. Further north, immediately on the border with the Maschukulumbe country near M'Beza, I found two groves of these magnificent and striking south central African palm trees which the Matoka call *kahuma* (or perhaps *ki-Huma*). I found them mostly growing on very slight elevations, either singly or in small groups dispersed around villages, kraals and fields. Or I saw them in plains as in M'Beza growing in dense groups.

Until we reached the Ki-Bondo village the terrain was dropping slightly and gradually towards the east and then the north-east. That day we saw zebra, kubunda antelope, eland, and Harris antelope and we recognised fresh tracks of lion, hyena, kudu and gnu.

The chief of Ki-Bondo was a relative of Sietsetema's who was, however, at the same time his subject. His name was Sebelebele. Since the inhabitants of this village had just freshly burned over all the fields immediately surrounding the village we could not find even a small space to establish our camp. Thus we had no choice but quickly to clear a section of the nearby bush covered with high grass and thus prepare our camp site. My men began their work with machetes and assegais, yet since this went all too slowly two of the natives set fire to the grass while ten of the others stood ready with branches in order to beat the flames down in the following moment. In this fashion they were able to create a camp site of about twenty square metres in a very short time. Yet in one of the bushes a small twig was still burning and we had been lying on the blackened and still warm ground only for a few minutes when we saw a huge flame licking up behind us which brought us all back on our feet in a second. In no time the fire had caught the dry strips of grass to the left and to the right and the bush, too, burst into flames. It was hard work until we finally extinguished with branches the dangerous fire which threatened our supplies in the immediate vicinity. We literally fought for our lives with the raging element. I had come out the worst of all. My eyebrows, my moustache and the left half of my hair were singed and I had light burns on my hands. We had just succeeded in extinguishing the fire when the chief and his retinue appeared. He brought us two goats as a present, his wives brought us grain, and I bought on this occasion two of the beautiful clay pipes which are equipped with a long stem as well as coal tongs going with it. None of the good people of Ki-Bondo had ever seen a white man before.

Sietsetema's people had seen the unfortunate Mr Thomas who later was murdered by the Matoka in the south-east. Also some of the inhabitants of Mo-Monquembo had been to Schescheke and had had some contact with Europeans. Yet for the inhabitants of Ki-Bondo we were creatures from another world. Thus we caused great amazement and were stared at all the time. They would have liked to touch us continuously, in particular, our hair. As usual my wife was the centre of admiration and when she happened to comb her dark blonde long hair in the shade of a tree these people with their short curly hair were almost out of their minds. They were shouting and called on all who had stayed on in the huts to do some work or who had already left us to come back. They clapped their hands and shouted over and over again 'Kauke, kauke, monati' (look, look, how beautiful).

The women were delighted most by the fact that my wife had the longest hair and not we men.

The journey of 7 July was not very interesting, but the following one was all the more of interest. The 22 km which we covered until we reached Moëbas kraal[1] provided a series of magnificent and changing scenes. We first passed through a wood which looked almost like a forestry scheme with its regular small trees. It was an all too real proof that some decades ago a terrible woodfire must have raged through it and destroyed the wood in this area.

After we had passed through this wood of young trees we reached in the fifth kilometre one of the magnificent tropical forests which had not been touched by fire for centuries. Probably every European enters this kind of a tropical forest with a deep awe of Mother Nature who with her overwhelming power even becomes a killer of her own offspring in the depths and shade of such a forest. We were filled with the same awe. The vegetation was impenetrable as in the tropical forests in Brazil. The giant trees were closely intermeshed with lushly growing underbrush by means of lianas and creepers. Unfortunately every thick tropical forest is a paradise for carnivores and great caution was needed to pass through these two kilometres of forest. In the seventh kilometre we reached a deserted village with a primitive water conduit for catching the rain water. From these ruins onward the landscape became very pleasant. Long valleys intersected by others were bordered by underbrush or partly overgrown with thick bush. They were interspersed with broad clearings covered with high grass or with sandy hillocks.

These valleys and forest clearings were all the more fascinating because of the numerous animals of which we saw more than on any other day before. Since I went first together with Leeb and my wife and was far ahead of the slow train of porters, we tried to shoot one of the animals but they did not allow us to sneak close enough and some of the daring attempts to shoot from a distance of 500–700 m were merely wasted ammunition. That day I thought of my hunting companions at home who have only hare, deer, fox and partridge which they can hunt. I wished they could have been here even for one hour so that they could have had a glimpse of this great animal paradise. At first we saw several groups of zebra in their own 'family circles' but occasionally also accompanied by magnificent reddish brown kakatombes approximately as tall as a red stag. The next game we saw was a large herd of gnu in the middle of the valley. These seemingly plump blackish-grey animals stood there with their heads down as if they did not notice anything. Yet they were actually fully alert and watchful. As soon as they realised the slightest danger they threw their heads back for a second, bleated low and after they had trotted around in a circle several times, they galloped off into the valley with their tails upraised. Soon we could no longer see them. Behind them herds of impalas were rushing through the thickets near us with some pregnant female animals among them. All of a sudden we clearly heard what was the roaring of a lion very close by. No doubt this animal paradise offered a full range of delicacies to the king of beasts. We had just disturbed a herd of warthogs rushing away from us when Boy warned us of a buffalo herd which was approaching a maize field of the kraal toward which we were going. But the most magnificent of all I saw that day was a herd of at least seventy Harris antelopes which were lying close together in the wood. When we came near the animals all jumped to their feet and rushed off in full flight. There were animals of all age groups and colours ranging from a pure brown to glistening black and they had such beautiful horns that I did not know what to admire first about these animals. Of the larger antelopes in southern Africa the Harris buck has become the most valuable even though it is not the rarest. The magnificent horns of both sexes as well as the beautiful fur of the stag explain why these animals are so much sought after. Their great shyness and caution make it very difficult to hunt them and thus their fur is very valuable.

In the morning we passed through a little village called Kobo which was built on the slope of a sandy ridge and was attractive because of a few *kahuma* palm trees. Here we found a small interesting tobacco field established on one of the huge ant-hills which are very common in this area. The beautiful aromatic big-leafed plants did not grow closely together but were spaced out with dark pink blossoms right around the foot of the hill. They were surrounded by a thorn hedge in order to keep buffaloes, antelopes, gnus and zebra out of the field. Yet since many of these animals, especially the buffaloes, can by no means be held back by such dry mimosa brush, the people had built a hut on top of the hill made out of four poles and branches and covered with grass. From this post a guard, armed with assegais, had to watch and to defend the tobacco field during the night.

It was quite an exception that the people of this village were very friendly to us and gave us whites some beer and to our servants some maize cobs. Around sunset we reached Moëba's village. The few people who let themselves be seen did not inspire great confidence. On the contrary, I could not help but be slightly upset about them. We camped under a mimosa tree on a harvested field, the edges of which were all surrounded by high grass. I had chosen this place as camp site since the tree was more or less in the centre of the field and since in case of another fire we would have been safest in the middle of the field.

Slowly one after the other the porters, i.e. the people of Sietsetema who had favoured me so much, caught up with us. Yet instead of bringing the bundles as usual to the place where we camped, in this case under the tree, they stopped at the edge of the bush. When my servants shouted at them to bring their parcels closer they answered with derision and shouted back that they refused to carry their loads any further under any condition and that anyway they had carried them far enough. 'But you must carry further, you agreed to do so and your king ordered it.' 'Ha ha ha, the king can carry it himself, he got your presents, not we.' 'And your payment we agreed upon?' 'We now have changed our minds, we do not go any further than here and we refuse to go on for two days further still to Mo-Panza as we promised originally. We do not want to talk about it any more. Pay us now otherwise you will never get your things back into your possession.' Once again it was necessary to show my cold blood. Under no condition could I yield to these men—on the one hand because of the principle and on the other because Moëba could never have given me the necessary porters even if he had wanted to do so. He was unable and unwilling to denude his small territory of sixty armed men for two whole days. Thus I had no choice but to get the mutinous porters to carry my luggage further.

My orders that the men had to bring the bundles to the tree by sunset only caused loud laughter. In fact, the men became so bold that they came up with their spears and took up a threatening posture. My servants bravely took our side and the altercation between my faithful servants and the mutinous porters became more and more vehement. All of a sudden the situation became very serious, much more serious than it had been before in similar cases which I have described previously. Suddenly the dissatisfied porters raised their spears against us from a distance of at most six metres. This movement, however, made some of my servants so angry that they were no longer able to hold themselves back. With their spears and staves they leaped against the mutinous crowd. Only with great difficulty I managed in the last moment to restrain them from fighting and prevent bloodshed.

I realised that now the moment had come to prove the personal courage of the European. I handed my rifle to my wife and completely unarmed I went up to the leader of the mutineers and asked him to give me his bundle. He refused to do so but rather lifted his stave in his left hand and swung his spear with his right hand in order to defend himself. At this very moment I hit him a blow between his eyes with my fist. Since he had not expected this he fell over backwards with his stave and his spear and even knocked down a second man standing next to him. At that point my three white companions rushed up to me also unarmed and the whole crowd took to their heels, deserting their bundles like cowards. I grabbed the two budles next to me and quickly carried them to the tree and my men, black and white, did likewise. In a quarter of an hour all of our bundles were counted and lying under the tree. We guarded them from now on with rifles in our hand. Furthermore I armed some of my black servants and sent them out to fetch giant grass, firewood, and branches for our camp.

The hostile porters, however, retreated and tried to reach Moëba's nearby kraal via a detour. I then asked five porters who had not participated in the uproar and who now were bringing in their bundles what the actual cause of this mutiny had been.

'Monari,' they said, 'it was the fault of the man with the double eyes [the cross-eyed man]. All during last night and today on our journey he had talked people into it so that they finally decided to resist you openly.' 'What do you think was the reason for this young fellow to do this?' 'Well, master, he comes all the way from Sakasipa and that is very far. He had intended to catch up with you in Ki-Schindu and since he did not succeed in doing so he followed you until Sietsetema in order to earn at least a bit as porter. Now, however, he is so tired from the long way that he wants to return. Yet since he did not think that you would pay him and his four companions before they got to Mo-Panza they instigated everybody against you to refuse to carry any further so that you would have to pay us for two days' work what had been agreed to be the payment for four days. Monari, you can be sure that they have now gone to Moëba in order to influence the chief, over whom the Marutse ruler Luanika has no power against you'. (They wanted to say by this that in the direction I had taken Sietsetema was the last chief who was still under Luanika's power.)

And in fact in the evening a representative of Moëba's showed up. He was a very old man to whom I gave immediately a sitsiba as a present. When he said that I had to pay my porters now according to their work I answered that I would never do so.

In the evening all the porters came back, one by one, and they built themselves a forty-metre-long and two-metre-high protective wall out of grass and poles. Their ringleader had just arrived when it became dark. For the whole night they tried to persuade the porters, of whom some had begun to vacillate, to refuse to carry our parcels the next morning. Early in the morning Moëba appeared personally and complained that I had only sent him a small present. I did not mind giving him a little something in addition, which made him immediately somewhat more friendly. Fortunately I discovered on one of his insteps a broad and rather neglected wound which obviously had been caused by an axe. So I offered him my help which he accepted readily. Thus things were already much better and our friendship became a definite one when Fekete repaired an old musket for him. To show me his benevolence he gave me a bowl of maize and a few pots of beer as a present.

In the afternoon I made an astronomical determination of our location and visited Moëba's village. There I saw for the first time the style of Maschukulumbe hut construction. Of course, we could not really think of sleeping that night. The changed Moëba had arranged a big drinking-bout to which even inhabitants of the kraals in the neighbourhood had to show up with the necessary 'liquid'. My porters were their guests and in their honour, they were drinking, screaming, dancing and drumming all night long. It is unnecessary to say that in their honour we could not get any sleep that night.

When I arranged our bundles next morning for the departure the porters again refused to pick them up and to carry them on. I sent immediately for Moëba of whose friendship I now felt quite sure, and I asked him kindly to come into my camp. In the meantime I had ordered that all porters had to squat on the right side, my servants on the left side. We whites, however, and the chief resumed our seats between the two crowds. The friendliness with which the chief treated me was so impressive for the porters that only the five ringleaders stepped out of the group when I ordered that those who wanted to leave me should immediately step forward. The chief asked me whether I wanted to pay or whether I preferred to let them go since they had not done their full job. I told him that I did not want to have such scabby sheep in my service, yet that I wanted to pay them not for four days, but only what they deserved for two days' work. The actual payment they deserved was one piece of cloth for each of them. Yet I still promised them some blue glass beads in addition so that they were able to buy some food for their trip home. When the dissatisfied men nevertheless claimed their payment for four days, that is a full sitsiba, Moëba got up and declared that the malcontents had to accept my offer which was completely adequate for their services. If, however, they would not accept it by the time the sun was right above us I would not have to give them anything at all. This was the first time on our Zambezi expedition that a chief protected us against the porters who were subjects to neighbouring rulers. As insolent as black porters and subjects often are to their own sovereign, they behave in a servile and slave-like fashion towards a foreign chief if they have entered his territory and he treats them in an imperious fashion. Once again I had to assign Moëba's protection to my profession and to my treating his wound.

When I came to pay those five men three other porters asked me to pay them in the same way for their two days' services, which I did. Moëba promised to give me twelve porters to Mo-Panza. I did not really need twelve; however, I intended to relieve some of my servants so that they could hunt faster and more easily. I thought especially of those who had risked their lives for us so willingly during the last mutiny.

From Moëba I also heard more about the murder of the Matoka prince by the Maschukulumbe of which Sietsetema had already spoken. The prince was called Tschanci and Moëba's report sounded somewhat less favourable about poor Tschanci. Moëba claimed that this chief had not only stolen cattle from the Maschukulumbe but had been giving them trouble for years. He had attacked them in several predatory raids, and in the course of them he had killed several Maschukulumbe. Moëba gave me a little tube-like reed basket filled with salt as the Maschukulumbe sell it. This Maschukulumbe table salt is the best salt which is sold in the Zambezi area and it seemed to me to be produced from salt lakes as is the salt in the south.[2] In spite of his seeming magnanimity, however, Moëba did not forget his own advantage. This was proved by a secret instruction which he gave to the ugly old headman whom he gave me as a guide. During the mutiny of my porters this man had played the miserable role of a true hypocrite and I decided to be on guard if this man was supposed to lead our way. When we started out and I was seemingly busy with our bundles I overheard a conversation between the two of them and was able to learn the following. The noble king said to his courtier: 'Our people are going to carry the loads only for two days, and the white man will give them only a small sitsiba. Yet I want my men to get at least a large one so you will have to lead them on a detour to Mo-Panza so that they will need at least three days and then he must pay a large one.'

I tried to prevent this intrigue by always walking right behind this 'old gentleman' on our journey, never letting him out of sight. In addition I had already secretly called aside on the very first day one of the porters Moëba had given me. I told him that he and his friends would each get a large sitsiba as payment from me for their porter services up to Mo-Panza, but only if they would take the shortest way.

The man promised to do so and when I pointed out to him that the old headman intended to bring us to Mo-Panza via a detour he gave me an astonished look and smiled. When, later on, the train of porters again moved on, the 'old gentleman' had him as a 'permanent second companion'.

The trip from Moëba to the village of Ki-Kabura was 23 km long. It was an exhausting journey since it went over many hills. We bypassed several smallish kraals of independent and not very powerful Matoka chiefs. In the fifth kilometre we passed through Moëba's last village. Near this village two crossroads were branching off, one to the right and one to the left. The first one led to the village of Ki-Atschika, the second one in an almost northern course to the village of the murdered chief Tschanci.

In the seventeenth kilometre we again bypassed a few villages. In the twenty-second kilometre we passed the village Balila and in the twenty-third kilometre we camped near the village Ki-Kabura which was situated opposite the village Ki-Kambo. The whole day long we walked along a watershed and thus passed on our journey numerous little valleys which opened up on our right and on our left and finally ended in two big valleys which ran parallel with our course for about thirteen kilometre. They drained first to the north-east and then to the north.[3]

In the fourth kilometre I crossed a geological formation of mica slate in a south-east direction with a slope of seventy-five degrees (which very probably was gold-bearing). In the seventh kilometre I found conglomerates i.e. quartz reefs mixed with laterite and aluminium detritus.

In the ninth kilometre we crossed the Ki-Vuata stream and for the next three kilometres saw on our left in the west beyond the valley parallel to our course a large clearing. It was a slope without trees which at that time in the winter was a huge yellow brownish spot in sharp contrast to the surrounding dark woods. This big clearing is called by the Matoka *Kabance*. From various elevated points we often had the chance to look into the large long valley parallel to our course in the east on our right. Here and there we could see in it some kraals and small villages of independent Matoka chiefs peeping out from under the palms. In the far distance, about fourteen to seventeen kilometres away, the Ki-Sombo range came into sight.[4]

Interesting was the Ki-Rungunja valley which we entered in the thirteenth kilometre. Into it flowed a little stream with the same name which at that time of the year, i.e. during the peak of the dry season, was still half a metre deep. We crossed the valley where it became a narrow rock gorge. Then we climbed over a low watershed into the Ki-Gomatje valley which is linked to the Ki-Rungunja valley with which it unites near the place where we entered it. In the twenty-second kilometre we crossed the Ki-Monjeke stream. On our journey we left Moëba's area, as I mentioned before, and touched the territories of two independent Matoka chiefs.

We had rested for a short while near the kraal of the chief on the Ki-Gomatje river and when we started out again our old guide led us into an eastern course which did not seem the right direction to me. I let him go and asked that Matoka about it whom I had picked as my confidant. When I pointed to the old chief drastic cure. I intended to march on with all the might and strength of my body and my soul in order to break out into perspiration. By sweating I hoped to find some relief from my fever and my pains. Led by Boy and Mapani I began to walk ahead. In the beginning this march was terribly difficult. I had the good will yet I was lacking the necessary physical strength. Finally the desired sweat broke out and, thank God, it had the effect so often proved before. From one quarter of an hour to the next I was able to go faster; soon I was able to walk on my own and at the end of this day's journey I was marching again at the head of the train free from fever and relatively better.

When in the late afternoon I and my vanguard finally selected the camp site on the little Ki-N'onga river 4 km from Mo-Panza's village we could not yet see anything of our porters. They came trotting closer about one hour later in small groups. In each village which we passed they had to tell what these strangers actually wanted. And since their reports brought them many a pot of beer they did not make any effort to be brief or to hurry.

The last 5 km went through a shallow broad valley, the rich wild life of which exceeded everything we had seen so far north of the Zambezi. Numerous little paths which we noticed indicated that many huts of the Matoka were hidden at the wooded edges of the valley. These Matoka were already Mo-Panza's subjects. In the east his territory reaches even further south than in the area where we had entered it.

I decided to pay my porters here so that the old scene which unfortunately was to be expected again and which my reader knows all too well would not spoil from the very beginning the new porters whom I had to hire.

At this point I was very much concerned with bringing to an end the tradition of mutiny which my porters from the Zambezi had passed on from each group to the next so far. What would I have to expect if such scenes were to happen among the thievish Maschukulumbe? It was easy to foresee that they would side with the mutinous porters and would rob us. I hoped to prevent this danger by not letting the porters I had brought along get in contact with Mo-Panza's people. And I hoped to find those he gave me more content with what I offered them. This was the reason why I camped 4 km away from Mo-Panza's village. When the porters had arrived I separated them into two groups, into Sietsetema's people and into Moëba's people. The latter were not only content with their payment but even asked me to let them continue to carry my things. Yet I had to refuse them for the above-mentioned reasons and since anyway I wanted to have new porters. But in order to reconcile them a bit to this disappointment I gave them, in addition, some blue glass beads. The offer of Moëba's people to continue carrying for me had a good effect on the rest of my porters who had already worked out a plan of opposition. Certainly they had to shout, yet this time it was only to make a noise. They wanted to enjoy the pleasures of staging a mutiny but they did not think of threatening me any more. When the sun was almost down they all came to me one after the other and each of them declared all of a sudden that he was satisfied with what I had promised them at Sietsetema's—that is, with one big sitsiba. Since all of cheap, almost transparent, calico. One could see immediately that these people were very rarely visited by strangers, for our servants were received and fed just as warmly as we were. In the honour of our men a solemn beer banquet was proposed for that night. This feast was accompanied by such a deafening drumming and shouting that I had to ask them finally to stop the musical part of the festival so that we could sleep at least for a few hours.

Before we left next morning the Matoka came up with some elephant tusks in order to exchange them for rifles and ammunition. I sent them away, trying to explain to them that I was no ivory trader and therefore would not exchange anything for ivory. This appeared to be incredible to the natives, since for them the concepts of a white man and an ivory trader were identical. The Mambari, who were the black representatives of the Portuguese ivory traders and who were the only strangers who visited this area, only asked for ivory and all they had heard from them about the whites must have been concerned only with ivory. Thus when I refused their ivory they thought that we were probably not the 'true white man'. They simply could not figure us out. Since we refused their ivory we were lacking in their eyes the main feature of a white man, and yet the whole personal discription which the Mambari had given them probably hundreds of times fitted perfectly. In contrast to the Mambari we had light skin, long, soft and straight hair which was even blond.

Our next journey from Ki-Kabura onward stretched over eighteen kilometres and took us to the famous king Mo-Panza, the last independent Matoka chief on the frontier of the much-feared Maschukulumbe. This trip was full of interesting sights. First we reached the ford of the little Ki-N'onga stream north-east of Ki-Kabura. In the first six kilometres we passed six streams in as many shallow, basin-shaped valleys sloping towards the west-north-west and north-west. These valleys were separated by wooded or cultivated hills. In the first, second and fifth kilometres we passed by villages of which one, the last and biggest one, called Schambalaka, was to our astonishment enclosed with a fence of high poles. We had to go right through the village. In contrast to the villages we had passed through the day before the looks of its inhabitants inspired so little confidence that I soon gave up my plan to rest there for a little while. After we had obtained information about the shortest path leading to Mo-Panza's residence we immediately travelled on. From the fifth to the tenth kilometre we passed a rock outcropping which I will always remember because of the very strong attack of fever by which I was overcome there. This attack was so violent that I had to lie down at the side of our track since I did not have the strength to drag myself on. My whole body felt shattered. Once again I had another attack of those terrible asthmatic wheezings which I had not had since my blood-letting in the Leschumo valley. A sudden vomiting, however, gave me great relief. The asthma, too, vanished gradually. I was able to get up again and supported by Boy and Leeb could stagger on.

Since I did not want to get stranded along the way under any circumstances and since we still had to walk quite far over the wooded hills, I decided to risk a very were a people who were regarded and avoided by their neighbours as a *noli me tangere* and were even considered to be beasts in human forms. But I knew that Mo-Panza was the only Matoka chief who was living in a relatively good relationship with some of the neighbouring Maschukulumbe chiefs with whom he was even trading. He could, and indeed should, give me reliable information about them.

VI

The stay with Mo-Panza
and the journey to the border of
the Maschukulumbe

ALREADY THE EVENING BEFORE, 13 JULY, and the first night in our camp on the little Ki-N'onga stream Fekete had come back from his mission and had reported. 'Doctor, such a good old king we have so far not found among the Matoka.' I can hardly say how grateful I was for this news. For just now a friendly ruler was necessary if our plans were to succeed—now when we were on the verge of entering the Maschukulumbe area. Mo-Panza had already heard of our arrival before we ever reached him and he seemed to be overjoyed that finally the white men had come to see him, as he thought. 'For such a long time I have been waiting for the Makoa [whites]. I have heard that Monari [Dr Livingstone] and *Dsorosch-siani njinjani* [Mr Blockley, called the little Dochorosch, i.e. the little George, in contrast to Mr Westbech, the tall or big George] have crossed the big river'—and he pointed to the south—'to come up to us. And yet they do not come. I thought already that I had to die without seeing one of you. But now the Makoa have come finally. And as you say you are not alone but there are several of you. Indeed, even a *mosari* [married woman] or a *musezana* [girl] has come with you.' 'A *mosari*, Morena [prince]', I answered. And Mo-Panza clapped his hands with joy and although he was a very weak old man of about ninety years of age he knelt down and kissed the earth. As Boy interpreted for me he appraised himself fortunate that finally before his death his most ardent desire had been fulfilled—to see white Europeans who knew how to make calico and rifles. 'Mo-Panza gave me beer and sends to you, doctor, this pot with beer, groundnuts, and this maize, all these presents which Mapani and Jonas have just put down.'

I put together some presents for the king which were to be sent to him. Later I myself found Mo-Panza to be a good-natured man who in addition even had an equally good and honest old adviser—a fact which is even rarer among black chiefs. Yet this adviser was often pushed aside by Mo-Panza's brother, a hypocrite and a greedy creature of about forty years of age.

This lovable brother introduced himself to us the following day and soon became all too insolent in his claims and his importunity. His main goal was to get a rifle and a good deal of ammunition. He had planned on his own with the support of a group of compatriots who had possessed for quite some time some bad muskets, but without any ammunition, to make a raid into the border districts of the Maschukulumbe with the main aim of getting some cattle. In diplomatic terms I had not yet established any relations with the Maschukulumbe, yet one thing was quite clear to me: that I could not support such an undertaking in any way.

The same day, on 13 July, the king's old adviser introduced himself and asked me in Mo-Panza's name whether I was feeling somewhat better. I asked him for forty porters to bring my things into the king's kraal. Since my servants were supposed to help carrying the bundles it was not necessary to hire more than forty porters for this short journey.

Early on 14 July the porters appeared and we soon agreed with them on their payment: for as little as one tablespoon of small blue beads each they accepted the job. Out of respect for Mo-Panza I had arranged for the first time to make a festive entrance. Unfortunately, it had to be noisy as well.

Boy was walking in front with the waving Austrian banner which we unrolled for most of the chiefs. Behind him followed Fekete, then the rest of us, then the servants carrying the presents for Mo-Panza and finally the train of porters. The path which we had to travel was 4 km long. After we had crossed over two hills it led through something like a large basin overgrown with high grass which drains into the Ki-N'onga stream. After a march of an hour and a quarter we reached the royal kraal which was situated just as that of Schindu rather high up at the edge of a wooded slope amidst extensive maize and millet fields. We had not expected anything spectacular in this residence, just as we had not in those kraals we had visited earlier. As a rule the so-called royal kraals were miserable huts of a very light construction and thus they were very soon disintegrating. Since people never repair their huts all these residences north of the Zambezi look rather run down. Mo-Panza's royal residence, however, was the worst ruin of all the ancestral castles of the natives we had seen. The whole of the glorious residence consisted of a few huts, some of them full of holes, others completely ruined. They were not even built in the well-known rondavel style, but were made out of poles and branches and were covered with very defective grass roofs. A straw hut of our field watchmen at home would have been a Palazzo Pitti in comparison. The clay with which these huts had once been smeared had mostly fallen off and thus the wind was blowing happily through the numerous spaces, gaps, and cracks. Lizards, snakes and insects came in at night as soon as it became cool outside, and only the smoke of the fire burning inside kept bats and owls from entering the human quarters for the night as well. This terrible neglect of their living quarters struck me all the more since the women of the Matoka are otherwise well kept and have little work to do. I said 'women' and the kind reader might ask himself what the women have to do with hut building? Very much indeed, because among the blacks in southern Africa the women are the master builders. Among the peoples south of the Zambezi they still have this obligation besides all the work in the fields. Yet the huts of the Bechuana and Matabele are truly splendid buildings in comparison with the masterpieces of these lazy Matoka women who do not do any field work and are even helped with their hut building by the masters or husbands who get the wood and the clay for them. One of the main reasons for the bad state of their buildings might be the warm climate and the extensive woods.

These factors do not make it absolutely necessary to have the shade of a hut in the summer or the protection of a hut against wind and cold in the winter. These natural conditions cause a very lax method of building and it would be very difficult to be more demanding and strict about it. I was only amazed at how these miserable Matoka huts could give their inhabitants any protection at all against wild animals, especially since Mo-Panza's kraal was closely surrounded by grass two to three metres high. Between the huts were mimosa trees and two huge fig trees, the latter being fully decorated by their large dark leaves in spite of the winter. Their branches were laden with heavy fruits which were sitting densely on the branches in bundles and rings up to one metre in width. These figs are as small as the Italian figs, yet they contain hardly one fourth of their nutritive value. They are rougher and have a light brownish and orange colour. The natives prefer a lot of other fruits to these figs, even though they can use the fig trees, which yield such extensive shade and which offer their fruit to men without any labour, as pleasant shady roofs. From one of the mimosas was hanging a shield and several baskets which were very probably war trophies.

When our festive procession finally reached Mo-Panza's kraal both young and old were expecting us. None of them had ever seen a white man and you can imagine how they all rushed up to us. The question of what kind of thoughts we might have about them and their huts probably occurred to none of them. For these happy people their world comprised the entire world. At first we saw the two huts in which Mo-Panza himself was living, surrounded by the huts of his wives which were slightly better made. Very near was standing a young fig tree thick with leaves. This was the usual resting place of the king. Thus we were led into the shade of this tree to wait for the appearance of the king.

To the left we saw a collapsed hut and next to it the trophy poles of Mo-Panza which had fallen down because they were termite-ridden. These were dry, dead trees with several branches dug into the ground which carried, or once had carried, skulls of lions, leopards, hyenas, buffaloes and other animals as well as some booty of Mo-Panza's chiefs. Later I was allowed to choose from this temple of fame whatever my heart desired. Yet the skulls had suffered so much from the influence of the weather that I could not use a single one of them—not even a single set of teeth of these carnivores.

We had probably waited for half an hour when the old man, bent over his cane, dragged himself near with great effort, accompanied by his advisers and some unarmed servants. He was wrapped in a beautiful woollen blanket which one of the Mambari traders coming from the mouth of the Luenge had given him as a present not too long ago. He obviously wanted to impress us with this robe of state. He sat down on a straw mat and before us praised his luck again that our appearance had made it possible for him to see white men before he died.

Mo-Panza's long welcoming speech was not without a certain solemnity. He concluded with the following words: 'You see, when I say that since yesterday I consider myself very happy, then a voice is speaking to you which knows more than all of my people sitting around me. For this voice had been stilled already several times for ever and yet was brought to life again. I have been dead a few times [unconsciousness, probably as a consequence of brain haemorrhage] yet I became alive again. The God who is living in the blue of the skies and in the fast-moving clouds as the Marutse say, called me back to life. You could have seen me twice a day in the morning and in the evening lying on the ground and could have heard me expressing my great thankfulness to this God for such blessings. You can see that he heard me since I asked him often to send me Makoa in order to see them. They did not come for a long time and I have become so old and weak that my feet can hardly carry me any more. But now they have come after all and I welcome you. But do follow my advice and do not go where you have decided to go. Give up this plan. The Maschukulumbe are not people as you and I are. You only see a few huts around me here and so you might think that Mo-Panza is poor. But no, he is not. Numerous are his kraals and villages dispersed everywhere, and he has many villages in the valleys and right in the forest. There are many wild animals in my territory and elephants, too, visit us very often. My people never have to suffer from hunger and the Maschukulumbe come to us to trade with us.'

In the king's speech was something like the dignity of old age and his looks, especially his face, gave an impression of confidence, frankness, and naivity even though he was somewhat cross-eyed. Physically, indeed, the old prince was quite run down. His ankles and wrists were swollen with rheumatism and very prob-ably caused him much pain. I realised immediately that the mystical dimension of Mo-Panza's nature assigned our appearance to his god. This could only be advant-ageous for us.

I congratulated the king upon his recovery, wished him a long life still to come, and then I asked for a camp site. He listened to me, then he pointed to his right to a place under the most beautiful fig tree, promised to come back himself in the afternoon in order to talk with me, the 'white magician' about his disease.

When I heard that hyenas came up to the huts every night, this time I had my men build an enclosed round camp. Inside it they pounded in some pegs to which to tie our dogs. At the west side of our camp was the camp of my servants.

In the afternoon Mo-Panza indeed appeared and immediately he began talking about his old malady. As all Matoka believe about their diseases he, too, thought that his was nothing but an affliction with which a secret enemy had bewitched him to take revenge on him. 'In my sleep they let ants, termites, and snakes into my body and these now move around in my body and cause me terrible pain [the usual feeling in case of a partial or temporary paralysis which is comparable to having ants in one's limbs]. They pinch, bite, and prick me until I finally die [these are the attacks which cause unconsciousness]. When I then come back to life I feel somewhat better for a few days.' I promised the old man some medicine and then I got talking about the continuation of our trip and the porters I needed. At my request for porters on the very next day he shook his head. 'No, I sent some men to the border of the Maschukulumbe where I possess a herd of cattle since I want to

5   *Matoka (Tonga) chief Mo-Panza (Mapanza)*

give you one.' I waived this present immediately since I wanted nothing but to get on. Yet he insisted, since his malevolent brother was behind the whole thing. This black diplomat had already found out that I would not give a rifle to Mo-Panza and he now wanted to force me to do so by this rather clever move. The king had only very few cattle and they were therefore very valuable in this tribe. If I were now to accept a cow I had to give something very valuable in return as a counter-present, and the least was one rifle. 'Sir, give me porters at least to the Luenge river and not only to the first village of the Maschukulumbe.' 'If they are willing to go that far, yes. But I cannot force my people to do so. It is very far to the Luenge river. I promise you to talk with them. Many will come anyway in order to look at you and then we will see.' In the meantime the king provided us with a lot of strong *butschuala* and my servants with food. He would have done much more for us if his younger brother, who was his future successor and who did not see our appearance as an act of the gods, had not hindered him.

Among none of the Matoka tribes which I had visited on this trip had I found so many distinctive characters. I may say that one type is very evident among the Matoka of Mo-Panza. It is fairly common and indicates that these Matoka must have been in very close contact with the northern tribes before the invasion of the Maschukulumbe into the areas north of them. In some of these distinctive types, however, there seemed to be some Mambari blood which could be explained easily, as the Mambari have visited this area for a long time past for their ivory trade. These types are beautifully built men, at least of medium height, strong, and stocky. They have somewhat longer curly hair, many have aquiline noses and often a not too short beard on their chin.

I made some twenty sketches of the most outstanding types of Mo-Panza's people. Unfortunately, I lost them at Galulonga except for one (plate 6).

Many of the Matoka wear *impande* shells on their foreheads or in their curly hair; some wear them on their chest like Mo-Panza himself. Since they assign supernatural powers to this chalk shell, especially the power to protect the person who wears it from certain diseases, Mo-Panza had given an *impande* shell to each one of his favourite wives (he had a large number of wives) as well as to his

6   *Matoka (Tonga) men of Mo-Panza's (Mapanza's) village*

children. They were to be worn with a little strap on the chest. This gift did not fail to make a very deep impression.

Very soon, however, I made a discovery which I would never have expected from this honest king and his relations with the gods. I found out that the nature of his trade with the Maschukulumbe was nothing else than vulgar traffic in young girls and women. In Europe this would be punished with long imprisonment. He kept this trade going partly on his own, partly on other people's account. Since the Maschukulumbe like to buy women, the southern Matoka as well as Wanke's Makalaka occasionally come to offer them these goods. Yet most of these traders are afraid to go directly to the much feared Maschukulumbe and thus in most cases Mo-Panza acts as their middleman. He buys these women, keeps those whom he likes for himself and exchanges the others with the Maschukulumbe for cattle. It happens occasionally that these beauties run away. They do not have to fear that they will be handed back by the lesser chiefs in the east either as quickly or at all, as the young wives who had run away from Sietsetema were returned by his neighbours.

Mo-Panza, however, was not only a trader in women but, as I soon realised, a very experienced amateur in the subject himself in spite of his old age. Not only did he marry beautiful daughters of his own country, but also less beautiful daughters of the subchiefs in order to make them faithful vassals by establishing this blood relationship with them. The feeble old man does not even reject the widows of these subchiefs in order to enlarge his fields through their heritage, i.e. stretches of bush which they have already cleared. In short, this black prince of ninety years who had never before seen a white man could have given a French novelist many a magnificent inspiration for spicy episodes of an 'old sinner'.

At Mo-Panza's I met three Maschukulumbe who had fled from their area and had settled here. For the first time my people had the chance to see some representatives of the chignon-wearers about whom I had talked so often and who are ridiculed so much on the Zambezi.

On 15 July a 'true' Maschukulumbe showed up from the neighbouring chiefdom. He came with fourteen iron hoes which he had bought himself from another neighbouring tribe in the west and which he wanted to trade with Mo-Panza for a woman. Except for a calico rag of about one and a half square metres which was hanging over his shoulder this man was absolutely naked. And even this calico rag he had obtained earlier from Mo-Panza in exchange for some lechwe and puku skins. This wild Maschukulumbe was, of course, the object of our greatest interest. Immediately upon his arrival we realised that the Matoka treated him with a certain respect, but that they shunned him more than they respected him. We soon saw that the Matoka were in fact quite afraid of him so that he was paid more than the usual price according to the prevailing rates for what he offered. Even my wife and my servants looked at this free Maschukulumbe with a certain awe. This is one of the much feared people? Does he really look so horrifying that he inspires fear? He looks so apathetic and almost submissive and has already been squatting there for two hours and does not move. Only the rise and fall of his chest and the fact that he is lifting his eyes every now and then seem to prove that the 'frightening being' is not a mummy, but a real Maschukulumbe. I was sitting at the side with my diary in the shade of a huge sycamore and observed the man as well as the various onlookers.

The psychological study which I made with this Maschukulumbe sitting there so completely indifferent suggested nothing promising. I saw clearly from his hardly noticeable movements with his head that he was trying to follow the conversation of my natives who camped not too far from him. Only very occasionally he lifted his eyelids but then he looked at my wife and/or my companions and these looks told me much—very much. He seemed to pierce his objects with his eyes and out of his flashing eyes shone an incredible avarice and animal-like passion. After a moment he fell back again into his heavy brooding—his mind being far away. Precisely this apathy, however, was completely unnatural and was an example of the self-control of the Maschukulumbe. This man had never seen any Europeans but probably had heard of them. Now all of a sudden several of them stood before him, even a woman. Nothing would have been more natural than the same amazement and unreserved curiosity as we had experienced from others so often on our march. Instead he exhibited only an icy silence and a certain reluctance to be addressed. This proved to me that this man was neither good-natured nor stupid but for a black he was shrewd and bad.

The observation of this man warned me to be extremely cautious. I had seen something in this man that I had never observed before in a native of southern Africa. Even the wildest Matabele warriors had never impressed me as this man with his evil eye glancing around shyly under his half closed lids.

I could not help but realise that a certain feeling of fear was coming over me. I could no longer exorcise the evil eye out of my mind. This was a bad omen for me.

The following day, on 15 July, my wife was once again attacked by the fever and had to stay in her miserable grass bed. We hung a canvas sack filled with water on a shady branch exposed to the draught in order to cool the water as much as possible for her compresses, since this gave her some relief from the pains she suffered. I was near her resting place and was just trying to bargain for a sheep and several rather pretty clay pipes representing animal heads from a Matoka who had offered them to me in exchange for some small golden glass stars from Gablonz. All of a sudden my wife screamed loudly and jumped up from her bed in spite of her heavy fever. From under her bed crept a one and a half metre reptile which had come in from the outside through the grass and branch fence and from there under her pillow.

My wife had heard the rustling and had thought it was a mouse or a rat which often bothered us. But then she felt that her pillows were lifted slightly and when she raised her head the snake's head hissed at her from out of the grass. When my wife jumped up the entire cobra became visible as it tried to escape into the dense grass. A. soon as they recognised the frightening snake the blacks hastily rushed out of the camp in full flight, whereas I threw an axe at the snake and Leeb hit it

with his butt. Both of us hit it directly and in a few minutes the reptile had ceased
to be dangerous for men. Its spine was smashed in two places.

7   *Interior of chief Mo-Panza's (Mapanza's) council and reception house*

The same day, after she had recovered slightly, my wife visited Mo-Panza in his
largest and best hut which served as a reception hall (see plate 7). The description
she gave of this reception chamber made me interrupt my drawings of the royal
kraal and visit Mo-Panza in his splendid building, taking a little present along.

When I entered the rather spacious hut constructed from poles and wicker-work I needed some time to find my way about since it was semi-dark in the hut. In the middle of it a fire was burning, the smoke of which escaped through the numerous holes and cracks in the wall. On the other hand these holes had an advantage as the blue sky of that sunny July day could be seen through them. The basic cover of the naked walls was dirt. Furniture or decoration of any sort did not exist, but instead there were many empty beer containers and some rough logs as support to keep the *palazzo reale* from collapsing.

The old monarch was sitting on a miserable bed constructed out of poles. On one side of him towards the wall several men were lying with their faces on the ground. They had just arrived to bring the usual tribute of beer in huge clay and wooden pots. On the other side the king's minions as well as his fine brother were busy drinking. Their throats seemed to be like an endless pipe which led into a vacuum underground for they were simply pouring this bad brew down and one could not see that they swallowed at all.

The huge drinking cups were emptied, were filled anew, and emptied again until one big pot was pushed aside and the next one had to be dragged near. It was then emptied in a similar way and in an amazingly short time. Large yellowish brown rats were running around and playing everywhere. They were left in peace and they knew it very well and obviously enjoyed the animal-loving attitude of their human room-mates.

In the close vicinity of this dwelling were some of the better, somewhat more, rainproof and windproof huts in which the temporarily 'favourite' wives were living. These huts were situated here and there without the symmetrical circular arrangement of the Marutse or of some of the Betschuana tribes. Mo-Panza, the man of the great landed properties, the king who was highly respected by the other Matoka chiefs because of his relations with the much feared Maschuku-lumbe was, indeed, only a poor man.

If one considers the good water conditions and the fertility of the soil in the area belonging to Mo-Panza the prosperity in his country should be considerable if the king and his advisers would care more for the well-being of the country. The little country could perfectly support twenty times the inhabitants with cattle and agricultural goods, yet at this point I would estimate that Mo-Panza has about 2,000 subjects.

At this visit Mo-Panza gave us a calf of about one and a half years as a present. I did not want to slaughter it but to have it driven with our mules behind our train in order to use it later, perhaps as a pack animal. Yet this animal had never experienced what a rope is. I had hardly tied it when it broke its rope and escaped for good. A second calf which I was offered by a Marutse, a friend of the murdered king Sepopo, I did not accept because he asked for ammunition in return.

This Marutse, one of the most faithful followers of Sepopo, was a refugee who had fled here after Sepopo's death in order not to be killed by Waga-Funa.[1] He had recognised me immediately and had told me that he had seen me for the first time in 1875 at the court of his king in Schescheke. The memory of these blacks is indeed amazing as well as their eyes and their ears.

On 16 July we left Mo-Ponde, Mo-Panza's residence, in the afternoon after I had again given the king some presents and after he again had warned me of the Maschukulumbe. 'Look,' he said, 'if you leave them alone and go there'—and he pointed to the east—'then you will come to the place where the Luenge flows into the Zambezi. You can go north from there avoiding the Maschukulumbe and you get to Lake Bangweolo, of which my old friend [i.e. the king's first adviser] has already told me.' Once again he gave orders to those of his people who had agreed to carry my things for one sitsiba through two Maschukulumbe territories until the northern border of the third one—this meant up to the Luenge. I had made the condition that they would have to carry either to the Luenge or not at all.

The fact that I was this time in the pleasant situation of being able to act in such an independent and determined fashion I owed in the first place to the favour of the old king, yet in an equal degree to the friendship of the old adviser whom the king had just mentioned. This old man who showed so much geographical knowledge did not only hold the chancellory in Mo-Panza's kingdom but prac- tised medicine besides his political activity. Strangely enough he did not treat me as a rival but as a colleague. Since he was highly respected among his people his protection helped my enterprise considerably. He advised sometimes one, some- times another to go with us to the centre of the Maschukulumbe country up to the Luenge. And with his authority he succeeded in banishing people's fear so that we left in good spirits.

The memory of the days spent at Mo-Panza's were for a long time a ray of hope in the dreary hours to come, for soon everything was to be changed.

The first march from Mo-Panza northwards was more than eighteen kilometres long and led us directly north, to my great satisfaction. The hilly country sloped in this direction. In the first valley I found the Ki-Atschova stream and in the second one the Morube stream on which the village Buerva was situated. It was surrounded by lush fields and we rested there for half an hour. In this village Mo-Panza's daughter was living, a hard working and modest woman to whom we gave some presents. Here we saw many big calabashes sitting in the forks of the trees around the huts in which the Matoka kept certain magic, charms, medi- cine or fermentation for their *butschuala*, i.e. millet beer. We established our first camp near the village Musosa situated on the right bank of the Monjeko river, the most beautiful stream of the northern Matoka territory. The northern bank of this river is overgrown with a dense forest, rich in game, where one can find, among other animals, huge herds of elands, gnus, zebras, and buffaloes.

In the Musosa village, which lies attractively hidden under several *kahuma* palms and huge mimosa trees, only a very few families were living—occupying seven huts. It is the last relatively large settlement of the Matoka before the Mas- chukulumbe border. Chief Tschinganja gave us a friendly reception and gave us groundnuts and other wild fruits as presents. The Monjeko river has a water- power comparable to that of the large Marico. Its banks are covered with loess and in its deeper pools are numerous crocodiles. Its river bed is quite interesting since like the Jordan it displays three water channels, each used in a different season of the year. At the time of our visit, which was during the lowest water level in the winter, the stream was flowing through a simple and rather narrow channel of about six metres in width. After the first rains and in the fall it is flowing through a higher channel of double the width, yet during the rainy season in the summer after the greatest rains it flows in a very broad bed lying even higher up—like a third level—which is much larger than the first two. The dominant stone structures which we found on our journey of 16 July were iron bearing conglomerates. That day we had left the northern Matoka hill country and we were standing at the beginning of a vast plain limited only in the distance in the east by a mountain range. In the west it was limited by laterite ridges and towards the north the plain seemed to drop to the Luenge. This plain stretching far in front of us to the east, north-east and north was supposed to be free from tsetse flies according to the reports of the Matoka. Here we found some of the cattle posts of king Mo-Panza as well as of some of his chiefs who were not a little proud of their small cattle herds. Thus the Matoka possessed only a very small number of cattle, half of it in the farthest south on the Zambezi and the other half in the farthest north, again along the border. The cattle on the southern border are of the Marutse breed —tall and with fine coats—whereas the cattle of the northern border are of the Maschukulumbe breed with small cows and only medium-sized oxen.

The report about the tsetse fly seemed to me most unlikely since I found that further down at the river, and especially on the opposite bank, even during the winter season, at that time tsetse flies occurred in much greater numbers than in any other area north of the Zambezi, all of which unfortunately we had found to be everywhere infested by this detrimental insect. The tsetse fly thus was also present in this plain. I believe that the cattle in this area was well accustomed to the poison of this fly, but because of this poisonous insect the animals had stayed so small, i.e. had degenerated. In the same way the Matoka can only breed rather stunted sheep, goats and dogs in the tsetse area.

The morning of 17 July 1887 was one of the most exciting ones on our whole trip. This day we were to enter the long-desired Maschukulumbe territory, still virgin land for the European. We started out very early. The first 5 km we marched in a north-eastern course, then directly north. Our next camp site was to be seventeen kilometres further from our last one.

First we followed the Monjeko river, which offered various interesting scenes with its jungle-like vegetation. Its banks, along which our narrow path was winding, were about twelve metres high. In the third kilometre we passed a few huts. This was the village with the proud name of Diabora where the most northern Matoka lived along this route. In the fourth and fifth kilometres we passed through and admired the first large grove of those magnificent *kahuma* palms, the tops of which were full of huge clusters of fruit. I had never before seen so many specimens at the same place and I had never observed any fruits on these palm trees. The description of the fruits which I have already given to my reader was taken from the observations made in Diabora.

We stopped and rested under these palms in order to enjoy for quite some time the delicacies which these beautiful giant trees were offering us. Here I even found a second species of palm unknown to me, with thin trunks bent several times almost in a knee-shaped fashion. They were as tall as the *kahuma* palms yet their leaves are similar to those of the date palms. The area through which we passed that day would be ideal for the establishment of a big city. The soil is fertile for gardens and fields, there is loess in the river for brickyards, and the river which is flowing all year round could be used easily for irrigation purposes. The Luenge river is close and is probably navigable down to its confluence with the Zambezi. There is ample wood on the left bank of the Monjeko, excellent pastures for cattle, and game in abundance all around.

I have already told a lot about the rich animal life I found in the areas I passed through on my expedition north of the Zambezi. Yet all of this is by far exceeded by the number of game we saw in that plain on 17 July. I must, however, mention that we were here at the edge of the area where fire-arms were known, as well as in a territory where the Matoka did not dare to hunt because of the Maschuku-lumbe and where the Maschukulumbe did not dare to hunt because of the Matoka. The various kinds of game we saw were not even shy. Had we passed through such a game park south of the Zambezi how much would we have indulged in the pleasures of hunting and collecting. But here we were all the time under a slight depression. We were in Maschukulumbe country. We already intended to establish our camp that day in the first Maschukulumbe village. Our thoughts were constantly revolving around this interesting tribe and their country which was as yet completely unknown to Europeans.

We had gone ahead when all of a sudden one of our porters came running up to me and asked me to wait until all the porters had caught up with us since they felt safer under the protection of our guns now that we were soon to come to the first Maschukulumbe settlements. Also, they said, our *Pici-Namahari* (female donkey) was so ill that she could not walk any more and therefore the last porters and Oswald, to whose care I had entrusted this sick animal, had stayed very far behind. They were talking about the donkey I had bought from Rev Coillard which soon afterwards had turned out to be sick and thus did not serve us for anything. I myself or our servant Muschemani drove the other mules. This precaution had very good reasons. First of all, these animals were heavily laden, and secondly, I knew that donkey and horsemeat are the favourite delicacies of lions which they prefer even to human flesh. Thus I always had an eye on the donkeys during the whole journey. When I stopped to wait for the last ones of our train and had just decided to leave the sick donkey behind the following morning, Oswald came up to me and reported that he had left the donkey behind as dead. On our journey back one and a half months later we learned that the animal was still alive in that first Maschukulumbe village and that she was carefully guarded like a strange treasure that had fallen from the skies. And not only was the donkey happy and perfectly well but she had even brought forth a male colt which was just as attractive as his mother was serious. It was admired and gazed at even more by the Maschukulumbe than its melancholy mother. These tribes had no domestic animals other than cows and dogs, and thus our donkey was gazed at in the various villages through which we came on our further journey just as camels, bears or elephants are stared at by our European peasants when a group of tight-rope walkers is travelling through. Often people were standing so closely around us that we were hardly able to move. And if it happened that one of our two donkeys started to neigh the whole crowd rushed away, especially the women and children, and fled back into their villages. People really did not seem to be able to get used to our donkeys even though they called them very significantly the 'zebras of the foreigner'. Even less well did the cows of the Maschukulumbe get along with our long-eared donkeys. They were sniffing curiously at them and they even attacked them. Often, however, these two faithful beasts were attacked by the dogs of the Maschukulumbe who also thought that these poor tired animals were zebras and they pursued them furiously which often caused real danger for us. Yet more about this in a more suitable place.

Our poor goats had to suffer just as much from the Maschukulumbe dogs. Whenever we entered a kraal we were forced to drive the goats between us in order to protect them. This fact in itself proved what kind of an isolation the Maschukulumbe had always created around themselves. The domestic animals which their neighbours were breeding were completely unknown in their country. This seclusion also had another effect which was very disadvantageous for their only domestic animal, i.e. the cow. They were unable to improve it by crossbreeding with other races as the Betschuana had done by crossing their cattle with the Damara and Zulu cattle. That day while we were waiting for our porters I observed a new type of termite hill. They were the lowest which I had so far seen in southern Africa and they even had a new shape. They were hardly twenty to thirty centimetres high and the hill was bowl-shaped, dropping slowly towards the centre which had a big entrance opening. The diameter of such a laterite or loess bowl of which the outer wall usually dropped sharply and steeply was between half a metre and one metre (normally seventy to ninety centimetres). I found these hills at the bottom of the valley yet even more frequently on the wooded slopes of the laterite or rocky loess ridges in Moëba's and Mo-Panza's areas. Finally the porters came near, one after the other.

As a rule there were four or five marching in a group. I had them all gather together and then rest for a short time. Then we marched in an unbroken column up to the most southern Maschukulumbe village which I was told was no longer very far away.

To the right and to the left we saw much game. In the west beyond the Monjeko river we recognised some large huts built in the style of the Matabele huts yet we did not see any human beings. When I asked, Mo-Panza's people told me that this was a deserted Maschukulumbe village. In the wake of some quarrels which had broken out the year before between the Maschukulumbe and Mo-Panza's subjects (which however had soon been settled) the Maschukulumbe had abandoned this settlement and instead had established the village M'Beza which we now were approaching.

'*Hela, Hela, Batu, Batu ahacho, Hela Ki-Maschukulumbe!*' 'Look, look, people, look there are Maschukulumbe,' one of our servants whom we had sent before us as our scout all of a sudden shouted. All of us stopped and looked in the indicated direction in which the first Maschukulumbe supposedly had appeared in their own territory. And, indeed, four people were approaching us. Soon we faced the first Maschukulumbe on their own territory.

VII

The Maschukulumbe
The area between M'Beza
and Kaboramanda

THE MUCH-DISCUSSED FIRST ENCOUNTER between us and the Maschukulumbe was rather stiff on both sides. This embarrassment, however, had quite different reasons for each of the various parties concerned.

We Europeans were somewhat restrained because of the importance of the moment. My black Matoka carriers showed signs of fear while the first Maschukulumbe whom we surprised so suddenly did not know what to do. Should they run away and call their brothers in the village to take up their arms or should they simply stay in the place where they were just cutting reeds for their huts or should they come up to us?

When my people called to them they came closer. The oldest one among them was a true Hercules of about 40 years while the others were all young men. They were all naked and were carrying light but long spears; in fact these were the longest spears I had ever seen among the blacks. The shafts were 2·5 m long and had 'matotele' as points which were small assegai irons with barbs on one or both sides.

The blacks recovered amazingly quickly from their surprise since the rumour of our coming had travelled rapidly ahead of us. Unfortunately, it had also brought the news that we were coming from Luanika's empire and that this royal neighbour of theirs whom they hated with passion had ordered the Matoka chiefs whom we had visited on our journey to take care of the transport of our baggage. Luanika's mere agreement with our journey had discredited us in the eyes of the wild Maschukulumbe to such an extent that they regarded us as enemies from the very beginning and detested and hated us equally.

We could not have brought any worse recommendation than to have been Luanika's protegés. The raw Maschukulumbe did not make the least effort to hide their feelings: we could read them in each of their looks and after one hour we knew what the situation was. I still hoped to secure our position, half of which was already lost, by means of my profession as 'witchdoctor'. This had already helped us often on our expedition. Yet after a few days I had to realise with fright that even this ultimate protective talisman did not work among these Maschukulumbe. We were Luanika's people, they said, and how could they possibly trust us? We were Luanika's spies, and how could they not be afraid of us? We were mortal enemies of the country and how could they possibly spare us? We were traitors who had come into their country under the pretext of being compassionate physicians—how could they possibly let us live and allow us to travel on?

They had, indeed, heard of white people, they said. Some of their people even had seen whites in earlier years around Sepopo. Yet these were probably—what we too were undoubtedly—nothing other than whitewashed Marutse who were spying under this cover. We had to be Marutse whether we were whitewashed or had been transformed into white men by some magic. No Maschukulumbe whether of high or of low status, whether old or young, whether man or woman, would accept any medicine from us even if I were willing to give it away. People avoided us and shunned us as evil witches.

This was the sad truth which I recognised right away during our first days of travelling in Maschukulumbe country. I had lost the talisman which had been so valuable for the success of our expedition among the tribes north of the Zambezi and I had lost the respect which my profession otherwise had claimed everywhere. On what should our prestige be based from now on and what could substitute for the power which Stanley or Cameron had possessed amidst hostile tribes by means of their large numbers of faithful porters armed with guns which favoured their expeditions? I had counted on the magic of my profession as a physician. I had thought it would substitute for Stanley's guard and I think I need not feel ashamed of this error.

My profession as a physician indeed had rendered us priceless services ever since we had left civilised South Africa. It was only my profession which had enabled us to continue our trip among the Matoka. It had been the blind fear of the European doctor who was thought to be a greater magician than the local witchdoctors. This had protected the few white members of our expedition on the deserted paths through the forests deep in the wilderness, even if one of them had been ill and had to stay behind or had lost his way accompanied by those thievish porters.

My medical profession had won us porters even from hostile chiefs and above all it had helped to keep together the thievish porters and to discipline them when they began to mutiny. The best proof, indeed, for the power of my profession were those twenty 'faithful' Matoka porters with whom I had reached the first Maschukulumbe village. And now our authority even among them had become shaky. Even though they knew that the accusation by the Maschukulumbe that we were spies was completely unfounded, they were quite impressed that no Maschukulumbe was willing to accept any medicine from us and that they all despised my remedies. My instinct told me that I could no longer trust my twenty Matoka servants. Later, unfortunately too late, I learned that they had cheated me from the very first step we had made into Maschukulumbe country.

The shortest way, that is a worn path leading from the south directly north to chief Kasenge,[1] crossed the Monjeko river near the village Musosa and led to the west of the river through dense woodland down to the Luenge valley. My porters, however, led us along the right bank of the river and in a half circle towards our aim, always intending to desert us at the next best opportunity since they were fearful of accompanying us to the Luenge into the heart of the Maschukulumbe country. On our journey north I did not know this and I realised this unfortunately much too late—only on our painful retreat. In addition, the behaviour of the Maschukulumbe became more insolent from one day to the next. I realised that they as well as my Matoka porters slowly began to question our prestige. They no longer believed in our invulnerability and in the certain healing power of my medicines by which the Maschupia, Matoka, Marutse and Matakala had sworn. Thus we had to recognise that the obstacles on our way were to become more and more dangerous the further north we penetrated. I understood completely why a man like Livingstone had not been able to traverse the highly interesting Maschukulumbe territory about which he, too, very probably knew through reports of the Matoka. At that time, however, such an expedition would have been much easier since in those years the Maschukulumbe were still living on good terms with the Marutse.[2] It only took a few days for this situation, which had changed in such a completely unfavourable way, to become quite clear to us. No pondering or interpretation of this situation could help us; the facts spoke for themselves.

Yet let me come back to the events of 17 July, the day when we entered the Maschukulumbe territory. The abovementioned representatives of this tribe pointed out to us the nearest path to M'Beza without a word and disappeared again in the high grass.

In front of us a large plain stretched. It appeared to be totally overgrown by the much feared giant grass, except for a few high mimosa and fig trees and the two types of palm tree—the fan palm, *ki-mahuma*, and the *ki-sizaru*, a kind of thin-thin-stemmed date palm which the Matoka call *ruseme* and the Maschukulumbe *runkomane*.

First we came through fields and passed some huts which were only inhabited during the time when the field work is done. The fields were small but the most carefully kept ones I had so far found among the blacks. Around and through the fields they had dug small ditches for the excess rain. The vegetable beds were elevated and well kept and those in which they plant sweet potatoes still showed some of the huge bulbs which taste so delicious when they are roasted.

The fields, of course, were situated right amidst the high grass, thus surrounded by a natural wall which in the wintertime was dry and rustling. In order to frighten the game away they had twisted the grass together along the edge of the field into bunches. Two of these bunches, which were about half a metre apart, were always tied together at the top into a big knot. It would have been more effective to cut off the branches of the mimosa trees growing around there and put these up as a fence. But this would have been men's work and these black lords of the creation shunned this work, of course. For among all the men of southern Africa they are probably the worst lazy-bones. The careful field work was exclusively the merit of the women. The huts which we saw were different from the deserted dwellings which we had seen on our march north. They were of the Betschuana type—however, much narrower and instead of a two metre high side wall they had almost three metre high walls. They also had a circular grass roof which, however, does not hang as far down over the wall as over the huts of the Betschuana.

The walls are constructed in the following way: two poles are driven into the ground, both rather far apart, and the space between them is firmly packed with bundles of maize stalks. From inside and outside they are rather poorly plastered with clay; sometimes this is only done from the inside. The rather small diameter of these huts (about three metres) was striking in contrast to their height. We had passed the small fields and while walking we had startled kabunda gazelles which were rushing away from us. By now we were approaching the southern M'Beza village.

All of a sudden I saw some pointed black objects moving back and forth in front of us and glittering in the high grass. I called two of my Matoka porters to ask them what that might be. I learned that this was a Maschukulumbe hair-style and one of the longest ones which well-to-do young men usually wear. Indeed, this was the case. A little path was winding in front of us through the high grass along which a young Maschukulumbe was running in order to bring the news of our arrival into the nearby village. When we left the high grass and got to a somewhat elevated clearing we saw the village opposite us. The free space in front of it was filled with naked blacks. Each of them was balancing an almost one metre high hair-style which sat perpendicularly on the backs of their heads. My wife as well as my men could not help but shriek at this sight. A few moments later we had reached the first inhabited Maschukulumbe kraal where we were followed immediately by some armed men who did not ask us for permission. They accompanied us to the village centre which was situated slightly further north. This was the actual residence of the most southern Maschukulumbe chief Ka-Kumamba. This subtribe of the Maschukulumbe which we had reached first was called Bamala.[3]

The Maschukulumbe village was situated on a free space in the middle of a grass thicket. It was enclosed by poles and the huts were standing rather closely together and formed a circle with a diameter of about 200 m. The space between every hut was closed by the poles so that it was only through one single entry that one could reach the centre of the village. Four of the huts were standing somewhat separated from the others and were not enclosed by poles. They were inhabited during the night by female slaves. The enclosure and the walls of the huts were not very strong and no protection against wild animals. Men, women and children kept pouring out of these rather neglected huts. The old and the young men as well as the boys were completely naked. The women grabbed some poorly cured lechwe skins which they wrapped around their hips rather carelessly using the hind legs of the animals as strings and tying them togerher under their bellies. This was their only clothing. At no other place and among none of the other dark tribes of southern Africa had I ever seen such sparse and sloppy covering of the women as I saw here among the Maschukulumbe. Every man without exception was wearing an elaborate hair-style. Most of them were about thirty to forty centimetres long, standing either slanted backwards or straight upwards on the backs of their heads. But one of the men was wearing his hollow rounded hair piece in a horizontal position and thus distinguished himself from the others as the chief and ruler of this little village.

In most striking contrast to the men all the women, to our great surprise, had completely clean-shaven heads. Only girls up to twelve years were wearing short twisted strands reaching downwards about ten centimetres, whereas boys of the same age were wearing their hairstrands twisted upwards from their crowns on which the base of their headdress was later supposed to be. Girls under 12 years were wearing belts around their hips from which were hanging to the left and right some fringe-like straps to which they had tied shells, and hollow metal cases not dissimilar to cricket cocoons. This was a kind of tinkling decoration which was meant to be a sort of charm.

What struck me especially about the behaviour of these people was an insolence which was almost comparable to that of the Matabele. The guides who were imposed upon us without any explanation, the instructions which later were given to our porters and servants, and many other things immediately aroused my suspicions which unfortunately only too soon proved justified in every respect. First of all our servants had to make quite an effort with their sticks to keep the village dogs, a kind of strong, yet stout, whippet, from attacking our dwarf goats and our donkeys. Goats and donkeys were unknown not only to the Maschukulumbe but also to their dogs. In defence of the latter I have to admit, however, that they were perfect hunting dogs trained to go for lechwe. Cattle as the only domestic animals make up the main wealth of the Maschukulumbe. The good pasture and the relative ease of cattle raising have made the Maschukulumbe tribe extremely lazy. The cattle herds which often number more than 1,000 head enable them better than the Zulu or Betschuana to work very little. There is not much of noble and human feeling in the Maschukulumbe, but if they have such feelings at all as those which we call affection, preference, respect, care, and pride they concentrate these feelings exclusively on their work and their care for the well-being of their cattle.

What friendly feelings they had for us right in the first Maschukulumbe village and how hospitably they planned to receive us was proved by the very first reception ceremony, i.e. the convening of the council of war under a single huge mimosa tree at the south-west corner of the village. We were told for the time being to stay in the meagre shade of a small mimosa tree at the south end about 120 m away from the village. Since we came from Luanika's empire and very probably with his permission they were not sure whether they should allow us to camp and to sleep in the vicinity of their village at all.

In spite of the severity of the situation we could not help but smile whenever we looked at the crowd of people squatting under the single huge tree. These pitch-black figures formed a strong contrast to the grass, which appeared ochre coloured during the winter drought. And with their tall headdresses they resembled holy servants of the inquisition who also wore tall, pointed and narrow black hoods. The war council finally decided to let us stay for that night under this tree. The determining factor was that if they refused to accept us we would very probably go on to the next Maschukulumbe chief in the north and thus would neither buy any food in their village nor give any presents to their chief. In addition they immediately sent out runners to the east, west and north, as we found out later, in order to inform their neighbours about the arrival of the whitewashed Marutse spies and to warn them to take precautionary measures. They felt too weak to attack us directly and to chase us out of their borders. They could not count on our Matoka porters, as they knew that in spite of all their fear and in spite of the fact that they would have liked to retreat, Mo-Panza favoured us and would punish them severely upon their return home. Thus they refused in spite of all incentives to join their own force with that of the Matoka against us. Accordingly, the Maschukulumbe in that first village were content with squeezing as much out of us as they could. When our porters were questioned by them, they told them about the treasures in our packages and especially that we had many *impandes* (amulets), precious *burungu* (glass beads) and *ko-empele* (skirt-sitsibas), as well as various secret remedies which made anybody who carried them bullet-proof. All of this spread like wildfire from hut to hut and attracted more and more crowds of Maschukulumbe until we were so densely surrounded by them that we could no longer move at all. If we had had to defend ourselves we would have been unable to lift our firearms, let alone to use them. My black servants were so much intimidated by the crowd of Maschukulumbe that they had crept between our feet and between our bundles of baggage. Most of them had such an expression of fear in their faces that even the traiterous Matoka had to laugh aloud. At that point I saw by chance that some of the bold Maschukulumbe boys had chosen to sit on our big tin chests containing the cartridges. And struck by a sudden inspiration I shouted to the leader of the Maschukulumbe who was standing not too far away from me, 'Look, chief, these boys are sitting on the powder for our guns.' The man who was just trying to reach over the heads of the crowd in order to get a glowing pipe of tobacco dropped the pipe when he heard my words and screamed that the *mushemani* were sitting on the fire of the guns of the white man. At the same time he tried to get out of the dense crowd of people, striking out furiously to all sides. The Maschukulumbe did not quite understand what this man meant, yet they realised well enough that he and they were in danger. They rushed away, all in different directions, and from then on they came neither close to us nor close to our baggage for the rest of the day.

Finally the chief appeared with his wife and repeated his permission for us to establish our camp there. Now only two things were of importance. Firstly, we had to watch our belongings very closely and, secondly, I quickly had to buy the most necessary food supply. In both I was successful.

It was out of fear rather than from vigilance that my blacks this time obeyed perfectly when I ordered them to sit there for the time being and to watch the wall of our camp built with our parcels. For some yellow and lavender coloured glass beads I bought cheaply some hay for our camp as well as poles to support the camp wall. The Maschukulumbe simply pulled the poles out of the fence around their kraal and were laughing when they were dragging them near to us, thinking to themselves 'tomorrow or the day after tomorrow the strangers will probably leave and then we will get our poles back again'. Yet I had some of the poles cut up for fire wood. The saleswomen, two thoroughly ugly and bald-headed persons, protested strongly and immediately, yet in vain. We also bartered milk and dried meat for our Matoka porters. The honoured chief brought us beer as a present for which he received in return glass beads, a sitsiba and, for his wife, a large and a small piece of cloth. Finally, they brought us two cups of flour which they had ground between two stones, differently from the Matoka and Betschuana who pound it in wooden mortars. Yet we did not buy the flour since we found it too expensive. In general, I found that the Maschukulumbe, even though they are, as we observed, not heavy *butchuala* drinkers, do not grow as much grain as they need and buy most of it from the Matoka and Mankoya in exchange for lechwe skins and cattle.

When the crowd disappeared in the evening we could finally breathe freely again. The Maschukulumbe go to bed rather early, and so did the king and his wife, both decorated with numerous ivory bracelets and several *impandes*. The noise, the shouting and the pressing crowd around us for so many hours had exhausted us so much that we lay down one after another right on the ground while Oswald and the servants were preparing dinner. They began to make ours as well as their own beds with the giant grass I had bought. After a few minutes we were fast asleep and then after dinner we began to take turns for the night watch —each of us being assisted by two blacks. We tied the donkeys to the mimosa trees between us and the servants' camp to protect them against wild animals. One of them was so ill that he could not get up from the ground. When everything was in order we all lay down around the high burning fire except for the guards who were sitting outside the glare of the fire in order to watch better. The noise in the village of these people who went to bed so early soon subsided. It was a beautiful calm night, but our minds were unable to calm down. Every little noise made us nervous. In the silence we could clearly hear the crackling of the fire of our porters and every now and then the lowing of the cattle gazing over to us and the unusual fire at night. We could hear the howling of a pair of hyenas and the neighing of a zebra. In the clearing in front of us we could clearly see gazelles and an antelope the size of a reedbuck grazing quietly. Maybe they felt safest from the carnivores here in the vicinity of human beings. And indeed they are safest here until civilisation comes also to these areas and puts firearms into the hands of the natives.

The next morning we had the chance to watch the Maschukulumbe at work as barbers fixing their hairstyles in all stages. We saw some dandies walking around with fully made up giant hair arrangements, while others had only started or had them half prepared. I was trying to draw the portraits of these blacks and I was successful in it. When later at Galulonga all of these drawings except for one sheet were pulled out of my portfolio and were lost together with the determinations of longitude of our trip north of the Zambezi, I tried months later to make pencil drawings from memory of at least the most notorious of our enemies. I made a sketch of one of them and then I called one after the other of the six blacks whom I had still kept as my servants and who had accompanied us to the Maschukulumbe. And I was only satisfied with my sketch when all of them separately recognised the person immediately and called him by his name. Since I did not find the tall hair arrangements on old people it appears as if these giant coiffures had only become fashionable during the last twenty years.[4] The hair is smeared with some fat and a black metallic powder until it glistens. It seems to be resistent against vermin. The sight of such giant hairstyles is terribly funny. These people have to carry their heads so stiffly that the hair, which stands up straight into the air sitting on their short bodies resembles the long neck of a giraffe. The heavy weight at the base of their head soon causes such a hypertrophy for the muscles of their temples that they become visible as strong ligaments like those in the front and the rear of their necks.

After several years and depending upon the individual the temple muscles weaken and atrophy. The spear-shaped braid becomes a droopy pigtail dangling more or less downwards and pulling the skin of forehead, face and temples downward. Thus, it prevents its wearer almost completely from making a fast movement and makes it completely impossible to run.

What a lovely fashion! The men wear hair arrangements up to 110 cm long. Yet, as many a female reader will note, the women appear clean shaven. Well, this clean shaven state has its good reasons. It is proof of the spirit of female self-sacrifice. The girl whom a man buys for himself (and among the independent Maschukulumbe the woman too has a say whether she likes or dislikes this or that man) has to sacrifice her kinky hair to her master after she has become his wife. Our beauties give their chosen partner one curl; the Maschukulumbe beauties give him all. And yet this is not enough for him. In addition, he shaves his slaves and those whom he has killed in a battle and he buys hair from the surrounding tribes. Then he orders the local hairdresser to make for him—according to his liking—a fist-shaped coiffure, or the many-tiered one, or even the giant hairstyle. Such a giant hairstyle, all in all, according to the local prices, costs as much as a strong ox for which we Europeans had to pay nine to ten metres of calico. The making of such a hair arrangement is a work of art which takes weeks if not months. We were able to appreciate such a coiffure since we had the opportunity to watch a Maschukulumbe hairdresser at work. His 'victim' was a dandy of about thirty years. Naked as all the rest of them, he was lying in a semi-reclined position with the lower part of his body on a lechwe skin. His upper body was leaning so heavily on the lap of the hairdresser that his head came to rest on the hairdresser's right knee. The fancy hairstyle in the making had already reached one third of the required height of 1m. The hairdresser had in his right hand a strong 20 cm needle similar to our upholsterer's needle. In it was a long, well-twisted thread of bark fibre. He wound the fibres around short strands of hair which had been twisted together previously. These were then attached to the existing top ring of the hairpiece. When one of the kinky strands of hair became too short the hairdresser added with his left hand a new supply of kinky hair to that particular strand. Soon this new strand was firmly tied to the rest of the hair structure. Thus, the bark thread, which at the beginning of this elaborate coiffure is tied to the original hair, literally twists spirally from the head up to the thin and fine pointed tip of the hair arrangement. It gives the whole construction a certain degree of firmness. The thread is smeared with the hair polish which I mentioned before. Thus it looks like genuine hair on first sight. The process of twisting and tying the hair and thread together is done with so much force that the structure appears fine and very firm without looking heavy. The object of labour, that is, the vain man, is not clamped into a vice. Accordingly, the hairdresser, in order to complete his work of art, has to do his weaving with such force that when he is pulling the thread, not only the head of his client, but occasionally even his whole body, jerks convulsively. This procedure must be very painful to the vain client and very exhausting for the hairdresser. Both, however, stick it out with great patience even if it takes weeks and sometimes even months until the giant hair arrangement is finished. It takes so long partly because it is so painful and partly because it is very difficult to get enough hair at the proper time. The highest goal of the vain martyr in terms of his physical appearance is the completion of his coiffure; his personal vanity does not go beyond this. The epitome of all material ambitions is a large herd of cattle. A head-dress and a herd of cattle comprise the ideal of greatest earthly happiness for the ordinary Maschukulumbe. For the Maschukulumbe chiefs it is a head-dress, herds of cattle, and human skulls. After that perhaps comes the pipe. Women, war and hunting are of second-degree importance. The drinking of alcoholic beverages, to which other Bantu tribes are so much addicted, does not play any role at all among the Maschukulumbe.

Because their heads are clean shaven the Maschukulumbe women are all the more ugly—even more so since only very few of them have pleasant features. I was told by the Matoka that the Maschukulumbe men, if they are cattle owners, have as a rule eight wives each. This might have been the case in former times, but I found in each household only one wife and with some chiefs, two wives. The friction and petty jealousy often leads to fights. Then one group occasionally tries —by a pretended attack on some cattle post—to divert attention from the main kraal which they then attack all of a sudden. They kill all the women so that the enemy remains weak and is not easily able to increase its strength at the natural birth rate. In such cases many hide their women and children in the bush to make it difficult for the enemy to kill the women. In areas where such raids have occurred too frequently the sub-tribes are forced to buy women from neighbouring foreign tribes. Prices for them vary substantially. Along the Zambezi a woman costs a cow, or a canoe, and sometimes even only a woollen blanket. Along the Luenge she costs fourteen hoes, which is substantially more. In order to buy wives the Maschukulumbe themselves visit the kraals of neighbouring tribes where they often find some 'in stock'. Or some representatives of the neighbouring tribes visit the Maschukulumbe with their precious commodity. They come only into the villages along the border, since all the neighbours fear to penetrate into the interior of Maschukulumbe country. The women dealers, however, never offer their most beautiful and strongest women for exchange. It is only the ugliest ones whom the Maschukulumbe can get. This is why we found that Maschukulumbe women left nothing to be desired in terms of ugliness. In addition, these women are never in a good mood since they consider it their greatest misfortune and shame to be sold as wives to the wild Maschukulumbe. The neighbouring tribes, however, with whom the Maschukulumbe trade and who sell them women, never offer them the daughters of their own tribe. They rather buy these women themselves, mostly from southern tribes such as the Matoka and Makalaka. They place these among their own women, but if they have an opportunity for a good barter they dispose of those women who do not please them. Thus, with the exception perhaps of a favourite wife and all the wives of a chief, every wife can be sold by her husband. Exceptions in all cases, however, are women who are daughters of chiefs or of free men of the tribe. (Among the Matoka these are only free Matoka and among Mankoya and Mabunda these are free Mankoya and Mabunda.) These women are married to free men. Among the Makalaka of Wanke this does not hold in all cases since even free women can occasionally be exchanged as objects of barter.

Among the northern Zambezi tribes the Marutse women have the greatest respect among their tribe, after them the free Maschukulumbe women, i.e. the daughters born to a cattle-owning Maschukulumbe and a true Maschukulumbe mother or a slave chosen as a favourite wife. We saw truly pretty Maschukulumbe girls only three times. They proved the saying to be true that 'Beauty is the highest gift of the gods to a woman', even if it is translated into the black race. These three girls were true little devils after whom the men were literally running; who gave orders to the men; and one of whom told us that they did not want to have any husband, i.e. did not want to get married. The father thus could not, as is the case among the Matoka, plan their future as he wished.

Early in the morning of 18 July when it was still cool we set out to continue our journey and left the first settlement of the Maschukulumbe. The day's march was 17 km and it led in a north-western direction to a pond which is called Moka-Ruange[5] by the Maschukulumbe and which belonged to the next chief to the north. In our third kilometre we crossed the Ki-Monjeko river and in the fourth and fifth kilometres we crossed two of its tributary streams, one of them being called Ki-Bukura. The Monjeko takes a north-north-eastern course and flows into the Luenge. The countryside was flat but up to the fourteenth kilometre overgrown with high grass and thus the crossing of this plain was one of the most difficult trips in the Luenge area. The path was winding continuously and we could hardly see 3 m in front of us in the grass thickets. Thus we were walking between these high grass walls without any view. This was not only uncomfortable but also very dangerous because this area was teeming with buffalo herds and lions which usually follow them. Nowhere else had I seen even the Matoka porters proceeding with so much fear and timidity. These men, who usually show so much courage in their encounters with wild animals, were already literally wet with sweat after the first kilometres.

I only want to report a few things about the adventures of this day. A few paces beyond the village I spotted a kabonda gazelle similar in size and colour to an steenbok, but somewhat bigger. It lives mostly in small herds. It is marked by a black tail which is noticeable from a long distance in contrast to the beautiful reddish-brown skin of the animals. This is why some tribes call it the black-tailed buck. I shot at a distance of 150 m and I even heard my small Winchester bullet hit; the animal however, jumped to the side and soon had disappeared out of my sight into the high grass. We followed the little footpath leading northwards parallel to the stream, but a few minutes later we heard the shouts of some persons rushing after us. We stopped to wait for them. They were the guides whom Mo-Panza had assigned to me. They reported that we were on the wrong path and that we would have to cross the river to reach the next chiefdom. When we thus turned left and walked towards the river we heard our little dog Sydomoja barking furiously in the giant grass to our side. One of the guides left us immediately in order, as he said, to see what was the matter. The barking of the dog made him rather suspicious. He thought that the dog had spotted a wild animal and was now barking at it or that some beast of prey had chased him behind a bush. We certainly waited in order to assist the guide with our arms if necessary. However, this was not necessary. The man soon returned carrying a kabonda gazelle. This was the animal which my bullet had hit between the shoulders. It had been able to flee off to the side about fifty paces away from the spot where it had been wounded. Then it had collapsed and was spotted by the little dog who had stayed behind us. I was very happy about this success because it was the first animal of this kind for my collection. I had it skinned immediately and only afterwards did we continue our journey. We crossed the Monjeko at a place which had been dammed and made shallow by many reed bundles which people had thrown into it.

People had built this original bridge not only in order to have a path through the river and to be safe from the crocodiles, but also to be able to fish. In the dam were two narrow openings at the mouth of which people had put simple reed fish traps which appeared to produce a good yield. While the Marutse use large and well-made drag nets and bigger and better baskets for fishing and are also very good at spearing fish with special and beautifully made spears, the Maschuku-lumbe are much more backward in their fishing techniques—as in most other spheres as well. Their laziness, which is the cause of their inferiority, even goes so far that they buy their fish-traps from the northern Mankoya even though in their area there are masses of excellent reeds and numerous pliable bushes, i.e. enough material to make traps.

On our further march, while we were passing through that dangerous tall grass which I have mentioned before, we were carrying our rifles in our arms ready to fire as we always did on such a 'pleasure procession'. On our narrow path we crossed many broad tracks. These tracks led to the river and were used by various kinds of wild animal, especially herds of large eland and numerous gnu, zebra and buffalo herds. Once, and sometimes even twice, daily they go to the little Monjeko stream to quench their thirst. The buffalo go there also to swim and to roll themselves in the mud. At each of the wider tracks we stopped for a moment and listened to hear whether perhaps a buffalo herd was approaching in which case we would quickly have retreated into the grass in order to let these dangerous wanderers pass. After about the first half of our march we reached an area where the grass had burnt down and where quite a number of trees were growing in clumps. We just had reached this clearing when Boy, who was walking ahead of us, pointed out a high and thick cloud of dust approximately six hundred metres to our left. At first we could see nothing, but then the wind blew the dust further to the side and we recognised a buffalo herd galloping towards us. When the buffalo saw us they stopped and suddenly turned around. We were surprised about this strange cowardliness and began to follow this herd. Yet we were not able to fire a good shot. Since I did not want to follow this herd too long I returned alone and ordered the porters to continue their march with my wife, Leeb and Mapani as leaders. Then I left them and veered to the west in order to shoot some game and thus to raise the spirits of my Matoka porters through a rich meat soup. And, indeed, I was successful. From afar I saw a striped gnu near a tall ant-hill next to a pond overgrown with reeds. I sneaked closer through the water using the hill as cover. Then I climbed the hill and shot. The bullet shattered the right hind thigh. The animal turned around twice in a small circle and began to run. About 500 m further on I caught up with him and killed him with a shot into his forehead, at a distance of 60 m. He was an old bull living by himself and probably an outcast from his herd. Even today I regret that I did not skin him and have his skin sent back to the Zambezi at a time when I still had the Matoka carriers at my disposal.

That day we continued to see much game. For the last kilometres we walked along a wooded slope. We then pitched camp by the pond which I have mentioned earlier. My kind reader can well understand that my carriers welcomed the venison with loud shouts. And there was even another piece of game for us that day. It was an eland bull which Boy killed in the vicinity of our camp site. We made full use of its meat which is preferable by far to the tough meat of the striped gnu. First of all, we ate a lot of it. Then I decided to stay one day longer in order to make the rest of the meat into biltong. I planned to use a few Maschukulumbe to transport the meat which was to be loosened from the bones and cut into long strings. On 19 July several Maschukulumbe families came to us from the nearby village. We bought some maize as well as dried sliced yams from them and paid for it with gnu and eland meat. When I asked how they hunted they told me that they make pit traps along the paths leading to the usual waterholes of the game. In this way, for example, they had caught two buffaloes in one day about ten days before and had speared them in the pit. These Maschukulumbe frightened my Matoka porters so much by some of their reports that the leaders of the Matoka came up to me to say that they refused to go any further and would not carry our bundles any more. 'You cannot desert us here in this wilderness! I do not think that the nearby village has enough porters. You promised and you took on the job to carry our bundles to the Luenge. I know very well that you led us on a detour and not along the shortest route. It is your own fault that we are not yet on the Luenge.' 'No, we do not want to carry any further. Already the people in M'Beza threatened to kill us because they wanted to carry for you in order to earn something for themselves. Only the fear of our mighty king stopped these people from harming us. If they had carried your things they would probably have led you the wrong way today on the march through the high grass and then they would have killed you. Even to us they did not point out the right path. They sent us on the wrong path which you took first. Then we met an unknown Maschuku-lumbe who came from the new chief in the east, the son of the recently deceased king Ki [Si] Namandschoroschula, who rules over the Wuenga a sub-tribe of the Maschukulumbe.[6] This man told us secretly the right path to Kaboramanda[7] and then on to Kasenga. This is why we called you back and brought you to this path. But now we cannot go any further with you, no! Otherwise we shall be killed by them—and only so that the Maschukulumbe can get possession of the payment we will receive from you.' 'Why don't you hide the sitsibas in an empty drinking vessel, then they won't see them and will think that I had already paid you at home?' 'No, we won't go a single step further.' 'Is this your gratitude for my get-ting you good food and even having bought for you Mokanda beer from the Mas-chukulumbe?' 'No, we shall not go.' 'Well then you will have to go. I and my people will find our way to Kaboramanda. You are not the first mutinous porters as you probably have already heard. Sakasipa's and Moëba's people did the same, they also refused to go any further. However, you are not the first ones whom I am going to force to follow me with my bundles through my *Malemo*—just as I did with those people. I shall leave Kamuso *gasutzana* [early tomorrow morning] and you will follow me. Why should I be afraid about my belongings among you? You know very well that I am a *Njaka* [witchdoctor].'

The mutiny of my porters also had an effect on my black servants. I got the im-pression that they were on the verge of deserting me. These servants who usually did not waste much of their time with the porters, and in fact were often opposed to them and helped us faithfully to watch the crew, had been whispering secretly and constantly with this horde of Matoka porters during the last days. I had never seen them doing that before.

I could not reach any agreement and thus I left early in the morning of 20 July i.e. only I, my wife and my travelling companions. Oswald intended to stay be-hind together with Fekete, but I did not allow it. We had to put all our eggs in one basket. My reputation as a physician, or rather as the witchdoctor which I was considered here, was too well entrenched among these Matoka. I did not have to fear that they would not follow us with the bundles. I was convinced that we would have been killed by these Matoka several times before had it not been for this respect and fear of me as a magician. As long as I was able to use these Matoka as carriers in Maschukulumbe country I had to maintain my prestige tenaciously.

After all, I had already seen when visiting the first chief's residence that we could not expect anything good from the Maschukulumbe. Indeed, I had to fear that the difficulties of hiring porters and the complications they then would make would be even greater than had been the case among the Matoka. And from them we had been forced to suffer so much that we had almost thought that our whole expedition would collapse because of the lack of porters.

The trip to the kraal of the next Maschukulumbe prince Kaboramanda was almost fourteen kilometres long and followed a north-north-western course. This stretch was rather interesting because of its vegetation. In our second kilometre we came to a swampy pond with reeds closely growing around it and we passed through the fields belonging to the Motande village. They were situated on a laterite rise of 4 m surrounded by bush. This rise dropped towards the north into a basin-shaped valley draining into the Monjeko stream. This valley, as well as the somewhat lower plain at the northern slope of the hills, is covered with a large palm forest measuring 18 km across. Kaboramanda is situated in the middle of this forest and thus has an enviable location—even for a dream castle. Yet this gorgeous landscape has its disadvantages, too. During the floods only the ant-hills and the palm trees growing on them stick out like little islands from the water which stagnates like a pond for quite some time. The bush is rich with game since antelopes, zebras, gnus and buffaloes feel much safer on the open plain with its short grass than in the giant grass. Yet here, too, the lion often takes up his stand and stalks the game for hours against the wind, hidden behind ant-hills or small palms until the grazing game has come close to him. We had passed through Motande and its fields where I found those strange grain storage containers which can take approximately 300 kg of grain. They are thickly smeared with cement and decorated with crude paintings. All of a sudden my Matoka guide came running up to me and brought me the pleasant and surprising news that he did not know which path to take. The villagers refused to show him the way to Kaboramanda. 'You are lying, man. You know it and just do not want to find it. I shall go myself and I shall find it', I said. 'All right, but we won't go any further,' he answered, 'we must sleep here tonight because my men ate so much last night and the night before that they cannot move any more.' This then was the reason. And in part this might have been true, because the people had gorged themselves with the gnu and the eland the whole night long in a way which was rather disgusting for us to watch. Even the half-roasted intestines they had gulped down. The blacks are in this respect themselves half animals. If they had to provide their own food they starved, but when I gave them meat they were as greedy as vultures. In order to be able to eat even more they had been screaming, jumping, shouting, gesticulating and beating themselves. When we got up in the morning from our primitive beds the gluttonous men were still sitting around the pot and were still stuffing it in. Their otherwise sunken—literally hanging—bellies were horribly blown up and their eyes lay deep. Some were suffering from tremendous headaches and were staggering away to throw up. This is the way the blacks live. In their own families some are more moderate with venison—but only some. The majority gorge themselves incessantly as long as there is something left. I know cases where only a few men fell upon a whole buffalo or gnu and ate it up without leaving anything. Thus I understood quite well that my porters, after having eaten in one night a whole male gnu and a quarter of an eland, were no longer able to make a long march with a load on their shoulders or heads.

'I am going,' I said finally to the chief who was staying behind. 'You have to follow me.' There were several paths leading away from the village in a fan-like fashion. I chose one leading north. I had walked about 700 m when the chief came gasping behind me. 'Now I see', he said, 'that you do not know everything and that your *malemo* [medicine, charm, poison] does not serve you well because you have chosen the wrong way.' He was laughing at me scornfully. I was sorry that I had made an error and had exposed myself, yet I was still trying to use this situation for my own ends. I told him harshly that he none the less would not know the shortest and most direct way either. 'I should not know it? I know it very well since I have walked it once already myself,' unintentionally escaped from his mouth. 'The way is there where this woman is walking.' We immediately turned left and followed the indicated proper path leading from west to north. The man stopped and watched as we walked on. Furiously he drove his spear into the grass since he had said too much, I, however, shouted at him 'Ha, ha, *Kosana, Mona a Mo-Panza* [chief and man of Mo-Panza], my *malemo* has loosened your tongue very well and it had disclosed how many lies you have told today.' The man and my black servants, who had caught up with us in the meantime, followed us. We took a rest after eight kilometres by one of the many ponds in the shade of some palm trees. We rested there for a full hour until about ten porters had caught up with us. The others were not yet to be seen. Finally we left the place anyway in order to reach Kaboramanda soon.

Since the first ten porters had appeared I felt quite relaxed. I knew that the others would follow, too. The makuluani palm forest[8] through which we passed that day was the most beautiful and gorgeous one which I had seen on the entire trip. The trees were not very close together. Generally, between two and five trunks had grown up together as if they came from one root. But these individual groups were about ten to fifty metres away from each other. Dead leaves and even more the large thorny leaf-stems have been lying around here for decades since the tough palm fibre does not rot easily. The trees were overladen with fruit and the fruits were over-ripe. Numerous lion tracks proved that these carnivores had a good time here. All the more I was surprised about the light-heartedness of the two Kaboramanda men who, naked as usual—one in front and the other in the rear—were driving a herd of cattle of more than a 1,000 head to their pasture. 'So few', said Boy who was walking next to me, in one of the few Dutch phrases he knew, 'Very probably the lion prefers a fat eland and the fat zebras to these almost skin-and-bone cows. If he comes the Maschukulumbe will anyway desert their herd and run away.' 'But why', I asked, 'do they drive them to pasture that late; nowhere else is this done among you blacks?' 'Well, this has two reasons. One is that they are afraid of the wild animals who roam about until well after sunrise.

On the other hand, however, the Maschukulumbe like to sleep long until the sun is high', and Boy pointed out the location of the sun at about 10 o'clock. We understood and appreciated this explanation.

We came across two large zebra herds, one of which was very shy. The reason was perhaps that they had been hunted by the lion in the morning. They now were afraid of men, too, who normally leave them in peace in this area. The males rushed away in the lead. Every now and then they stopped, turned to the side, and then stared at us with stupefaction. Meanwhile ahead of and behind them the herd was galloping on. The leaders made one jump to the side and then stormed ahead again—neighing, and snorting with their tails raised high and completely conscious of their freedom. It is an extremely interesting and beautiful sight to see a herd of zebras of about sixty animals galloping across a central African bush clearing lined with the dark green of the tall *masuku* trees and towered over by the slender fan palms with their broad and magnificent tops. Good fortune made it possible for me to experience the great and rare pleasure of seeing this beautiful scene several times. It is a delight for one's eyes and heart. And it is deeply engraved in my memory.

VIII

From Kaboramanda
to the Luenge River

and Bosango-Kasenga
The kingdoms of Kaboramanda

AROUND NOON WE ARRIVED IN KABORAMANDA, the largest settlement we had yet seen in Maschukulumbe country. It was the residence of King Kaboramanda.[1] There were also several other chiefs living there whose rank and influence were just as great as that of the king. Yet they recognise him as their head. In Kaboramanda too, these blacks behaved true to their characteristics. They turned out to be late sleepers and lazy-bones of the sort which cannot be found to the same degree among all other tribes of southern Africa. We entered the 'town' towards noon—about 11 o'clock—and yet we did not see a soul, neither outside nor inside the large empty courtyard which was surrounded by huts arranged in a circle and was also used as a cattle kraal. Everybody was still in deep slumber. Only after we had walked through the settlement and had settled down for a rest on a low soft slope did people finally notice us. Then, however, they began to scream, shout and yell. This proved to us sufficiently what kind of excitement and nervousness our sudden arrival had upon the unsuspecting black dreamers. Before my porters had yet arrived we took up our stand near some bushes and we began to collect branches in order to build a camp wall quickly. We had thought that some people from Motande which we had passed on our way had rushed here to announce our arrival and to arrange an unpleasant welcome for us. Even though this had not been the case we still had a rather rough day. After they had finally noticed us we became the subjects of greatest interest. Young and old, men and women, chiefs and everybody—literally everybody—rushed up to us shouting. How they ogled and stared! Each of our movements, our dress, our language, our food— everything—was observed thoroughly and then was discussed animatedly. Many things were incomprehensible to these good people who were standing around us like harmless children overwhelmed by astonishment and surprise. Every now and then one particularly clever chap in one cluster offered the others his own opinion and explanation. We noticed among those people a few chiefs in particular with slightly aquiline noses and with handsome, almost magnificent figures and a proud carriage. One of them had a plain white piece of linen wrapped around himself just like a toga—another had a plain blue piece of linen. They reminded us some-how of Roman patricians. Their coiffures, however, which were hairpieces fifteen to twenty centimetres long sticking out horizontally from the back of their heads, resembled more those of Roman matrons.

For the cloth of these 'togas' they had exchanged cattle in the east with the Mambaris. They then had the slaves of the Mambaris sew together lengthwise these pieces of material, two to two and a half metres in size.

The chief, dressed in white calico, came first to our camp. He entered it proudly accompanied by two women who were carrying something. He gave them a con-descending sign to unpack their baskets. They pulled out a lechwe skin, two little baskets filled with good salt, a piece of tobacco, and a calabash filled with fat. All of this they offered for barter. The chief did not say a single word to us—neither himself nor through his servants. From his self-confidence I gathered that he had probably often had contacts with Mambaris and had at least heard of the white man. Since I did not need any of the things he offered and since on the other hand I did not exactly want to expel the man from our camp, I just left him standing there with the two women standing behind him. He stayed at the same spot like a statue for two and a half hours. Only every now and then he uttered a word over the heads of those who were surrounding us in a close circle. Then as quietly as he had come he finally went away. As soon as he lifted his foot from the lechwe skin his two women came and packed up everything. Then they stole away behind the mighty man. If I had had porters I would have bought everything from him merely for a good relationship with him, but like this I had to let him go unsatis-fied.

The Maschukulumbe porters who had carried the eland meat for us now asked for their payment. I met their demand with Gablonz (i.e. blue cut) material. Around sundown, after people had stared sufficiently at us so that they no longer seemed to fear or to be afraid of us, a few men who were already known to us came from M'Beza. They brought a message from the chief there. Shortly after the arrival of these messengers the attitude of our admirers changed. They began to be bold and even insolent and started to threaten us.

Flocks of people pressed closer to us up to the flimsy wall of our camp which we had made by stacking our bundles atop one another. The wall tumbled inwards and one or two of the agressors fell right into the middle of our camp. My porters, who in the meantime had all arrived, were lured into the huts. They soon came back to announce that they would not continue the next day to carry my bundles under any condition. My black servants literally hid among us. Their great cowardice which they showed so openly was quite harmful for us. The circle of the increasingly noisy crowd became bigger and bigger. My porters joined the crowd and began to describe what kinds of things were in our bundles. By this the greediness of our enemies was stimulated to the utmost. Some of them even grabbed our bundles and tried to take them into their pos-session. They intended to use them as a pawn, not giving them back before they were paid. Of course, I did not tolerate this. When the situation became more and more critical with every passing second I suddenly had Oswald blow the trumpet. The people were paralysed and struck dumb with astonishment. They all stared at this golden glittering thing i.e. the trumpet. Before Oswald could laugh at all the astonished faces or blow another strong flourish, one man in the crowd, who might have been in the battle with Luanika's troops, began to yell and shout. In a trice the crowd dispersed with such speed that they tumbled one on top of another. This sight made even our porters laugh. They shouted after the crowd which was running away that they should not be afraid and should rather resume their positions again. The black who had caused all that confusion had been standing in front of the mouth of the trumpet, which he thought was the much feared firearm. Thus, he had provoked the great panic. The scene, however, was repeated even more dramatically than before when the people came back again to stare at Oswald and his trumpet. One of them was so courageous that he reached over the heads of his fellow men to touch the trumpet in order to find out whether it was warm or cold. This was just the right thing for our musician. At that very moment he blew such a tremendous blast that the blacks literally fell down screaming. Those who were standing next to us almost tumbled into our laps and between our feet screaming at the tops of their lungs. As soon as Oswald had recovered from a fit of laughter caused by the unheard-of effect of his dear trumpet, he blew a gay little piece. The blacks, who had meanwhile recovered, came somewhat closer. Yet that day we were no longer molested by the Kabora-manda people—but, on the other hand, all the more by our own porters, and even by our black servants. The porters, who had already seen the trumpet in action in honour of Mo-Panza, nearly died with laughter at the frightened 'stupid' Maschukulumbe. In comparison they felt immensely worldly-wise. Yet their attitude changed quickly. They all appeared shouting loudly in front of me and demanded their pay. They carried on wildly. They wanted to impress the Maschukulumbe before whom they normally were humiliated like dogs. They felt terribly important and worked up their courage by shouting. They even tried to pay themselves by grabbing a few of my bundles. My patience was at an end. Since my blacks, who in the south at Mo-Panza never would have tolerated this kind of a thing, were now merely watching it without challenging the porters, I decided to act quickly. I called Leeb and we grabbed our rifles and got ready for battle. I shouted at the porters who were drawing nearer, to take their hands off my possessions and retreat quietly to their fires. 'Everybody whose hand reaches out for my things is going to hear something from my *tlobolo* [rifle]. This should not be pleasant for him.' That helped. Without answering a single word they retreated. But until the dawn of the next morning they had long discussions with my servants. I was absolutely sure that these conversations were not in the best in-terests of our expedition and I was thus on my guard. I got up very early, I woke up my wife and the two of us watched for the women who went to get water in the morning in order to ask them the shortest way to the Luenge. They pointed towards north-west and said 'Bosengo-Kasenga'. This we could not comprehend since the nearest point on the Luenge was said to be directly north. Only later we realised that their direction was correct. An unobstructed path went to Bosengo whereas the nearest point on the bank of the Luenge could only be reached by canoes through lagoons and grass and reed thickets, and even then only with great difficulty. Yet at that point we did not know this. We were suspicious when they pointed to the north-west and later preferred to continue our journey in a northern direction. That morning not a single porter (except for one of the guides) wanted to move. They told us that under no condition would they go any further. They demanded their pay, but without being insolent as they were so often otherwise. This time they rather tried to get it by complaining. 'Firstly,' they said, 'we are tired. Secondly, we are afraid to penetrate any further into this area, since on the Luenge we will be killed because of the calico with which you are paying us. And lastly the people of Kaboramanda threaten to kill us if we go any further with you and deprive them of the opportunity to fleece you.' That the last argument was no lie I had already realised the evening before. 'No,' I answered, 'you have to go along at least to the Luenge. You told me yesterday that the Luenge is quite near and I shall give you some glass beads in addition to your sitsiba.'

I decided to go ahead even though this time I literally had to force myself to do so. That day I really feared that the men would not follow us and show up on time. However, I stuck to my decision. They told me that it would take a full day's journey to the Luenge.

Maschukulumbe do not wear any clothing except for a cowhide thrown over their shoulder. Very few wear a piece of calico similar to a sheet (called *kubu*) which they wrap around their body like a toga. As porters, so they told me, they demanded for each day's journey such a *kubu*, i.e. four metres of calico per person while the Matoka served two to six days as porters for two metres of calico. I would have had to pay 180 m of calico from Kaboramanda to Kasenga even though this stretch had already been included in the payment of Mo-Panza's Matoka. Thus, I would have had to pay double. When we Europeans left the camp, only Boy, two other servants, and the guide of the porters followed us. We came to a path leading north. For a long time it led along under beautiful fan palm trees and then into a landscape not dissimilar to an artificially planted English park. Herds of kabonda gazelles and reedbucks swarmed around us on our right and on our left.

Never before had Boy displayed such timid and nervous behaviour as that morning. Once again he was the 'old woman' and not Boy, the leader of my small group of servants. Again and again he looked back, stopped, listened, and listened again. This was so obvious that I felt almost certain that my servants had conspired with the porters, who anyway had been intimidated by the behaviour of the Maschukulumbe, and that they were plotting against us.

After we had walked slowly for about one hour, covering at most 1.5 km Boy suddenly began to shout. His shouting was an answer to a call coming from the rear. Since Boy had stopped we walked on much more slowly. Suddenly I heard several times 'Boss, Boss' shouted in such a piteous wail that we could imagine the frightened look on Boy's face without seeing him. We stopped until he came up to us gasping. He was running like a hunted animal. Instead of using more lengthy words I shall draw a sketch of him as his appearance is firmly fixed in my memory. Boy was an image of terrible fear. Although he could hardly get enough breath to talk he reported that the second guide had just informed him that the Maschuku-lumbe had taken the bundles away from the porters, had beaten several of our servants, and had even killed one of them. My companions became very worried at this news. Only I knew what was really happening. And laughing into his face I told Boy that the whole thing was a lie and that he was only trying to threaten us so that we would return to Kaboramanda, would pay the Matoka and my servants, and then would have to take Maschukulumbe at any price to carry our loads.

Under no condition, however, were we willing to return because then we would have been much too weak before our many enemies in the camp at Kaboramanda. Since one of the porters who had come along with us was carrying cartridges I had him come to me and had him put his load in front of me. Then I sent him back to convey the message that all my servants and porters should come to us. Otherwise I would throw the *marumo* (all sorts of projectiles, i.e. lances, spears, assegais, but also lead, cartridges and other ammunition of the Europeans) way over the palm trees into our camp. If he saw that the Maschukulumbe had taken away a single load then Mapani, to whom I had lent a rifle, should fire a shot into the air. This would be the signal for us to shoot from our position into the village which from here was still visible between the palm trees.

The reader will understand that this threat was only a booby-trap since I was firmly convinced that the whole thing was only a shrewd plan to get us all back to Kaboramanda where our situation would have become rather critical.

Boy wanted to keep the messenger from going, yet I did not allow this. We waited seated. The messenger took the shortest way back which was not in the direction from which the voice that supposedly had frightened Boy so much was once again to be heard. The calls were coming from much closer. Boy wanted to answer them yet I stopped him. I ordered everyone to hide behind the bushes in front of which we were standing so that the man who was calling and would appear at any moment in the clearing before us should not see us. When I ordered Boy and one of the porters to come with us the two refused to move. Yet since my intention was to convict Boy either of ignorance of the situation or of perfidiousness, and since I wanted to reassure my people who began to get worried, I grabbed both of them by the neck. I pushed them forward by force and then threw them down to the ground rather harshly. Then I quickly took away from Boy the rifle which I had entrusted to him and gave it to Fekete. My companions looked at me with surprise, they could not understand my behaviour. But after a few words everything was clear to them. 'Listen carefully to the caller. Don't you hear that the caller from whom Boy got his "frightening" news approaches us far too slowly? For if these words were coming from someone who is escaping and rushing to us in a great fright they should become clearer and clearer with every minute and the caller should have reached us five minutes ago. I think that this bogy is slowly coming closer quite leisurely, assuming that we are much further ahead. This is the best proof for all of you that the whole thing is a wicked conspiracy supposed to intimidate us.'

Boy was trying to catch as much as he could of my words which I spoke as low as possible. And indeed, his face began to take on a friendly expression and to cheer up. He began to understand me. Was Boy really innocent, knowing nothing of the conspiracy? Could he have been a deceived instrument and was his fear true? These thoughts were whirling through my mind. The changes I noticed on the face of the leader of my servants soon convinced me that Boy had nothing to do with the whole plot, that he was indeed suffering from great fear inspired by the porters and the Maschukulumbe during the past night, and that now the leader of the porters coming behind us had thrown him into a true fright.

This observation relieved us greatly and we kept completely quiet. Then we heard the same calls again. The words seemed to be uttered even faster and in great fear. Peeping through the leaves of the bush we soon spotted the man whom our small group was awaiting desperately, each with a different kind of feeling. Indeed, it was the first guide of the carriers; Boy had recognised his voice correctly. He was walking along slowly. In a leisurely fashion he took a pinch from his reed tobacco-pouch which was hanging around his neck from a strap. Then he stopped, looked around, and then walked on carefully. He had already passed through half the clearing, stopping several times, and had come as close as fifty steps from us. Calmly and coolly bending his upper body backwards he once again burst out in that frightening call. But this time he had not yet finished his cry when I rushed out from behind the bush. I reached him so quickly that his cry died in his throat. Realising that we saw through his game he stood petrified, anticipating the worst. All my people, even Boy, were on to his tricks and without allowing him a word or even stopping him we turned around and went on. The culprit, too, had recovered from his shock. He turned around in order to report the failure to his companions and to tell them that my *malemo* (medicine, charms) was too strong, that nothing would help them, that I knew everything and that they had to follow me. We had hardly walked 1 km when we heard behind us the slapping of the porters' sandals hitting the hard and dried-out path.

The porters had struck and had refused to move, but when we had not come back in spite of the 'bogy' they sent behind us, the situation changed considerably. The same Matoka carriers who had tried so hard to intimidate us the day before in front of the Maschukulumbe, now all of a sudden began to be afraid among the Maschukulumbe of Kaboramanda who pressed around them closely. They were glad to leave this place. Since they were afraid, however, that the Maschukulumbe would not let them go at a low price they threw them the eland meat which was hanging over the fence of our camp and which was supposed to be carried after us by Maschukulumbe porters. When they caught up with us they used the excuse saying that the Maschukulumbe had taken my food away from them by force. I knew very well that the Maschukulumbe were very keen on venison and also that they considered hunting too much of an effort. Thus, the unautho-rised present from my servants was very welcome for them. While they—in some cases even master and servants—were fighting for the meat among each other, our porters used this opportunity to disappear into the nearest bushes. Thus, they cleared the camp which they had not been willing to leave in the morning under any condition unless they were paid.

The journey of 21 July was 27 km long. It led us in the first ten kilometres in a north-north-western direction, then for 5 km west by north, then for 6 km north by west, and it ended in a north-north-western course in Bosango-Kasenga. The turns in the sixteenth and twenty-first kilometres were almost at right angles. There was in fact a direct path in a north-north-western direction from Kabora-manda to Bosango yet it had not been shown to us by the men, even though one woman had pointed it out. A second path branched off in the twelfth kilometre and both then linked up with the main path in the twenty-first kilometre. So we had taken a longer detour which was very hard on us in particular on that hot winter day. Yet I had passed through a more interesting area than if I had taken the direct way through the bush. For the first 3 km it went through the mukuluani palm forest which I have mentioned before. Then it went through a sub-tropical wood similar to that in the lower Tschobe valley with respect to the arrangement and distribution of groups of trees which, often surrounded by dense shrubs and liana growth, were a magnificent sight. It was here that almost all our carriers finally caught up with us, together with a delegation of Maschukulumbe which was probably sent on our behalf to the next chief. From the fourth kilometre on we had this wood on our left whereas on our right we had an open plain covered with high grass. This plain was delimited far in the east by an overgrown laterite ridge but in the north-east it appeared to stretch endlessly. The whole plain was a huge thicket of giant grass through which the Monjeko flowed. During the dry season there were many fens and ponds while during the flood season it looks like a single lake. In that time this area is exclusively populated by waterbuck whereas at the time of our journey, i.e. in winter, the giant grass was teeming with many different kinds of game.

In the seventh kilometre our path crossed a densely overgrown sandy ridge stretching towards north-north-east. It was traversed by such broad buffalo paths that at first I thought there might be a large cattle herd of the Maschukulumbe nearby. However, a close inspection of the tracks and assurances from the blacks convinced me that there was an extremely large number of buffalo living in this area. Of course, it would have been rather unpleasant for us if we had suddenly encountered such a herd of buffalo in the bush which formed impenetrable under-growth in places. Fortunately we were spared such an encounter.

When we walked up the low laterite ridge there was an incident which con-vinced us clearly that the Maschukulumbe who had proved to be considerably more arrogant in Kaboramanda than in M'Beza would become bolder every day. For an hour already some Maschukulumbe had been walking next to us. They were the delegates sent by the chief of Kaboramanda. They also were under secret orders to observe us closely and, so to speak, to study us on our journey. I do not know whether these men were instigated by our porters or whether they did what I am going to relate now on their own initiative with the intention of making us feel their power in their own territory. All of a sudden two Maschukulumbe stepped in front of me at the head of the column. They blocked the small path and called on me to stop and wait until all the porters had come close, since some had stayed behind and could easily be killed or robbed by their comrades, i.e. the inhabitants of Kaboramanda. I kept cool and said 'When I left the camp I ordered all porters to leave too. Yet they refused to follow me. It is their own fault if anything happens to them. If my belongings should be stolen in the course of this, I shall go and get them back.' Boy translated my words for the two of them and as soon as he had finished I ordered them to get out of my way. When they did not move I pushed them aside and continued on my way. They stood there astonished at the side of the path. Later they stayed behind and did not bother us any more, as they had done before when they had made remarks while they were walking alongside us and even at times had juggled their spears. On that sandy ridge overgrown with bush we got into such dense areas that I myself became slightly worried about the fact that some of our porters still lagged far behind. Thus I stopped in a little clearing for an hour's rest and awaited the last stragglers.

Only when everybody had finally arrived did we go on. Until the fifteenth kilometre we marched in a west by north direction. Stretches of bush alternated with clearings overgrown with giant grass and some shade trees. Between the twelfth and thirteenth kilometres we passed a second laterite ridge and between the fourteenth and fifteenth kilometres we passed another such ridge; neither was as densely overgrown with bush as the first one.

In the twelfth kilometre we reached a kraal and here a second path branched off towards north-west. This was the direct way to the place of our destination. The Maschukulumbe who had accompanied us stayed behind here. After they had talked with some of the villagers, most of whom were working in the nearby fields, the latter refused to show us the right way. Instead they pointed to the north and indeed we took the northern path. In the fourteenth kilometre we reached a second village fenced in by high poles. We followed the path through the village until we came to the edge of the bush and were standing at the edge of a valley through which the Monjeko which here perhaps was called the Luenge—was winding. Yet numerous lagoons blocked our way. There was no kraal anywhere in the high grass and the much sought-after Bosango-Kasenga was not to be seen. I was absolutely positive that we were in the Luenge valley and that Bosango lay further westwards since the broad paths branching off to the north-west at Kaboramanda and the one in the twelfth kilometre led there. I was sure that we had only to go straight westwards in order to hit one of the two paths. The heat was great that day; in this area we had been less able than usual to walk in the shade; furthermore, we had only had a very light snack early in the morning in order to get out of Kaboramanda quickly. Accordingly we were all as tired and exhausted as if we had walked 25 instead of 15 km. But there was no time for complaints and hesitations. We simply could not stay here; we had to go on towards the west in order, first of all, to find the right path. Thus, I followed a strictly western direction. To our right the area was covered with giant grass bordered by high reeds in the distance. Every now and then along the lagoons we found boggy areas covered with short grass in which hundreds of crested cranes strutted. Large groups of lechwe and occasionally puku were grazing. We were too tired to fire a single shot and walked on quietly. In the area before us the Maschukulumbe had burnt the grass and we soon reached this blackened stretch. Fortunately the wind was blowing the fire westwards so that this little bushfire could not harm us. The heat of this southern African winter day was so great that we were hardly able to walk in the hot sand. The heat from the ground came through the soles of our light desert boots. Finally after 21 km we found the path we had been seeking. It followed here a north-north-eastern course across a small elevation in the valley and then entered a group of trees which limited the horizon. When we got closer we could see in the setting sun some huts under the trees which soon turned out to be the much desired twin village Bosango-Kasenga.[2] Even though our path for the last 6 km had gone straight through the Luenge valley and although the double village was supposed to be situated on the Luenge we still could not see anything of the Luenge River itself.

Bosango-Kasenga was situated on one of the numerous slight elevations in the Luenge valley which rise about eight to twelve metres above the river level (figured on the basis of a normal water level during the winter). These elevations run parallel with the river. Close to the river they are overgrown with high sycamores and huge mimosa trees. Further away from the river, however, they are covered with dense bush. These elevations originated in earlier flood periods. During the summer floods these elevations form small islands on which the natives build their huts and kraals. The whole day long and, in particular, on the last stretch of our march, we saw thousands of ant-hills as big as haystacks and overgrown with thick grass. In between large herds of zebras, striped gnus, eland, and kabonda gazelles grazed. At times we even saw reedbuck and oribi here and there.

Our moral victory over the porters and their Maschukulumbe collaborators had cheered my servants up somewhat. Boy even had the courage to venture off the path to stalk game. Shortly after our arrival in Bosango he came with the good news that he had shot an eland bull and a zebra mare. Faced with the prospect of fresh juicy meat the porters and the Maschukulumbe were immediately ready to go back with Boy in order to get the game. When I learned that the 'ruler' was living in the western part of Bosango I sent a messenger there to find out under which of the sycamore trees growing between the two villages I was supposed to pitch camp. One cannot simply stay under any tree; some of these trees are consecrated to ancestors and others are used as council meeting places by the Maschukulumbe.

While I was considering all this three Maschukulumbe introduced themselves to me as subchiefs. They told me that I could not see the village chief Siambamba[3] since we were Luanika's spies and Luanika's men had years before (i.e. in 1882) taken away all his herds and had killed his men and women. Furthermore the chief was ill, so they said, and demanded that I gave some blankets as presents to him and his three subchiefs (i.e. to the three gracious gentlemen standing in front of me). I told them 'Indeed, he shall get some yet; my companions will have to greet him in my name and will have to bring him personally my blankets. Otherwise I shall not send anything.' I said this because I had realised immediately that the three subchiefs were trying to blackmail me.

I also decided to pay the porters right away as already they were sitting around my servants again trying to persuade them to desert us. They told them that they could not survive for three days and that the Maschukulumbe had decided to exterminate all of us. All too clearly I could realise the effect of these words on our servants whose faithfulness anyway had wavered in recent days. Thus, I wanted to have the black sheep removed as quickly as possible.

When I got down to paying them one load was missing. 'Where is the man?' 'Nothing is missing.' 'Yes, I am missing one bundle and I am not going to pay you before it has been brought here.' The intentions of our porters now became perfectly clear. They discussed the situation among themselves and then they explained that the man had fallen ill and was lying far away in the fields. 'I do not pay before he is here'. Then a few went in order 'to look for him' and in a very short time the quickly 'found' sick man came striding up to us energetically. We laughed about this clumsy trap and the blacks laughed with us even though they were ashamed. I gave the men one and a half sitsibas instead of the one which they had agreed upon. I was glad that I had been able to make them carry my loads so far into the heart of Maschukulumbe country. I would have even given them two sitsibas if they had not been so rebellious and had not made such disgusting scenes. Without grumbling they all accepted their pay except for one man. He was one of the leaders and exactly the one who had incited his fellows and the Maschuku-lumbe against us. More than anybody else it was he who had tried to persuade our servants to desert us. This man did not get as much as one of his mates and he got literally furious about it. He rushed into nearby Bosango and with loud shouts he informed everybody that we were nothing other than Luanika-Lebosche's[4] spies and had come to count the number of cattle in order to report it to the Marutse king. I am sure that any other traveller would have sent a bullet behind him from the camp right through his head since his incitement was like oil on the flames of the Maschukulumbe. We were to realise the effect of his behaviour immediately. Soon a crowd of howling natives accompanied him to our camp. We posted ourselves in front of them. Holding our guns before us we did not allow them to come close. During this event revolution, so to speak, broke out even behind our backs. The porters tried to incite our servants and instead of disappearing the previously paid porters started to grumble about their pay. Taking advantage of the threat of the Maschukulumbe they tried to squeeze something more out of us.

I told them to go away. 'No, we are hungry.' 'All right, then take the zebra meat in addition.' They took it but remained seated and continued to try to talk our servants into deserting us. Since our servants, however, were not prepared to yield right away to their arguments the seducers declared that they would only leave the next morning. Their attitude suddenly changed. They became quiet except for the first ringleader who now turned to accuse them. He called them dogs and asked them whether they were afraid of us five Marutse spies. This was really too much. I aimed my rifle at him and surrounded by the Maschukulumbe he retreated into the village. Half of our servants as well went with the porters to the village in order to hatch new schemes undisturbed by us. These men returned only after midnight and their discussions with those servants who had stayed behind went on for a long time. We were awake all night long since we could not block this conspiracy. Around 3 o'clock in the morning the ringleader showed up again and even had the courage to creep in the dark up to the grass wall. He pushed the grass aside cautiously in order to sneak into our camp. I watched everything and at the moment when he tried to climb in, I hit the thin grass wall with the butt of my rifle. The man screamed and fell over backwards. Then without any further shouts he ran back to the Maschukulumbe village and the porters and servants went back to sleep. The day was already dawning when we who had been on guard all night long lay down on our miserable grass beds. My wife and Oswald took over the watch for the next couple of hours. Finally Aurora announced the coming of the day. Never in our lives had we longed so desperately for the sunrise as during those days which we spent in Maschukulumbe country. In the sunlight we felt relieved. We could breathe more freely. In spite of sleepless and anxious vigils our hands clasped the rifles firmly. In the daytime one at least can see one's enemy eye to eye but the night, indeed, is man's enemy.

Our situation then was already highly critical. I called Boy and Mapani and tried to persuade them to stay with me. They seemed to consider it. This, however, caused the porters to refuse to leave Bosango. When I threw them out of my camp they, indeed, left, but settled down a hundred metres further on under another tree. They were determined not to go until my servants joined them so that all together they could start to travel south—or until another solution materialised, perhaps through the hostile interference of the Maschukulumbe. The latter, however, seemed to be more reserved than the Maschukulumbe in M'Beza and Kaboramanda, but this attitude suggested caution in pursuing their hostile plans rather than any peaceful intentions. In order to put the chief in a favourable mood for us I sent Fekete with two of our servants to him. The natives told him that the chief was not in the village, yet Fekete entered the chief's rounded palisade court, the periphery of which was partially occupied by the huts of the Maschukulumbe. Fekete ordered Boy to ask a girl for the hut of the chief. The girl did not know that the chief was not at home to strangers and pointed immediately to the hut in which the chief supposedly was. When the men who were following Fekete slowly realised this they ran after him and tried to prevent him by force from entering the hut. Fekete, however, pushed them aside and boldly entered the hut.

On a miserable bed covered with cowhides the naked chief was lying, truly a pitiful creature. The hut was filled with the putrid smell of a neglected, pussy wound. One of his shanks was covered with boils from the ankle up to the knee. They had already partially affected the bone. The chief answered Fekete's greetings kindly. After the very first words had been translated my representatives realised that the chief knew nothing about the demands of his people. He seemed to be completely satisfied with the blanket they offered him and he promised immediately to give us porters. When Fekete advised him to see me for help for his festering wound the king did not respond. Yet I was grateful for the good news which my messenger brought back. Even Boy, the fearful, told my servants the truth and shouted across to the porters how kindly my representatives had been accepted by the ruler of Bosango-Kasenga. And after this change of the situation I became somewhat hopeful that I might keep the servants in spite of the previous experiences.

All too soon, however, before I was able to take any action on the favourable prospects for our expedition, they dissolved. Shortly after the return of my messengers the three subchiefs, who are already known to my readers, showed up again led by a giant of a man to whom we soon gave the nickname 'Village Knave II'. They pompously sat down in front of us, called Boy and ordered him to tell us that the king had given our present to a woman slave since it was too poor for him. He had demanded that we should give presents to all of them and should send him a better blanket. He could not give us any carriers and he also would not have any boats to ferry us across the Luenge River. He did not want me to treat him. We had anyway only come to do him harm. During these two days while we were sleeping in the vicinity of his villages his wound had become worse and tomorrow he would have to be carried away, they said, to get out of our hostile presence. In vain, I assured them of the contrary. Instead of defending us and telling the Maschukulumbe how many sick people I had healed my servants were so intimidated that they refused to translate our words for the king's messengers. The worst of their message, however, was the news that the ruler of this area intended to withdraw from our presence. Thus any possibility for fruitful negotiations would have vanished. My servants hurried across to the porters who were still camping under the tree. The Maschukulumbe followed them and they all talked and negotiated quietly. Later I learned that the Maschukulumbe told them that the king would leave for two reasons—firstly, because we would be attacked and massacred and he would not feel safe from our bullets in his hut and secondly, because he wanted to get out of the evil spell which we were supposedly exerting according to the three subchiefs.

I realised that my twenty servants were lost and that I could no longer count on them. 'But what', it all of a sudden occurred to me, 'if I were to try to win over the three subchiefs?' I called them and gave each of them a blanket. To one of them, the giant, who looked the friendliest, I gave the best one. I told him secretly (that much I knew of their language) that he should come back again the same evening to get a second present.

He came and even brought some sweet milk as a present for my wife. He told me that the king was completely satisfied with his blanket. (There was no more mention of a slave woman.)

Well, I was glad about this and I gave him a sitsiba which I had rolled up so that it looked like a scarf. I promised him another sitsiba for each boat which they would lend us to cross the river. I was told that the Luenge was quite near even though we could not see the slightest sign of the river.

When it became dark my servants all asked for a sitsiba as a present and for their total pay, since they would have to leave us. 'No,' I said, 'I am not paying any of you. You committed yourselves to go on further with us if I would give each of you one sitsiba.' 'We shall go back even without pay,' they answered, 'we do not want to be killed by the Maschukulumbe.' 'As long as you stick to us faithfully, nobody will do you any harm', I claimed. But it was in vain. Immediately half of them moved all their things over to the porters for the night. Thus they demonstrated, so to speak, physically their departure from the job. Among those who left their things in our camp even though they were sitting together with the other crowd, was Boy. He came back to us after midnight and asked for a rifle. I no longer wanted to lend it to him because of his dubious behaviour during the last two days. 'For what do you need it?' I asked. 'There are lions in the vicinity. The Maschukulumbe are afraid and we have to protect them.' After a short while Boy again came up to us claiming that he just had heard some lions and that I should allow him to fire just two shots into the air. Since we were all watching him I handed him a rifle. Yet as soon as I had done so I realised how unwise this was since he could easily have shot me or one of my people before we could have shot him down. I believe firmly that this had actually been his intention. He became afraid, however, when he realised how closely all of us were watching him in the bright moonlight. I had given him only two cartridges for the Werndl carbine. These he fired quickly into the air and when he wanted to have more I simply took the rifle away from him.

Muschemani, our sick servant, disclosed to us two days later that it had been Boy's intention to run away with the rifle. Whether he had planned to kill us he did not know. Boy had thought that we would no longer be awake at midnight and he had based his original plan to steal a rifle on this assumption.

The next morning we heard loud yelling and shouting in both villages. The Maschukulumbe were running back and forth. The Matoka porters mixed with them. As the ringleader had again joined them they still showed no signs of leaving. I ordered them to leave the place otherwise I would chase them off with some bullets. I realised all too well that this crowd in the end would get my servants to desert us and to flee. Their desertion, however, would have been the worst fate that could have befallen us there. When the porters began to jeer at me we got ready to shoot and this threat helped. These creatures jumped up and half an hour later there was no porter left in our immediate vicinity. Our black servants, however, had stayed behind in the porters' camp. If only Boy had not been such a coward! He, who enjoyed such great respect among the porters that we whites had often distinguished him from the others because of his other good qualities, now infected all his fellows with his fear and shook their usual faithfulness and loyalty.

The yelling and shrieking in the two villages between which we were camping increased. Soon some Maschukulumbe showed up, their chests, necks and faces whitened with chalk. Each of them was carrying a spear decorated with a tuft of feathers. We looked at them in astonishment without knowing that this meant war and hostility. My servants, however, were so frightened that six of them ran to Bosango in order not to be attacked; they thus became deserters. Soon afterwards we saw them, however without their things, walking south-westwards together with the carriers and a group of Maschukulumbe into the bushes surrounding the valley. Boy ran after them and came back with the report that he had been invited like all of them over there to spend a day and a night in festivities with the king in his kraal in the bush. They would slaughter an ox and much beer would be drunk. I let him go. A strange train now left Bosango. Some of the fantastically painted Maschukulumbe carried a wooden stretcher with a man lying on it. He was Bosango-Kasenga's ruler, the man with the festering wound who let himself be carried to another kraal so that he would not be present during the planned attack on us. Several women followed with beer. A few children and some men made up the rear-guard. When we saw the porters leaving we were glad that we were finally rid of them, not knowing that they would come back again during the night.

The day passed rather quietly. Our servants were lying around obstinately and refused to do any work except for Jonas, Kabrniak, Muschemani and Siroko. The giant showed up again. He was very friendly and brought some fish and flour etc. to exchange. He accepted the glass beads but only at second-hand—namely from my wife. He confessed, with Jonas translating, that his colleagues had persuaded the chief to leave Bosango but he did not tell us that an attack was planned. In fact, from his later behaviour, I would almost believe that the giant had not been let into the secret of this nefarious plot. In order to make him even more obliging I presented him with a set of rifle medals which the Viennese firm of Witte had given us. And after my wife had strung them onto a thread he strutted like a peacock around our camp with the necklace of medals around his neck. He even brought his two wives to introduce them to us and they seemed to be rather friendly and not as ill-humoured creatures as all the other women we had met so far in these areas. Their friendliness caused Oswald, to our astonishment, to make a laudatory oration on the Maschukulumbe. He claimed that they were not as bad as we always thought. Since in his speech he every now and then used a Sesuto word our striking servants understood him. They interrupted him with *Naja-naja* (no, no) to indicate that Oswald did not understand the Maschukulumbe at all and that they were anything but good!

It became dark and the night fell quickly. This night I shall never forget even if I live to be a hundred years old. Already at dusk the hyenas began their usual night howling. With these sounds the painted Maschukulumbe and also the porters returned. Boy consulted with them at a little distance from us. The result of this consultation was that those servants who still had their things in our camp now began to pack their belongings and to roll up their bed skins. For me this was a clear sign that they now really were prepared to leave and to escape. I told this to my people, but nobody wanted to believe my words, Oswald in particular. I suspected that our servants would not just simply leave but would try to rob us in order to get their pay by force since they were not going to get it otherwise as they had broken their contract. In order to prevent such a raid I immediately made a counter-plan. I ordered the camp fires extinguished, pretending that the bright light would hurt our eyes. I had a cooking and night fire made forty paces to the left and another thirty paces in front of us at the end of the servants' camp. Thus our camp was dark while there were many fires around the porters' camp which gave a lot of light. I called Leeb, who understood the situation best of all, and we sat down in the dark part of our camp with the carbines in our hands, observing closely everything which was going on outside. My wife, Oswald and Fekete were sitting at the cooking fire. They were laughing at funny tales which Mapani and Jonas were spinning. The sudden gaiety of the two servants confirmed my suspicion even more that they were trying to deceive us and to distract our attention from the camp since these two servants especially had been rather ill-humoured, rude and insolent during the days before. In the other camp we could see that my servants were seriously preparing for their escape. They dug up the ground and took out the treasures which they had hidden there without anybody noticing it. Among these things were the sitsibas they had already earned, strings of glass beads and a number of stolen trifles which were no use to us such as empty cartridges, rifle medals, etc. All of this they wrapped into skins which they then carried a few metres into the dark of the night. Muschemani and Siroko had wrapped themselves in their blankets and were lying at the first fire in front. They kept away from the strike. Then Chimborasso came and shook both of them awake. He succeeded in making Siroko waver. Mapani came from the cooking fire with his cooking spoon still in hand pretending to be completely innocent. He posted himself next to the fire and without stooping down he talked with Siroko in a low voice as I could see from the movement of his lips. He talked to him at length until Siroko, too, got up, grabbed his blanket and other belongings, and then joined the others in the camp on the other side. Mapani left also and only Jonas stayed behind. Under no condition could I let Jonas run away as well. He was my best interpreter and was somewhat personally attached to me. I simply had to keep him. I called my people and had Oswald observe Jonas. 'What, Jonas should run away? He is as faithful as a rock, Doctor', he said. 'Stay close to him,' I said 'I expect at any moment now the sudden flight of the servants if they do not shower us first with their spears.' Oswald sat down in front of Jonas without any arms. 'Oswald,' I said 'where is your rifle? You must arm yourself.' Oswald asked Leeb to hand him his carbine because at this point the expressions and glances of the ever so 'faithful' Jonas made him suspicious as well. He got up from his camp stool so that he could react more quickly in the case of an escape by the suspect. 'Leeb,' I said, 'help Oswald—otherwise Jonas might run away from him.' My wife and Fekete, to whom the behaviour of the servants was now all too clear, took over Leeb's watch. Jonas had heard my orders and before Leeb was even able to leave our camp Jonas threw down his blanket from his shoulders between Oswald's feet. With a shout he leaped forward and was welcomed by the yells and shouts of the other servants. In the next moment he disappeared into the dark in the direction of nearby Bosango. Leeb ran after him, but immediately some of the servants got up to protect Jonas. Afraid for Leeb's life, I ran a short distance after him to call him back. Soon he was at my side and all of us retreated into our camp. There was shouting to be heard from the village and people were coming nearer. They were the Matoka porters. They mixed with our servants—their ringleader in their midst waving his spears high over his head. Some of our servants, unarmed, approached their former camp situated right next to ours. They seemed to be still looking for something. Behind them, as we could see clearly, a few armed Matoka were sneaking closer. Each of us was on guard at one side of the camp. Leeb and I stood guard together on the side which faced the servants' camp. It was divided into two by the trunk of the big sycamore tree and thus could not be watched very well by only one person. I was watching the right, Leeb the left. All of a sudden he shouted 'Thieves, thieves!' And with a single jump the two of us were outside in front of our camp. One of the Matoka had pushed through the grass wall and was trying to grab the towels which happened to be lying on top of our bundles. He had already pulled them out when we jumped up to him. This sudden attack, which they had not expected, caused a terrific confusion among the blacks. Everybody ran and rushed about without any plan and order with the aim only of getting away. In seconds the place was deserted. I hesitated for a moment and I heard my people shout 'Shoot, shoot.' 'No!' I shouted back and then ran after my servants. I ran until I reached the area between the two kraals which constitute Bosango. I heard the flapping of the sandals of my fleeing servants before me, yet it was so dark that I could not recognise anything. A bullet fired into this group of deserters would have been, indeed, well deserved but that was just what the Maschukulumbe were waiting for. They hoped that we would shoot into the night and thus provide them with a good reason for their attack, so that they could say that we had shot at them first, that we had shot into their huts and thus had broken the peace. This was my consideration when I gave strict orders not even to shoot the hyenas who came to get the bones scattered around our cooking place.

The fires served as my guides like lighthouses and I returned safely back to our camp. That indeed, was a sad evening. Frightened by the screaming of the blacks my donkeys and goats had freed themselves and we had to look for them first of all in the darkness and to tie them fast again. Then all fires were put out except for the one small outpost fire at the end of the servants' camp. Before all of us, including my wife, went on our night watch we gathered for a quarter of an hour around this watchfire. Our group had become very small. No words came from our lips but our eyes said more than words. Oswald was gazing at the ground, Leeb's eyes were seeking mine with the question, what should be done? My wife held my hand as if she was afraid that any moment I might have to rush out again into the dark night and perhaps for ever. She tried to hide her tears and was bending down deep over the fire.

Never before had I heard the flames crackling so hatefully and so scornfully as that night. I felt as if I was standing right in the fire. The ground became hot under my feet, I was panting and I had difficulty breathing. There we were deserted and just at the moment when we were about to make such an important step forward by crossing the Luenge.

All of us felt that the desertion of our servants had brought a catastrophy upon our expedition. Henceforth the question of porters and of our penetrating further north was completely in the hands of the Maschukulumbe. We felt instinctively that under these conditions we would no longer be able to proceed much further; none of us, however, considered returning with our former porters.

The warm tears of my wife which began to fall more frequently on my hand brought me back to reality. I tried to console her, my white companions and myself and to cheer us up. Of course, little of comfort could be said since our situation was plainly desperate. Only by a miracle could we be saved. And yet we all agreed 'onwards to the north!'

While we were standing there distressed and quietly racking our brains for an idea for salvation we heard a husky laughter coming through the deadly silence of the night in our immediate vicinity. All of us looked to the spot from where it came. Only then did we discover Muschemani, the Makalaka who had been squatting all that time next to the fire. He alone had stayed. He whom we always mistrusted was the most faithful soul of all.

I slapped him on his shoulder and now wanted to hear what he knew. Yet it was too dangerous to stay too long at the outpost fire leaving the near camp unguarded. Also, it was personally dangerous to be in the light of the fire and thus a target for the spears of enemies who were perhaps sneaking up on us. Thus we put out even this last fire and went back into the camp where each of us mounted his guard for this night. There I sat down with my carbine in my hand so that I could look over to the hostile camp and listened to the report of the 'last faithful'.

'Ha, ha, ha, indeed,' he said, 'they had intended to leave you a long time ago. Boy—Boy is a snake even though he is from the same tribe as I am. Mopani, Siroko, Kabrniak, Monohela, Katonga and Moruma did not want to leave. They did not want to leave "Missis" killed by the Maschukulumbe but the others persuaded them and so they ran away along with them. The Maschukulumbe will still kill us tonight, so they said. The Matoka were instigating the Maschukulumbe, telling them that your sacks contain many valuable *impandes* and many other beautiful things. The Maschukulumbe promised some oxen to the Matoka if they would make us flee and they promised not to kill us if we would run away.' Needless to say after this report, which left nothing to be desired in clarity and brevity, I could not get a wink of sleep that night in our camp.

The extinction of all fires made the enemies give up their planned attack in the dark. Later at night we enjoyed moonlight. Yet we did not notice anything suspicious except for the howling hyenas roaming about. Shortly before daybreak

Muschemani noticed something dark in the bottom of the valley towards the south-east. We all strained our eyes. Indeed, there was something which seemed to move and to come closer. '*Batu, Batu*', the black was whispering. Yes, these were people approaching in single file. About 300 paces before us they stopped and then suddenly turned left towards Kasenga. They had probably thought that we were asleep. When they realised that we were awake they retreated. They were about sixteen that we could count.

Early in the morning the giant showed up. This time he had thrown a piebald oxskin over his shoulders—otherwise he was, as usual, completely naked. With affected regret he listened to the tale of our servants' flight. Then he jumped to his feet and pointed south into the distance where—as Muschemani with his experienced eyes confirmed—the group of our servants were marching southwards through the bush. Their retreat sealed our deplorable fate and yet we could not allow them to notice any trace of distress or depression if we at all wanted to get away from Kasenga.

The Maschukulumbe believed that because of the flight of our servants we were completely at their mercy and consequently very depressed. Yet we were laughing and joking as if nothing had happened and in order to confuse them completely I decided to go hunting together with Leeb about six kilometres away. Later on I never dared anything like that any more. Before I left I called all my people and handed each of them a rifle. Then I indicated this and that with gestures so that the Maschukulumbe began to feel alarmed and many even left the vicinity of our camp.

Hardly a third of a mile away from camp we found numerous game. Leeb wounded a male zebra with a bullet and I killed him quickly. 'The shooting helped,' my wife said, 'the giant and his Maschukulumbe withdrew from our camp when they heard the shots.' When later on we still shot at some game from our camp the blacks even asked us not to do it again since it was too frightening. We tried to exploit the friendliness of the giant to get as much as possible out of him. First he gave me a herd boy to watch my animals so that I could have Muschemani all the time with me as translator. We gave the giant presents again and again in order to get him more and more on our side. Indeed he became so docile that he literally obeyed my wife's words. It was only sad that his influence on his own people was so very weak. In general, I found the relationship between the chiefs and their subjects among the Maschukulumbe to be the loosest existing in all of southern Africa. Thanks to the giant we paid the lowest prices in exchanges for food and in our purchases of firewood and drinking water. With the help of Sesuto my wife began to ask him about the Seschukulumbe language and he translated willingly all the words she asked. The most important ones we took down. After a few days we were able to get along with the Maschukulumbe even in the absence of Muschemani. As often as we were alone with the giant I discussed the question of the porters which for us was the most burning issue of all. After a lot of talk back and forth he finally told me about the decision his compatriots had made in this respect. His report was even more disadvantageous for us than we had expected. The conditions they had set up for the transport of our things proved to be 300 per cent more expensive than those we had to accept from the Matoka. And those had seemed to us already very onerous. The conditions under which we were to get porters here were the following:

1 From our camp to the Luenge river women were to carry our loads so that they, too, could earn something. Their pay should be glass beads.
2 From the Luenge on, as was usually the case with all other tribes, the men were to carry our loads—but only to the next village.
3 This next village should never be further away than one day's journey from the place of departure—because the Maschukulumbe want to sleep at night in their own huts and want to drink the milk of their own cows in the evening. If the next village were further they would drop our things, go home for the night, and come back sometime the next morning in order to carry the loads further but not for too long so that they could be back home in the evening. In general, however, the villages are situated rather close together.
4 The payment for each trip, regardless whether it was a quarter of a day or two days long was one *kubu*, i.e. two sitsibas of 4 m calico each. This was along the Luenge the value of one ox which costs in that area about 12 guilders.
5 Payment had to be made before the departure.
6 Chiefs and subchiefs, etc. claimed special presents in the form of sitsibas, *kubus*, glass beads and other glittering things.

I had expected to find less stiff conditions than among the Matoka where we had to pay porters for two to six days' service two metres of calico each and some foodstuffs. Of course, this payment had been agreed upon only after much effort and many difficulties and had only been granted to me as a doctor after a cure which had enhanced my reputation considerably. Here among the Maschukulumbe, as I said before, I had unfortunately no chances at all as a physician and this was our misfortune. I had hoped to find increasingly better conditions of wages the more we penetrated further north, i.e. into areas which had been touched already by Arab traders coming from the east coast. Yet I found instead increasingly worse ones. After the first shock of these exorbitant demands was overcome we began to comprehend them. The Maschukulumbe simply understood very well that we were in their power absolutely and completely. They could press us as they liked, we could scream but, in fact, we could do nothing against it. Thus we were for them a rather rich object for robbery.

The reasons why their demands were stated in the given form are so interesting that I want to explain them in some more detail. That they were asking for one *kubu*, i.e. two sitsibas of calico, had its reason in the Maschukulumbe fashion. The fashion of the Matoka, Mankoya, Matabele, Makalaka and Mabunda, i.e. to wear aprons of leather and animal pelts as aprons, or calico sitsibas or belts as clothing, is not known to them. Only when it is very cold do they wear a roughly cured cowhide thrown over their shoulders, or if they want to dress at all in foreign clothing they wear a piece of cloth equal in size to a cow-hide, i.e. a blanket. Yet since only calico is imported by the Portuguese *mambari* across the border they use as official coats two sitsibas of calico (i.e. two pieces of 2 m each) sewn together lengthwise.

They asked for payment in advance since they wanted to leave it right away at home so that they could not be robbed in the next village. These petty potentates are constantly at war with each other; they steal each other's cattle if they happen to be grazing in the neighbour's territory, etc.

The Maschukulumbe do not go beyond the next village since every settlement which could even half way claim to be called a village has its own ruler and he can raid the neighbours even if they are of the same tribe.

Because of their great cowardice and laziness, as they are not used to working, the act of carrying our loads for a whole day is extremely exhausting for them. It would be even more so if they had to carry our loads for two days, i.e. about four to five hours each day.

Finally, the fact that they wanted to drink the milk of their own cows each night has not only as a reason their desire for their home village or their childish fear of unknown areas, but was rather an expression of their jealousy of their own wives. There is a shortage of women among the Maschukulumbe which causes the 'beauties' to be much desired and to act quite coquettishly. This is why the 'masters of the world' do not want to sleep even one night outside of their own huts.

I tried to ease these onerous conditions as much as possible. Despite the support of the giant, I succeeded only in one point. This was that the women as carriers were eliminated completely, and instead the men were to carry our loads straight from our camp into the next village north of the Luenge. This rather useful agreement caused open hostility from all these black furies since they did not want to be left out of action at any cost. The giant was put to flight twice by the women of the village Kasenga and hardly escaped being beaten up by them. Such is the nature of the authority of a second-rank Maschukulumbe chief.

As unfavourable as the question of porters was, I also learned, thanks to my generosity, some favourable things from the giant. One thing was that after the departure of my Matoka carriers the inhabitants of this twin village did not feel strong enough to attack us. He had strongly advised those who had assassination plans against such an attempt in view of our arms which were much feared everywhere. On the other hand, he was afraid that the two villages would not be able to provide me with the necessary number of porters since one group of men had to guard the chief in his residence in the bush and another had to watch the cattle. In spite of all these peaceful-sounding reports I took measures of greater caution after the escape of our servants. In particular, I broke up the camp of our porters so that our camp stood freely in the open. Accordingly it would not be possible for enemies to creep near us that easily or to threaten us with fire. It was quite obvious that the enemies could lay fire to the grass walls of our servants' camp at a time when the wind might have blown the flames towards our camp. Muschemani, the last servant, now had to sleep in our camp. In order to make this possible without any danger for us I gave him soap and had him wash himself thoroughly in one of the nearby ponds. Then I gave him some mercury ointment as pomade for his hair. I ordered him to throw away his dirty blanket and gave him a new one. The bundles which had been stacked along one camp wall now were piled up in the middle of our camp. We slept around them during the nights.

In order to find out finally how far the Luenge river was from our camp—and it could not be too far since the Maschukulumbe often brought us fresh fish for sale —I observed them through my field glasses from the top of a huge nearby ant-hill. I realised that the river had to lie about two to two and a half kilometres further north. Its old and partly dried-out bed was situated on our side. It was teeming with large flocks of waterbirds from which I gathered that it was free from crocodiles. Here, too, the Maschukulumbe usually fished. Even though we had been used to seeing a number of otherwise shy species of birds moving around the blacks' kraals in a rather tame fashion, we were quite surprised about the be-haviour of the crested cranes, the pied crows (*corvus scapulatus*) and the huge trum-peter hornbills. Nowhere else had we seen the first and the last species so tame. Never before had we been able to get as close as forty paces from them. Ever since we had entered the region of the northern Zambezi I had been forced to give up the collection of birds; thus we had no reason to betray their confidence in any way. There was also plenty of game very close to the camp.

At the end of July all of a sudden a true passion for building broke out in the twin villages. They were partly repairing badly damaged huts and they were partly building completely new ones. They went about this with a half-heartedness and laziness which would have upset even our most ill reputed village carpenters. People build here for three to four months in order to be finished by October immediately before the rains set in. Here, too, the work is done by the women; the men only bring them the building materials. But what a difference between the industriousness of the Betschuana women and the attitude of the women of these tribes, even though they have all the material they need right there—even a good sandy clay for plaster which the Betschuana women have to get from far away.

While making these observations, however, I did not forget my journey for a single moment. Because of my insistence the giant was finally persuaded to make some efforts to get people from the neighbouring villages and thus to get together a sufficient number of porters. I was promised porters for 25 July; however, they only wanted to carry for us as far as we could get in one day. Since I feared this I insisted that we had to get at least across the Luenge on that day. After long per-suasion they finally granted me this and our Village Knave II asked me which direction we wanted to take on the other side of the river. He suggested that we should go northwards. But because of the large swamps we would first have to go eastwards and then north-westwards in order to go through a narrow pass to reach as quickly as possible a 'pale face'—as we were—who was supposed to live two days' journey beyond the border with the Mankoja. The last confession I could get out of him by means of several brass combs which looked very good in his hair was, 'the Maschukulumbe south of the Luenge are bad, and I do not know myself why you have not yet been killed. Yet we are antelopes in comparison to those who live across the river. They are hyenas who do not spare us, their brothers, if we show up over there. You have to reach the Mankoja fast, otherwise your death is inevitable.'

A piece of cloth was his reward for these true words which among the Maschukulumbe are so rare. The chief ran hither and thither until he had mustered together the number of porters he thought to be sufficient; even women and children came along with the carriers. It was a loud crowd of about 200 people. The women were shouting at us and were threatening us with their fists. In fact, some of them joined forces and tried to chase some of the men away by throwing stones and the firewood which was lying around at them—just so that they would get the porters' job to the Luenge. I ordered the crowd, which was surrounding us closely, to stand back. Only after they had withdrawn on all sides to about twenty paces did we get busy with our loads. We arranged them in two rows side by side; there were about seventy-five pieces. Then I got out some raw linen, died calico, and the 2 m long colourful sitsibas sewn together from sackcloth. I let the people choose one of the three kinds. With one voice they all shouted for the last and least valuable kind. Then we fixed two sitsibas to each load and after we had made sure that each bundle had its payment properly attached we quickly stepped back and gave them the sign to pick up the loads.

That was a merry yelling and shouting! In a jiffy the screaming crowd rushed to the loads. We could see nothing but a heaving clump of people out of which every now and then was sticking a spear and in which innumerable hands and feet were in hasty motion. When this clump dispersed smaller groups were formed. While about half the porters took their loads a little to the side to indicate that they were paid and were willing to carry for us, others came up to us, threw their loads in front of our feet, swearing that they had had no pieces of cloth fastened to them. Of course, the calico pieces had been stolen from these bundles, had been hidden by the women under the skins hanging down around their legs. Thus, willy-nilly, some loads had to be paid for twice. This was one of the advantages of advance payment to the porters! But now we could no longer keep the reserved and composed attitude which we had tried to show. The men left some of the loads sitting and we observed how they were folding up the stolen 2 m pieces in order to get away with their booty more easily. The next moment I jumped right into this gang of thieves. They escaped as much as it was possible in this dense crowd surrounding us. I could only get a hold of two sitsibas which they dropped. My wife, who was uneasy about my daring in jumping into that mad crowd, had followed me, yet before she knew it she was encircled by men and women who held up torn pieces of calico shouting that we were trying to cheat them and had only fastened one piece of calico instead of two to each load. Of course, there too, the second piece had already been stolen. My poor wife, however, did not know how to get out of this crowd. One of the men twisted his piece of calico together and threw it before her feet and the closely-shaven women were thrusting themselves at her like furies with raised fists. I had just about worked myself out of the crowd which had formed itself around me when I heard my wife's desperate call: 'Emil, Emil, my carbine!' I pushed those who still were pressing me aside with the butt-end of my rifle and rushed to help my wife. Yet as fast as I tried to get there, I came too late. Rosa had got rid of her oppressors by herself. The man who had thrown his piece of calico at her feet had then grabbed her dress—obviously to tear it from her body. She very quickly had hit him so hard between his eyes with her fist that this clumsy hero fell over backwards, knocking down two other heroes standing behind him and inadvertently hitting a woman's eye with his arm. Thus, Rosa was free when I reached her. The other aggressors had withdrawn quickly—the women trying to preserve their military honour by threatening us with their fists even from a distance.

Finally I, together with the giant, succeeded in getting some order into the masses. He was shouting loudly—ordering the Maschukulumbe to start on their march. But then all of a sudden the people shouted: 'No, no, not today, but only tomorrow.' When I heard that I called Muschemani and he had to translate: 'According to our agreement the loads have to be carried right now to the Luenge.' There were interruptions such as 'The Luenge is far—we won't reach it today.' 'This is not true,' I said, 'the sun is still high.' It might have been about 10 a.m. Finally the train started to move slowly, but very unsteadily. I took the giant by his arm. 'Come, Morena', I said and tried to pull him slowly to the head of the train. 'Muschemani,' I said, 'tell them that if the loads are not at the Luenge when the sun will be there—and I pointed overhead—then these rifles will throw bullets from there into their huts and will set them on fire sparing neither men nor women.' For a moment everybody became quiet. The giant—accompanied by four blacks—came with us and while walking he shouted back at his compatriots that they indeed should follow soon. They should be glad that we were leaving their vicinity and our magic thus could no longer harm them.

Only some followed us and with hesitation. After about two and a half kilometres from Bosango we got to the deep river. It was 120–150 m wide and flowing slowly. Its bed was about four to six metres below the bottom of the valley. This was the reason why we had not been able to spot its reeds and its banks overgrown with papyrus stems. The place where we were to cross it was exceedingly bad and could not have been more ideal for an attack of the Maschukulumbe.

On a peninsula, overgrown with prickly reeds and situated four metres below the river banks were a few dugout canoes. At most they would carry two to three people, but their workmanship was not nearly as good as that of the Marutse canoes. On a clear, swampy spot the men dropped their loads and ran away. Only very few stayed on, among them the giant. This place, however, could so easily be covered by spears thrown out of the high grass from above that in case of an attack we would not have had any shelter and could not have resisted the missiles too long.

Thus, just as quickly as they dumped the loads we picked them up again and carried them into the centre of a clear spot. Reeds were gathered quickly to protect us slightly, at least, against the spears of the Maschukulumbe should they have attacked us from above.

When we counted the loads I found that one was missing and that some of our food supply i.e. the fresh zebra meat tied on some of the bundles, the dried fish which we had bought and two calabashes filled with eland fat, had been stolen. I got over the loss of this food, yet I told the giant that I wanted to have the missing load back as soon as possible. He asked around among his few companions who had stayed, where this bundle was. One of them gave him the answer that it still was lying in the camp we had just left, since there had been no carrier for it. Twice they had stolen the pay from it and then they still left it. They probably thought I would not realise the loss and they had planned to let it sit there until the evening and then to take possession of it.

The giant promised—of course, for a further present—to go and get the load and after he had left Muschemani said that the giant as well as all the others would never show up again even though they had been paid to carry our things from the north bank of the river to the next kraal. About an hour later, however, the giant showed up with the load to the surprise of all my people. Now I wanted to cross the river. Yet this again meant arming ourselves with much patience. We had anyway to realise that the time of our forced marches was over and that each step forward had to be paid for with incredible sacrifice of time and money. Here at the Luenge we were stuck for the moment on a small peninsula.

The Maschukulumbe who were hired for the day had a vested interest in letting this day pass by without doing much. Neither good words nor threats were effective against this policy. All of a sudden they felt so tired after that much heavy work that they first had to return home to get something to eat. Also, they said, only two of the owners of the canoes were there and the other two had to be fetched. Thus we had no choice but to let them go. Yet I called the Village Knave back, took him aside into the dense reeds, and took the sitsibas I had promised him as pay and quickly wrapped into them another one. When he left he promised for sure to come back the same evening.

The labours of this day had been hard; we were very hungry and now felt the loss of the stolen food supply doubly hard. The water of the Luenge which is not as deep as the Zambezi, was dirty and of a dark green colour. This came from the numerous swamps on both sides of the river lying partly higher and partly lower than the Luenge. From them dirty and rotting masses of vegetation slowly but steadily drained into the river.

At 4 o'clock the canoe owners arrived. There were fifteen men. Yet after they had been paid two sitsibas (4 m of calico) each for every canoe they went about their job in such a relaxed fashion that I was afraid that they would hardly have loaded the canoes by nightfall. Thus we gave them an energetic hand and loaded the canoes more heavily than they would have liked. We could see through the plans of these overly clever fellows who wanted to drag out the crossing of the river into the dark night in order to be better able to steal things and drag them away.

As soon as the blacks saw that we were working ourselves they no longer

8 *Holub's party crossing the Luenge (Kafue) river*

moved a finger and had us alone load the seventy bundles, in the process of which I even got an unintended free bath.

Finally the canoes were laden for the first time with a total of twenty-eight loads. More we could not entrust to these nutshells which hardly held two people. The first column was led by Oswald who always had great confidence in his influence on the blacks. Then Leeb followed on the second trip with twenty loads, the third one consisted of my wife with twenty-two loads, then followed Fekete with thirteen loads and two dogs, then Muschemani with the goats, then the giant with one of the mules and finally I with Jacob.

As I mentioned before, big animals are not transported in the canoes but have to swim across next to the canoes. Their heads are kept above water by means of their halters. For donkeys this kind of a journey across the river is much more dangerous than, for instance, horses or oxen because of the crocodiles, which are particularly fond of donkey meat. In our case the two mules, in addition, behaved as stupidly as possible. They did all kinds of things to prove correct the prejudice which people have against their mental abilities. Jacob especially tried constantly to jump into the canoe so that I had a very hard time preventing it from overturning.

It was late in the afternoon when I as the last one approached the shore. My wife who had been watching my somewhat dangerous crossing with some apprehension was just stretching out her hand to help me get out of the canoe when I saw something which made my blood boil.

In the next second I was back again in the canoe and grabbed the giant by his throat. '*Bona meschi, meschi*' (look, water, water) I shouted. His companions came quickly in their boats to help him but my people also rushed to my support even though they did not understand my behaviour. But in two minutes' time everything was clear to them as well. They had not taken us to the other bank of the Luenge but to a swampy island, where—after the Maschukulumbe had disappeared with their canoes—we would have been marooned. There they wanted to let us starve since it would have been impossible to escape because of the many crocodiles, and we had no food supply. After we had died all our possessions would have been easy booty for them. This nefarious plot was very cleverly thought out but they did not succeed. As long as we still could lay our hands on even one canoe the odds were in our favour because of our arms. Soon the giant and his noble companions felt our carbines on their chests and this sensation induced them quickly to seize their rudders and take us to the high genuine north bank of the Luenge. We had to employ all our caution to watch that none of the canoes disappeared for good in the dense papyrus while darkness fell.

Yet the efforts and labour of this horrible day were still not over. Since we had only four canoes they had to drive repeatedly back and forth between the southern and the northern bank of the island and we had respectively to load and unload the bundles in a hurry, to keep an eye on everything, and always to hold our rifles at the ready. This was a terrific demand on us. To carry the bundles one by one would have taken far too long. Thus, we each had to take two at a time—i.e. sixty to seventy kilogrammes. Right at the first attempt to carry such heavy loads we got stuck in the swamp. There was nothing else to do but quickly to take off our pants and shoes in order to walk the short distance unhindered by the net-like grass growing high and in profusion out of the swamp. Yet we soon had to give up the attempt to carry two loads at once since we still sank into the swamp half way up our thighs. We could hardly even work our way through with only one load. Soon we were bathed in sweat and black with the mud of the swamp because on each trip we fell down once or twice, caught in the net-like grass. It was getting completely dark and we had to hurry even more to finish our work quickly. 'Four more loads, Doctor', Fekete finally shouted as he heaved two yokes with cartridge containers, i.e. two heavy loads, on to his shoulders with enormous strength. 'Quick, get the goats and the donkeys', I shouted. The goats had to be carried into the canoe and when they were sitting in it with Musche mani, they began to jump. The canoe tipped over and new efforts had to be made before they could be loaded into the canoe a second time and could be ferried across. Then came the last two bundles, one of which was the tent wrapped around its poles in which our flag was rolled up and in which we kept our spare rifles safely.

The last great difficulties were caused by our mules. With quite some effort they were dragged to the boats, yet when they walked into the water their legs got entangled in the net-like plants. After we had freed them and had finally taken them to the opposite river bank we again could not get them out of these plants growing along the water. We had to push them back into the water, to turn them over on their backs and then we dragged them across the dangerous patches of vegetation lying on their backs with their legs sticking into the air.

Finally everything was on the north bank of the Luenge! The blacks were in a hurry to get back home and I was not a little surprised that they had the courage at all to return home in that dark night. We were alone and very worried about what would happen next. The Village Knave, who was the only one I could trust, had promised me, induced by a present, to show up early in the morning together with the porters, but who could guarantee this? Anyway, we had not much time to think of the next sad morning. With incredible efforts we had actually crossed the river together with our luggage and our animals. Our loads, however, were sitting at the water's edge and first had to be transported up the slope of the river bank. It was impossible for us to spend the night down there in the swamp and yet it was just as necessary to stay with and watch our luggage. The slope was only a few metres high; however, being deadly tired as we were, we hardly survived this new effort. The blackness of the night and the crocodiles approaching the river banks strained our nerves to the utmost. I hurried up the slope. Boundless elephant grass covered the river bank up there. Because of its dryness it was rather dangerous to sleep there in this season. Thus I called my wife and Oswald and asked them with their bayonets to cut down the grass for four to five metres around and to throw the straw obtained from this on a pile for our beds. The rest of us hurried down again to carry up our loads. This time Muschemani helped us, too, since his charges, our goats and donkeys, were already lying up there near my wife and Oswald. Even these creatures were so exhausted from wading in the swamp and swimming through the river that they had no desire to eat. It was extremely diffi-cult to get up the slope. The loads seemed to be incredibly heavy and to become heavier and heavier. Our exhaustion increased rapidly. A few hours before when we were still loading the boats each of us lifted and carried one load easily. Now all four of us had to join forces to lift up 40 kg and to put them on our shoulders. Finally carrying the loads became completely impossible and there was no other way out but to tie a strap around each load and thus to pull all our luggage slowly up to our camp. In the meantime they had cleared a place of 8 m² and we began to pile up our luggage. By midnight this was done. Yet even though we were dead tired nobody thought of sleeping. From wading through the swamp most of us were wet; the night, however, was chilly. Therefore we had to look for the pack-ages with our reserve clothing and had to change into dry clothes. Only then we could think of making a fire. Yet where to find fire wood? There was no wood at all around. Along the river we certainly would have found some drift wood yet because of the crocodiles we dared not go to the edge of the water in the dark. Then Oswald detected an old fish trap lying on the river bank and Fekete saw not far from it a broken canoe. This marvellous discovery was greeted by us with loud shouts of joy and a few minutes later the blows of an axe could be heard booming through the quiet night. Soon the canoe pieces were flaring up in two fires which warmed us up. Under the effect of this warmth we all fell asleep except for Leeb and Oswald. For them it was impossible to sleep since they were bothered by an intense feeling of hunger. They searched through everything for something ed-ible. The result of this clearly thorough search was twofold. The first one was that except for two fish which soon were sizzling over the fire, the Maschukulumbe had stolen all the food. The second result was that of those things which had been carried loosely, an axe, a bayonet, a saw, two shirts and several other pieces of Oswald's clothing had been stolen. And Oswald always had such great confi-dence in the blacks!

I woke up early on 26 July. My people were still sleeping deeply and quietly around me. 'Chu, chu' came from the river as if it was being shouted through a megaphone. It was the snorting of the hippoes which woke me up from my world of dreams and brought me back to reality to remind me of my terrible hunger. I grabbed my Winchester. Perhaps I could make out a living creature, for instance, a bird in the reeds who would be the victim of my bullet. On the island which could have become our grave I recognised an *ardea goliath*, the most malicious species of the malicious heron family, the magnificent goliath heron. In order not to frighten my people with a shot I shook them awake and only then I fired. His neck shot through, the bird fell into the reeds—yet how to get him?

While we were thinking about this some shouting on the opposite bank of the river towards the south caught our attention. And indeed, what I had doubted so much yesterday had become true. The Maschukulumbe appeared among the high reeds, led by the giant. An hour later they were with us together with the dead heron. The appearance of the Maschukulumbe porters at the north bank of the Luenge after they had already received their pay the day before was one of the few honest deeds which we have experienced during our stay of several weeks among these tribes. Unfortunately, however, I have to say even their decency was blemished. Four of the porters who had received their payment the day before were missing; in their place four other men had appeared who wanted to carry the loads of the former. Of course, they wanted to be paid in advance for their services.

Before I leave the Luenge I must still remember our tame baboon Pit. After we had finished the exhausting work the night before on the swampy island and were about to leave for the north bank we had not been able to catch the animal. Of course, we were sure that, as usual, he would swim through the river and follow us—however, what about the crocodiles? In spite of our exhaustion we were worried for the life of the baboon to whom we had become very attached and we all—each on his or her own initiative—grabbed our rifles as soon as we heard a splashing in the water which indicated that he was trying to swim across. We succeeded in scaring the crocodiles away by our shooting so that Pit safely reached our shore even though a few hours later than we. When we greeted him and shouted loudly 'Pit, you are back again!', the animal went literally out of his mind with joy. He showed his teeth, chattered with them, and clung to Oswald, his favourite friend, with his wet legs.

Throughout our entire journey north of the Zambezi up to 25 July, the day when we had left Bosango-Kasenga, we had almost nothing but bitter experiences. But all this was nothing in comparison to what we were to experience daily for four weeks from 26 July, the day when we crossed the Luenge. On each of the following days until 22 August there was at least one event which entailed most unwelcome consequences for our Austro-Hungarian Africa expedition.

Yet let us follow the events. On 25 July I told my porters that I intended to go straight north where a range of hills, stretching from north-east to north-west for about fifty kilometres marked the northern border of the Maschukulumbe territory. There was a cut in these hills and in it a narrow pass through which a path was leading. I had to follow it to get out of Maschukulumbe territory north of the Luenge by the shortest route. Unanimously, the carriers refused to go in this direction. Among their fellow tribesmen north of the Luenge all of whom they fear as their enemies, Njambo's,[5] Zumbo's[6] and Masangu's[7] people, who live in the direction of this narrow pass, were supposed to be the worst and most dangerous. My porters were only prepared to go west-north-west or north-east. In the first direction, so they told me, the Village Knave's father-in-law was living. But the Maschukulumbe territory stretched twice as far north there than in the straight northern direction which I had chosen. In addition—and this argument weighed most of all—this stretch was for the most part full of impenetrable swamps. These two reasons unfortunately made me give up this course. Since I had to swallow a bitter pill anyway I chose the north-eastern direction. The high grass and the tall reeds around us hindered our view and when I asked how far it was to the next village the Maschukulumbe told me that we would be there in the afternoon. Under any circumstances they wanted to be back for the night at Bosango-Kasenga. They would not go any further than just before the village Nikoba.[8] Otherwise, they were sure to be killed.

Our way at first led us through harvested maize fields and then through the dangerous high grass and reed thickets. Already during the first three kilometres I could see that it was impossible for the five of us to watch the porters properly and to keep them together. After four kilometres fortunately the left bank of the Luenge was mostly burnt out and at a reasonable distance from the river were some well-used zebra tracks. We were able to use one of them as our path from which we could watch and look around fairly well. The path led alongside one lagoon but in our fifth and sixth kilometres it led straight through two other lagoons stretching from the north-west right across our path so that we simply could not avoid them. I shall remember them for the rest of my life. It was difficult for the Maschukulumbe to get through these two lagoons although they could move about as agilely as monkeys since they were naked. The net-like grass hindered them from walking. One had to help the other and already after crossing

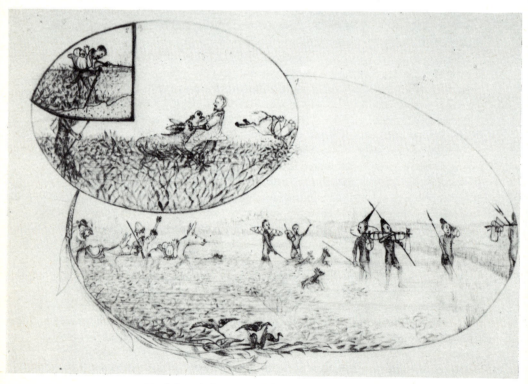

9   *March through the swamp north of the Luenge (Kafue) river*

the first lagoon the whole group had to rest for a full hour since the men were so exhausted from passing through this water. Their exhaustion in the water proved to us immediately what we had to expect for ourselves.

We tried to cross at several places. Finally, we chose one where the zebras seemed to wade through. I first asked Oswald and Leeb to try to get to the other bank. To our satisfaction they succeeded although only after considerable efforts. Yet they were only encumbered with light things. These two were supposed to stand guard on the other side in order to protect us with their rifles while we were trying to work ourselves through the swamp. Much more difficult, however, was the crossing for Fekete Janos, who was trying to carry my wife on his back. With her clothing it was absolutely impossible for her to take even two steps forward in the net grass. Like a true Hercules Fekete tried to do his difficult task and my wife tried to make his noble deed as easy as possible. Not a single minute longer than necessary did she want to be a burden for him and the moment that Fekete reached an area in the water which was not that overgrown with reeds she jumped down and got to the other shore on her own. I was the last one and after Muschemani had barely managed to bring the goats across one by one I now had to drive the donkeys across. I had already succeeded in getting my two mules through some patches covered with grass and even reeds—at the deepest spot the water reached up to my armpits—when we got caught in that terrible net grass. The two mules were trying hard to keep their heads above the water and I could hardly move forward. Jacob, the stronger and more agile of the two donkeys, helped himself forward by pulling out again and again his front legs which were completely entangled in the red creeper. Then he jumped and tried to swim. In this way, indeed, with very quick movements he got across the dangerous vegetation floating 0·5 m below water level and reached a more shallow and less entangled spot. But even so there would not have been much hope that the animal could have reached the other shore safely with his load if Muschemani and Fekete had not rushed to his support and helped him out of the water. The second and much weaker mule, who was an exceedingly block-headed animal, became absolutely stuck. Although the animal might have drowned in the meantime I hurried forward, swimming across the most dangerous spots, in order to give my rifle which I did not want to lose in the river to either Fekete or Muschemani, who were busy with Jacob about twenty metres away from me. Then I rushed back to the mule and realised that he was no longer able to keep himself above water. The animal was snorting and trembling violently. I had to untie his straps and to take off his load of more than sixty kilogrammes and his saddle since otherwise there was absolutely no salvation for him. When I had taken off his load the donkey was able to keep at least his head slightly above water. I tried to reach the shore as quickly as possible with my burden. But, still weak from the exhaustion of the day before, I was hardly able to drag myself those 60 m through the swamp. With such a load on my shoulders I could not think of swimming. That I finally reached the opposite bank of the lagoon was due only to the fact that the porters and my people at this spot had to a large extent already torn the net plants open and thus literally had cleared a path for me. When those resting on the shore saw me with my load they all rushed to my help. Before I returned again to my poor 'asinus' I took off my clothes since they were soaked and bulky with water. They would have hindered me in my work to come. When I got to the animal I first of all began to free his legs. The grass which was entangling them tightly had to be pulled off blade by blade and then I had to trample it down. After I had freed his legs in this way I lifted his front and dragged him forward until he felt that his extremities were free. He then tried to work his way and to move forward on his own. Of course, the poor mule still got stuck several times but by means of the procedure just described I reached the opposite bank with him in an hour's time. This was our fate at the first lagoon. In order to be less impaired in my movements in the second lagoon I kept only my jacket and my shirt on and in this outfit I again carried out my pleasant duty as the group's donkey driver at the end of our train.

Yet I suffered greatly for this. In my calculations I had not taken into account the most important factor in the tropics, i.e. the sun. By the end of the first 200 m I felt a burning sensation on my legs which soon became very intensive and then turned brilliantly red. A sunburn on my lower body made its effect felt. This, indeed, was a bad day's march. Only in the water of the lagoon did I feel some cooling relief. This second lagoon was not quite as difficult to cross. It had only occasional deep spots and it was possible to wade through the whole lagoon in a zigzag path along which it was hardly more than one metre deep.

From the 2nd km on we had left the actual river bank behind and were following a north-eastern direction marching on a secant while the river on our left described the arc of a circle. We came to the Luenge again in the seventh kilometre. Since at this place a little stream called Muschongo flows into the river and has washed a deep depression in the river bank, I fetched from our porters, who were resting at the mouth of the stream, the package with our used clothing. I carried it a little upstream into the depression so that I could get out those things I needed without being watched.

On the first day of our march I could already observe that work and effort are unknown concepts for the Maschukulumbe. Like our spoiled children they constantly complained that they were tired and hungry. At our first resting place an old man and several women from Bosango-Kasenga were already waiting for them; they had obviously reached there by a shorter route. They had brought some food for the porters—mostly dried fish and milk upon which they fell immediately. Only after a rather long rest did they start out again. With great effort I finally succeeded in getting for all of us together two small dried fish from them —a very meagre refreshment after the exhaustion of that day and of the day before. Despite our great hunger I did not dare to shoot a head of game although we had met everywhere zebra, lechwe, and waterbuck. If I had shot an animal the Maschukulumbe would not have left that place for hours because of the feast. Since they wished to return to Bosango in any case in the evening it would have been impossible to test their honesty by asking them to come back the next day, once again. Thus we dragged ourselves on even though we were hungry.

In our tenth kilometre we reached the river a second time after having left it again in the seventh kilometre. At this spot we saw several hippoes diving up and down in the river. Fekete and I succeeded in lodging some bullets in the heads of these clumsy water dwellers. Yet it was impossible to wait until the sunken animals drifted to shore since the carcasses of these animals only rise to the surface four or five hours after their deaths.

In the thirteenth kilometre the path followed a somewhat northern course and in the sixteenth kilometre we again came back to the river and a lake-like lagoon around which we had to walk. On its opposite shore was the goal of our first day's journey north of the Luenge. It was the Nikoba village belonging to a Maschuku-lumbe chief who lived nearby, somewhat east-north-east in Diluka. The lagoon was a sac-shaped bay. Only close to the river were its banks overgrown with high reeds; otherwise the shores were bare. In the shallower parts of the water we could see the notorious net grass and in the centre of the lagoon high reeds, papyrus plants as well as net grass were growing high above the water level, indicating that there was a swampy island. The lagoon was, as I shall report later, an important source of income for the inhabitants of Nikoba and Diluka and was known all over as one of the most important hunting grounds in Maschukulumbe territory.[9]

IX

Our stay in the vicinity of Nikoba and Diluka

WHEN WE APPROACHED THE NIKOBA VILLAGE after our march of more than seventeen and a half kilometres I decided to pitch camp on the slope near the lagoon which was overgrown with low grass. Our porters had already dropped their loads on the ground and were just about to run away when a herdsman, who was watching a herd of over eighty head of cattle, approached them. He told them that this place formed the border between the territory of king Njambo[1] and that of the ruler of Diluka. This news induced the porters to pick up their loads again and to carry them closer to the village. I found this place I had chosen rather suitable since we had quite a clear view from there which would not have allowed any enemies to sneak close without being noticed. Furthermore this place was about 500 m away from the village, so that in case of attack we would have been able to cover a sufficiently large area with our rifles, before the enemy would have been able to use their spears. We would not have liked to be closer to the village for just these reasons, especially as we soon got into high dry grass which, if it had been set on fire by enemies, could have become very dangerous for us. About 200 m from the first camp site we passed a small harvested maize field of barely thirty square metres. It was surrounded by high grass on all sides and was the only bare place we could see far and near. Under no circumstances did I want to approach the village any closer than this spot. Therefore, I gave strict orders to halt, which also seemed rather welcome to our porters, since they were terribly afraid of the inhabitants of the twin villages. In an instant our bundles were lying on the ground.

After they had exchanged only a few words with the inhabitants of the village the men hurried back and very probably crossed the river in the same canoe which the old man and the women had brought after them.

We immediately began to build a camp wall by piling up our luggage. Because of the lack of bushes there was no other material for fortification. We did not dare to leave our camp for a longer period of time in order to cut trees without risking our lives.

That night we moved for the first time into a camp of a kind that we had to

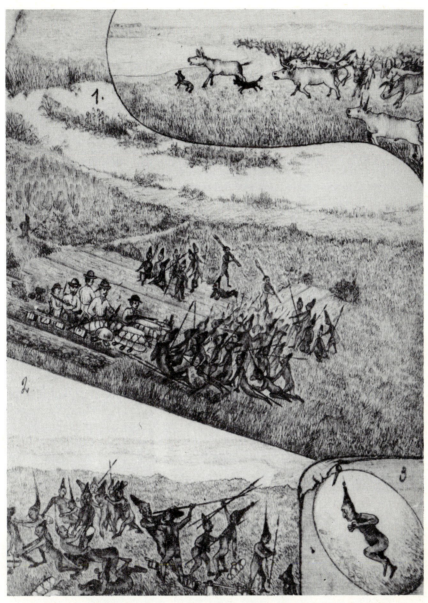

10   *Holub's camp at Nikoba village and the fight between his Maschukulumbe (Ila) carriers*

maintain from then on in Maschukulumbe country. A miserable wall of bundles was from then on the bastion of our safety. The short camp wall was two metres —the long one a little over three metres long. Both met at a right angle and this angle was our 'huge fort', our bastion, and the resting place for my wife during the night. This camp wall, however, was only a solution for as long as we were still in the possession of our loads, the number of which had already shrunk to seventy. Each day of course this wall became smaller and weaker. We often sat in this camp for hours and indeed even for days with our rifles constantly in our hands even during our meals. In front of each of us lay an open cartridge box, each with 100-500 cartridges. During the first night we made big fires along the open sides. We realised soon, however, that we had to reduce these fires to just the coals since we were unable to see the Maschukulumbe in the light of the fires when they were sneaking up on us like snakes. These fires were rather more harmful than useful for us, since they blinded us and by throwing bright light at us made us easy targets for enemies. We were thus forced to rely on our ears and on the sagacity of our last three remaining dogs: Witstock, Daisy and Sidamojo.

That night we all felt, even though we were not talking about it, that the harshest time of our journey had come. The events of the last two days had already made us doubt whether we would be able to reach the northern border of the Maschukulumbe territory alive.

Soon after our arrival the representative of the chief came from Diluka. He was a lame specimen, covered with leprosy—like boils and scars. In spite of a bad relapse of fever Oswald in his usual humorous way nicknamed him 'Limpy' in Viennese dialect. Since I thought him to be the actual chief I gave him the usual presents for a Maschukulumbe chief. This induced him to sell us some fresh lechwe meat for glass beads. When I asked him how he had come by the game we got the answer that puku and lechwe skins were the most important trading goods of the twin villages and that Maschukulumbe from far and near came to exchange cattle for these skins. The fellow tribesmen exchanged these skins again at the border with Mankoya, Mabunda, Matoka and Matakala for salt, corn, tobacco, arms, women, calico, glass beads and blankets. In certain seasons these riverain antelopes are hunted systematically, but otherwise they trap them by digging pits in the game tracks. They stick spears into these pits so that the animals hurt or impale themselves when they fall in. This is the way they kill these animals. Are these really human beings who murder the poor game in such a horrible fashion? All predators kill their prey quickly. And yet the Maschukulumbe—human beings—impale antelopes with two to three spears or only pointed burnt wooden sticks on which these animals slowly shed their life—bleed, starve, or die of thirst. Only rarely are these covered pitfalls checked every day or every other day. Fekete once found a poor impaled gnu and shot it dead immediately to end its suffering. I myself once fell into such a pit which was covered perfectly with dry grass. Only my presence of mind caused me to stretch out both of my arms to the edge of the pit. Thus I kept myself suspended and saved myself from being impaled on a pointed mimosa stick which was as sharp as a knife.

The behaviour of the few Maschukulumbe who visited us that evening put us on guard—always two of us both before and after midnight. Our entertainment during the whole night was the howling of a couple of hyenas which are found inevitably around every Maschukulumbe village, the roaring of some lions and the almost uninterrupted neighing of vigilant male zebras on both the far and near river banks. Otherwise nothing remarkable happened that night. Early in the morning a group of natives came from Nikoba and soon afterwards a second group from Diluka with an old ugly man as a leader. He tried to introduce himself as the true ruler over this area. 'You are camping on my field, who gave you permission to do so? Have you already sent me some presents?' Instead of myself Limpy answered him not in order to defend me but in opposition to the old man. The altercation which followed only confirmed my previous observations that the power of the Maschukulumbe chiefs over their own subjects is almost non-existent. This subchief resisted his chief openly. 'This may be your land but this field, as well as the area around me here, is mine.' This land dispute which, of course, was rather unpleasant for us, caused such a quarrel between the two —each supported by his people—that they soon began to threaten each other with sticks and arms. In their faces and by their gestures they expressed a bestial fury such as I had never observed before among fighting blacks. I realised that I had to pay a second time, yet since it was the second royal present in the same place, it was certainly not as generous as the first one. This seemed to antagonise the old man even more against Limpy. The latter probably would have had the worst of it if he had not been supported by an ally who was worth at least ten men in the entourage of the old man. This was a Herculean Maschukulumbe who seemed to be even taller because of his dandy-like hair arrangement piled up rather high on his head. When this black fellow, to whom Oswald gave the honorary name 'Hadschi-Loja', realised that the situation had become somewhat critical for his bent and lame friend, and that he and his followers were beginning to retreat before the fists and sticks of his opponent, he came forward and posted himself in front of the old man with his arms akimbo. He began to snort like a furious bull. Without even lifting a hand against this new opponent and without saying a single word the old man withdrew together with his followers from the field he just had contested. This proved that as chief and ruler he had no power here. When we asked about him we learnt that this giant was a potentate of a village about two kilometres away in the south-western direction on the other side of the Luenge river. Not only was the quarrel terminated but friends and enemies were soon talking with each other as if nothing had ever darkened the mirror of their hearts. Yet this cordiality might have been very dangerous for us. Muschemani had overheard their conversation, during which they agreed to cut us down without any previous open attack. For this reason I did not allow any armed Maschukulumbe to come close to us. While we were standing we had our rifles cocked and while we were sitting we were holding them on our knees. Whenever armed men tried to approach us quickly, we immediately raised our arms. This always had the desired effect and they retreated instantly. Only the fear of our carbines kept them from throwing their spears at us from a distance of forty paces. This unpleasant and rather nerve-racking situation had already lasted for about three hours when the whole troupe of about eighty people (there were over fifty men and the rest were youngsters) withdrew a little to the side—not in order to retreat but merely to take counsel about the situation. Since they did not know that Muschemani understood their language for the most part and that even we had already learnt quite a number of Maschukulumbe words in Bosango, they spoke rather loudly. Thus Muschemani could catch some of their words. Soon he gave us a report in his usual manner. He remained squatting on the ground with his head on his arms which were in turn resting on his knees. He was smiling and without opening his eyes any further—his lids were usually half closed because of an old eye disease—he gave us in a completely indifferent tone the crucial news: 'Hm, hm,' he said, 'these people over there—they say that they are going to come now to stab us with their spears and whichever of us they cannot stab, and the dogs, donkeys and goats, will have to be thrown into the big water [i.e. the lagoon].' I gave Muschemani a rifle and since we were facing our enemies at the open side of our camp we all went behind the long camp wall and put our open cartridge boxes next to us on top of it. All of us, even my wife, were ready to shoot. We would have been able to shoot forty shots without having to load our rifles again. Yet I gave orders that nobody was allowed to shoot even if the spears fell right next to us. Under no circumstances could we afford to draw their blood first. The situation was indeed rather critical, yet in spite of this I still thought it would be the best for our cause if we were to avoid any bloodshed. I hoped to bring this about by displaying an utter fearlessness and cheerfulness and by making sneering remarks and gestures about the various creatures who were approaching us in two groups.

I was not mistaken about this primitive race; and the experience we had then was to help us later on several times—in fact the very next day when the situation was much worse. The Maschukulumbe had thought that we would retreat and hide ourselves when they advanced upon us. Instead they found us laughing but with our rifles pointed at them. This stupefied them and their quick strides became slower and slower with every second. I told Muschemani in a low voice that he should not shoot before I had fired myself but that for the moment he should take aim at Hadschi-Loja. When they reached the field the blacks stopped and formed one single big group. All, however, were staring at Muschemani and even began to duck their heads. As soon as I recognised this sign of their cowardice I rushed up to Muschemani, and putting my hand on his naked shoulder I shouted in a loud voice so that all our enemies over there could hear it, 'As soon as the first spear draws blood you shoot the *mona umutunja* [giant]!' And I pointed my rifle at Hadschi-Loja, who had retreated into the high grass and had thrown himself down heroically on his belly so that nothing was to be seen of him but his face, his shoulders and his half-finished hairdress. '*Mona umutunja, mona umutunja*', I shouted across to this coward. Muschemani, however, got up, took two steps forward and tried to take aim at his black head. The giant began to snort like a wounded bull while all the others escaped singly or in groups—either running away upright or crawling on their bellies through the grass. I called Muschemani back; the danger was over; and an hour later there were no strange blacks around us any more. Indeed, the 'tube of fire' still has the same effect on primitive races today as in the times of Cortes and Pizarro.

Only then could we afford to get some rest. Some of us quickly started a fire and began to prepare a quick meal while my wife and Muschemani, both well armed, tried to drive our donkeys and our goats, who were grazing at the lagoon, somewhat closer to our camp. With our bayonets Fekete and I began to cut down some of the elephant grass which was growing in high bushes on the other side of the field. By this means we tried to get a clearer view—at least towards that side.

Not an hour had passed when Oswald's trumpet gathered us together again. People were coming from Nikoba singly and in small groups. Yet they were unarmed, as we soon realised. Of course, we did not point our rifles at unarmed people and we did not hinder them from entering the small field where we were camping. Smiling, i.e. making a wry face in their usual manner, they sat down on the ground between the camp walls and the high grass. The striking friendliness of these Maschukulumbe made me suspicious from the very first moment. And this suspicion grew with every minute into a strong dislike. Shortly before these people had attacked us with their weapons and had only withdrawn out of fear of our seven rifles. They were fifty men who with a truly bestial fury had tried to kill us for several reasons. These same people now came up to us with smiling faces, talked to us, and suddenly began to be interested in our method of preparing food. Who could dare to trust them? I decided to be on guard and told my people about my feelings. All were of the same opinion. Only Oswald was unable to give up his usual attitude. 'Well, these blacks are not as bad as you think, Doctor. They are coming without arms. You have to consider this, Doctor. And they are so much afraid of our rifles.' 'Maybe,' I said, 'yet for several days past they have been after our lives and of that we can be sure. The smiling enemy is much more dangerous than the enemy who is storming us in full fury.' As if our counterparts had understood Oswald's words, they got up and came even closer, this time towards the shorter camp wall. They lay down on their bellies right next to our bundles. Not too many of them could find room there in this way, since on that side the high grass began at a distance of only 4 m, while on the open camp sides there was at least a distance of 20 m separating us from the high grass. Ever more groups of people came from both villages. My suspicion grew more and more. Even my companions began to get worried about the ostentatiously friendly behaviour of these men lying on the ground or squatting in the grass—at least in as much as they were visible. When the group of people had almost reached the number of eighty I tried to end the matter. I jumped on top of the luggage wall in order to look around. I shouted: 'Oswald, Leeb, step forward quickly without your rifles and approach the blacks lying in front of me as if you want to take the grass away from them which we have cut for our camp and on which two of them are lying. If these people do not yield willingly then lift them up by force, but without using arms.' Then I jumped down and we grabbed our rifles in order to protect our men who were leaving the camp over the low wall. Shooting was not necessary and Oswald and Leeb succeeded in pushing four of them back. I began to explain to Muschemani loudly and with gestures the reason for our action. He was supposed to translate this immediately for the Maschukulumbe into the Setoka language. (Most of them understood Setoka which Muschemani spoke very well, even though he was not a Matoka himself. He did not speak to them in Seschukulumbe in order not to disclose that he knew their language to some extent.) I had him say: 'Black are the hearts of the Maschukulumbe, my *molemo* [medicine, charms] has told me so. They came with friendliness in their faces, licking our hands like the *matscha* [dogs]. Yet they are hyenas in the skins of dogs. Because while we are thinking that they have come as friends, their little boys are creeping through the high grass, each carrying several spears which they secretly throw and push through the grass to the last ones in the group. Already I can see some people of the seemingly unarmed men who are armed.'

And, indeed, this was so. After this speech, however, it did not take long before those who were lying or sitting on the ground slowly got up one after another except for four: the old man, Limpy and two others who remained sitting at the edge of the field. After they had realised that we had seen through their perfidious ruse they no longer concealed their arms. The boys returned to the village carrying the spears openly over their shoulders. We were safe from a real attack because of our rifles.

Soon a new change of scene took place. Women came from Diluka in order to sell us chickens and milk cheaply for glass beads. The four Maschukulumbe who were still present soon began a loud conversation with these women. I did not think this was of any importance and ordered Muschemani to use this time to rush quickly to the lagoon—if necessary twice—in order to fill our water containers and our cooking pots with water. This black chap, however, who was just busy cleaning our pots and plates, asked me in his usual indifferent manner to allow him to stay still for a moment. He said that he would soon finish his job and that he would also listen to what those over there were saying since we were again the subject of their wicked tongues. When this fellow finally got up and was about to go off with his water containers he told me that the old man (who was the chief and the husband of two of these women) had ordered the women not to bring us any food upon punishment of a beating. They also were to inform the women of Nikoba about this on their way home. The old man claimed that we had too many *impandes* (conch-shells as medicine) to protect ourselves. By this device we could see through all their plans and attacks; this was why we should be starved. There were no arms which could kill us. After these words the women turned around and went back with all the foodstuffs. The men, however, remained there squatting in the same place.

Later that afternoon two Maschukulumbe men and one boy came from Nikoba, each of them leading four dogs on a leash. They walked in a stooped position. When we got up to look around they asked us to lie down and pointed to the lagoon and, in particular, to the opposite shore. The old man told us in Setoka about their intentions. Thus we learned about the importance of the lagoon for the inhabitants of the twin villages. 'Over there on the other side of the water a herd of our most sought-after game is coming. Its skin is our most valuable barter object. It is in greater demand than the skin of the puku or other game. One of the Muschemani [herd boys] who are specifically on the look-out for this purpose has just reported that the lechwe are coming nearer. These antelopes which graze together with other game in the grass plain occasionally come in the afternoons to drink at this big water. If this is the case then Njambo's herdsmen or ours approach them clandestinely from the rear using the cattle herds grazing near the lagoon as cover. Thus they drive the game without frightening it slowly into the water. The dogs then race around the water and thus prevent the antelopes from reaching the banks. On the lagoon, however, there are hunters lying in their canoes. They then spear the animals. Therefore—stay as quiet as possible so that my people together with the dogs can get into that big herd over there.'

Even though such a hunt would have been interesting to watch I was glad this time that the lives of these poor animals were spared. From the north—that is from the direction of Njambo—a few Maschukulumbe came carrying tobacco on sticks over their shoulders. They wanted to exchange it for lechwe skins. They frightened the antelopes which were to be hunted so that they ran away. When these men came closer to our camp and saw us they all of a sudden stopped as if rooted to the spot. We were the first Europeans they had seen. They intended to come right to our camp yet the old man and his followers did not allow them to strike up a conversation with us. When these strangers left I gave them a handful of glass beads and whispered to their leader '*Wuena ke-empele*' (You—an apron), which the man understood immediately. He nodded with his head and followed Limpy to Nikoba accompanied by the old chief of Diluka.

As I realised later it was quite a misfortune for us that we were only able to speak to those four tobacco carriers who belonged to a neighbouring Maschukulumbe tribe after they had been thoroughly indoctrinated by our enemies. That evening the leader came to us with one companion. From all the Maschukulumbe whom we had seen his looks most inspired us with some confidence. Yet later on he was to become a traitor. I asked him whether in fact a white man was living at the border. He assured me that one white man was living with chief Masangu and was exchanging calico, blankets, and glass beads for ivory and that another one was living beyond the border far towards the north among the Mankoya and was hunting elephants. Since I had not yet heard anything about this stranger from the people of Nikoba and Diluka I felt inclined to believe this man. Yet everything he said was only lying and cheating.

Before sunset, after they had milked their cows, the women as a rule showed up with some fresh milk. Often they also brought chickens and other barter goods such as wood and salt. Yet today they did not come. The order of the old man was obeyed. I did not want to slaughter one of my five dwarf goats since they were pregnant. And as they were a special kind, slim and small like steenbok, I was planning to take them along until I reached the next sea coast. Well, it was not the first time on this expedition that we went to bed with 'grumbling stomachs' and began our night watch.

In the meantime it had become almost dark. Nightjars began to fly about and from the reeds we could hear every now and then the individual call of the bittern and the noisy chorus of the night herons. We were still sitting and talking around the smouldering coals when Fekete and Muschemani, our guards, reported that some figures were approaching us from the east. Since they were walking on the well-trampled path I figured that they were not coming as enemies, otherwise they would have been sneaking through the high grass. I had Fekete watch these people while the rest of us concentrated all our attention on the elephant grass at a 30 m distance from us so that we would not be attacked from the opposite side while we were attentively watching the people arriving on the path. After all we could cope with such a strategic ruse. Finally the dark figures came quite close. They were women from Diluka, the very same ones who were ordered not to bring us any food. They came secretly with milk and dried fish. We gave them glass beads and even doubled the amount of the usual price. They then rushed back into the village as fast as they could so that nobody would notice their absence. I do not know whether I should marvel more at the courage or at the vanity of these women. They risked their lives for frivolous trinkets, i.e. a few glass beads.

Early the next morning our 'friends' showed up again. It was the old man with a large crowd of followers. He claimed more presents, since he had not been satisfied the day before. For the second time the unpleasant and annoying attack scene of the previous day was repeated. This time it was even less convenient for us, since Njambo's four men were watching this, even though they themselves remained quietly in the background. So far the individual Maschukulumbe chiefs had proved to be so jealous of each other that a joint campaign against us was out of the question. In the presence of his neighbour we could have shot all the followers of a Maschukulumbe chief down to the very last man and yet the onlooker would never even have lifted a single spear for his fellow tribesman. Later, however, when we were approaching the northern frontier and when the chief realised that otherwise we would escape them, their greediness got the better of their jealousy, and thus the chiefs on the northern Luenge joined their forces against us. I was always afraid of this possibility and this was why I found the presence of those four strangers so inconvenient.

As was often the case at politically tense moments our situation became much more serious due to an unexpected cause. This was our two donkeys. That day, just as the day before, we had a very hard time preventing the dogs of the Maschukulumbe from harassing them as well as our goats. Thus the animals kept close to our camp anyway. Yet by noon the donkeys had strayed a little further than 150 m away, and the threatening attitude of the blacks did not allow us to send Muschemani after the animals. What I had feared, indeed, happened. The dogs of our enemies which had been let loose chased the donkeys and they took to flight.

Unfortunately they were running along the lagoon where about one kilometre further away Njambo's big herd of thousands of head of cattle was grazing. After the mules had run directly into that herd they again recovered their sense of direction which is characteristic for these animals in southern Africa. They immediately returned on the right path. This time, however, thousands of cattle were chasing them. Yet our mules were much faster; they could have escaped quite easily if only the dogs had not constantly run between their legs and thus slowed them down. When I saw this I shouted loudly to the Maschukulumbe and had Muschemani translate it—that they should call their dogs back immediately otherwise I would shoot one of them. By then the cows had come very close to the donkeys. Yet these cruel creatures, who would have welcomed the death of my animals which carried the load of four porters, incited the dogs even more. Thus I rushed out of camp and at the very moment when one of the curs was again rushing by Jacob and trying to bite his nose I fired a shot from a distance of 70 m. The bullet pierced the dog's chest and it collapsed howling. The first few bulls who were Jacob's closest persecuters stopped as if they were suddenly rooted to the spot, but Jacob and his companion trotted up to the open side of the camp braying. My wife threw a bit of millet in front of them as a reward for their clever return. The death of the dog could not have been any more welcome for the Maschukulumbe. Now they had a reason to blackmail us as much as possible. Shouting wildly, all the men, women and children jumped up brandishing their spears. Hadschi-Loja in particular behaved in a rage—but all this from a distance. The very same shot which had incited them to such a fury had tamed them at the same time. It was the first time that these people could see with their own eyes the effect of the firearm of which they might have heard before. One stroke of lightening meant death. This destroyed their courage. They did not dare to approach our camp. Instead about ten or twenty people split from the crowd, ran to the dead dog and stared at the carcass without, however, touching it. A little later I saw the four strangers coming closer to the camp. They had to pass us in order to return home. I called them and tried to start some negotiations with them for porters. King Njambo who was not living far away should supply them to me for very good pay. I realised well enough that I would not get any porters here.

The dog had belonged to the limping subchief and he now claimed 10 m of calico as compensation. Instead of 10 m I gave him calico for one *kubu* i.e. 4 m. When we left the choice of the material to these tribes it was strange that when they were shown unbleached calico, broad rolls of linen, colourful calico (such brands as Neunkirchen, Kosmanos, Holeschowitz, Liesing, Blaudruck and Fellmayer) as well as those 2 m pieces sewn together from small samples of colourful sackcloth, they always chose the latter, by our concepts the least valuable material.

The dog was still being stared at; indeed, the whole crowd had gathered around his carcass. Finally people dispersed and went back to their huts. Only now did we have some temporary peace and quiet. We began to grill our few pieces of dried fish.

In the afternoon our guard—this time my wife—gave the signal that a group of about 100 Maschukulumbe were coming from the north. They were also seen by our enemies in the village and since they thought that these people came 'to pay us a visit', 'our good neighbours' came in order to await the strangers in front of our camp. The newcomers were already the porters I had asked Njambo for! As soon as our good neighbours had learnt this Hadschi-Loja took the leader of the group somewhat aside into the grass. The leader was smeared heavily with cow fat and glistened already from afar. He was a young prince of the royal family and wore a huge hair arrangement. After a short while the prince came back and declared that his people would not carry our things for us since we had not given all the presents the people of Nikoba-Diluka were demanding. We would still have to pay 6 m of calico for the dog. I tried to counter these accusations by asserting that I had given more presents here than in Bosango and Kaboramanda. Furthermore, in the end he (Limpy) had only claimed 4 m. Through Muschemani I said in Setoka, 'No, all these have treacherous and poisonous tongues. They would have robbed us and they would have killed us three times already if our *tlobolo* had not frightened them. Tell them, you son of Njambo, that we five are not afraid of them and their friends and next time if they should attack us once more I shall not wait until their spears are falling on us or even draw our blood. No, tell them that I shall shoot them like that dog there if they attack us—even before they throw their first spear.'

Njambo's men stepped back and sat down about a hundred paces away to our right. Then all of a sudden the old man came up to us with his subchiefs and offered to give me his people immediately as porters. This turn of events I had not expected in the least and at first we did not even understand it. Then our opinions differed greatly, so that we literally first had a council of war as to how we should react to this sudden abundance of porters. 'They think those people will spoil their business', said my wife. 'Yes, that is true.' 'They want to earn something as well', Oswald objected. 'Yes, they want to rob us since we five cannot watch all of them.' 'They plan to attack us on the road', said Leeb, 'now that they have support from these new spear bearers.' 'Well, that's possible, too.' 'Is Njambo's town so close that they can still get there today?' asked Fekete. 'They do not stay a night away from home and for this we should have to pay 4 m of calico per man.' 'You are right, Janos, the kraal must be very close, otherwise these strangers would not yet be here in response to the message which I gave only today at noon asking for porters. Indeed, this is it. The old knave wants to give us porters now so that on our way to Njambo it will get dark and then it is not possible to watch even the nearest porters. This rogue believes that we shall lose everything we possess in this way.' Even though we were speaking German Muschemani understood the tenor and nodded assent, confirming it with a loud '*e-he*' (yes, indeed). I was determined and told the old man: 'No, we do not want to go now, at least not with you, but with those over there.' 'And why not with us?' 'Because you are bad, worse than hyenas. Because you are a gang of thieves and we do not want to go with you through the night.' 'But we want to go and you have to go!' suddenly 'dear little

Hadschi' shouted. He should have been the last to interfere as he did not belong to Nikoba-Diluka. He was about to jump forward and to attack us when the men next to him wrenched his spears from him. Yet he tore himself away from them and jumped right in the middle between us and the blacks without any arms. 'What, you are not going?' shouted the giant. 'No, I would not dream of going with you.' 'You must go, we shall kill you, we shall trample you to death. You shall go.' 'No.' The man then became so enraged that he was jumping up and down in front of us like a furious baboon. He was hissing because he was no longer able to scream or to talk. Foam came out of his mouth and when he became somewhat slower his movements became more regular. I do not know whether this was intended or not. He got into some kind of rhythm and had worked himself into a war dance. The crowd behind him began to hum and this applause made his voice come back. 'Master,' Muschemani called, 'watch out!' A war dance in such a situation meant danger for us—the greatest danger, indeed. I saw that those men squatting on the ground began to jump up and to stretch their arms grabbing their weapons tighter or picking up those spears which were lying on the ground. Should I shoot the giant down? Look how he again distorts his face.[2] Again he was relapsing into a state of blind fury. The applause made him mad. With his arms he reached mechanically behind himself while he was jumping madly. He obviously wanted weapons. What should I do? I had to act fast, very fast. The lives of all of us were hanging by a thread. Suddenly an idea crossed my mind and immediately I put it into action. My rifle flew into my wife's lap and unarmed except for the knife at my side I jumped into the arena where the giant was dancing. I tried to imitate his furious leaps while laughing and screaming. I tried to parody him and I jumped even more madly than the huge clump of fat in front of me who was dripping with sweat. Making the wildest grimaces I tried to breathe. The giant stopped. He stood there with his torso bent. His body, his hands and feet were trembling so that he was hardly able to stand; his eyes were literally popping out of their sockets. His voice seemed to have given out. I kept on jumping until loud guffaws and roars of laughter brought me back to reality. Then I stopped. It was the Maschukulumbe who were screaming with laughter. I had defeated the giant. I had ridiculed him in front of his own people. A cold shower could not have had any more stupefying effect on Loja. He still was standing there on the same spot after I had already returned to my people. Finally his friends took him away. Njambo's people left too, and only a few people from Diluka stayed on. Who would have thought that they should constitute a new threat for us? They, these few people, wanted to make themselves a name. They alone wanted to have the glory all for themselves 'of wiping us out'. One of them went away, yet he soon returned to the rest of them with a glowing piece of wood. Before we could prevent it they began to set the grass on fire along the edge of the field at a distance of 20 m from us. Fortunately there was no wind blowing. The fire would keep us warm, yet at the moment at least it could not harm us. Nevertheless, we began to cut down the high grass behind the camp walls with our bayonets. 'Look, they are going to burn their *empele* [calico, apron] and their *burungu* [glass beads], too', one of our enemies shouted all of a sudden. And just as quickly as they had set the fire, these seven men tried to extinguish it again. They began to throw the loose humus soil with their hands onto the crackling and slowly burning flames until the fire was put out. As they had noticed almost too late, the fire was endangering not only us, but their villages as well. Then they ran away.

How many such days had we still to expect? How long would this torture still last? Even Oswald, to whom the blacks always had seemed to be innocent little angels, was that day convinced of the contrary and did not say a word. He soon wrapped himself into his blankets. He had reported ill and, indeed, I could see his fever attack from looking into his face. And today it seemed to be a relief for him not to have to join the conversation in the evening and not to have to make a concession.

When a little while later the women showed up again with milk, two cups full of flour and fish we interrogated them about the white man in the north. They obviously had not yet heard anything about him. The women left and a quarter of an hour later we heard loud shouting and screaming in Diluka. We were quite astonished since the Maschukulumbe normally went to bed early and never made any noise during the night. Soon everything was clear. They had caught the women returning from their forbidden trip and very probably had punished them hard.

The next morning, on 27 July, the two villages were as if deserted. Only an old woman passed by our camp with a pot on her head. My wife quickly decided to ask even this creature about the supposed Portuguese.[3] So she followed her all on her own, caught up with her, and the old woman gave her exact details that a man who looked just as we did was living with Masangu on this side of the narrow pass which has already been mentioned several times. We believed that woman and gave her generous presents. All our aspirations, however, were to reach this white man as quickly as possible. One week later, on our retreat, I learned that the whole report of this woman had been a vicious trap. She was one of these vain old women who had been bringing milk for glass beads every evening and who had been caught during the last excursion. They were all supposed to be beaten up and our informant was even to be killed since they had provided us clandestinely with foodstuffs. In order to escape this punishment they had volunteered to give us a report about the white man. This was to make us even more determined to follow the route through the swamps to the narrow pass, so that en route we could finally be attacked and killed. We had no idea of all this, nor of the fact that Njambo had already been won over to this plan by messengers and had agreed that men from Nikoba-Diluka would join his men for the attack. For the first time in the history of the two sister tribes his men were supposed to fight side by side with their fellow tribesmen.

Around nine o'clock a large crowd of Maschukulumbe showed up, led by their chiefs. They wanted to porter for us. As in Kasenga we were supposed to give each of them 4 m of calico in advance as their payment. 'How far is it to Njambo's kraal?' The men were pointing with their right hands to a celestial point which indicated that we could be at Njambo's in at least two hours' time. 'For such a minor service I shall not give two sitsibas, never.' 'We shall go on to Massangu.' 'To those hills over there?' 'Yes.' 'You are lying. I have never seen a Maschuku-lumbe yet who has told the truth.' 'No, we shall go beyond Njambo's residence.' 'Do trust them, Doctor,' I heard our negrophil Oswald whispering, 'so that we can finally get away from here.'

We fastened the pieces of calico to the loads. The two chiefs got 5 m more of calico each as a present along with some Pforzheim theatre jewellery. Then we stepped back, however, allowing the porters to approach only five loads at any one time. This went on until they had picked up the first twenty loads or so. But then the rest of the men rushed to the pile of remaining loads for fear that they would not get anything to carry, i.e. to steal. My companions and my wife as the last one were hardly able to work their way out of this dangerous crowd. Besides the inhabitants of Diluka-Nikoba, people from the southern bank of the Luenge had also come, among them some of Hadschi's subjects. They all were fighting madly for our parcels so that even the two pieces of calico, each 2 m long, which had been fastened to the bundles were ripped into pieces. In a very short time this struggle developed into such a row that blood was flowing on my right and left. I was wedged tightly between several of them so that I had to use the butt of my rifle to free myself and to gain my mobility. Unfortunately I lost my hat in this scuffle. My wife was terrified at this scene and at the same time she was worried about our possessions. She had not enough eyes to watch everything. All of a sudden she called, 'Look how they hit each other with their spears, their own fellow tribesmen!' Then again she shouted 'Emil, look at that thief, look at Hadschi! He just now ripped off the two calico pieces from the bundle he took to carry. And he has given the cloth to his wife who ran away with it, hiding it under her skin apron. Look, there she is running!' The bundle in question was lying unattended on the field where he had thrown it to indicate that no payment had been attached to it and that thus there was no porter for it. The above described mutual friendliness with which the carriers treated each other induced me to talk a little more seriously with Mr Hadschi. I was trying to look for this wanted man and detected him when he passed me coming out of a thick crowd of people. I grabbed him immediately by his throat and demanded the calico from him pointing with my rifle to the load. The giant was so surprised by this sudden attack that he was not able to utter a single sound. I shook this chap until he bit his tongue. At that moment, however, I heard the following words: 'Emil, you are mistaken, the other one is the Hadschi, I used the wrong name.' Well, that was that, but I could not afford to have them realising my error. I touched that man's chest with the cold steel of the mouth of my rifle. He fell backwards and almost pulled me down on top of him. Then he began to scream that he had not stolen anything and I pretended to believe him and let him loose. That man ran away in a hurry and shouted to his people that they should give up carrying for us. They did not let him repeat this a second time. Most of them anyway had wrapped their payment around their foreheads or their bodies and they now rushed off simply throwing the bundles they had picked up for carrying to the side. Then we had to get out new pieces of calico, measure them and distribute them. While in my heart I was actually rather glad that I did not have to see that miserable giant and his gang any longer, Oswald was shouting loudly to catch my attention. He reported that some twenty porters had already started off on the way and now were walking rather fast, probably with the intention of disappearing with our loads all together. I comprehended this dangerous situation rather quickly and I ordered my three companions to stay there together and watch the porters in our camp. I myself took my wife by her hand and we rushed after these twenty honourable gentlemen. They were moving so fast that we could hardly get any closer to them. Suddenly two of them stayed behind and we soon caught up with them. They were two Maschukulumbe one of them being a very old man. They had left their bundles in the path and were trying to escape. I blocked their way, but they refused to carry their loads and did not do so until I took my rifle from my shoulder. While these two delayed us in this way the other eighteen had gained a good 300 m start over us. The area was overgrown with short grass and the whole valley was covered with thousands of ant-hills as big as haystacks. They began where the ground ascended slightly. While we were still stuck with the old man Oswald caught up with us. He was driving a young and strong Maschukulumbe in front of him by pressing the mouth of his Winchester into his naked back each time when he wanted to stop. This inspired the lad again with energy and strength. I put the load of our old man, who really was exhausted, on his shoulders as well, kept my rifle diligently close to his skin and in this way we moved ahead. Oswald, however, stayed behind, since some porters followed behind us and he had to watch them. We were very lucky that there was no elephant grass growing near our path.

We had not marched for long when we recognised Njambo's village in the distance. When we had approached as close as several hundred metres to Njambo and just felt that we could begin to breathe freely we suddenly saw with horror that the eighteen porters were cutting our loads open with their spears, pulling out calico garments, etc. and throwing them to some boys who came running up to them with baskets in their hands from the village. At the same time a group of Maschukulumbe men were coming towards my porters welcoming them with loud shouts of cheer. My efforts now were concentrated on preventing these two groups from meeting. Thus I ran as fast as I could in order to catch up with my porters and got them to stop. I called them, yet instead of stopping they began running to an isolated mimosa tree about 300 m away from Njambo. There they dropped our loads. Then they tried to get to the men from Njambo coming towards them. Yet I had already blocked their way and was aiming my Winchester at the first one of these thieves. The moment that I levelled my rifle he turned around and, followed by the others, rushed back again to the tree where they again picked up the stolen parcels.

I stayed at the same spot with my rifle ready to shoot. Yet I was standing there unprotected—a good target for the spears of the Maschukulumbe who were coming to help their fellow tribesmen. It was a critical moment. For several minutes I was suspended between life and death. My carbine was pointed all the time at the thievish carriers while my eyes were glancing across to Njambo's people. How was this to end? One minute after another passed. There was a noise behind me. I could clearly hear something gasping. What was it? I turned my head around quickly. Was it a Maschukulumbe sneaking up on me? My bullet had to beat his assegai. Yet it was no Maschukulumbe—it was my wife who had seen my trouble from a distance and was running up to me with her rifle in her hand. Now we were standing back to back and had an easy task to watch the two uncertain groups closely until our men with the other porters came close. They finally reached us in great distress and with sad faces since several of our loads had been stolen on their march. The porters from the very beginning had practised the tactics of splitting into several groups in order to make it difficult to watch them. Some had stayed behind, had opened the parcels, and when Leeb had looked back at some point, they had disappeared with parts of their booty.

These miserable thieves probably would have stolen even more, especially since they were very swift-footed, if my people had not fired a few shots after them over their heads in order to save at least some things. That helped. One of them dropped a whole load and two others dropped some linen. The last thief who dropped his stolen parcel in fright from the sound of the bullet was no less than the ruler of this area, the old man, the chief of Diluka-Nikoba who was trying to drag away some shirt material. Heavily laden with these things my servants had just caught up with us.

Before I continue with my report about our stay at Njambo's, the events which I have chosen to describe in my next chapter, I have to recall that moment when we saw for the very first time the famous trophies of a Maschukulumbe chief. This was a moment which we—I and my wife—shall never forget.

In the very first moment when my wife joined me in order to support me she touched my shoulder and said in a low voice, 'Look over there!' I first looked at her and was not a little frightened when I saw that all the blood had left her face. I thought that my wife was wounded since a fast sprint such as she had just run does not make one's cheeks pale but rather red. When I asked her she gave me the same answer, 'Look, over there!' I turned my head to the left and for the first time I saw that frightening, notorious trophy of which we had already heard often but which we had never really seen in any village yet, so that we believed the whole thing was a legend. Here, however, it had become reality.

Some metres behind us to the left was a tree or rather a dead barkless trunk, not very high, which the Maschukulumbe had placed there. The short dry branches were sticking into the air like fangs and on each of them, except for two, human skulls were sitting. Most of them had been pecked clean by birds of prey and were bleached by the sun. Some of them, however, revealed by lumps of flesh that they had been put on this horror scaffold not too long ago. Between these skulls were hanging some weapons which told us to whom the skulls had once belonged. Mostly these had been peaceful traders of neighbouring tribes. According to their weapons they were Mankoya (bow and arrow), Marutse (harpoon assegai), Makalaka (ordinary assegai). They had come to exchange corn, fish traps, tobacco and weapons for the skins of riverain antelopes or cowhides. The Maschukulumbe had began to quarrel with them on purpose or they had attacked those whose skulls they stuck up here. The rapacity and bloodthirstiness which was grinning at us from that trophy pole told us all too clearly that we would be killed among these people as soon as we were no longer able to protect ourselves. This skull pole also told us that it would not do us any good in an extreme emergency to throw before those greedy Maschukulumbe everything we had, except for our instruments, diaries and cartridges and to say to them 'Here, take everything. Just let us get safely to the border. Do not fear that we might return to Luanika in the south and shall betray you. We are going to the north.' Even this sacrifice would not have saved us. We ourselves were our only salvation, our courage, our strength, and our firearms. In view of these skulls swaying in the breeze which seemed to be grinning a horrible welcome to us, our courage became the courage of desperation. 'Well then, let us take up the unequal fight. If we must die it shall only be at a high cost!'

X

Our stay at Njambo's
March to Galulonga

I DROPPED THE THREAD OF MY TALE at that moment when my servants finally had reached us and we were all united again. To the left the porters had sat down with our loads under the big mimosa tree. From the right Maschukulumbe were coming from the village to link up with the porters and to divide the loot among themselves. My very first tactical task was to prevent this.

Our porters tried several times to move away from the vicinity of that lonely tree under which they had dropped our loads, yet when threatened by our rifles they always ran back again. The Maschukulumbe from the village retreated again towards the village and formed a group there when they saw my people coming. They were Fekete Janos, Ignaz Leeb and Oswald Söllner. Five carbines seemed too dangerous for them. Their retreat gave us some breathing space so that we could concentrate our attention on our porters. Seldom had I seen in people such fear and weakness as we could observe in most of these twenty thieves. We walked up to each of the twenty porters and ordered them to pick up their loads. They did this without any resistance. When we examined the packages we found that they had stolen things from twelve out of twenty. In particular three were almost entirely robbed of their contents and were stuffed instead with dry grass.

'Where are our belongings? You sons of a bitch have stolen them!' '*Ehe*', the thieves answered, grinning with satisfaction. They confirmed my suspicion smiling in the most insolent fashion as if to say 'Yes, indeed, that goes without saying. What else did you expect?' At a given sign from me Oswald and Fekete each grabbed one of the chief thieves by their necks. I grabbed a third one myself by the arm. I had firmly decided to take these sly birds before Njambo and to demand that he punish them. This was a daring step to take but, on the one hand, this was one way of getting some of my stolen goods back and, on the other hand, I wanted to prove to Njambo that I was not afraid of him despite his 300 spear-bearers. Deep in my heart I was certainly worried—for with only a superficial glance around I could tell that never before had I dealt with such a mighty Maschukulumbe chief.

My wife and Leeb stayed behind in the camp. In order to facilitate their job
—since they could easily have been attacked by those seventeen thieves during
our absence—I let the remaining porters go knowing very well that I probably
would not get back even what had been stolen by the three chief thieves whom
we were holding by their necks. In the meantime my wife had come up to us
quickly in order to go with us.

As soon as Njambo realised what our intention was concerning the porters he
came walking towards us together with his subchiefs. He was dressed in full rega-
lia, i.e. he had wrapped a colourful plush blanket around his shoulders. Back in
1875 I had heard about Njambo at Sepopo's in Schescheke. (Njambe in contrast to
Njambo means in Marutse the invisible god living in the blue of the sky.) And on
this trip ever since I had reached the Zambezi area I had heard bad things from the
Matoka and the Marutse about this cruel tyrant. Now I was to get to know him
personally and, indeed, I was to experience the full blackness of his character.
Njambo was in his fifties, not large, but rather of slight stature. His face featured
an aquiline nose so sharp that one rarely sees such even among Europeans. The
corners of his mouth were twisted upwards so that even in moments of greatest
agitation he always looked the same, seeming to smile in good humour. His eyes
were small. One could read clearly cunning and astuteness in them. They seemed
to me like the eyes of a cat-like animal of prey squatting in front of his victim—his
eyelids half closed. Yet under the half-open lids he followed every movement
intently in order to leap up suddenly in the best possible moment to catch his
victim who had slowly been lulled into a state of indifference. Like all Maschukulumbe men, Njambo, too, had his face and the front part of his forehead clean
shaven. He was wearing the obligatory hair ornamentation—which, however,
was rather small and ordinary—on the back part of his head.

When he reached me we all greeted him and I sought justice. I pointed out the
looted packages lying in the grass and the thieves who had pleaded guilty.
Njambo's Mephistophelian face melted into a diabolic smile. If ever in his life a
smile had come from deep in his heart, this one did. He was the initiator of the
robbery and his people were the receivers of stolen goods. Now I approached him
as a judge in my cause. He really was delighted. 'Hee, hee', he was giggling and
his entourage supported him with 'ho, ho'. The chorus, however, joined in with
the battle cry 'Pah, pah'. This battle cry was like a 'salve'. It was our greeting from
this chief—and thus a very bad omen. There are moments in one's life which after
decades are still as vivid in one's memory as if one had experienced them every
day since. Just like this I can still hear in my heart that refrain of the hangman and
his assistants 'Hee, ho, pah!'

'Do you think I have the right to punish the subjects of a foreign chief?' Njambo
answered smilingly. 'Go back to Diluka and take these thieves before their chief.'
'Their chief himself is a thief and has stolen things from me. Furthermore these
stolen goods are not with him but with you in your huts.' He ordered me curtly
and cuttingly, 'Let these people go!' What else could I do then but to let the
thieves loose? They were received with open arms near the village by their fellow

tribesmen, screaming with joy, and by Njambo's warriors.

Only after they had run away did Njambo thank me for my greeting. I was trying to suppress my bad temper and the memories of the last hours. I tried to show a friendly face and greeted him and his royal entourage once again. I had Fekete deliver the presents to Njambo and ask him to give me porters as far as the border—if possible the same day—since the Diluka-Nikoba porters who had originally promised to carry my loads to the border had run away. 'Yes, you shall have porters, yet not today, but tomorrow.' During these negotiations more and more warriors had gathered around us so that I found it best to retreat to that mimosa tree which I have mentioned already several times and to build with our loads a camp wall of a type which would at least give us a little protection.

Before we left a boy appeared with a slightly damaged clay pot containing milk. Njambo told us the following in his smiling fashion through Muschemani. He pointed to the sweat on my wife's and my forehead and he pointed to the milk 'You are exhausted from walking, look at the sweat on your faces. Refresh yourselves; the milk is cool and will be good for you.' We had anyway already looked at the milk with great desire. Such was our luck.

A Maschukulumbe does not drink from a damaged container. Why then did they offer us one? The milk, however, had a noticeable greenish tinge. 'That milk is poisoned', it suddenly occured to me. We thanked him for the present. The king let us go saying that we should stay longer, that he and his people wanted to trade with us, too, and that they intended to buy *impandes* in particular. Over and over again there was that false idea that we were *impande* traders. While I was trying to contradict this error I hit the pot with the milk slightly although unintentionally. Some of the milk spilled over and Witstock, Leeb's dog, licked it up eagerly.

That very day Witstock fell ill, vomited and the next day perished from convulsions and very violent pains. That was the effect of the poisoned milk which that smiling devil had offered my wife and me in such a friendly and sweet way as refreshment.

We built our camp with its walls of bundles facing the village. At the corner of our short camp wall was the tree and at the two open sides a shallow, dirty and swampy pool in which cattle bones were being bleached. It provided us with some protection. The skull tree was about 200 m away from us, if I remember correctly in an east-south-eastern direction. At the western side we dug the hole for our cooking hearth and here we also stuck in the pegs to which we fastened the goats and donkeys during the night.

Women and some men came up to us; the first brought much sweet milk and many chickens. Since I was not sure whether they would soon refuse to give us food here as well, my wife bought everything they brought us. We immediately killed almost all the chickens and cooked three full pots so that in an emergency we had enough food for three to four days. It struck us that many men were leaving in twos and threes hurriedly to the west, north-west, east and north-east. I suspected that these might be messengers who were quickly to gather Njambo's entire armed force which lived dispersed on the plains as herdsmen. By the following day my suspicion was confirmed by facts.

All these messengers were bearing two to three harpoon assegais whereas normally they always carried only one spear each. It also struck us that three Maschukulumbe sat down at our fire without asking us for permission and that they refused to leave until I finally poured some foul-smelling carbolic acid over their naked feet. We soon realised that they were spies whom the king had sent to our camp as permanent observers. The presence of these spies became rather annoying for us even though they were sitting at a little distance from us. We had to take clothing and fresh underwear from our packages, had to prepare the calico for our next porters, had to get out the glass beads as barter objects for food and had to choose presents for Njambo's subchiefs. On these occasions, of course, we could not avoid them looking into our loads. Only once did they get up to run into the village from where people were calling them. Yet they came back and called on Muschemani to get Pit. Under the strain of the circumstances we had not noticed that Pit was missing. Immediately upon our arrival he had rushed into the village where he was playing all kinds of tricks. He rushed between people, inspected their storage vessels intently, etc. etc. People let him do this. They had never seen a tame baboon and they seemed to have great fun with the animal. Yet their amusement appeared to have changed suddenly when Pit jumped at a magic calabash which had been placed on a special pole near the king's hut and which was supposed to contain special charms. Then they shouted 'Pah', and Pit was driven out of the village. Since they were afraid, however, that he might come back clandestinely they called our black servant through those spies to tell him to chase that ape to the camp where we tied him up immediately. Later the king's messengers appeared with the broken calabash and demanded payment for it. After long negotiations I could not help finally giving them 2 m of calico as compensation.

In the afternoon we saw to our surprise several porters coming from the north. Already from a distance we could tell that they were strangers. They came close rapidly. They were three men, one boy, and behind them bringing up the rear were two Maschukulumbe. The three first men, however, judging by their thick and beautifully groomed kinky hair hanging down below their ears and by their weapons consisting of bows and arrows, were true Mankoya, i.e. from a tribe living north of the Maschukulumbe. They brought the well known cake tobacco, a product of their country, to exchange it for lechwe skins.[1]

I was very eager to talk with these Mankoya unobserved. Unfortunately they did not stop when they marched by us. When they visited us in the evening they had already been indoctrinated by the Maschukulumbe. And when they sat down near our fire it was not really possible to talk with them since the Maschukulumbe spies immediately came closer in order not to miss a single word. Yet since one Mankoya knew Setoka I succeeded in telling him my intentions anyway with Muschemani translating in a low voice. I talked to them in the firm belief that they would be glad to see for the first time some Europeans who now would bring calico, etc. to their fellow tribesmen without wanting precious ivory in return.

More than anything else, however, I was interested in hearing about the supposed Portuguese in more detail from the Mankoya. Of course, I had no idea that
my informant had been won over already to the plan to draw me into a trap based
on the phantom of this Portuguese who had never lived.

I asked them in much detail about this European. I had already written a letter
to this Portuguese which these Mankoya, whom I regarded as God-sent angels,
were to bring to him. In order to arrange it so that I could give this letter, plus
payment for its delivery, secretly to the Mankoya squatting closest to me, I
shouted a few words to Oswald to rid me of my troublesome listeners. He did this
in a rather original fashion. Oswald let Pit lose from his chain. The ape was
friendly and grinned at him in return as usual. Then Oswald pointed with his
hand to the spies who had edged closer and closer until they were 2 m from us. He
said in a harsh voice: 'Pit, look, they have chained you.' In one jump Pit leapt on
top of these two. They rolled over and the women standing a little further back
laughed at them, though they tried to keep a straight face. Yet Pit kept on teasing
them without harming them. They finally had to hide behind the women. In the
meantime, I had rolled up one sitsiba (2 m of calico) into a fist-sized piece. While
everybody's attention was drawn to Pit I passed it unobserved to the Mankoya
squatting next to me by letting it slip to the ground out of my sleeve. The black
dropped his big cheetah skin tobacco pouch over the calico. Then he quickly bent
down and in the next moment letter and calico had disappeared into his skin bag.
The behaviour of the Mankoya confirmed my belief that he had seen the Portuguese at Massangu's as well as my assumption that the path through the narrow
pass, the true trade route to the north of the central Maschukulumbe tribes, indeed
went through Massangu's kraal.[2] I was now certain that this man was decent and
honest even though he was acting cautiously with respect to the Maschukulumbe.
I could not imagine any treacherous intent on his part, yet his behaviour was in
fact thoroughly mendacious and deceptive. Otherwise I cannot report anything
bad about the Mankoya in general and I believe that this man was simply acting
under the influence of the Maschukulumbe. I heard later that my letter was delivered to Njambo and either was burnt by him as witchcraft or was set aside and
thus at some point could fall into the hands of another traveller together with my
diaries.

In the afternoon I sent Fekete with Muschemani to Njambo to bring him a
present and to ask him to give me porters for certain by the next morning, 30
July. He promised this, yet he did not keep his word as I had anyway expected.
The clearly visible Maschukulumbe reinforcements which were coming to
Njambo on the evening of 29 July and in the morning of the following
day induced me to be on guard all night long with all my people, except for
my wife.

Even though I sent for him several times the next day, Njambo only showed
up in the afternoon. Muschemani told me that the king had taken from our
porter-thieves of Diluka-Nikoba all the stolen calico and all the glass beads, leaving them only with some brass jewellery and some of Oswald's clothing. He was

busy distributing 4 m pieces of red and white dotted calico among his chiefs. Later Muschemani reported that the king had bought in exchange for our calico some tobacco, pipes and spears from the Mankoya and the Maschukulumbe who had come from the north. From others he had bought millet, maize and beer. This news was soon confirmed because the Maschukulumbe traders who stopped for a while at our camp on their way home were carrying some rolled up calico pieces openly tied to their spears.

As I have already said Njambo showed up in the afternoon with his entourage and told me that he could not give me any porters since the presents I had given him were so small that he could not see them. 'And what about that which you stole from me via my porters?' 'That I did not take from you but from them. You can be glad that I punished them.' What divine justice in the country of the Maschukulumbe. This was a new paragraph in the code of penal law. Thieves and robbers are punished best by the judge taking away most of their booty and keeping it for himself.

Njambo's territory is probably the largest of the Maschukulumbe areas. It measured twenty to thirty kilometres from south to north, stretching from the village Galulonga[3] in the north down to the Luenge. From east to west I would estimate its extent to be forty-five to fifty kilometres. I should think it has twenty small villages, 450–500 able-bodied men under arms, a total population of 850–900 people,[4] about 7,000 head of cattle and perhaps sixty to seventy dogs. (There are only these two domestic animals in this area.) The area is situated, as I said before, on the northern or left bank of the Luenge. It consists of river flats overgrown with high grass, numerous lagoons, and swamps. The flats can be divided into three zones. The one on the river has the highest growth of grass, is rather flat and, depending on the bends of the river, it has a width of three to twenty-six kilometres. It is followed by another rather high-grassed zone full of ant-hills the size of haystacks. There must be more than 100,000 of these ant-hills. The northernmost zone is overgrown with shrubs, is full of reed-covered swamps, and every now and then there are groves or merely groups of high shady giant mimosa trees. The area is abundant with game—mammals and birds. The game to be found is mainly lechwe, puku, kabunda antelopes, eland, striped gnu, zebra, hippo, hyena etc.

Since Njambo made no arrangements whatsoever to provide us with porters I decided that day to make an attempt on my own to go to the Portuguese and to ask him for porters. I knew that these traders, whether they are Portuguese or Mambari, have their own servants or hirelings in large numbers whom they use on all trading journeys no matter how distant. These men have to go as long or as far as it pleases their master. Thus, I could not only hope to get porters from a Portuguese, I simply had to dare this last attempt to save us.

I knew too that my people would be able to deal with the blacks during my absence, which anyway should not have lasted longer than two to three days. They would not spare their attackers whereas I was the one who was always trying to prevent any bloodshed whenever possible. I am absolutely convinced that most African travellers would have used their firearms directly during those attacks in Diluka and on other occasions. Perhaps this would have intimidated the enemies more. Yet it is not impossible that each shot might have provoked the enemies so much that they would have attacked us incessantly and we finally really would have been defeated.

The mountain range which limited our horizon, stretching from north-west to east-north-east, was about thirty kilometres from our camp. It was the watershed between the Luenge and another river flowing parallel to it. We could all see clearly the pass which I have already mentioned several times and over which the path to the Portuguese supposedly went. Thus I could rightly hope that I should be able to reach Massungu's village, still on our side at the foot of the hills, by the next morning if I marched all night long. The day after that I could then be back in our camp at Njambo's with the desired porters. I decided to go providing that the night was clear so that I could use the stars as my guide. I intended to take little Daisy along so that with his bark he could indicate to me if and when I was approaching a kraal or if and when a wild animal was approaching us. My people, however, who thought that such a march was foolhardy, were trying to talk me out of this decision. Yet when they thought it through carefully they realised that things could not go on like this. We would never be able to reach the northern border of Maschukulumbe country alive if we had to go on fighting calamities similar to those we had had to face during the last days. Something decisive had to happen. Several times already our deaths had only been prevented by a fortuitous joke at the decisive moment or by a mere coincidence of fortunate circumstances! A single wrong action, a decrease of our strength, or the dozing off of all of us after the exhaustion of the day and several sleepless nights could destroy us all. This is why I was determined to go, and yet in the end it did not happen. There were two reasons which persuaded me to stay. One was the strong reinforcement of armed men in the village and the conviction that they were planning an attack during the night so that I would have to stay in the camp. The second reason was that the night happened to be pitch dark so that I could not possibly have found my way without a guide. Had I gone anyway, my people would never have seen me again. I surely would have died in the swamps, the existence of which then, however, on 30 July was entirely unknown to me.

In the evening the wind increased and developed into a south-east gale which howled gloomily through the dark night. It was all the more surprising to us that the Maschukulumbe who otherwise are lazy people and go to bed early and do not get up until late, stayed up unusually late that day and made a lot of noise into the night. Perhaps—since they were too cowardly to attack us during the day —they were going to use the night as cover for an attack and were working themselves into a trance for it by singing, shouting, dancing, beer-drinking and brawling.

I stayed—and this decision saved me from lingering death in the swamps and was very advantageous for my people during the attack on our camp which, in fact, did take place that night. It was one of the most terrifying nights on this whole journey. The icy wind blew across the plain and made us shiver. We could not keep a warm fire going in such a storm because of the fire hazard. Neither could we lie behind the low camp wall since we had to be on guard. A single mistake and the consequences might have been the worst possible for us. It got darker and darker. The howling of approaching hyenas blended with the shouting and rejoicing coming from the village. Bands of two- and four-footed robbers joined in noisy chorus. If we only had had twenty-five well armed Zanzibaris we would have laughed at Njambo's activities, but like this it was different.

After the wildest war-whoops a sudden quiet fell. We soon heard clearly the shuffle of feet from the distance, i.e. from the village. They were coming out, they were gathering in front of the village for the attack. Our situation was desperate. The many ant-hills around us provided welcome cover for the enemy. In addition, it was impossible to see further than ten metres in that darkness. It was as if heaven and earth had conspired against us.

Because of the strong wind I even had the smouldering coals put out. Oswald kept his eye on the flats. The rest of us turned our eyes towards the village. Of course, we could not see much, but we could hear. That the enemies were gathering in front of the village I could guess from the fact that the hyenas which usually sneaked around the village every night were suddenly quiet. Probably they had been chased away by spears; in any case, we heard them anew ten minutes later about half a kilometre further west.

'One has made himself a little fire there', Oswald whispered to Fekete who had crept up to him since his post was closest to him. Fekete directed our attention immediately, yet cautiously, to this development.

But already we saw a large blaze suddenly flaring up directly to the south about 800 to 1,000 m away from us. Oswald had only seen a little spark and a few seconds later we already saw a blaze. And in the following minutes this 'little fire' exploded in the west in width and height so much that within an hour the plain was converted into a sea of flames over several miles square. This fire had been caused by the fact that one of the herdsmen had not put out the fire which he had made during the day near a barren ant-hill. The enemies, of course, had noticed this blaze with anger since its bright flames hindered their attack considerably. The bright blaze soon lit up our camp like daylight and equally the Maschuku-lumbe village as well as the ant-hills. Behind these the bandits had sneaked up on the harassed and deadly tired strangers. Now they were stuck there as they were afraid to leave their safe hiding places.

The unintended bush fire had frustrated their attack which could not have been thought out any more crudely nor in a more diabolically simple fashion. The crude thing about their plan was that the blacks thought that all of us were asleep every night.

One of these nights while fast asleep we were supposed to be taken by surprise. At their first bark our dogs were to be killed with a few spears. Then the whole group of attackers, about fifty to seventy men, were to throw their spears at the dark clump of us lying on the ground before we were able to grab our guns. The attackers were then to run away immediately, whereas we, either dead or wounded, were to be left to our fate. No Maschukulumbe was to leave the village for the direction of our camp for days and nobody was to approach our camp until the vultures circling overhead and swooping down to our corpses would indicate that we were all dead.

The giant fire in the plain had prevented their diabolical plan and had saved our lives this time. Whose fault was it that the fire flared up? I do not know his name yet I am grateful anyway for his unintended deed. When any of our enemies went into the space lit up by the fire and tried to get from one ant-hill to the next they became as visible as a black human figure in daylight and were an absolutely clear target for our rifles. Yet at the same time the fire which had frustrated the attack of the blacks showed them, too, that we whites were not asleep but on watch. In the red light of the flames they saw us moving about in our camp and in particular they saw the barrels of our rifles flashing.

The human skulls lit up by the flames and sticking out in sharp contrast from the darkness behind us seemed to be grinning down at us from their pole. Their greeting meant: 'Caution and vigilance'.

We were vigilant, indeed. We soon saw how the enemy was slowly withdrawing from one ant-hill to the next until they had reached the village. For an hour the Maschukulumbe made a great noise in the village, then it slowly became quiet. This time the Maschukulumbe really went to bed, as was proved clearly by the barking of the hyenas who were again sneaking around the village.

The fire in the plain, however, raged on until the next noon. This was not the first big bush fire during the night which I have seen on my two African trips. However, it was, undoubtedly, the largest one and was the most frightningly beautiful sight which I ever saw in that respect. The grass around us at a diameter of half a kilometre had been grazed out and trampled down as it was the constant habitat of the thousands of head of cattle of the village. This pasture thus became for us a belt of salvation from the blaze. The fire had probably extended itself furthest in the south. There it might have penetrated as far as 30 km until stopped by the Luenge and its lagoons. I need not mention specifically that it was only because of the raging south-east gale that this bush fire grew to such incredible dimensions yet at the same time also into such magnificence.

Finally the morning dawned; the barren plain lay naked in front of us. The day was cold and the wind so gusty that we did not dare to light a fire among our loads. From time to time the wind was blowing clouds of smoke and acrid gases towards us. We were all very tired and physically as well as mentally exhausted. Yet there was no time to complain or to meditate. We had to get busy and to become active.

That day, too, more Maschukulumbe arrived in the village as reinforcements, and I realised more and more that Njambo was the most powerful among the Maschukulumbe chiefs. More and more I felt pressure to get out of his sphere of influence with my people. We had a council of war and came to the following conclusions. In case Njambo would not give us any porters I and my wife, followed by Muschemani and the donkeys, were to start out to go to the Portuguese and then come back with the porters to pick up Fekete, Leeb and Oswald who, in the meantime, were to transform our camp into a small circular laager.

. After that decision was made I once again sent a messenger to the king to ask for porters. The king let me know that he had no porters. I sent a messenger a second time whereupon he came himself with his 'state council', all looking rather thievish. They were followed at a little distance by over 300 spear bearers and many women and children. 'I want to have presents.' 'I have already given you many presents.' 'I want to have more!' 'You got a great deal from the stolen goods of the porters from Diluka and Nikoba.' 'That is all nothing. I want to have *impandes*, glass beads—big, beautiful, colourful glass beads and blankets.' I gave him some glass beads. 'That is not enough, these are not beautiful and big.' And yet they were big blue golden stars from Gablonz. He did not like them but gave them away immediately to one of his knaves and I had to give him new ones. The same thing continued to happen until Njambo had taken 3 kg into his possession. Then I refused to give him anything more. Three kilogrammes of these beautiful glass beads represent in this area the value of at least six oxen. Then he wanted to know what I would pay the porters if they were to carry my packages to the next village which as he thought was about three hours away. I intended to give 4 m of blue calico worth one big ox in Njambo's country. Yet they did not want this calico and demanded 4 m of the sewn sackcloth design (from the Smichow cotton mill, formerly Przibram). I got that out, as well. Then the king said that this was too little for three hours' work. He pointed out the time, describing with his hand a section of the sun's orbit in the sky. I should give more. All these tortures were dragged out on purpose so that I had to open many packages and he had a chance to find out what the content of the various loads was.

The final effect of this long conversation was that the people asked by Njambo whether they wanted to carry for us shouted in hundreds 'We do not want to porter!', unless I were to give them the handkerchiefs and the blue calico. Yet I did not agree. My journey was still long and every metre of calico very valuable and the further north up to Tanganyika the more desired it was to become. 'All right, you do not want to carry for me. Then I shall go to the 'Lekva' and he will give me his porters.' My words made Njambo stop short, even though he knew very well that the Portuguese for whom I was looking did not exist. He was obviously afraid, as I now realise, that I might get more willing porters from the chief of Galulonga and would come back with them to get us out of his grip. He seemed to be on the verge of giving in when his thieving counsellors again swung him around to repeat 'No'. After that I decided simply to break off all negotiations and to start out immediately with my wife to go to the Portuguese. First we had still to rearrange some of our parcels. Then I told my people that in case the blacks were willing to carry our loads in spite of everything—which I actually expected would happen—they should start out with them and should inform me about this by firing a volley of shots, otherwise, however, they should avoid any shooting.

After all that had been arranged I took my rifle with 170 cartridges, my wife took hers with sixty, and Muschemani carried a double-barrelled rifle loaded with buck-shot. Yet before we left I had Muschemani our interpreter, tell Njambo the following: 'If you should let your people carry for us after I have left they will probably try just as the previous porters to run away with my things. Now do you see this vessel?' I put a little bottle on an ant-hill in a direction where there were no people, fired and splintered it into atoms. 'Well, the same thing as happened to this vessel will happen to each of your men who try to run away with my goods —their heads will be crashed.' Smiling, as always, with half-closed blinking eyes he said: 'Yes, do this, that is right.' After this final demonstration which made the blacks feel somewhat uncomfortable, I left and we went northwards. The path, however, went to the north-east and led to a village called Galulonga on the right. But I wanted to avoid it and march straight to the narrow pass in order to reach the Portuguese as fast as possible. I had no idea that behind the next hills overgrown with high grass deadly swamps were hidden. We might have been walking for 4 km through dense grass (which, however, was burnt down in places and thus allowed us a limited view to the hills in the north and north-east) when we heard shots fired exactly in the sequence we had agreed upon. Njambo's people had decided to carry for us. This made us happy for a moment. But our only aspiration and desire was to get closer to that range of hills and its narrow pass. Each step seemed to bring us closer to our salvation and thus we marched on energetically, especially since we knew that our people were following. I went ahead with the two little dogs. Then came my wife and the two dwarf goats plus the two laden donkeys driven by Muschemani. At the tenth kilometre we reached a deep swamp.[5] Since we could not cross it we were forced to go out of our way to the right to avoid it. There we met two blacks hunting in the high grass. One of them was a Maschukulumbe and the other, to our great delight, a Mankoya armed with bow and arrows. We asked them the way and gave them a few glass beads. They pointed to the north-east. They said we would have to follow the path because that was the only way to get through the swamp. Repeatedly they mentioned the village Galulonga which we absolutely had to pass since no other dry route would lead to the narrow pass and to Massangu's kraal. Galulonga seemed to me to represent a danger for the three of us. I also did not like to take a detour. Thus I pressed on directly through the swamps. I realised already, however, that the narrow pass was much further away from Njambo's village than I had estimated from there. From our camp I had thought that it was hardly thirty kilometres and now I saw that it was still at least thirty kilometres away from our temporary position. Because of the clarity of the African atmosphere it happens very often that Europeans make such an error even after years of wandering through the African wilderness.[6]

The sight of the narrow pass and the nearby northern border which meant salvation from our agonies had a great effect on our nerves. We overcame the alarming feeling caused by the cool brown swamp water which was seeping into our shoes and we made a path directly to the north.

I hoped to reach Massangu's village, supposedly situated on this side of the narrow pass, and thus the Portuguese, by 3 o'clock in the afternoon so that we could be back for the night with my people. This goal spurred us to hurry even more. Yet after the first 200 paces it was clear that any kind of speed was absolutely impossible here. Each step forward had to be made with the greatest of efforts. The water was totally overgrown with reeds and the mud, which in the beginning was as deep as fifty to sixty centimetres, became deeper and deeper. It was of a dirty brown colour and its smell was terrible. Every fifty to sixty metres ant-hills as big as haystacks stuck out of the water like little islands covered with saro palm bushes or reeds.

We were wading in our shoes. My wife went first. I drove the donkeys after her and the black was following with the goats. If it was difficult for us to lift our feet out of the mud and the grass entangled in a mat on the ground, it was even harder for our beasts of burden with their pointed hooves. Anyway I had only laden them with half loads, but even these were soon too heavy for them and it became worse and worse with every step. Jacob knew a way out by jumping from one spot to the next. He was the more intelligent and stronger of the two donkeys. The other one, however, simply stopped. I had to lift out his front legs, then to lift up his whole rear body and to push him forward. This was the only way of moving this animal forward. This effort as well as the weight of the two rifles on my back meant that in a short time I was dripping with sweat as much as with swamp water. And soon I was so tired that I could hardly keep myself standing on my legs. My whole body was shivering as if in a fever and I had to lean on my rifle as on a walking stick. Poor Muschemani was somewhat better off since we had trampled something like a path for him. He only had to help the goats along every now and then. The work with the donkeys became harder and harder since my power to get the animal forward faster weakened. My wife went ahead with Jacob who was following her in big jumps like a faithful dog. I lagged behind more and more. Finally I no longer had even the strength to lift up the animal once more. Against my own wish I had to sit down in the swamp water to rest for a while. Only when my wife who got worried about me came back to help me, was I able to get up and to follow her for a few steps. I had to leave the poor animal behind yet since I saw that his feet were trembling just as mine and that he finally went down on his knees under his load I took the load off his back and dragged it to the next ant-hill. My wife did the same with his saddle. We went on, but terribly slowly. Again and again I had to rest, sometimes right in the swamp, sometimes on an ant-hill. All strength seemed to have left my body. Suddenly I got warm, then hot. A fever attack had seized me. With the outbreak of the fever the rest of my strength declined rapidly and I felt as exhausted and as weak as I never had before in my life. Mechanically my feet tried to wade through the swamp. Finally even that became impossible. I gave my wife my rifles to bring them to the next ant-hill and I stayed behind. Muschemani came to me and my wife rushed back to help me. With an incredible effort I could still get myself to the place where the rifles were lying but then I broke down completely.

I had the feeling that I would not survive the next half hour. In addition, there was this disgusting, nearly choking, odour coming from the swamp which made my already laboured breathing even worse. I seized my wife's hand and asked her to forgive me all the horrors and dangers of this journey in as much as they were my fault and I said farewell to her forever. 'I shall not last very much longer. More air, I am choking . . .'

My wife is not one for sentimentality. She pressed my feverish hands to her breast, tore my shirt open and then she leaped up. 'Is there no possible help?' She climbed higher up the ant-hill and then I heard her shouting once and then again. She had spotted three Maschukulumbe far away at the edge of the swamp as they came out behind a huge herd of grazing cattle. 'Shout at them to come here fast, very fast.' I had not believed that I could be saved. I would have stayed here over-night and then would have been choked by the night vapours of the swamp. Then I heard that human beings were coming! WAS THAT POSSIBLE? I tried to get up and to see them with my own eyes. Our enemies! 'Good heavens, en-emies?' Rosa shouted, 'they are human beings, saviours. They are coming without spears.' 'They are herdsmen,' the black shouted, 'they have not yet heard anything about us. They have no idea what went on in the king's kraal. No, I can see the as-tonishment in their faces at the sight of you. No, Baas, do not fear, these people come to help you. Look how they are waving at us. They are warning us not to go on.'

The slightest gleam of hope often works wonders. With Rosa's and Muschemani's help I pulled myself up and saw myself what I did not dare to be-lieve. This was help in an emergency. Three Maschukulumbe stood at our side ready to do everything we wished. We immediately gave them our sackcloth as a present to prove our friendliness towards them. Then they began their work of rescue. One of them took my wife on his shoulders and the other two carried me until we got to shallow waters and finally reached the northern bank of the swamp. Here we rested while they went back. One of them brought Jacob's load, the other his saddle, the third carried two of the weakest dwarf goats. Musche-mani brought the rifles. Jacob had come through without any help.

From the spot on the edge of the swamp where our carriers had put us down we had walked at most 500 paces and suddenly at a turn of the path we stood in front of the twin village Galulonga. In front of us was Leeb, around whom were sc-attered about twenty of our loads. The surprise on both sides was tremendous. I had a bad time. 'Did you not see the Portuguese, Doctor?' 'No, we were at the edge of death and without these three Maschukulumbe we would have perished in the swamps. But you Leeb, how did it go with you? Tell us.' Before that, how-ever, I gave our three life-savers generous gifts and they promised to get us the second donkey and his load. But then Leeb began to talk and I shall give here a short summary of his report:

'Soon after the doctor had disappeared out of our sight Njambo came to us and said that he would allow his people to carry our loads for a present of one blanket. We gave it to him. At a sign from the king a hundred porters came. Yet they rushed in sheer fury to grab the loads. In short, all the scenes of attempted theft which had occurred in Bosango were repeated again. Finally the men began to move. I ran to follow the first twenty porters and I shouted to my companions to do the same, each with twenty porters. Soon some of my porters left the path. When I was about to shoot at them I was hindered by the raised spears of two closely-knit groups of blacks who had run along to follow us closely. Njambo, the devil, had kept his word in this respect. While I was following those of the twenty porters who had left the path into the dense grass, the others who had stayed on the path cut open our parcels and handed their loot to some women standing in the grass. I realised only later that they had been posted there with baskets by Njambo for exactly that purpose. The men then stuffed grass into the sacks and tied them again with bark fibre as they had been tied before. All that happened so fast that I did not notice it at first. I drove the fugitives back to the path where I did not see anything suspicious. I only met women whom it seemed to me were carrying corn or bush fruits in their baskets. In these baskets, however, were all our stolen glass beads, sackcloth and brass goods. I realised about this robbery too late. Only here has everything become clear to me.' With these words he was pointing to our loads. 'Here,' he said, 'the porters dropped the loads and ran away. When I caught on to this bold robbery the thieves had long since disappeared in the high grass and reeds so that I could not even fire a single shot after them.'

'Where are Fekete and Oswald? And where are the rest of our things?' 'They are not yet here.' Women and children were gathering around us. I gave them glass beads and got them to bring our things about 160 m further south to what seemed to me to be a deserted kraal. It was an elliptical place 4 m wide and 7 m long, partly filled with clumps of soil from an ant-hill and enclosed by maize stalks. It had openings towards the east, north-east and south-west. Next to it was a similar partly destroyed enclosure, and I found this place, in which the blacks dry their corn after the harvest and where they protect it from their cattle, quite suitable for a camp. In any case, this seemed to me to be the safest stronghold in this vicinity.

We got maize stalks from the nearby broken ring fence and closed with them the third opening towards the east. While my wife sent the women off to get some milk and something to eat Leeb together with Muschemani began to repair the damaged sections of our enclosure and to narrow the second opening. They put clumps of earth against the walls to enforce them at least above the ground. In the evening Fekete's and Oswald's arrival was announced. Supported by Leeb I walked a little way towards them.

Imagine my horror, my dear reader, when I saw them coming with only five porters bringing the scientific instruments and part of the cartridges. In total, they were not even carrying four full loads. 'Where are the other porters?' 'Run away. Everything is stolen. Suddenly in the midst of our march the porters rushed away in all directions at an unknown signal. It was impossible to fire upon them because of their armed accomplices who had accompanied us on the right and the left.

Some who realised that they had stolen cartridges or scientific instruments were very disappointed. [Fortunately Leeb and his porters had already brought earlier the two little boxes with my diaries.] They threw these things away and quickly divided the other loot up with their neighbours.' Fekete had saved these things which were useless for the blacks by going to Galulonga and hiring five porters who now were bringing the rest of my belongings. Unfortunately we soon realised that the inhabitants of this village were just as thievish as those from Njambo. On the short march through the village they had skilfully opened several of our packages and among other things they had stolen my wife's blankets.

When we examined our belongings more closely we were missing, among the most important things, 7 bundles of glass beads, 3 bundles of calico, 5 bundles of blankets, 2 bundles with Oswald's entire clothing, one bundle of Oswald's and one of Fekete's camp blankets and spare clothing, 1 bundle of my best clothing and 2 bundles of my wife's clothes and underwear. The remainder that was missing comprised cartridges. Half of the things were missing from three of the packages Leeb had brought. These were mostly my wife's and my spare clothes. From the other bundles several parcels of sackcloth, glass beads, jewellery, brass rings, etc. were missing.

It had become true: with each step further north things got worse and worse. In fact, after this robbery we were already at the brink of disaster. In the final analysis those actually responsible for our sad situation were the nineteen servants whom I had hired for the entire trip, but who had deserted us in such a cowardly fashion at Bosango. Had they stayed with us things would never have become so bad. While I and my companions were talking of them in not exactly the most flattering terms and while my wife was looking around for the women whom she had sent for milk, suddenly eight blacks in skirts approached. My wife looked at them closely and then she suddenly shouted: 'What does this mean? These are no Maschukulumbe. Emil, come quickly. My God, these are our people.' We all jumped up, rushed to the camp, and found Rosa's words confirmed.

Eight of the deserters who had caused all our misfortune by their escape had come back to us. I saw Mapani, Jonas, Maruma, Kakatombe, Siroko, Mononumba, Stoffel and Plati. In their flight they had gone as far as the dear old Matoka King Mo-Panza, who is already well known to my readers. Mo-Panza had listened to their report with astonishment but he did not allow them to finish it. With harsh words he condemned their miserable cowardice. He said they were responsible for our death and that we were probably already killed. But just as certainly they all would have to die, because as soon as the Marutse King Luanika heard that they had deserted us in the midst of his enemies he would send out messengers to kill each and every one of them.

After these words of Mo-Panza all intended to return. Yet Boy, the coward, who otherwise had proved to be so useful for hunting and other necessary jobs was against this. He talked eleven into staying with him at Mo-Panza's. The other eight who now were standing in front of us had picked up all their belongings to go north in order to look for us. Mo-Panza had given them food and they had found a shorter way than the one we had come. Thus, they reached us on 31 July.

'We were hurrying to get to you,' were Mapani's last words, 'because in the flats between our place and the Luenge our eyes were often attracted hither and thither by beautiful gay colours and we saw that these were Maschukulumbe wearing your blue, red and white calico, your clothing, and other things. Our hearts were seized with incredible fear since we could not believe that you had given all that to them as presents. No, we had to believe that you were already killed and that they had robbed you.'

In order to preserve discipline I turned away from them when they arrived and squatted down next to us. I had to show them a strict face even though at the bottom of my heart I was rejoicing in the fact that they had come. When they wanted to talk to me I walked off sideways asking my wife to listen to them. I was unable to hurt them, this was quite clear from the beginning, yet they had to be punished and only when Rosa and our companions asked me to forgive these repentant fugitives did I finally give in.

I then accused them of cowardice and asserted that we never would have got into this situation if they had stuck to us faithfully. Then all shouted at the same time: 'We would never have left you if it had not been for Boy who had been whispering into our ears for weeks not to go on. It is totally Boy's fault. Boy is responsible for it all!'

The remorse of these poor chaps was quite genuine since—as we now heard —the Maschukulumbe had not made it easy for them to get to us. They had to give up their blankets, their calico pieces, the glass beads around their necks, and even almost all of their spears only to be permitted to travel through. People told them that we were dead, others reported that only two of us were still alive. Again from others they heard that everything had been taken away from us and that we were running around naked and without any arms.

Yet they were not diverted from their purpose. They went on and finally reached us. I told my wife to give them a few metres of cotton—without my apparent knowledge—so that they could buy themselves some spears from the inhabitants of Galulonga. This they did the same day.

The next day, 1 August, I sent Fekete, two of my servants and the three Maschukulumbe to drag the donkey which we had left behind out of the swamp. They succeeded in doing so but Fekete and the two blacks could not understand how we had ever been able to get out of that swamp alive as exhausted as we had been. That day I established relations with chief Uschumata-Zumbo.[7] I urged him to return our stolen goods and he urged me to give him his presents. Among the people of Galulonga there was a man who incidentally was the father of one of the three herdsmen and who tried to persuade the chief to give our stolen things back. Yet he was unsuccessful. On the whole this man took our side and we owed him a lot that day. For his good will I gave him better presents than the chief. Since I did not see him the next day during the battle, it appears that he had been strangled that night by Zumbo. He was the only one who knew nothing about the supposed Portuguese at Massangu, yet he advised us strongly to get across those hills as soon as possible which we were anyway trying hard to do. He said we would be completely safe there.

The range of hills stretching from north-west to east was a ridge with two saddle-shaped depressions in the north and north-north-east. Several other cone-shaped hills rose in front of it in the east. I took the liberty of calling this range the Franz-Josef Mountains in honour of my highest benefactor, His Majesty the Emperor.[8] Their northern slope is the border of Maschukulumbe territory in the north. These hills are rocky and sparsely wooded. In the centre lies a semicircular valley jutting to the north which encloses the large Galulonga swamps.

That day the same Maschukulumbe who, as a stranger in Diluka, had inspired us with so much confidence because of his friendly face and who had told us so much about the Portuguese at Massangu showed up. He was chief of a village in the east. His tongue was this day just as friendly as the first time. Yet his words contradicted those of our new friend entirely, especially with respect to the Portuguese. We were quite confused as to our decision.

The return of my eight servants was like a sign from heaven and thus I planned to end the critical situation as quickly as possible and to go to the Portuguese on the following night. I decided to take my wife, Leeb and seven servants along with me, as well as the bundles of calico and glass beads, in order to secure them, 4,500 cartridges and instruments, in brief, only those things which the people did not want anyway were to remain in the camp. I intended to leave four rifles behind for Fekete and Oswald and the two blacks, Mapani and Muschemani. These were just as many rifles as we planned to take along. The camp made from maize stalks offered more protection than our usual makeshift camp of the one metre high parcels, placed in high parcel walls at right angles. The border, i.e. the range of hills, was at most 28 km away. Massangu as we were told, was living about one hour from the hills on this side. Thus it would not be difficult to reach Massangu and to be back in our camp at Galulonga by nightfall. Fekete and Oswald agreed with my plan entirely. They only asked me to come back before nightfall. They were sure that they could hold the camp with four rifles during the day against the whole Maschukulumbe gang. Yet they were afraid that they would be too weak at night.

I intended to start out at 2 a.m. and to be at Massangu's around eight in the morning. I wanted to be back home by noon in order to attack the blacks from the rear in case our enemies were to make an attack on the camp. Yet in order to find my way through the night it was necessary to find out more details about the path leading to the narrow pass. Every now and then we asked the women who came to sell us milk where Massangu was living and we always got the same answer: 'There, at the narrow pass.' We observed several groups of tobacco sellers. They were Mankoya or Maschukulumbe coming from that direction. Since they were, however, covered with mud up to their chests we concluded that the swamp through which we had come the day before stretched even further and that the paths from Galulonga to Massangu passed through it.

This was a very unpleasant observation, yet in order to be sure I had to find out more. To the people in the village it seemed to be clear that we intended to go to Massangu even without porters. Thus we were not only watched carefully, but —as I found out later—messengers were sent to Njambo that same day in order to call the Maschukulumbe hordes gathered there quickly as the 'most suitable moment for the attack had come'. Around noon some Maschukulumbe came to our camp and reported without being asked by us that the route to Massangu went directly westwards. The way the speaker behaved proved that it was a clumsy trap. In the afternoon we saw this 'trustworthy' face—which is already known to the reader—several times around our camp and Fekete swore firmly that this was the same person who had concerned himself so much with the thief of our blankets when he was passing through Galulonga and that most probably he had been involved himself in this theft. We noticed, too, that individual Maschukulumbe as well as small groups of them were loafing around our camp and the twin village at a distance of about 300–500 m. They were probably keen to see whether and when some of us would start out on our way to Massangu. In order to confuse them as well as to find out some more about the route there I sent Leeb together with Mapani and two other blacks to hunt for some water birds along the banks of the lagoon from which we had been rescued. Actually, however, he was supposed to find out where the footpaths from Galulonga went by which the Mankoya to-bacco traders had come from the north. He was to see whether these paths led directly to the narrow pass, and, in brief, he was to determine himself which direction we should take. He was also to find out whether the swamp in which we had been lost stretched so far to the east that we would have to cross it on our way to the narrow pass. I ordered Leeb specifically to make inconspicuous road signs for himself so that we would not miss the right paths to Massangu during the night. Furthermore, I had Fekete with two blacks stand guard about 100 paces from the camp where they could see far to the north and, as it seemed, along the swamp. This guard had to watch Leeb constantly so that in case of an attack they could intimidate the attackers with bullets. Leeb returned safely and confirmed our suspicion of the 'trustworthy' face. After Leeb had recognised on his walk that those paths leading northwards between two tall trees were the ones going to the narrow pass he suddenly saw our confidant sitting on an ant-hill. Shortly after-wards he came up to him and asked Leeb through his translator, Mapani, whether he was looking for the road to Massangu. That, he said, was just this path going north. He would like to accompany him (Leeb) only he would have to get some of his companions and his arms because of the lions and the buffaloes in the swamp.

When Leeb answered that he was neither looking for the path nor intending to go to Massangu but had only come to hunt for birds, the man came very close to him and began to touch Leeb's Kropatschek rifle, that terrible weapon for the Maschukulumbe. 'Step back, Master,' said Mapani, 'this man plans something bad.' Leeb did so and had Mapani tell him that if his rifle suddenly threw out iron and killed him while he was playing with it that would be his own fault. This sound advice disturbed our confidant so much that he quickly ran away so that

Leeb thereafter was able to accomplish his mission undisturbed. Leeb finished his report saying: 'I hope these two trees have become fixed in my memory so that we can find the paths out of the village even in the dark.'

In the evening the old Maschukulumbe, whom I have already mentioned complimentarily, came to us. He brought me the news that people were planning to attack us on one of the next days. We should get lots of reeds in the following days to strengthen our camp wall. Furthermore, he told us what he heard secretly from his son—because of his friendly behaviour towards us they did not confide anything in him—that the village chief would not give me any porters under any condition. People were only allowed to sell us foodstuffs for one more day. In this way the chief hoped to finish us off very shortly. He would get everything which we still had packed in our parcels and what we were wearing on our bodies into his possession. Our heads would be stuck on the poles on both sides of Galulonga —my wife, however, he wanted to get alive in his hands!

Under these circumstances the decision to dare the indeed perilous attempt to break through to Massangu became reasonably easy. This now was our only salvation. When it had become completely dark and quiet in the twin village I put some of my blacks on guard behind the next ant-hill while we dragged big clumps of earth from a deserted and broken ant-hill to our camp in order to enforce our camp wall with them. We built it up to a height of about one metre. Then I called our guards back in, I had food cooked for the next day, and held a last council of war.

The full plan, parts of which I have already related, was the following: Fekete and Oswald were staying behind to occupy our camp. With them were staying Mapani, the most able of our returned servants, as well as Muschemani so that he could get some rest. Both Oswald and Muschemani were not too well. We were supposed to be back by the evening of 2 August, even if we did not reach the Portuguese or if he refused to give us any assistance. At 1 a.m. promptly we should get ready to leave, making no noise if possible. The Maschukulumbe should have no idea whatsoever that we were leaving. If some of them were to come to our camp during the daytime, Mapani was to tell them that we had seen buffalo early in the morning and had decided to pursue them. Our bedding was to be arranged in such a way as to appear that my wife was still asleep in the camp. We, however, would first go about 300 paces directly to the north-west towards the swamp, then we would start on the path to the north by avoiding the village and would follow this path in order to reach Massangu as fast as possible. Every one of us felt that the decisive moment for our expedition had come. Either our march through the night would bring help and rescue or the Maschukulumbe would succeed in dealing us the final blow of extermination so close to the verge of freedom. We all felt that the next twenty-four hours had to bring a decision. After all that had been discussed in detail we distributed the bedding (four blankets) which had been saved among ourselves and tried to sleep for a few hours to gather new strength. I tried in vain to fall asleep. I was watching with the guards and slightly after one o'clock everything was ready for our departure. We bade our two companions farewell and on leaving Oswald whispered into my ear: 'Please, Doctor, be back at night. During the day we are not afraid of the Maschukulumbe but at night we two whites are not able to cope with them!'

2 August 1886

'READY?' I WENT FROM ONE TO ANOTHER of my men who were squatting on the ground in order to make sure that loads, arms, and food supply were in order. Then I sneaked over to Fekete and Oswald and shook their hands to bid them farewell. None of us knew that this was to be the last handshake. Then I gave the sign for departure and we left the camp. In order not to draw the enemy's attention to our departure we had made all preparations in the dark and had not spoken a single loud word. Like ghosts we swiftly slipped into the open and sneaked down to the swamp, then along the swamp edge to the north-east to find our paths.

When we approached the village in that way the greatest caution was necessary because the village dogs could betray us all too easily. In fear of them we sneaked along the pathless swamp as cautiously as if we were on a hunt for mountain cranes. We had to avoid every branch and every stone so that no noise whatsoever would disturb the silence of that pitch-black night. Those who were walking in front had to stoop down and grope along the ground with their hands for any impediment. In the meantime the four men who stayed behind in the camp were listening into the night with their rifles in their hands in order to rush to our support in case of any emergency. Yet they could not hear a thing and soon they were glad that we had found that path so quickly and safely. In fact we soon reached the trees which Leeb had described to me as those between which that path was supposed to go. And indeed, we found a path and followed it. It was not, however, the main path but a side track which only further in the swamp linked up with the main path. In the beginning this was a well-trampled path but it soon disappeared completely in the swamp so that in the darkness of the night we soon found ourselves standing deep in swamp water in a pathless thicket of reeds. There was no going forward, only backwards. We all knew that we were on the wrong track, yet where was the right path? During the night we could not search for it—thus we had to turn back.

Dear reader, can you imagine the feelings I had when we were forced to direct our steps back again to Galulonga? I would have liked to cry if only I had been able to do so. We rested at an ant-hill, forced to wait until dawn. I took it on myself to stand guard since nothing was further from me than sleep. My wife and some of the blacks volunteered to watch with me yet I did not let them. They had to strengthen themselves for the exhausting march which lay ahead of them. There was no fear that I would not hear if some Maschukulumbe approached us. My nerves were so jittery that I would have heard a mongoose squeaking near us. In fact, today my wife and I still suffer from some kind of an insomnia as a memento of those painful night watches. I can rarely sleep longer than four hours today, and this only with interruptions. In my wife's case the consequences are that she often wakes up from her sleep sobbing and moaning and calling for me. She dreams each time that the blacks have torn her away from me or have killed me or our companions.

It was not yet dawn in the east when I pushed on again for our departure. The blacks appeared to be somewhat ill-humoured and afraid of the swamp. Only reluctantly they picked up their loads again. Leeb and I first went up and down in the swamp until we finally discovered at the crack of dawn those spots in the water which were free of reeds and thus were the path. Then we went on. The swampy ground was so soft that my wife could move only with the greatest effort and I had to carry her for about 150 m. For me, too, this march was very exhausting. I slipped repeatedly and each time both of us took unwillingly a very unpleasant mud bath. The same happened to one of the blacks who lost in the incident the bag with the 500 spare cartridges. Yet he did not tell me a thing. The water became deeper and deeper and soon seeped into our high boots. We thus changed into our low shoes and gave the boots to the blacks to carry. When the depth of the swamp increased so much that we had to wade in the water up to our breasts at certain places walking became so difficult that neither I nor my wife realised that we had lost our shoes and the blacks their sandals in the swamp. We first felt a burning and then a stinging pain. When we had climbed the nearest of the ant-hills which stuck out of the swamp here every thirty to sixty metres we saw the trouble. The many thorns, as well as the sharp reeds and palm leaves lying in the swamp, had lacerated our naked feet. My wife asked for her high boots, yet she got only one of them. I too, got only one. The missing boots had obviously slipped from the stick of our porter Siroko while he was passing through a deep spot in the swamp. And he had not noticed it just as the other one had not noticed the loss of our cartridges. An attempt to find these lost objects was completely unsuccessful and we could not afford a second attempt in view of the advanced time of the day. The sun had just risen fully and we had to reach Massangu and that range of hills in the north by about 9 or at the latest by 10 o'clock. The swamp, however, appeared to be very extensive. In the north-east and the south-west it seemed to be at least as wide as thirty to forty kilometres.[1] Our march became more and more exhausting not because the depth of the swamp had increased, but for the two reasons mentioned before, i.e. that we got more and more tired and exhausted with every hour and that our feet, covered with many wounds, began to swell and to hurt terribly. Some of the blacks had stayed far behind yet we could not wait for them. Onwards we had to march, onwards, in order to reach finally the end of the swamp. We were fortunate in that we met neither crocodiles nor buffaloes which were so common there. Our rifles were full of mud and had to be cleaned immediately on the first island. My wife complained much yet she carried herself bravely and marched on as well as she could. As true gentlemen we at first tried to find the 'best' way for her. It went always 'Come here, Rosa', 'Come here, Missis', until she did not want to follow us any more because often these tracks in the water were separated by prickly reeds. In passing through some of these patches my wife had hurt herself on pieces of wood; in others she had slipped and fallen down. Finally she found out herself what I had suggested to her before but what she did not want to believe in the beginning—that the widest strip of water in the middle was probably the oldest and deepest yet also the clearest with the fewest obstacles and the fewest thorns. Our march became slower and our halts on the large ant-hills protruding from the water became progressively longer. How we would have liked to stay much longer, yet we had to hurry. Onward we went along the tracks leading directly towards the narrow pass, the sight of which became clearer and clearer in the sparsely wooded range of hills. Our march from Galulonga had already taken six hours. Mostly, i.e. except for one kilometre, our journey went through the swamp. Finally I, walking ahead, stepped onto true mainland and our vitality increased again.

On our journey through the thirsty land between the Limpopo and the Zambezi such a swamp, in spite of its bad water, would have been very welcome. Yet on our trip north of the Zambezi water was one of the worst obstacles.

Fortunately we had no time then to think about the uneven distribution of earthly goods. As soon as we had revived ourselves a bit we washed our wounds out and cleaned our rifles superficially. We stayed half an hour more until our stragglers caught up with us. One of them, Siroko, did not come at all. We met him only on our way back.

The trees were in clumps like those of an English park; here and there were a number of huge candelabra-shaped euphorbias. One could see that during the summer the water probably covered even larger areas. We had walked for about 400 m steadily uphill when Mapani announced that there was a village to our right in the trees about 300 metres in front of us.

And indeed, this was so. A twin village, one of the largest ones we had seen, was lying in front of us. The huts formed an almost complete circle. The missing section, however, was open and not as was usual among the Maschukulumbe closed with poles. It was 8 o'clock in the morning. Since these tribes as a rule sleep until 8 and often until 10 o'clock these inhabitants, too, seemed to be still fast asleep. Yet soon we came to the conclusion that these were no late sleepers but that the village was deserted. The usual palisade fence was missing, as well as the herd of cattle. No, that village was not inhabited, it was deserted. Our hearts which had begun to beat faster with joy when we spotted the huts had to calm down again. This was not Massangu's kraal.[2]

We went past the village—yet now our dilemma began. Some twenty almost equally trampled paths went in all directions from north-north-west to north-north-east. Since just those three paths leading to the narrow pass seemed to be the most insignificant and the least used ones we had no other choice but to wait some time and orient ourselves. Suddenly there arrived, so it seemed, completely unexpected help. A group of Maschukulumbe and Mankoya tobacco traders came quickly walking down the western path. We stopped them and asked them the way to Massangu. Without being frightened these blacks seemed to be so perplexed by our sudden appearance in the bush that they rushed away to the side. Then they stopped and stared at us. They did not seem to understand the word Massangu and they said that a chief named Massangu did not exist in this area. Through Mapani I tried to sound out the Mankoya yet they pointed to their Maschukulumbe companions and did not dare to say a word. The latter pointed to the village and told us that it was inhabited. Before we had reached the village they had run there and got the late sleepers out of bed. Since dressing does not take a long time among the Maschukulumbe very soon a crowd of about 100 blacks came streaming towards us. They were followed by several dogs who certainly were not the image of vigilance here. One giant, surrounded by almost forty armed men, introduced himself as chief. The rest were women, youths and children. Some of them were interested in my blacks, yet I did not allow them to give any information but only to ask for Massangu. These Maschukulumbe who were true hermits in the swamp obviously had not yet heard anything about our arrival in the areas of their fellow tribesmen. They had never before seen a white man and perhaps not even heard of them. Finally their astonishment, muttering and alarm somewhat subsided so that I at last could make myself understood through Mapani and Jonas. I then asked the chief for Massangu. 'Massangu', he said, 'I do not know a king with such a name here. On this side of the hills no other chief is living. I am the only chief over the whole land up to that narrow pass. One of my subchiefs is called Massangu but he is no ruler of this area, he is my subject. Ha, ha, ha, Massangu a king? Who told you that?' In the beginning I could not believe that we had been cheated so much and I asked for the 'Portuguese'. These people did not understand me at all until Jonas asked the chief whom I presented with a horse-blanket whether or not a man with just such white skin as we had was living close by one of the next chiefs in the north. 'No, no', was the answer. These blacks obviously were not initiated into the plan of the others in the south who intended to divide the whole loot only among themselves. While the chief was still talking to us in this way a man pushed his way up to him from behind through the crowd of people. He then whispered something to him. The chief jumped up and when he stepped up to us again a few minutes later he said that the white man was living at Massangu's. The newcomer was one of the returning tobacco traders who had seen us the day before in Galulonga and who had left Galulonga that very morning. I did some cross-questioning of the chief and this man and the two got so confused in their answers that I realised soon that the white man I was looking for was probably no longer there but that he once had been there. Now one could only see his fields and the hut he had once inhabited. It was now quite clear that the whole story of the 'white man' was a lie. I only put one more question 'Which way leads to Massangu?' The blacks themselves did not know this for sure and finally pointed out to me a path to the north-east. I told them that I would not take that one but rather the path leading to the pass. And I asked 'Who is living there?'—'You will first find a village of the Maschukulumbe, then a second one where Mankoya and Maschukulumbe are living and then a third one where only Mankoya are living.'

How about going there—it suddenly crossed my mind—and persuading the friendly Mankoya to serve as my porters? This try could hardly have been harmful if in two hours we could have been there. Very readily the chief gave me three guides, even though I had only asked for one. 'Mapani,' I said, 'sneak up closer to the chief without disclosing your intention and try to overhear what kind of orders these three are getting from him.' Mapani did so and reported that the next chief was a vassal of the one standing in front of us and that he should not allow us to leave before he, the chief, came there, which he would do the very same day.

We left the place in apparent friendship and went north. Yet we had hardly gone a few steps when I was seized inexplicably by great disquiet. I was overcome by the kind of suspicion which seized me often on my journeys when I was heading into great danger. As we were walking my newest plan to go to the Mankoya and to continue our journey supported by their help seemed to be less and less practical and wise. I began to analyse all our chances logically and found that I was plunging into an adventure of rather dubious outcome.

The idea that—after the Portuguese had disintegrated into a chimera—help from the Mankoya was a very problematic proposition became more and more powerful and convincing. Perhaps these Mankoya were only subjects of a Maschukulumbe chief since we had already met some in Galulonga and some who had settled in the last village.

We had put two kilometres behind us, but these worries overwhelmed me so much that I decided to proceed only one more kilometre in order possibly to get a view out of the dense bush to the narrow pass and the paths leading up to it. If there were no very favourable views I intended to turn back immediately. I called my wife who was marching on bravely in spite of her wounded feet and I told her about my decision. First, however, I wanted to have absolute clarity on one question. I stopped and called the guides as well as all my servants to me. I had my servants ask the three guides where we were going. 'To Massangu!' 'But he does not live in this direction.' 'Yes, he lives there.' 'When will we reach him?' 'In the evening.' 'But your chief said around noon. You are telling nothing but lies.' 'No, it is true, all is true.' 'Do you know what this is?' I showed them my rifle. 'No.' 'This is the weapon of the white man,' Mapani shouted, 'you will fall down dead if you do not tell the truth.' 'Is that the weapon with the lightning with which Luanika has killed the people from Kaboramanda and Bosango?' they asked, by then already trembling and shaking. 'That is the one.' 'Where do you lead us?' 'Not to Massangu but to a brother of our king.' 'Where does Massangu live?' 'Further towards the setting sun.' 'Are there Mankoya living at your king's brother?' 'No.' 'How long do we have to walk until we reach the first Mankoya chief?' 'The sun rises twice and sets twice before you get there. For he does not live at the border and the path through the mountains is bad and rocky. Your feet are sore and bleeding and the rocks are very hot from the sun.'

The fear of our carbine had finally pulled the truth out of the hearts of our three guides. I gave the sign to turn back after we had come as close as 13 km to the range of hills.[3]

Suddenly, but only then, the diabolically simple plan of the Maschukulumbe from Galulonga became obvious to us with frightening clarity. There was not only no Portuguese, but there also was no King Massangu. In Galulonga they had planned to divide us in order to attack us in the swamp and the occupants of our camp simultaneously. Now everything was decided. We had to return quickly. Not only by the evening as promised but by noon did we have to be back in camp. As soon as my people heard my decision they shouted loud with joy. Even my wife felt relieved; she grabbed my right hand and a tear from her eye dropped on it. The return to Galulonga where we had not experienced a single happy moment now seemed to all to be the beginning of better times, so terrifying had been the march through the swamps.

First we directed our steps back to the village we had just left. The villagers came running towards us in surprise. Since my wife and the servants were so very tired I decided to wait a few minutes firstly to buy some milk for all of us and secondly so that we could pull at least the worst thorns out of our legs and feet. While we were waiting for the milk I had a chance to concentrate my attention on the village before us. In contrast to other kraals of this tribe the pointed tops of the cone-shaped grass roofs were decorated with antelope horns, and with buffalo, zebra and even lion skulls which gave them a very distinctive appearance.

Ten minutes had passed and the milk had still not come. Yet we observed a very great commotion in the bush. It was simple to guess that the herdsmen were being called to gather together in order to attack us later in the swamps. 'Onwards, get going', I shouted and we moved on. When some twenty men tried to hold us back and to block our way we pushed them aside and hurried on to the swamp. My poor wife and the blacks had to be content with swamp water to quench their great thirst. They all wept a quiet tear that they missed the cool milk but we could not stay any longer to negotiate.

The chief sent two guides after us who, in spite of our repeated refusal of their services, followed us as spies for some distance to see what we actually had in mind. Before we had reached the edge of the swamp a whole group of their village companions had already joined them. If that six hour march had been exhausting the two hour march back was even more exhausting. Only the hope that it perhaps might still be possible to rescue the camp and its occupants, undoubtedly already under attack, gave us literally superhuman strength to get through the swamp with our wounded feet in two hours. Finally the southern bank was near. We were already passing through the deepest spots—those parts overgrown with nympheas where we had struck the first palm thorns. We were already wading through those slippery and treacherous reed thickets full of holes where I had slipped and fallen down for the first time when I had been trying to carry my wife. Finally the ant-hills became scarcer and the reeds less. One and a half kilometres ahead of us the tops of the cone-shaped grass roofs of Galulonga became visible (which according to our experience of that day's journey seemed to be situated on a slightly elevated peninsula; perhaps it is even an island—I did not examine the environment in the east). 'Galulonga in sight', I shouted and an expression of general satisfaction was the answer. We approached the last deep swamp which actually drained the swampy soil and perhaps was a part of the Luenge. It was about eight metres wide and almost one metre deep. Beyond the deep water were about 600 m of shallow swamp. Then dry land, the territory of Galulonga began.

I was the first to step into the water. Immediately after me followed my wife, Leeb, Jonas and Maruma. I had hardly taken a few steps when my attention was drawn to a light gleaming object in front of me in the reeds. I went closer and soon the object became clearly distinguishable. It was a piece of clothing, a shirt. 'Rosa, Jonas, quick, come here, look there.' I shouted. Just then Mapani shouted quite alarmed 'Look, there is Fekete.' 'Fekete?' 'Yes, Master, for sure.' 'Well then disaster has struck, the camp has been looted and Fekete is trying to escape.' I shouted as loudly as I could, 'Fekete, hello, Fekete.' 'Yes, Sir, I am coming.' Soon we could hear his feet splashing as he ran through the swamp thicket. The short period of time until Fekete reached us seemed like an eternity. Trying to catch his breath he reported in a few words the catastrophe of the Austro-Hungarian Africa expedition. 'Doctor, all, but all is lost. Oswald is mortally wounded, the camp looted.' And how poor Fekete looked himself. He was barefoot without a jacket and with torn and blood spattered clothes. In his hand he carried his rifle. Close behind him Mapani and Muschemani then appeared. One of them carried two rifles, the other one just one. Yet otherwise except for their weapons they carried nothing. We all gathered quickly around Fekete. Yet I had still the presence of mind to place some of my blacks on some ant-hills on guard behind palm bushes so that we would not be taken by surprise by the Maschukulumbe while we were listening to the report of my faithful Fekete.

'What has happened?' Quick and broken sentences came out of the man's mouth. 'Early in the morning Muschemani drove the goats and donkeys to their pasture about 100 paces away from the camp. Suddenly he rushed back and said "The Maschukulumbe were about to kill me. They were yelling at me from the village and I happened to be so close to the village that their spears could reach me. I thought already that I was lost when one in the crowd shouted 'Look, he has the four front teeth knocked out like we have. He really belongs to our tribe.' 'No, he is a Makalaka', another one said, 'that son of a bitch has to die.' By then most of the crowd were shouting at the same time 'Yes, yes, he is a Maschukulumbe, he has no front teeth, we won't kill him.' I, however, drove my goats back to the camp. I walked fast but I did not run lest they think that I was afraid of them. Behind me came some Maschukulumbe, some of whom came up very close to the camp wall."' 'These', Mapani interrupted Fekete, 'were, as we only now know unfortunately, the emissaries of the secretly allied tribes who had all been called up and were already ready for the attack, either in the reeds towards the south or in the village towards the north.' 'These five men began to tease Pit, our baboon, who was on a chain and playing around in front of the camp. I was sewing sacks as I had been ordered to do and I was sitting with my back towards the entrance, so that I did not see what was going on there. I had just cut a piece of canvas for a sack when Oswald touched my shoulders and said, "Listen, I am mortally wounded, bring me to safety." I thought Oswald was joking but his face pale as death and his torn and bloody shirt riddled with spear holes proved only too well his words to be true. I leapt up, "What on earth has happened?" "I'll tell you on the way, come quick, let's get away from here and follow the Doctor." He had grabbed his Winchester and was staggering out towards the swamp. I was still standing there speechless when I was brought back to reality by loud shouts and shrieks. I saw the blacks rushing towards us in large crowds from the village and from the south. Mapani, however, and Muschemani who had left with Oswald suddenly called me. I turned around only to see Oswald collapse. I rushed out to him and lifted him up. "Away from here, away from the vicinity of these devils. Quick, take me to safety", he gasped. We carried him towards the thicket hoping to find some protection in the reeds. We got there safely and it was, indeed, high time. The miserable wall of maize stalks had already been overrun by the blacks and like a swarm of wasps they were descending on the camp. These events had happened so suddenly that I was without my jacket, without shoes, without cartridge pouch, in short, just as I was when I had to hurry and help Oswald. Thus I was not able to rescue a thing.'

The evening before Fekete had put my general diary into his jacket so that he could rescue at least these important notes in case of an attack on the camp. Now I heard that everything was lost, literally everything—the rest of our equipment which we had rescued before with so much effort, the 4,500 cartridges, our tent, our flag, the valuable instruments and all my diaries. The loss of the latter was probably the worst that could ever have happened. These thirty-two books contained all the explanations of our extensive collections. These books—apart from my companions—had been my best friends on this journey. Up to that 2 August, the day of the last attack, I had entered into them so to speak all scientific results of this expedition on 2,000 closely written pages and with 700 sketches. Now I had to hear that not a single one had been saved. The thought that through the loss of my diaries my reputation as a scientific explorer and, to a certain extent, even the justification of merely talking about my difficult journey, had been taken away from me was terribly depressing and shattering. This thought made me oblivious to all the much more urgent problems concerning our personal deliverance. I was standing there indifferent and completely crushed when Fekete called me back to reality by asking 'And what now?'

'We can no longer go south, Doctor, because there it is teeming with black enemies. I saw Njambo's people and the thieves from Diluka and Nikoba among the

11   *The attack at Holub's camp at Galulonga (Lulonga)*

crowd, too. We have to get to the Portuguese—this is our only possible salvation.' 'This salvation has turned into a soap bubble. There is no Portuguese living on this side of the border. This news was a trap for us. At some point a Mambari seems to have come as an elephant hunter to the Mankoya far beyond the border. On this fact the Maschukulumbe built their tissue of lies and their nefarious plan. Also, we would not be able with our wounded feet to pass through the swamp once again, apart from the fact that this attempt, also, could not be made without a fight.'

I had recovered my senses and I sent someone to the two groups of guards to find out whether they had seen anything suspicious. Those looking towards the swamp reported that the area in front of them in the direction from which we had come had begun to teem with Maschukulumbe. 'That's what I thought. We have no choice but to go south. And how could we go north? How could we ever get through over several hundred kilometres to the next European settlement on Lake Tanganyika without boots, clothed in rags, without any barter objects, and with only 300 cartridges? That would be impossible. After a few days, even if the blacks had not detected us, we would die without any treatment from over-exertion.' If there was still any salvation for us at all, it was in the south. We had lost everything except for our rifles and those could possibly save us. The main thing was to wrest our lost camp back from our enemy drunk with success. Perhaps there were still some things to rescue. And thus we marched with true defiance of death straight to the camp, having decided to dare a battle of desperation. We simply had nothing more to lose, but much to gain.

Thus we surprised the enemy who thought us still far away, so much so that they fled the camp in a fright. On our way to the camp I sent Fekete with Leeb to the right into the reed thicket where Fekete had laid Oswald down, to see whether he was still alive. My deputies found our poor companion dying. Some of his inner organs were already protruding out of his spear wounds. I shall remember Oswald Söllner as long as I live as one of my best friends. But out of due deference to the truth it has to be said here that the cause of his death was his philantropic attitude towards the blacks. The misplaced confidence he showed them always and everywhere cost him his life. If he had encountered the blacks who were teasing Pit that morning of 2 August with his rifle over his shoulder none of them would ever have dared to lift their assegais against him. Yet they did so because he reprimanded them strongly while carrying no weapon.

We reached the camp soon. 'Cartridges and diaries.' This was our war-cry. There were the two boxes for my diaries—overturned. These people had no use for my diaries—that was why we had always packed them by themselves into two little boxes so that the blacks would leave the 'useless things' behind even if they were to steal the other bundles. Yet one of the boxes was empty and the second one contained only six diaries—only five, however, were completed. While I was looking around I saw some candles still strewn about, some boots and a little box with fifty Winchester cartridges. In a second all this was in our hands. The diaries were wrapped quickly into Leeb's scarf.

'The Maschukulumbe are coming back already. We are lost, we are dead.' our black servants shouted and they dropped their bundles on the ground, if they had not yet done so before, in order to flee. Only by threatening to shoot them did we hold them back. We now turned around and marched directly towards the village—firstly to intimidate the enemies by our advance, rash as it was; secondly, however, to recover perhaps some of our possessions in the village. The camp was 160 m south-west of the village and 400 paces south a deep swamp was stretched right across the path to the south. After this swamp there was a reed thicket about one kilometre wide and beyond that lay the flats of the Luenge valley covered with ant-hills and partly overgrown with elephant grass and bushes. Since the grass was mostly burnt down the plain literally looked like an endless ugly field of stubble. With hasty steps I walked towards the village always looking around for my diaries. What luck! Here and there I saw some lying in the grass and I grabbed everything I could get. Before the village about 100 of the enemy had posted themselves waving their spears. They received me with shouts and screams, but they retreated anyway. The village itself was densely packed. Those who had come up for the attack on the camp from the southern swamp, had set out to return to their Luenge villages immediately after the plundering in order not to have to share their loot with those who had not acquired anything. They were re-inforced by those who had been following us from the north through the northern swamp. They had, however, arrived after the act. The men retreated before me into the village. I did not see that another band of men bent low was sneaking along the swamp to throw themselves between Oswald and us. I had already picked up nine diaries. Around me some Korans were scattered, further away some single boots, writing paper and the tripod of my theodolite. I picked up the ninth diary—fortunately it was the cartographical one of our tour north of the Zambezi without which it would have been impossible to write this second volume of my travelogue. While I was picking this up I suddenly heard to my right and to my left in front of me the war-cries of three Maschukulumbe bands rushing to attack me. At the very same moment I saw a few steps in front of me my black writing portfolio. It was open and contained my drawings and astronomical measurements. Next to it in the grass were lying two red and one white sheets. These were two determinations of latitude and one determination of time. One leap and I was in possession of these two objects with which, however, I retreated immediately. Even though I retreated slowly and had my face and my rifle turned to the enemy my retreat merely served all the more as an encouragement for them to attack. They saw how much the books I had in my hands impeded my ability to shoot and defend myself. Indeed, since I had dared so much for those pieces of scraps which seemed to them so useless, they might even think that I would rather not shoot at all than to throw away these papers. This consideration raised their courage even more. Some had leapt up the nearest ant-hill and with shouts incited the reluctant ones to attack me since for a few minutes I was standing isolated and rather far away from my people. My wife realised my dangerous situation and forfeiting her own safety she sent Leeb and Fekete to my support, while she took the musket out of Mapani's hands to protect herself. Thus I was able to reach the camp without getting wounded.

The enemies were obviously very annoyed that I escaped. They then concentrated all their armed forces and in a dense swarm they pushed between our camp and the place where Oswald was lying so that it was impossible to think of rescuing him or even of recovering his corpse.[4]

These were the circumstances under which we had to design our further war plan. We were unable to hold our camp. A breakthrough to the north would have been sheer suicide; only in the south was there still some glimmer of salvation. There I knew the territory, there I knew that we could get to the Luenge by forced marches and cross it in order to reach those chiefs who, as the reader remembers, had so strongly advised us against the whole expedition to the Maschukulumbe. Furthermore, marching to the south brought us closer to European civilisation and its sphere of influence.

The situation was so clear that none of us wavered, even for a second, about what to do. With one glance to the north, I said a last farewell to Oswald's corpse, handed my diaries to one of our blacks, ordered them to hand me two of the bundles of calico which we had taken to the supposed Portuguese and had brought back again. I left three of them in the camp and then gave orders for our departure to the south. I left these parcels behind since I knew for sure that fifty to sixty and possibly even 100 of the enemy would descend upon them and fight over them. We laid out this bait in order to gain time and to get a start on our enemies. I indicated the direction of our retreat and sent our blacks ahead of us. We Europeans, however, kept the enemies constantly beyond the range of our carbines. I gave my people a kind of briefing or marching order so that even in case some mishap would befall me they would still be able to reach the southern bank of the Luenge alive. It was thirty to forty kilometres to the Luenge. The route to it first went through a shallow swamp, then through dry reeds, and then across flats with trees and overgrown with grass. I thus advised my people the following:

'You have to reach the swamp before the enemy and you have to cross it fast so that you do not have to fight in it. Otherwise you would be lost if you were forced to do so. Once you have waded through the swamp,' I continued my order, 'take possession of the next reed thicket. Then fire four or five shots at your enemies and then move on quickly through the north-western reed thicket towards the Luenge. Once you get out of the reeds you will see in the south-western direction a group of some high trees. From there keep a south-south-western direction and you will reach the Luenge in the evening. You will have to cross it the same night. Only in this way can you find salvation with God's help. Otherwise it will be impossible, because if you have to fight you will be overwhelmed by the numbers and if you cannot cross the Luenge tonight, you will have to suffer death from starvation.'

While I was explaining all this we had almost reached the swamp. Then two of my servants who were carrying the calico parcels said: 'Master, we cannot fight if we have to carry. Our feet, which are so sore, are aching so much that we hardly can walk even without any load.' 'Perhaps you can manage in spite of it', I answered, 'Remember that we have nothing else to buy food from the Matoka if you do not carry these loads.' However, fifty yards further I realised that the men were unable to drag these packages any longer and I allowed them to drop them.

The Maschukulumbe had reached the camp long before this. Half the men from the left flank and some fifty men from the centre were already fighting merrily with each other for the packages we had left behind in the camp. Yet the rest of the blacks took to our pursuit and were coming closer in quite a threatening fashion. They saw through our plan and were trying to get to the swamp before us to force us to deviate from our march to the south. The race was a rather unequal one. We were utterly exhausted from our march early in the morning, our feet were sore, our clothes wet and heavy. The blacks were naked, had eaten, were healthy, had slept long and thus were fast and as mobile as monkeys.

Thus they overtook us even though they were running in a pincer movement. Their two wings began to close us in on the sides while the centre temporarily stopped and did not make any sudden advance. Had the centre pushed forwards as fast as the wings we would soon have been in a battle. While watching the execution of this manoeuvre I realised a considerable weakness of the blacks which could be quite advantageous for us. They lacked a unified command. Each chief, who was king in his village, commanded his own band. Thus one band was attacking, another retreating, or the same one was retreating and attacking at the same time depending upon the nature of the orders the leader was giving. In brief, the whole operation lacked any kind of plan. I decided to exploit this fact as much as possible. In the meantime we reached the edge of the swamp. When the enemies realised that we could escape them if we crossed this obstacle, all flanks started advancing and we were in danger of getting their spears from three sides simultaneously.

The situation had become very dangerous. If we had to fight in the swamp proper we were lost. Therefore, I decided to let our rifles talk. Initially, I only wanted to allow my people to fire over their heads until Mapani reported some of the words he had overheard—namely that one part of the blacks were supposed to rush to the opposite bank of the swamp and to set the dry reed thicket, which was across our line of retreat, on fire while the others were supposed to throw their spears without pause until none of us was still alive.

Hearing this I gave orders to shoot, but with the instruction merely of wounding and not killing these cowardly beasts. This was a fight for our lives—nothing more nor less. Their spears were already flying against our dogs who were barking furiously at them. My wife barely rescued her favourite dog, little Daisy, whom she still has today. The first volley of shots which I had ordered fired at blacks on this trip crackled. I aimed at the left flank, but I shot beyond it intentionally. Fekete and Leeb shot into the dense crowd at the centre and wounded two men, one in his arm, the other one in his leg. Both fell to the ground screaming. Whether or not the blacks were aiming at us I cannot tell; in any case they missed us.

The effect of this one volley of shots was incredible. The whole crowd stopped as if they were rooted to the spot. A further attack or a continuation of their pursuit was momentarily out of the question. Many rushed to the wounded; others were threatening us and screaming from the top of the ant-hills to which they had already retreated. We, however, used this advantageous moment and 'hurried' through the swamp in as much as one can speak at all of 'hurrying', since we had to wade through the water up to our chests. Suddenly I saw that my wife seemed to be rooted to one spot trying in vain to go forward. Before I could get to her Fekete, who was walking behind her, had worked his way to her and pulled all the meteorological instruments from her body which she had been trying to save in the last minute. He lifted her up and thus helped her onward. We had luckily passed through the deep swamp which was the most dangerous spot for us. We had hardly stepped on to the southern bank, which was overgrown with reeds but only slightly swampy, when we realised that individual Maschukulumbe were sneaking around and hiding in the reeds. The shots had scared them sufficiently too and in a friendly tone they shouted across to our blacks, who were walking ahead of us, to kill us. Since I understood this suggestion I cast a somewhat closer eye on my servants. Yet they rejected such suggestions with indignation, shouting back at the Maschukulumbe 'Nja—ja, so you say, but once we have killed our protectors then it will be our turn to be killed by you. Never, we have not come back to our masters', they mumbled among themselves, 'in order to kill them now. You devils.' They threatened the Maschukulumbe with their fists. Strangely enough, one fact, which we would hardly have imagined among such wild, uncivilised people, had made them terribly angry with the Maschukulumbe. This fact was that they had killed Oswald. Oswald had always treated our black servants well and had given them many a good titbit while he had been our cook. After the 'Missis' he was the next best liked by our black companions. If on our retreat one of Oswald's murderers had come close enough they would have pierced him with their spears and I would have been unable to prevent them.

To observe this reaction and feeling among our blacks made me quite happy. Yet, I have to admit I was even more touched by the fate of Pit, our tame baboon, who always had been Oswald's friend and for whom Oswald died. When Oswald had been treacherously attacked by those five Maschukulumbe Pit leaped at them and received in return a spear in his legs. The monkey had pulled this weapon out of his wound and ran after us for 15 km barking fearfully. We could not take him with us since he was continuously barking and whining loudly and thus would have disclosed us to our enemies all too easily. Also, we would have been unable to carry him when later on he could no longer have dragged himself on, and thus we had to shoot him. Unfortunately we were unable to perform this act of charity for our donkeys and goats as well. We saw them, when we were approaching the camp, standing and whining, each with a spear sticking in their bodies. Even today the memory of the sad fate of these animals is a painful one and this not only because I am an animal-lover in general, but because I had so many opportunities on my journeys to appreciate the great services these animals do to us men. We got out of the reeds without any accident and reached a somewhat higher 2 km long flat space covered with grass and full of ant-hills. There we left the path leading to Njambo and I took a south-south-western course towards a place which appeared to be clear except for two groups of trees. On our right and on our left on the grassy plain we saw some Maschukulumbe individuals at a distance of over 500 to 700 m. When we came near they lay down flat on the ground behind ant-hills to let us pass. All these Maschukulumbe wore some pieces of calico around their bodies which indicated that they belonged to that crowd of about 200 who had fled upon our return from the supposed Portuguese right after plundering our camp. They were now on their way home. That all these Maschukulumbe were so obviously and carefully avoiding us I could not really understand. I had never considered these people to be courageous, especially not if encountered individually; however, now they seemed to be incredibly cowardly. My blacks explained this fact in the following way: 'They had left Galulonga and their fellow tribesmen with the promise that all of us would be killed in the swamps. Then they heard our shots and saw us marching safe and sound along the southern bank of the swamp. They did not realise that one of us was missing and that was why they were so afraid of us.'

I was absolutely sure that in spite of all the fear caused by our shots we would soon be pursued again. Yet the further we marched the more evident became the contrary. Still, their words were ringing in our ears 'Go ahead, we shall either find you dead or shall kill you without much effort'. But none of us had comprehended these words, none had understood the meaning. But that very day these words uttered with such assurance were to become vivid for us.

We had safely passed through the ant-hill flat and everything seemed to be going well beyond our expectations. Only the pain of our wounded feet became more and more noticeable. Until then our mental agony had still suppressed our physical pain, but now our wounds required our attention. One after another we sat down to pull the thorns out of our flesh or to clean and to cool our wounds with wet grass. Yet if we wanted to reach the Luenge and in particular the ferry landing I knew we had to hurry very much. Again and again I had to ask my people individually to suppress their pain, if possible, and to follow me and my wife as quickly as possible. Even though walking was very troublesome for her she kept proceeding bravely and was among the first in front. She had picked up and put on the lone boot of mine which the enemy had left behind in the camp. Yet her terribly swollen foot and leg forced her all too soon to take off this narrow club-shaped boot and this was only possible with the greatest effort. My blacks did not carry anything except for their spears and my fourteen diaries tied into two pieces of cloth as well as four thermometers we had saved. Their sore feet, fatigue and hunger had such an effect on them that they refused to carry my diaries any further and dropped them three times. Finally I had to carry them myself taking turns with Leeb and Fekete.

Beyond those flats covered with ant-hills the terrain sloped very slightly and we stood at the edge of a black expanse which appeared to be endless in the direction we had to follow. From a distance we could already tell that this was a burnt-out area. None of us was thinking any longer of the bush fire which had developed during Njambo's attack that night and which had done us such a superb service at that time, in fact, literally had become our salvation. Soon, however, all too soon, we were forced to recognise that, instead of high grass there was only stubble ten to twenty centimetres high, covered with ashes. It stretched for half the distance between the flats covered with ant-hills which we had just left and the Luenge. This was for us walking barefoot a dreadful and possibly insurmountable obstacle. We found ourselves faced with a new trial which by far threw into the shade all the frightening experiences we had gone through and had suffered on this journey. Only Leeb still had shoes, but a kind of so-called veldskoen, i.e. a very thin type of shoe which is very common in South Africa as they do excellent service on the dry soft ground. If he had had firmer shoes, he could have walked with heavier steps, thus breaking some of the stubble for those following him. As it was, however, this was not possible. In addition, he was already limping himself and was happy that he was able to drag himself onwards at all.

A number of my kind readers have probably tried occasionally to walk bare-foot either when going swimming or in the countryside and have then realised immediately by the pains such attempts cause how effeminate our feet especially have become because of our wearing of shoes. What would they say if a criminal judge were to make a delinquent walk across fields of wheat stubble? What, how-ever, is wheat stubble in comparison to those finger-thick, woodlike remnants of the two to three metre high South African grass which grows so densely that it is impossible to walk between the stubble? If we had had sandals we would not have got away without wounding the parts around our ankles and our calves but we were barefoot, our feet sore all over, and our ankles swollen. With these feet with which we would hardly have been able to drag ourselves across parquet floors, we now had to walk for several kilometres across this stubble field, and this, *nota bene*, after we had been marching that day since 2 o'clock in the afternoon under the African sun, tormented by hunger and the worst mental pains, and—as well —after we had crossed through large swamps.

I shall leave it to the fantasy of my reader to imagine the agony of this march. I omit to describe how each step tore new cuts and wounds into our blue-red swol-len and bleeding feet and what pains were caused by placing our feet on the ground when the ashes, the dust and, at deeper spots, the mud penetrated into our many wounds. Each step forward was accompanied by moans and pitiful screams caused by most agonising pains. My wife suffered most, yet an attempt by the blacks to carry her was completely unsuccessful, because even the leather-sole-like thick skin of these children of nature could not withstand these spikes. I dis-tributed my jacket which I had torn in pieces so that my people could keep their wounds somewhat clean. As soon as one sat down, however, all had to stop be-cause we could not leave anybody further than 150 paces behind. In addition to the great pain and the exhaustion of our bodies we gradually became very thirsty. After three hours of marching the great thirst became such a torture that our exhaustion under the influence of the blazing sun increased to a numbness and lite-rally to a mental confusion. Some were laughing, others were staggering on, quietly staring in front of them with a vacant gaze. In our plundered camp my wife had found a bayonet which she had buckled onto herself. But gradually even this light load became too unbearable for her. I tried to carry it for a while yet soon I flung it away since it became too troublesome.

Gradually one after another was overcome by a terrible feeling of stupor and indifference towards the dangers. This feeling increased to an absolute despon-dency. I myself was overcome by a similar feeling. My head was buzzing strongly and I was completely indifferent to the impending dangers, a feeling which I had never known before in my life. Whenever one dropped down with exhaustion I had to hear the words: 'I would rather be killed than to live on through this tor-ture. No, Boss, it's impossible, I cannot go any further.' At such moments, which hit my soul in spite of my half unconscious condition, I had to use forceful and convincing words—I was forced to mention the harpoons of the Maschuku-lumbe, those *maruma* with barbed hooks, in order to get those who had fallen down back on their feet and to persuade them to walk on. One thing, however, became clear, i.e. that under these conditions we would not be able to reach the Luenge that same day. And yet this was the most important and primary precon-dition for our salvation.

By the next day the news of our escape would already have reached the Mas-chukulumbe living on the Luenge and they would have attacked and killed us in the swamps or in the lagoons.

My plan for our salvation was based on the premise that we would still reach the northern bank of the Luenge that evening, that is, at a time when the natives were certainly not thinking of us and would have left their canoes unwatched on the river bank. These canoes had to bring us to the southern bank without them knowing about it. If we were to be successful then the conditions for our salvation would have become converted from a possibility to a probability. If, however, the news of our escape were to reach the Luenge people before us they would hide their boats and would let us move up and down the river banks for days or even weeks so that we would use up our cartridges for shooting game as our food, and only then would they attack us and murder us easily since by then we would have become half-dead skeletons.

My companions, black and white, understood that I was right and they marched on again. They had to suppress their pain so much that they were gnash-ing their teeth. After we had walked onwards for another 3 km we were all so exhausted, particularly because of our incredible thirst, that I myself thought that we could not move any further. Suddenly we caught a glimpse of a few trees which helped our orientation. We were in the vicinity of Njambo's village. We had to pass between these trees and another cluster of trees which became visible at a further distance to our left close to the village of Njambo, the robber chief. Then we had to keep further to the right, i.e. to the south-west, in order to get to the lagoons and on to the island on which they had marooned us, but on which, too, at least one boat was hidden in the reeds. Under the trees we saw some huts which were a cattle post of Njambo. From there a woman came right across our path. She was carrying a huge bundle of grass on her head which shaded most of her face. When she dropped the bundle to rest a little she suddenly saw us 400 paces in front of her. She screamed and ran as fast as she could towards Njambo. Some Maschukulumbe came out of the huts, yet they kept at a distance of 500 m from us. At that very moment these blacks were the most unimportant beings in the world to me, because I had spotted something else.

Was it possible? I saw a pied crow alighting at a spot about 300 m away. Was there water? My companions stopped and shouted all at once 'Nunjani' (birds). Yes, these were birds. 'Hasi meci' (no water), said Mapani who was chewing on a wet grass root which he had dug up from the ground with the bayonet which he was then carrying.

'Polocholo ischile' (dead animal, carcass), said the others—'Na ja, meci, meci' (No, water, water), I shouted and tried to run there. But in spite of my best intentions I was unable to run. 'Could it be possible, my God, my God', my wife was whispering. Her tongue and her mouth were so dry that she could no longer speak aloud.

The old proverb 'man's extremity is God's opportunity' once again was proved to be true. Our pace quickened automatically and soon we reached that spot. It was a puddle, the water was shallow and very warm. Yet what difference did it make after all. It was water. We stopped there for a full fifteen minutes. In the end after we had bathed our feet as well we left this place rejuvenated. When I looked around at our departure to see if anybody was pursuing us I saw that a number of Maschukulumbe were perched in the trees at a distance of 1 km watching what we were doing.

With incredible pain we dragged ourselves on, more and more quiet and staring dully ahead like people who have nothing to hope for any more. Yet we came closer and closer to the end of this burnt-out area. And far away in the south-east a single high tree indicated that we were in the vicinity of Diluka. The prospect of possibly still reaching the Luenge that evening gave us new strength. Around 4 o'clock we had left the burnt area and came to tall elephant grass lying on the ground. Months ago when it was still young and tender, the flood had pressed it down. We now walked over it as if over soft cushions. In the distance we already saw the rise with the tall and shady sycamores of Bosango which served us as road signs. We now followed the shortest way right across the flats straight in that direction towards the old landing spot. Objects which on first sight we thought to be people turned out to be game (zebra, lechwe, and puku), which allowed us to come as close as a hundred paces. And yet we could not shoot even though a true wolf's appetite had overcome my blacks merely at the sight of these animals. Not a single shot could be fired on this side of the Luenge and even twenty to thirty kilometres beyond the river on the other side if we wanted to reach the south bank of the Zambezi alive. Around 6 o'clock we reached the first lagoon; we crossed it and the second one in shallow places. From there we did not go any further since the sharp eyes of the blacks of Bosango might have spotted us. Soon we found a hiding place where we rested until the night was setting. Under its cover our dangerous crossing of the Luenge would be made. When it had finally become dark we crept on hands and knees through the low grass towards the Luenge and, indeed, we accurately reached our old landing spot. A large ant-hill in an old maize field served as our cover for crossing the last hundred paces to the river bank. Here we rested again and I sent one man up and down the bank to hunt for a canoe. Then we searched the maize field for old maize cobs, but unfortunately we could not find a single one. Instead I found a piece of half-rotten pumpkin peel as big as an egg. What a lucky find. We cut it into tiny pieces and each of us had a quarter of a bite—which we ate with the greatest of pleasure and the desire for more. While we were sitting there cooling our feet with water naturally the full experiences of that day were the subject of our conversation. We almost had to assure each other that we had succeeded in what had appeared to be impossible and that we were standing alive at the Luenge bank. Soon my blacks brought us the good news that they had seen a canoe on the nearest island. They were pointing to the spot and I recognised it immediately. Indeed, it was just the same island and there was the place from where we had crossed with the loads on our backs. Over there at the bank of the island was a little canoe pulled up on land. It was a dug-out at most $2\frac{1}{2}$ m long, a nutshell, on the possession of which, however, our lives hung.

The question was now how to get the precious canoe into our hands? Well, during the daytime we would have been able to make a raft out of reeds in thirty minutes, yet at night we could not go to the swampy places where the nearest reeds were growing. I called my blacks and talked with them a long time. I offered them three blankets, payable at the Zambezi, if one of them would have the courage to swim through the river in spite of the crocodiles in order to get the canoe. Their consultation with each other took a long time, but finally Musche-mani and Siroko jumped into the deep water. However, one of them by the river bank immediately hit a crocodile with his foot. In a split second they were out of the water again and none of them had the courage any more to dare another attempt.

'If you don't go, I must go. I shall go—but I know very well that if the crocodiles catch me none of you will ever reach the Zambezi. What can you do without a leader? Until today you have obeyed my orders and you owe your life to the execution of these orders. The crocodiles will see my white skin from afar. Your black skin, however, they might not recognise so easily in the dark.'

Yet all kept quiet. To each of them his own skin was too precious to sacrifice it for the others. Then I tried to appeal to the passion called greediness whose power over people of all skin colours is supposedly so great. I offered to the courageous chap who would dare to go the musket which Mapani was carrying. Immediately the Marutse Monohela agreed to go. Slowly and quietly his dark body slid into the water. The rest of us were all standing in a dense crowd on the river bank, Mapani with his spear lifted high in the air to drive the crocodiles off. Our hearts

were beating audibly. Our life was dependent on this heroic deed. If this courageous chap were caught by a crocodile none of my blacks would dare it and I
would have to sacrifice myself! None of us was saying a word. Yet the man had
hardly entrusted himself to the water when all of us Europeans knelt down—the
blacks around us did the same since they saw us doing so—and emitted a deep and
fervent prayer out of our anxious bosoms towards the stars. We prayed that this
courageous man would succeed in saving us. And our prayer was heard; our good
star which had saved our lives in many dangerous situations again shone upon us.
Monohela had reached the bank of the island and had taken possession of the
canoe!

When I asked our blacks later why they had knelt down next to us, Jonas said,
looking downward, 'Baas, it was Mapani who said "Look, our masters are talking
to their *Njambe* [invisible deity according to the belief of the Marutse]. Come let
us do as they do. The God of these whites is powerful. He will help."'

Monohela swung himself into the canoe. Since he had neither rudder nor a pole
however, the boat kept spinning around in a circle until Mapani advised him how
to use his hands successfully as a rudder. Soon he was back in our midst. We welcomed him warmly yet quietly in order to avoid anything which might have
given us away to the Maschukulumbe. I was pretty sure, however, that these long
sleepers would only leave their huts if there was a very unusual noise.

I now intended to transport us all one by one to the opposite river bank by
means of the little canoe. Fekete was supposed to be our ferryman. Yet the very
first attempt to bring Leeb across was a failure. The boat was too small to take two
people. Leeb and Fekete fell into the water, fortunately still at a rather shallow
spot near the river bank. We had to get a bigger boat yet those existed only on the
other side of the river where the natives kept them hidden in the reeds. I offered
Mapani the double-barrelled rifle which Jonas was carrying if he would cross the
river in the little canoe and would bring back the biggest one of the boats lying in
the reed thicket. Mapani went to work immediately. He had quickly made himself a rudder by means of a bayonet and soon pushed the canoe away from the
shore, glad to be able to earn himself a second rifle so easily. We were lying
quietly on the shore intensely listening into the night which was becoming darker
and darker. For a long time we did not hear anything except for the playing of the
crocodiles. Suddenly, however, we heard a different kind of splashing at the tip of
the island.

We knew what this meant: Mapani had returned with a boat which was able to
carry two people. In an amazingly short time we were then transported one after
another across to the island which we then quickly crossed on foot while the boat
was ferried around it. Yet when we intended to cross the second, much wider arm
of the Luenge a new obstacle blocked our flight. That day we had to drink the bitter cup of sorrows until the very last drop.

For an hour before heavy clouds had begun to gather and obscure the stars.
When we were just about to leave the island a windstorm broke which made it
impossible to cross the broad Luenge in a boat such as we had at our disposal—let

alone to cross it so often until we all were on the south bank. On its very first trip the waves would have devoured our nutshell which stuck out of the water barely more than five centimetres. I knew that such storms fortunately did not last very long. It was about 9 o'clock, thus we could wait for a few hours and use them to recover slightly from our exhaustion.

We lay down by the side of a large ant-hill right at the water's edge. Since the night was chilly we decided to make a fire. Soon the fire was flaring up—broad but not high—in order not to draw the attention of the Maschukulumbe on the other side of us. This, indeed, was a real treat for all of us, in particular, for Leeb and Fekete who were soaking wet since their boat had turned over.

Mapani, Jonas and Maruma were on guard. I squatted down at the fire and soon fell asleep. My wife was watching, too, as long as I was sleeping and she had the blacks apply some cold compresses to her feet. I woke up around 11 o'clock and then took over the watch myself.

The waves were striking against the shore and the whistling windstorm was raging through the valley. Above us the broad sky was pitch black and still not a single little star was to be seen. Would this storm last longer? But if it did not calm down slightly by midnight we would all be lost. We still had to do a lot before the sun rose because we needed at least two hours to get across the river. Then it was one hour's walk through the swamps before we reached Bosango. Then would follow a half-hour detour around the twin village and finally we had yet to walk 6 km beyond this. All this, however, had still to be accomplished that very night before the day dawned.

Our salvation depended on our passing Bosango unnoticed so that the natives would not know that we had crossed the Luenge and our pursuers the next day. still would search for us north and not south of the river. The next to last hour of 2 August, the day which had begun for us at 1 a.m. was a very painful one for me and my companions. Would our salvation really be denied to us at the very last moment after we had struggled and achieved so much?

Still the waves were slapping noisily against the slippery river bank. Yet we could no longer be deterred. 'Mapani, onwards.' 'Baas, I cannot.' 'Mapani, we have to get across.' Finally I persuaded him to go anyway. On this first dangerous trip he took Monohela across with a firestick in order to put it down on the other shore as an indication of direction. We listened nervously. Finally he came back. Yet he reported that he was afraid that the boat would turn over on one of these trips. 'The baas apparently must die.'

I took Sidamojo, my rifle and the diaries along, kissed my wife goodbye, shook hands with Fekete and Leeb and then we parted without any tears. Perhaps we would see each other again, but possibly this handshake might be the very last one. I had to lie down flat on the bottom of the boat in order to press it down with my weight. The waves were splashing loudly and broke on the hollow little nutshell. Still far away, almost as far as the middle of the river, I heard the farewell of my wife. Thank God, we finally landed. I gave a sign with the firestick that I had landed safely.

It was exactly midnight when I set foot on the south bank of the Luenge. The second of August 1886, the day on which fate had allotted us so many frightening trials, had finally come to an end!

From the Luenge
to the southern border of
the Maschukulumbe

MAPANI WAS PADDLING BACK TO THE NORTH BANK while I walked up and down. I had our little dog Daisy whom I had taken along to search the reeds for wild animals or even for hidden Maschukulumbe. Yet the dog was padding back and forth without the slightest noise and soon I felt completely safe. I kept the little fire going, our guiding star in the pitch-dark night, and I listened by straining all my nerves for a sign which would indicate that the boat was coming. For a long time I did not hear a thing except for the neighing of the cautious zebras who realised our clandestine doings, and the wailing of the storm. Finally I heard the splashing of the rudder and soon the little boat brought my wife to the shore of salvation where she landed at a shallow place. I helped her out of the boat and again the little skiff went back. Mapani succeeded in getting one companion after the other across. It gradually became easier and easier since the windstorm began to calm down. It might have been 3 o'clock in the morning when all of us shook hands standing safely on the south bank.

A great step towards our rescue was accomplished, yet our salvation proper lay still at a considerable distance. Much still had to be done, much had to be suffered and tolerated before we could shout the great word 'saved'. The last man had hardly arrived when we began to wipe out the traces of our presence, straightened the reeds, extinguished the fire, and threw the coals into the water. Then we left the Luenge of which we all had only sad memories. On our trek north treacherous porters had intended to kill us here. The retreat across this river had been the most dangerous boat trip in my life. And yet we left this river going south with elated spirits because the first and the most difficult part of our flight lay behind us.

The march on which we started out on 3 August 1886 began immediately with difficulties since the whole bottom of the valley was burnt out for 3 km up to the twin village Bosango-Kasenga and it was very difficult to recognise on the wholly black surface the equally black swamp paths. I left the navigation in that pitch-dark night to my blacks whose sense of direction once again proved to be excellent as had been the case often before. In such situations the white man always does best by entrusting himself to the instinct of these primitive people.

I chose Mapani as our guide and gave him Kondongo and Maruma as advisers. I myself specified merely the places I wanted to reach. Mapani determined immediately at the Luenge our route, which he told me briefly: 'Master, because of the many swamps and lagoons along the river we cannot wander about too long in the Luenge valley, but must go straight to Bosango-Kasenga, using the shortest path leading there directly. About 400 paces before the twin village, we then turn left [to the east] in order to avoid Kasenga. Then we keep to the south-south-west in order to meet that path which leads from Kaboramanda directly here. On our way back to you we did not come via M'Beza and Kaboramanda because this would have been the long way round over which Mo-Panza's people led you. I believe that I can find again the shortest way which leads directly from Bosango-Kasenga to Mo-Panza without passing the two villages I mentioned just now which we would leave on our left [in the east].'

I agreed with his suggestion and thus we got going. With that amazing ability of theirs to find lost paths and to follow those which are hardly visible my blacks marched along between the lagoons and swamps and this even relatively vigorously in spite of their sore feet. We had all bathed our feet diligently during the night and the coolness of the night as well as the water had eased our pains slightly, so that initially we all marched on rather bravely. Yet this pleasure did not last very long. As already mentioned before, the dry vegetation on the bottom of the valley had been destroyed by fire so that the grass stubble soon cut open again our wounds which had just been closed. At swampy spots the mud again got into them. We had not yet gone far when the stinging and burning pain began once more. Literally without a sound we followed the path. And yet the night was so dark that the blacks often could only find the path by groping with their feet.

While we were limping along in this way, each of us trying to suppress his pain, we were suddenly alarmed by the puzzling appearance of light right in the darkness. We saw at a short distance before us, sometimes also behind or next to us, something white moving quickly back and forth. We stopped marching and at the very same moment the white spot stopped moving as well. Then it came slowly to us, closer and closer. Only then we realised that it was the white bushy tail of our faithful Daisy who with her usual eagerness was exploring the immediate vicinity, whereas our second dog with his sore paws was keeping close to the path near the very last of us. We finally arrived at the place where Kasenga was situated; we turned to the side, walked around the village and then walked in a stooping position about 300 m beyond it until we had reached the path leading to Kaboramanda. This path now was easier to follow since it wound through white sandy soil in clear contrast to the burnt black surface.

The day was dawning already when we left the path to Kaboramanda and then marched or rather limped on directly towards Mo-Ponde. I was very much for taking a short rest, yet on the other hand I had hesitations about it. My blacks were sure that we would no longer pass any Maschukulumbe villages and would have nothing to fear any more. However, what if they were wrong in this assumption, if there were still perhaps some villages in the dense bush on the laterite ridge, and if we were to stumble right into their kraals in the dark? Of course, the Maschuku-lumbe sleep long; however, their dogs are watching. Of course, we had nothing to fear at the moment from these villagers to whom the reason for our sudden return was unknown. But another fact weighed heavily. On it our salvation depended no less than on the manoeuvres of the day before. On 2 August our order of battle had been: to reach the Luenge at any cost by night, to cross it during the night, and to get out of the sphere of influence of Bosango-Kasenga by dawn of the following day.

This we had just accomplished. But the order for this day, 3 August was: to hurry unobserved as far as possible south so that we would forestall any rumour of our escape. Even if we were to reach occasional Maschukulumbe villages we would encounter undecided enemies who were not familiar with our situation.

If the goal of the day before had only been reached by physically and mentally superhuman efforts the goal of this day was no less difficult. It included the prem-ise 'to move ahead as fast as possible'. This premise might actually seem easy, yet for us it was almost impossible to fulfill for three reasons. These reasons were: the fact that our feet were sore, our general exhaustion and our hunger, and finally the fact that I was unfamiliar with the territory. The path which we just then were following was the nearest one leading to Mo-Panza. My blacks had used it when they had returned to me. Thus we knew, too, that a Maschukulumbe village was situated along the path. We would have to avoid it by walking in a large semicir-cle around it. Then we had to meet the path again and follow it southwards. In order to take proper advantage of all the territory we covered by our crossing the Luenge and of all the achievements of the day before I decided to take one and a half hours rest only after we had walked for 5 km beyond Kasenga,[1] and then to continue our march in full daylight. This short rest was welcomed by all of us. For reasons of caution we made only a very small fire. Since we had left the burnt over area and had reached a terrain covered with high dry grass our blacks quickly cut enough grass to make a bed for my wife. This had hardly been done when every-body, except for me and Leeb, who had taken guard duty, was already fast asleep. The bush was so dense here and we were furthermore in a kind of low country so that even in growing daylight we were not able to have a good view around us. I thus thought that we were far from any kind of human settlement and that I could grant my sleeping people one more hour of rest when suddenly we heard the faint crowing of a cock. Within a second we woke everybody and a few minutes later we were already marching again.

Only too soon we hit several paths crossing each other and found fresh human and dog tracks (from the evening before) which according to their direction made us assume that there was a kraal to the left (in the east). We turned to the right and continued marching with the greatest of caution. Our way went through an in-credibly dense low bush which often was very difficult to traverse. We were walking in such an arrangement that we whites went in the middle while two of our blacks were walking in front as a vanguard, two to our left and two others to our right as a protective detachment. They were all ordered to keep constantly in our sight in order to inform us of their observations by means of signs and whist- ling and other signals which they knew by then. Thus we came to a laterite ridge overgrown with bush and crossed several rather well-trampled paths and many tracks of cattle. These many paths confused us and the result was that on top of the ridge in the bush we suddenly found ourselves between some kraals. Now we had to exercise the greatest caution. I called all my people close to me and we sneaked onwards, always only a few steps at a time. Then we stopped and listened. Only if we had not heard anything suspicious did we slowly walk on again for a few steps. We bent the bushes apart cautiously after the path had been cleared of dry branches and leaves. Occasionally the cattle tracks were quite useful for us in this dense bush which they crossed in all directions.

We did not have to fear the Maschukulumbe late sleepers, yet all the more their four-footed guards. In addition we were afraid that our dogs would respond to the barking of the strange dogs and thus would give us away. This was why I had some bark fibre ripped from a bush and then had the dogs tied to it as to a leash. At the same time I ordered the blacks who were walking the dogs to watch them closely. They were to hold their mouths shut as soon as they might prick their ears upon hearing the barking of strange dogs and thus to prevent the treacherous barking of our dogs. Often we were creeping along on hands and knees and when at one point we heard human voices from one of the kraals we crept rapidly onwards and then lay down on the ground the moment the conversation stopped until it began again. Finally around 8 o'clock in the morning we descended the laterite ridge and reached several paths leading to the south. We chose the one closest to the west in order to reach Kaboramanda as fast as possible.

For one and a half hours we were walking along mostly under shady mimosa trees, but because of our increasing pain we had to stop and rest several times. At one of these resting places near a very welcome waterhole we encountered a large herd of kakatombe hartebeests. The animals were quite tame so that my people, who of course were forbidden to shoot, intended to kill a calf with their spears. Yet I did not even allow this. In spite of the fact that we were very hungry it would have been useless to kill the animal as we had to move on as fast as possible and could not even think of roasting the meat.

The further we went the more unbearable our march became, the more often we had to stop and rest, and the louder grew our complaints. Hunger, exhaustion, pain and the depression caused by our feverish condition fought a battle of life and death with our desire for survival and our energy.

Around noon we entered a palm grove; according to our opinion it was that of Kaboramanda.[2] The sweetish meat of the fruit shells of these palm fruits, however, could not satisfy our appetite since most of the fruits were still not ripe and thus were more harmful than nourishing. Of all residences of Maschukulumbe chiefs on our way back we had to fear most that of Kaboramanda. And to our great mis- fortune it was just in this very palm grove that my poor wife was finally over- whelmed by the dreadful pain in her sore feet. She fell down and was unable to move from the spot. The bandage around her feet had long since become useless because of the hard dry grass and the roots in the bush and she could no longer take any step without a cover over her feet. Again I tore off some more pieces from my jacket and even from my shirt in order to make bandages out of them for us all.

The moment when my poor wife fell down half dead and thought that she was to die will always remain before my inner eyes and will always be equally dreadful. It was the most tragic episode of the whole terrible retreat. I still hear her words of despair. 'I cannot walk any further, God is my witness, I cannot. Lord, have mercy upon me.' 'Rosa, please, pull yourself together only for half an hour more, only for one more half kilometre in order to get out of the vicinity of Kaboramanda. Look at our feet, look at mine, and at Fekete's. We all have the same pain but we have to move on if we want to save ourselves. Mapani, Marumo, come, come all of you, you have to carry my wife.' 'Master, we would like to, but we cannot, look at the wounds on our feet.' Finally I had wrapped the rags of my jacket around my wife's feet and I got her back to her feet again. I and Fekete were supporting her, so much so that we were actually carrying her, yet she complained and wept. The pains which she had been suppressing now for nearly twenty-four hours were too much, even for this heroic woman. 'No, let me die here, go on alone and try to save yourselves. The border is probably already near. I am not important. Only you, Emil, save yourself and your research. I cannot walk any further. I beg you, let me lie down and leave me lying.' 'No, never. Unfortunately we cannot carry you. Please, pull yourself together only for a few hundred steps then you can rest for a longer period of time.' 'No, I cannot. Go on, save yourselves and leave me my Winchester. I know what I have to do if the worse comes to the worst.' These complaints, and this heroism wrenched the hearts of us men. Of course, nobody thought of leaving her behind. We put together soft pieces of linen and wrapped her feet in them again, over that I put another piece of my jacket and the whole foot was tied up with palm leaf fibres. Thus we carried and pulled her on until it went downhill into a valley where there was short but soft grass. Once the hard uneven and sun-baked terrain lay behind us we made a great step forward. My wife was soon able again to step on the soft grass. In the beginning, of course, we had to stop and rest every hundred paces or so, yet in the late afternoon sun she was even able to walk on her own. The cool evening was some relief for all of us, yet on the other hand our ravenous hunger again began to bother us more and more. We tried to console ourselves that the border and thus safety was no longer far and so, suffering quietly, we sneaked on southwards, however no longer in single file. I, my wife, Leeb and Mapani walked first, the latter being our guide. Far behind us Fekete was limping. The others, however, had dispersed to the right and to the left, i.e. they were walking along the slopes of the valley and were looking for fruits and edible seeds to satisfy our hunger. Every half kilometre we took a rather long rest and then one or another of the blacks caught up with us limping and brought us something edible which he and his companions had found.

The valley through which we were thus passing with great effort became wider. In the distance we could already see a basin-shaped landscape with decorative palm trees which we believed to be the palm grove south of Kaboramanda. we were at most five kilometres beyond Kaboramanda since the village before Maschukulumbe huts above us and to our left. Soon we realised with fright that we were at most five kilometre beyond Kaboramanda since the village before which we were standing belonged to it. It was the western guard post of the chief's territory. Our fatigue and the heat made the distance we had covered seem much longer than it actually was. We had, indeed avoided Kaboramanda, yet we still were within its boundary.[3] This discovery destroyed our beautiful dreams of a night's sleep under palm trees. Pitiless, cruel fate made us move on and march as long as our sore feet could carry us. Under terrible pain, often crawling on hands and knees over bad stretches of our path, we still covered three more kilometres by nightfall. Finally we slept near the edge of a small yet dense thorn thicket and a small shallow pond surrounded by reeds. Since we had no axe we tried to break off some thorny branches to make a barricade, yet we no longer had the strength for it. Slowly all our servants arrived. With their spear tips grass was cut which we intended to use partly as our bed and partly as a blanket since it had already begun to become cold. In fact, by around 9 o'clock we were freezing miserably. We made two little fires. We four Europeans and our two little dogs lay at one of them, the blacks at the other one. In spite of our exhaustion we were absolutely starved and because of the cold we were unable to go to sleep. Therefore fires were made between each pair of us so that we could warm ourselves better.

That night we protected our camp against wild animals by sticking our heads underneath a thornbush. Our guard was also not the sort which one would normally have on a march through hostile territory. My blacks had soon fallen asleep and once I began to feel some warmth, my vigilance was gone as well, and we all slept without any guard. Thus we rested until sunrise, for almost eight hours merely under God's protection. Yet this rest and the coolness of the night were so good for our sore feet that we left our camp early, literally refreshed. Only the process of actually getting up was difficult. Our blacks had to help us to our totally stiff legs. But after we had done a few steps it was better. Of course, we skipped breakfast this morning just as we had skipped all meals the day before.

'Soon we shall be at the border', Mapani said, 'and then we can kill a piece of game and then we will no longer be hungry.' We had hardly taken a few steps along the path when Marumo, who was walking first, uttered a shout and pointed to a few bare spots on the ground to our right and to our left. When we came up we all recognised completely fresh, huge lion tracks. This lion obviously must have smelt us and probably had even looked at us closely during the night. Yet then he had gone back the same way as he had come without having disturbed us and without having done us any harm. Mapani was there on the spot and immediately voiced his opinion. One and a half hours later we found his opinion confirmed in all details. 'Look,' he said, 'this lion was not hungry—otherwise he would have chosen one of us and would have carried him away. This lion, in any case, killed a piece of game only yesterday—otherwise he would have preferred fresh human meat. Then the lion returned to the leftovers of his kill in order to eat it all up. And fortunately he was alone and a male, not a lioness, because the latter often kills out of sheer playfulness even when she is not hungry.'

After we had climbed gradually over one and a half hours our blacks announced that five Maschukulumbe huts were in sight. We stopped at that news and sent a few blacks to find out about this village. They soon came back telling us there were only three men in the small village as well as some Matoka porters whom we had used en route from Mo-Panza. We would have nothing to fear. On the contrary, we should take our revenge, kill the Maschukulumbe and loot the village. Our hunger—as well as the crimes done to us—demanded as much.

'You go behind us,' I said, 'none of you shall touch anything, otherwise you will regret it. These Maschukulumbe have done us no wrong. Why should they suffer for the crimes of their fellow tribesmen?' Our arrival caused great astonishment among the six men present, especially from the three Matoka. The Maschukulumbe were very mistrustful and full of fear, yet they gave my blacks some food. But I was looking for something to sell. Then Leeb announced that he was still wearing a scarf, the only object of that kind we had. For this scarf we bought about three litres of groundnuts which we ate a few hundred yards beyond the village called Motokoro.[4] We passed quickly by the few huts surrounded by corn and pumpkin fields and situated in thick bush. My wife walked first, yet since she marched the slowest I walked along with her while the others who were better on foot still stayed somewhat longer at the fire with the Maschukulumbe. My wife went on only with great effort. She tried to suppress her pain, however just there at the harvested maize field her wounds were cut open again and began to bleed freely. The pains became unbearable and she could no longer suppress them. When I looked at her I saw glistening tears running down her cheeks. At that very moment we passed the fire in front of one hut where some of my servants, two Maschukulumbe and the three Matoka were sitting. I recognised them as the three worst out of the group of Matoka porters hired from Mo-Panza. The latter are well known to my reader. These were the ones who intended to desert us on our march twice in Kaboramanda. They had instigated the Maschukulumbe against us in Bosango-Kasenga and they had made my nineteen servants desert us. By persuading and intimidating them they had caused them to flee. If any out of the number of my enemies on this journey deserved a bullet it would have been just these blacks. My hand was trembling when I passed them. They were staring at us, in particular, however, at my wife. Their strange stares made me feel uneasy. Mechanically my hand grabbed for the protecting weapon which I had not let out of my arms for days. Yet I pulled myself together and walked on. It seemed, however, that they had nothing bad in mind: they dropped their spears on the ground and followed us. Their eyes were following my wife and her tracks. What was that? Did I see properly? Yes, indeed, I saw only too well. Her feet were bleeding so much that each step left its trace in the sand. Before I could even rush up to her to wrap her feet somewhat better the blacks stood in front of us and clapping their hands they threw themselves in front of our feet. 'What do you want?' '*Schangwe,*

schangwe, Morena' came from their lips in response, 'What do you want, what is your wish?' 'Master, we Mo-Panza's children are greeting you. We have heard what has happened to you, your wife and your people and we pity you and your fate. Master, we want to help you.' 'You want to help me?' 'Yes, look, your wife cannot walk any longer, she will become a burden for you. You are still in Mas-chukulumbe territory. Their spears are still hanging over your head. Therefore, Master, allow us to carry your wife.' I did not believe my ears, yet I did not trust the Matoka either, with whom we had had only bad experiences. My wife was even more suspicious and thus we limped onwards and left them standing. After another half kilometre we reached a little stream. There we stopped for a rest. We made a fire to grill the groundnuts. There we were surprised once again by the arrival of the very same three Matoka. 'Master, two of the old dogs [i.e. Maschu-kulumbe] from that village over there started out after you left to hurry to Kabo-ramanda and to report you. The danger exists that you will be pursued. Therefore, allow us to carry your wife. For you others are able to walk faster than she. She is unable to keep up with you even for one more day.' Now I had to be-lieve the speaker even though I was unable to explain psychologically their change of mind. 'You really want to carry my wife?' 'Yes, Master, we do.' 'Rosa, Rosa, did you hear this? They shall, they want to . . .' but my voice failed me. I had bent over to look into the face of my poor quietly suffering wife. Her head was resting on her breast and she was sobbing loudly. Yet this time a smile of joy was shining through her tears. The terrible torture of walking was to come to an end for her—at least for a few hours.

'But listen, you people, I have nothing to reward your efforts not even a piece of cloth.' (A piece of sackcloth has such a value there that one could buy one fat goat for it.) 'No, Master, we do not want any pay. We shall carry your wife as long as we can, but in any case across the border.'

In truth I have not been able so far to report to my kind reader anything praise-worthy about the Matoka. The Samaritan deed which these three representatives of their tribe—otherwise evil and wild fellows—now did to my wife did not only reconcile me to them; it also proved to me that deep in the hearts of all human beings there is a residence of feeling which if you strike it induces even the barbarian to noble acts and such deeds which we would call ethical. This sensi-tivity induces me to believe in the educability of primitive peoples.

The Matoka began their work immediately. With their spears they cut a little tree for a carrying pole and collected palm leaves. A cured ox skin which served one of them as a coat for cold nights was used as the actual hammock. My wife was put on top of the skin, wrapped in it and then literally tied to the carrying pole by means of the ribs of palm leaves. We helped the porters to lift the burden on their shoulders and on they went so fast that I had a hard time limping behind. One of the Matoka had been given one of my big boots as a present from one of the ser-vants who had deserted us. I now got it back and thus I could use that day one boot while my other sore foot remained wrapped in a rag. Our way led through bush and across clearings. Every 700–800 m the two good porters took a rest while the third who was the least strong of them dragged their arms, foodstuffs and their cooking pot behind them. My other people stayed far behind. Only towards the end of the march when the two carriers began to get tired and had to take longer rests, did they come nearer and nearer until they finally caught up with us 1 km before our campsite.

The edge of a wood where the plateau descended towards a lovely valley, the stream of which flows into the Monjeko, was pointed out to me as the border of Maschukulumbe country.[5] Our porters chose as our camp site for the night a place 2 km beyond the little stream in thick bush. Thus we had reached the border of salvation. How it had been possible to overcome all that we had overcome we did not understand ourselves, and we shall never understand it. First of all we thanked God that we were saved, since it appeared as if our good star was still guarding us and the sending of the good-natured Matoka porters appeared to be a miracle. We were happy about all this and no less delighted were we at the prospect of finally getting some meat again after three days of the worst fasting. We were outside Maschukulumbe territory and thus were again able to shoot.

This valley with its clusters of trees was one of the most game-rich areas I ever saw. The first game I spotted were a few striped gnus. Covered by an ant-hill I sneaked forward, fired and wounded a gnu bull. After that little hunting episode I limped behind my caravan which in the meantime had reached the camp site on the clear little stream situated under tall trees. I had to take the one boot off since on my swollen feet it felt like an iron cover. Then I rushed to my wife who had not felt very comfortable in the improvised hammock, yet thanked God and the Matoka that she need not march any more herself. We made ourselves at home in the camp. I sent Mapani with a few men to bring in the gnu. That all of us who stayed behind urged those who were sent to get it to hurry as much as possible I probably need not mention. For our wolf-like hunger had become literally unbearable for all of us.

While we were arranging the grass for our beds and getting a fire going the blacks came back with the gnu bull. Soon he was cut up and my people were grilling some of the meat over the charcoal fire. We had no patience and began to eat the meat half raw. This tough bull meat which would probably never have become tender lay in our stomachs and caused the fever to flare up again. While we were sitting there talking learnedly about the toughness of the gnu meat, Mapani suddenly turned out to be a hidden Vatel or some other great master cook. He dug a deep hole in the ground, burned it out with a hot fire then filled it with ashes and charcoal. Then he threw the head of the animal with skin and hair right on top of it and covered it with a thin coat of ashes on which he kept a small fire going all night. Thus this gnu head was steaming the whole night. And the next morning we enjoyed a juicy and tasty roast 'tête de gnu'. Only one thing was wrong—it was 'not enough'. The meat of the skull was not sufficient for four people after two days of fasting. What would we have given for a cooking pot to prepare a meat broth in it. My blacks and the three Matoka were eating the ordinary gnu meat all night long and the following day, so that there were hardly ten kilogrammes of meat left on the second day even though the gnu bull had been the size of a grown donkey. According to our plans we were to start out south in the morning of 5 August. Yet Fekete's and my feet had become so much worse that morning that we were unable to take a single step. Therefore I decided, no matter what happened, to rest for this one day. Since she had been carried my wife's wounds seemed to feel less painful. Yet when she made the attempt to take only just a few steps she had such violent pains that she screamed and fell on her knees and had to be laid on her miserable grass bed. The inflamed ankles and tendons had become completely stiff overnight. On this day of rest to which we had been looking forward for three days we did not feel very well at all. As one says in Vienna, the exhaustion and the pain came out into the open only afterwards. I and Leeb also had some fever. I had to send those servants who were still able to 'limp' somewhat better hunting again. The rest of the blacks were sitting at the stream all day long and were bathing their sore feet in the cool water. Fekete had Mapani make sandals for him out of the gnu skin and got so used to them that he was wearing them until we got to the Zambezi. I myself tried such sandals several times yet I could not get used to them and preferred to go barefoot or with rags wrapped around my feet. The day of rest, as well as the fact that we had eaten again, strengthened us physically, and the feeling of safety tremendously strengthened us psychologically.

The next morning we started out early. The first steps even that day were still not very successful. Yet soon I got into the swing and was able to go ahead to shoot game, if possible. Leeb and the blacks took it on themselves to watch my wife who was again tied in her original hammock and was carried by the two Matoka. I soon encountered the largest herd of eland antelopes I had ever seen. These were at least seventy animals. Yet it was not possible to get closer to them and I did not want to shoot from a great distance—on the one hand because I was trembling from all the exhaustion and on the other hand because in our situation I regretted far too much any cartridge spent in vain. The further I went the slower became my steps. I had to take the rag from my feet since my heels were bleeding from walking and were very painful. Although I was walking slowly none of my people caught up with me which began to worry me. Yet since I had been told at our departure early in the morning that the village Masosa was very close I walked on hoping to reach it soon and possibly to buy some milk from these Matoka for three or four empty cartridges. My way led continuously over a wooded laterite ridge which at its eastern edge was washed by the Monjeko stream and which was very well known by the Matoka and Maschukulumbe for its abundance of buffalo. In my condition nothing was less desirable than to encounter a herd of buffalo. I was not a good shot and if I failed I was completely unable to climb a tree quickly in order to secure myself from the attack of a wounded buffalo. Fortunately the buffaloes seemed not to have the desire to see me and stayed away. Instead I encountered kakatombe hartebeests. When my eyes were following these beautiful animals, a young kakatombe calf bleating loudly suddenly jumped out of the bush so close to me, running back and forth in such a strange zigzag motion, that I was so absorbed watching it that I forgot to shoot until it had disappeared. In vain my hunger reminded me, but it was too late.

When we had walked a little further the country was gradually sloping to the east and to the south. I assumed that the south-east bend of the Monjeko was near and I was not mistaken. This march was over seventeen kilometres long. I had started out about half past five in the morning and it was perhaps 2 p.m. when I reached the Monjeko and soon afterwards the little village on its southern bank (to our right). Nowhere before had I observed so many tsetse flies as there. I sat down at the Monjeko stream which flowed only weakly at the bottom of the valley. While I was bathing my feet in the clear water I barely had the time to chase away the tsetse flies from poor Daisy who had run along with me all this time. That Daisy did not die from the tsetse stings can probably be explained by the fact that she had eaten long before some meat on the Limpopo which was poisoned with strychnine. I lay down under the shade of a tall mimosa tree and let my thoughts roam. Soon the villagers came out and stared at me in a stupor. I did not have to wait long until the first of my people showed up, then came the others, only my wife did not come. When I asked my people more and more worried questions as to what had happened they answered that the Matoka had been walking so slowly with my wife that they had gone ahead. The Matoka would probably come soon with my wife. Not only was I furious about this behaviour, even the inhabitants of the village began to scold my blacks for leaving the two porters alone with my wife in view of the numerous lions and buffaloes which made this area rather dangerous. In order not to be beaten up by the villagers some of my blacks hurried back and came just in time to help the exhausted Matoka cross the deep and steep bed of the little stream. Finally my wife was with us again after she had been literally untied from the hammock. Yet now she and the two Matoka began to shout at my people and for good reason. Especially the two Matoka were very upset about the behaviour of my servants. They should have stayed with them and at least helped them crossing the water holes. The result of the behaviour of my blacks was that the two Matoka who had carried my wife those two days for a total of 34 km refused to carry her the last 18 km—that was the distance still to Mo-Panza.

Only after we had calmed down the screaming and shouting Matoka somewhat was my wife able to put a word in and she told me in particular how much she had been in fear on that last stretch. The two blacks had suddenly put her down on the ground and had run away. Minute after minute passed and they did not come back. Then suddenly it occurred to my wife that they had deserted her and had simply thrown her away. Only then she realised that she never could free herself alone from the hammock. In short, she got terribly nervous and worked up, and began to shout and to cry. Even when the porters returned after a seemingly endless half hour she could not calm down.

The porters had simply become hungry and knew that near this place a little deeper in the bush there were some fruit trees bearing tasty fruit. Thus they had run there to get some fruit. They were very surprised about my wife's nervousness, in fact protested to her that she had even mistrusted them. Later they confessed to being a little ashamed that my wife had been in great danger of her life in view of the many buffaloes and lions in that stretch of the bush. Yet I have to repeat again that my blacks were much more guilty than they. The feeling of being saved and secure, however, quickly overcame this strain too, and we made ourselves comfortable in the village where we stayed overnight. I myself prepared a bed out of the softest grass which the Matoka women brought us for my poor wife who had suffered so much. They gave us milk, groundnuts, and cold polenta. Unfortunately I had nothing to give these good people in return. They, however, were again and again amazed that we had not only succeeded in traversing the Maschukulumbe territory to its northern border at Massangu but had also then got out of the country alive in spite of all the hostility of·its inhabitants. They themselves, so they said, would never have dared to go to the Maschukulumbe.

XIII

Return trip through the Matoka areas

From Masosa village to the Makalaka-Inquisi

EARLY ON 7 AUGUST WE LEFT MASOSA and in the afternoon we arrived in Mo'Mponde, Mo-Panza's kraal. On this stretch of our march I realised that man is his own worst enemy. For even though we were marching ready to shoot lion or buffalo at any minute our hearts were light since we had nothing to fear any more from man. The route we took was the same as on our march northwards. Fortunately there were no adventures that day. After all that terrible turmoil of the last days our minds really had calmed down by the time we entered the territory of Mo-Panza who before had been so friendly to us. Here we were planning to rest for a few days to let the wounds on our feet heal. In short, the fugitives and their plundered expedition were to be restored somewhat. Yet the situation had changed to our disadvantage. The old Mo-Panza was still kindly inclined towards us, yet his scheming brother, whom I have already mentioned earlier, now fell upon us poor half-naked whites successfully and even got Mo-Panza not to help us. Thus we would have left his kraal hungry if it had not been for an old subchief who took pity on us and induced the old king to give us some grain and a pot of beer for my men. The benevolent subchief himself, however, gave us 20 kg of maize, an old pot and a wooden spoon so that we were at least able to cook the venison and the grain. I attempted to get from Mo-Panza some rare examples of Matoka handicrafts and promised to pay him well with calico on the Zambezi to which he was supposed to send a messenger after us. I had chosen mostly rare objects, such as long-stemmed pipes with attached fire-tongs; head decorations made out of seeds, fruits, ivory and bird feathers; a shield made out of gnu skin; beautiful dagga-pipes; wooden bowls; clay pots, etc. Mo-Panza had already agreed to this deal when his brother tried to seize the opportunity to squeeze a rifle out of me. Only for this price, which I had refused to give him before, was I to get these rare things. Of course I did not agree to this. Because of this treatment I planned to leave Mo-Panza the very next day. Yet my people persuaded me to stay one day longer because of my weakened condition due to the fever. And so I did. It was, indeed, good that I stayed since I experienced a very violent attack of fever that night and the next morning. I would have been completely unable to walk anyway.

Yet the following day we had to get on, and indeed, even more than that. There was no way of staying on at Mo-Panza. The fever soon was to become as great a danger for us as the Maschukulumbe, now that we no longer had any medicine. We could not hesitate any longer and had to change our whole plan of operation. In hurried forced marches we had to get to the Zambezi (in as much as one can speak of hurrying with fever attacks and festering wounds on one's feet).

The most important event during our stay in Mo'Mponde was the arrival of the rest of my deserters. They did not dare to appear before us until the kind old sub-chief brought them to me and pleaded for them. What could I do? Their desertion which was the main reason for our disaster should have called for a severe punishment; however, in our situation such a procedure was not advisable—in fact, it was simply impossible. I thus made an admonitory speech and then forgave them. I refused, however, to accept Boy, the ringleader, and told him to beware that he did not fall into my hands otherwise I would shoot a bullet straight through his head since he was the biggest coward of all these rogues and the main cause for our great misfortune. Otherwise I took the deserters again into my service, but only until the Zambezi. I had to accept them at least to have porters in case of a severe relapse in our fevers as well as for the skins which I was still hoping to obtain before reaching the Zambezi. For these reasons I was glad to have with me again these eleven porters whom I knew well and who were pressing south just as I was.

Before I conclude I have to mention here one other incident which happened during our stay at Mo-Panza's. The very first night we were visited by a pair of hyenas who used to roam around the kraal every night searching for refuse from cooking or for some young goats. When Fekete was looking in the morning for his light veld-shoes which one of the deserters had given him as a present, he decided that they must have fallen off his feet during the night. He found only one on which his foot had been resting yet the second one was missing. We teased him that the hyena had pulled the second one off his foot.

Since we could not find the shoe anywhere in the end we believed ourselves that the hyena had taken it. I told Fekete to watch out during the next night so perhaps he could get an interesting skin which would have been the first one for our collection from our return trip. All the deserters who had stayed with Mo-Panza still had shoes. On our journey north we had given our servants worn, but still good, shoes. They had fled in them and now they gave some of us the shoes back since our feet were in such bad condition. For my wife a pair of shoes was padded with soft rags so that she could step on the ground again.

Night was falling. We had all suffered from fever attacks during the day so that we were all exhausted. Soon we fell fast asleep. Fekete was ill, too, yet he stayed awake. Suddenly we were shaken from our sleep by a shot. The hyena had come right into our camp and when he was leaving it Fekete had smashed his backbone with a bullet. While the animal was still trying to drag himself away I plunged a spear into his neck which quickly put him out of his misery. This was an exciting scene. It was bright moonlight as our entire camp got ready for the battle. The howling hyena was pursued by us all with spears, rifles and sticks with which to beat it. The Matoka village, too, was in an uproar, since people thought that the Maschukulumbe had dared to attack us and we were engaged in a battle with them. All the more delighted were they when they heard that we had killed one of the hyenas which had threatened the village every night for years. The animal was skinned that very night and early in the morning we cut his intestines open. In his stomach we found Fekete's shoe torn into four pieces and my companion had to have another sandal made for himself. The rest of us, by the way, had to convert our European shoes which we had got back into some kind of sandals as well. We had to cut holes into them at the sides and on the top since the mere contact of leather with our wounds was unbearable for us because of our many abscesses. Of all these shoes two held up until the Zambezi. I have kept them as a souvenir—although not a beautiful one—of that dreadful twenty-day march from Galulonga to the mouth of the Tschobe.

Our first day's journey was about sixteen kilometres long. It went through low, broken, hilly country which in the first half was sloped towards the west and in the second half towards the east. In mid-journey we crossed the valley of the N'Onga stream and its bed which was partly dried out. We crossed quite a number of small valleys to the side with little streamlets which entered the N'Onga valley. Four of them on the right bank and one of the left bank were larger and worth mentioning. In our sixth kilometre we passed a deserted village, in the eighth kilometre we passed the village Jankuba which was just being built and in the tenth the twin village Tschambiqua and Kabanzi.[1] From there we marched straight towards a range of hills running perpendicular to our route.[2] On one of the spurs of this range of hills in the immediate vicinity of the little village Kosora we pitched camp for the night. The panorama was quite picturesque. Beyond the pretty wooded hills beautiful rocky patches rose. Palm trees surrounded the nearby villages in which I noticed immediately a different style of hut.

When our blacks asked the Matoka to give us some food they refused to do so with taunts and jeers. Since we were very hungry, but could not yet rest there to cook the maize which Mo-Panza had given us as a present, we picked up here and there discarded pumpkin peels and 'refreshed' ourselves with this refuse. Our two little dogs, however, were chewing dry maize kernels. This was the only place from here to the Zambezi where people refused us any assistance and even mocked our misfortune.

I had intended to cover more than sixteen kilometres on that day's journey, yet from the ninth kilometre onward I was again attacked by the fever. Although I pushed myself to the limit I could go forward only very slowly. In the end I had to be supported and finally in the sixteenth kilometre I had to rest for that day.

Shortly after we had improvised our camp for the night we got a surprise visit from sixteen representatives of Mo-Panza. They brought the following news from the king: they had come as our guides in order to show us the shortest way. They were also going with us to find some work with me or some other European at the Zambezi. I did not like this whole story. We could not go wrong, why then this escort? I got suspicious. I would also have to shoot game for these sixteen as far as the Zambezi. No, I could not take them on. Anyway I had all the twenty servants from before in addition to the four Europeans; this caused enough trouble in itself. I did not sleep, but watched those sixteen during the night. I saw them having a lively conversation with the villagers. The next morning yet another six additional men from the village followed us without being properly equipped for a two-year journey, i.e. to stay long enough on the Zambezi to earn a rifle. After I had informed some of my servants about my suspicions I ordered these strangers watched closely. The next day provided us with so much incriminating evidence against these people that their intention became clear to me. I decided to get rid of them as quickly as possible. Mo-Panza's brother had sent them, seemingly in order to accompany us, but actually in order to attack us on the first possible night, to kill us, and to get our rifles into their possession. During our march we stopped to rest several times. I pressed them hard with questions until finally the whole plot became completely clear to me. 'How could Mo-Panza afford to let you go? He is not safe from the Maschukulumbe and he needs his people at home.' 'Why did Mo-Panza give you no food for your twenty-day journey to the Zambezi? He usually does so when he sends people there. Should we waste our cartridges on you to feed you with venison? Do you really think I am so stupid as to do so? Did I not heal several of your sick people before? Don't you think that I as *Njaka* [physician, magician] have looked into your hearts and into that of your chief who sent you? My *molemo* [medicine, poison, charm, amulet, etc,] penetrates deep, deep into people's hearts. Not Mo-Panza but his brother, the black hyena, has sent you.' I made remarks of this sort every now and then and all too soon I realised that I was right. In order to allay my suspicions they tried to outdo each other with kindness. In many of the villages we passed they bought for us pumpkin shells filled with millet and gave them to us in Mo-Panza's name. Yet they also enlisted five more assistants for their plan. Thus, by the end of our more than twenty-three kilometre long march of the first day my decision was made: I had to get rid of these people before sunset. On our march I asked them in a rather casual fashion where in the south (i.e. in our direction) Mo-Panza's last subjects were to be found. The answer was 'They were those whom we have just left.'

That was very convenient for us. 'And who is living towards the south?' 'For a good distance nobody. Then some independent Matoka chiefs, not as powerful as Mo-Panza.' 'And where is Moëba living?' 'Towards the west.' 'And Sietsetema?' 'Towards the south-west.' 'Good, that is completely correct.' The men whom I had just questioned suggested that we camp near the village we had just passed called Siketa.[3] It was situated on a divide and rich with fat-tailed sheep. 'No, I am going further.'

Thank God, none of us whites had a fever attack that day. I ordered us to march on in order to get away as far as possible from the last village so that in case of a possible attack the bandits could not get any support from the village. We had passed the range of hills which we had first seen the day before, called the Kosara hills,[4] and we now were descending into a very beautiful basin-shaped valley partly covered with tropical vegetation. Thus the pretty rock scenery, consisting of mica slate rising vertically out of the valley like old castles, appeared even more interesting. The valley itself as well as its side valleys were teeming with game. I was surprised to find waterbuck since I did not see any large body of water around.

'In this basin', the Matoka told me, 'the Marutse king Luanika-Lebosche has slain many Maschukulumbe. After he had stolen that large number of cattle from them in 1882, he went south. Here the Maschukulumbe of the southern Luenge tried to recapture his loot. They united in a group of several hundred men. Here in this valley they hoped to grab him. Yet the battle was too unequal. Luanika had rifles and the Maschukulumbe only had spears. Luanika let the enemies come as close as the range of their spears and then gave the order to fire at them. They fell like game and the king moved on unmolested.' We passed through numerous deep valleys with little streams and small flowing water courses, five of them worth mentioning. Beyond the heights of the hilly country we crossed the big N'Onga in which we found some water flowing still. This was, however, bound to dry up since we had crossed its bed the day before without seeing any flowing water. In the first half of our journey we came across a large number of Matoka villages.

As I said before, I went on for a further 5 km in order to get away from the village. Then I tried to look for a suitable camp site for the night. We found what we were looking for when we had left the hilly bush country and came to a plateau sloping towards the east, the south and the west. We pitched camp near a stream by a steep rocky outcrop overgrown with bush.[5] Before we moved into our improvised camp I would have liked to provide us with a hearty supper. I had hunted a fat eland bull but had not been able to kill him. I looked that day somewhat more graciously on Boy. I had given him Leeb's rifle for hunting purposes; however, St Hubertus, the patron saint of the hunters, did not favour him that day either, even though we had seen much game, especially gnu, kakatombe, eland, roan and sable antelopes and had heard buffalo, hyena and lion.

Meanwhile the question was how to rid ourselves definitively of our unpleasant escort that same evening. Our situation was as follows: we had pitched our camp on a rock terrace and the twenty-seven Matoka had put theirs up on a second one. We Europeans, as well as Mapani, Boy and Maruma, were each armed with one rifle—among them were two magazine rifles, one with fourteen and the other with seven cartridges. Thus armed we moved in front of the rocky outcrop in the protection of which they had pitched their camp. Our blacks with their spears were the second battle line. I had Mapani say as interpreter: 'You have come as our guides?' 'Yes, Master.' 'Where is the way to Sakasipa? You do not know?' Then one of them answered, 'Not even the inhabitants of the last village know it.' 'Such guides I do not need. I do not even tolerate them around me, for I know well enough that you are planning to attack us during the night and to kill and rob us. Therefore you are not allowed to pitch your camp in our vicinity, but only far away. And tomorrow I do not want to see any of you any more, otherwise I shall shoot down everybody who comes near me.' None of them answered a single word. 'Here is the millet which you have begged for us in the last village, take it as your food.' After that some of them began to roll up their skins in order to get ready to leave. 'Quick, get yourselves away from here. Before the sun goes down you have to be off!' We stepped back a few paces, they passed by indifferently and we let them go. I posted some guards, yet the night passed completely quietly —this last danger on the part of man was over.

The following day we passed several streams and a little river, all flowing to the north or north-west and probably belonging to the system of the river which we had come across in Moëba's area. Later the terrain was sloping towards the east to where several streams were flowing, too. In our twentieth (and last) kilometre of that journey there was again a stream flowing westwards. We pitched camp alongside it. We passed a deserted village, passed through protea and mimosa woods, found mica slate and granite. Both the stones were covered by a stratum of iron-bearing conglomerates on the elevations while in the valleys they had been transformed into limonite. That day we also encountered a group of Matoka who showed us a good path. We were, in fact, at the border of two Matoka territories east of Sietsetema. The next day we were to pass through the territories of several small chiefs and thus this information was very useful for us. This march of 11 August I shall never forget because of the great suffering my wife had to go through after a violent attack of fever. Yet in spite of this she was forced to keep up with us.

That day Sydamojo, our bitch, gave birth to a lone puppy, probably because she had been bitten by tsetse flies (even though Mr Blockley maintained that the animal was immune to the bites of this insect since she had been born in a tsetse fly area). She carried her puppy immediately into a deserted jackal hole. When we left this place the next morning she followed us with the little puppy in her mouth. Thereafter I had one of the blacks carry it in an old leather apron.

Our two marches of the next day were more interesting and less exhausting. We stopped at noon in the eleventh kilometre and camped for the night in the twenty-second kilometre. We went mostly in a south-south-western direction, first down a slope into a valley until we reached the bottom of the valley through which the Djesa stream flowed westwards. On this route we found much game. Boy, the best hunter among my people, to whom I had again given a rifle, that day shot a male zebra which was delightful booty for us. Ever since the day before we had been suffering from hunger, so much that my blacks had caught frogs for themselves. We were all dragging ourselves up the slope. We were tired and, in addition, I was shaken by fever.

When we reached Djesa,[6] where the huts were all surrounded by high poles because of the numerous lions, all the inhabitants ran out screaming. In vain we shouted after them to stay and that we would not do them any harm. These good people thought we were Marancian's band which had fled from Schescheke and was roaming in the area. They had beaten such a sudden and hasty retreat that we found a pot with a still warm dish of bush pig. My starving blacks fell upon it immediately, yet I drove them away with my fists shouting 'We have not yet become robbers and thieves in spite of everything.' Those who had sneaked into the huts and were beginning to pack up tobacco and household utensils which seemed useful for their trip back got an even worse beating. When the villagers observed from a distance that we were not robbing them, the men came close and were quite friendly, even servile.

Meanwhile Boy came back with the news that he had killed a zebra. My dear reader, you should have heard the shouts of exultation which my starving blacks uttered at this moment. Even we Europeans grinned rather happily. I promised the villagers that we would give them zebra meat in exchange for the wild pig which was already cooked. In addition, they gave us milk, some flour, and beans. When they saw that my wife was sitting on the ground they gave her a little wooden stool, in return for which I gave them two empty cartridges. They accepted them with pleasure and used them as hollow *gomas* (snuff boxes).

After they had warned us to be cautious since the area was teeming with lions we parted as friends. We Europeans especially carried away a grateful memory of the good inhabitants of Djesa. Below Djesa we crossed a deep depression, after which our path led us along a slope. The depression was sloping down towards the west and south-west. After a three-hour march we passed a village called Katwe. Here chief Samokakatwe was residing. His territory stretched some kilometres north and 6 km south of the Djesa stream. We camped in a clearing in the lush grass right in the middle of a *mopani* wood. The evening was cool but beautiful and the sky bright with stars. Since none of us that day had been overcome by the fever we all felt more content and even quietly happy—for the first time in weeks.

The following morning we marched on, with the wooded hill crest to our left just like the day before. We crossed over several laterite ridges which were running perpendicularly across our route. They were mostly shaped like a half-moon and became flatter at the end of the basin-shaped valley. We crossed four streams flowing westwards and in our twelfth kilometre we passed the village Kaunga[7] which was right in the centre of a small territory belonging to the Kaunga chief. In the eighteenth kilometre we entered the territory of a different chief and in the nineteenth and twentieth kilometres we spotted several villages to the east.[8] Only when night began to fall did we choose a camp site on the bank of a river rushing southwards.[9] Since that day my wife as well as Leeb and I had suffered from fever attacks we had had to take longish rests several times, as for instance at Kaunga. Therefore we got to sleep rather late.

The area through which we came was rich with game. We noticed in particular eland, roan and Harris antelope, kabunda gazelle, buffalo, striped gnu and zebra. In the bottom of the valley where the Makalaka Inquisi[10] forms extensive swamps there were a large number of hippoes. Carnivores were rather common. We saw hyena and jackal, heard several times the roaring of a lion, saw fresh leopard tracks in the bush, and admired a huge lion trap near the Kaunga village which consisted of a square surrounded by a double palisade fence. The inhabitants told us that the lions not infrequently attacked the kraals and villages during the night and that, although their fields are situated nearby around the villages, workers in the field were often driven back into the villages by the lions even during the day-time.

Right at the beginning of our march we met a kakatombe herd. We observed this time again a particularly characteristic feature of this most beautiful type of hartebeest. If such a herd is surprised by some danger or by a hunter all of them flee in the same direction in a closely-knit group. The calves are trained by the old ones to go in front. Only after they have disappeared in the wood or bush do the elders take to flight. They go first in a different direction and thus try to divert the carnivore or the hunter from the track of the young ones. Then by a large detour they try to catch up again with the young ones. If we got close to them again the whole scene was repeated once more. The inhabitants of Kaunga were extremely hospitable. They were not content like their fellow tribesmen merely to offer us only groundnuts, millet or corn but even brought us chicken and gave my wife some milk and sweet wild fruit. The friendliness of the inhabitants of those vil-lages we passed in late afternoon increased to a point when it became truly offi-cious. Thus I felt compelled to place double guards for the night. If I had had some quinine at my disposal I would have stayed there a few days in order to get valu-able trophies for my collection with the expenditure of only a few car-tridges—and with the help of the Matoka who are very experienced in beating and driving the game close at dawn or dusk.

The march on 14 August was probably one of the most interesting ones of the whole expedition north of the Zambezi. It was also the longest one since 10 July. Early in the morning we immediately crossed a rapidly flowing mountain stream with quite some effort. Then we entered an indentation of the Inquisi basin. The blacks told me that the river was the little stream which we had crossed at Sietsetema's. Yet I cannot believe their report. To my mind this river, flowing south-westwards, into which numerous little streams flow in the valley basin, is the upper Makalaka-Inquisi which we crossed again the same day in our twenty-eighth kilometre. By then it had become a broad and extremely attractive river with picturesque river banks. The ridge which had been on our left on our jour-neys on 12 and 13 August and along which we were marching bent eastwards at the spot where we crossed the Makalaka-Inquisi. Then the ridge turned in a south-westerly direction, sending out a number of spurs, mostly parallel to each other. Later the Makalaka-Inquisi cuts through it. The spurs of the ridge then form lon-gitudinal valleys which carry many subsidiaries flowing into the main river. Be-cause of this distinctive fan-like distribution of deep valleys and narrow ridges over which picturesque and steeply rising granite blocks tower, the first kilo-metres of our journey were very interesting. Unfortunately we suffered much that day from the fever, so that our journey proceeded only slowly. Gradually a characteristic symptom of this disease—an absolute indifference to one's own safety—overcame us Europeans. Without saying a word we were trotting on, following each other at rather long intervals. Only I stayed close to my sick wife.

On the paths leading to Mala, our next goal, we saw numerous buffalo and lion tracks. We were already so accustomed to these that they left us completely unconcerned. On one occasion I suddenly felt so bad that I had to sit down. My wife slowly went on alone even though just then we had been marching for an hour through a dangerous thicket of high grass which seemed to stretch until the village of Mala. Since my wife thought that I was close behind her she went on slowly only armed with a light spear which served at the same time as a cane. I had to vomit violently and I could not get up from the ground until Leeb caught up with me and helped me on. In spite of my extreme exhaustion I tried to get forward quickly since I had become worried about the safety of my wife walking alone. For I had seen a game track with many fresh lion prints entering the human path which we were using. At some places the high dry grass had been stamped down on both sides of the path. It appeared that lions had been playing there. The further we went the more worried we got and finally we began to shout. To our pleasant surprise we heard her familiar voice answering from the immediate vicinity. 'Why do you shout so loud? You are chasing all the game away and we won't shoot anything today either.' 'Yes, but the lion tracks. Don't you realise that one does not see anything else but these on the path?' 'Well, but they are old.' 'No, no, look, the dew has not yet fallen onto them. The lions must have been running along here shortly before us or must still be lying somewhere close to here.' Then we waited for Fekete, out of concern for his safety, and went on together to Mala. When this village, which was only a few kilometres south of our previous night's camp, finally came into sight we could judge how slowly we had been marching that day. It had taken us six hours to come this small distance. In a clearing before Mala we encountered a herd of gnu. Only the unpleasant taste of their meat kept us that time from shooting one of the animals. Because of the abundance of game we were hoping that day at least for a juicy buffalo calf and, indeed, our wish was fulfilled.

The inhabitants of Mala consisted of only two families who had four huts at their disposal—one of them being a stable for sheep and goats. We found these people in great alarm. Night after night lions came to their kraal. They could no longer drive their goats and sheep to the pasture. The lions even penetrated into the kraal. They leapt so often against the three-metre-high palisade that it became loose in the sandy ground and gave way to the carnivores who then entered the yard. When the inhabitants tried to scare the animals away from the fence with their spears, one of the palisades yielded to the impact of a lioness who had been jumping against it. The palisade fell into the yard and the inhabitants were barely able to climb the high watch scaffold erected in the centre of the yard. From that night on the inhabitants no longer posted themselves along the fence for their defence, but climbed even at dusk on to the scaffold which is represented in my sketch. There they spent their nights thenceforth in order to defend themselves, as well as their herds, from such an impregnable height. The lions, however, did not seem to respect this primitive fortification very much as we soon learned from the reports of the natives. 'Recently on a night when the lions had dragged three goats out of our huts and had eaten them we killed a lioness with our spears from this scaffold. Her skull is hanging on that pole, as you can see, Master. And yet the lions come back to us every night. Even the meat boiling in that pot there is from a half-eaten goat which the lions killed last night in this yard.'

On entering the compound the smell of the meat had pleasantly hit our noses and in a minute we all gathered around the large clay pot, the contents of which were momentarily the most interesting for us. With the words 'I shall give you zebra meat', I had already dipped into the bubbling pot and was soon distributing some pieces of the tender cooked meat to my white companions. The Matoka gave the rest of the contents of the pot to my blacks, although this was a dubious present to our mind since at the bottom of the pot only the intestines of that poor goat were cooking. My blacks, however, as I have already reported several times before, were not fussy and soon the pot was empty.

In other ways, too, the Matoka were very helpful. They gave me a pair of magnificent buffalo horns. This was the first piece and so to speak the foundation of the collection we were gathering on our trip home. When I gave it to one of my blacks to carry, I certainly had not the slightest idea that this second collection at the end of our labours would fill over seventy boxes.

For two empty cartridges the people also gave me the lion skull which was stuck on the pole. But the skin they had to deliver to their chief. According to the tradition of the Matoka the skins of all wild animals which have killed a domestic animal on a particular piece of land belong to the land-owner. And as much as they were intrigued by the empty cartridges which I offered them they refused to give the skin away.

I would have liked to stay overnight in Mala to secure a few lion skins for our collection. Yet in the past few days the fever had attacked my wife and Leeb regularly every other day. As just that day, i.e. 14 August, was free from fever I decided rather to give up a promising lion hunt and a few beautiful lion skins and to use this day as much as possible to march onward. Since I had no medicine I was in constant fear that a sudden severe attack of malaria might kill one of my people.

The people tried to keep us there at any price—at least for one night so that we could shoot, if possible, all their lions. If that day had been the fever day I surely would have done what they wished. As it was, however, I could only be sorry for them. They assured us seriously that they would have to leave this place because of the carnivores.

After we had revitalised ourselves with a hearty zebra soup and a zebra fillet we bade the poor Matoka farewell. I invited them to come and visit us at the mouth of the Tschobe and to get some presents there. From Mala we marched, as indicated, in the direction of Mo-Sinkobo, Sakasipa's town which according to the information of those blacks was four to five days away. From there we then would be able to get to the mouth of the Tschobe in three and a half days. The idea of reaching in a measurably short time the furthest outpost of civilisation electrified all of us.

In our minds we were already at the Zambezi, which seemed in the neighbourhood of Vienna. With these happy thoughts we walked on bravely and in the evening we were 28 km closer to home.

In the second kilometre of our second march of the day we crossed the ridge which split at this point. We walked through a very broken basin-shaped valley and through gorges until in our sixth kilometre we crossed a second spur of the ridge and entered a long broad and hilly valley. This appeared to be enclosed by the spur we just had crossed and by the main ridge. Its soil seemed to contain magnesia. In the hilly countryside full of gorges through which we first passed we found numerous lion and buffalo tracks. Boy asked me to give him five of my blacks to try out his hunting luck.

On our march through the brackish valley we saw many zebras and a herd of kakatombe hartebeest who drove their young calves to escape in the usual fashion before they themselves followed by an extensive detour. That afternoon the sun beat down on us in that treeless valley. We had to rest often but for short periods. Only around 5 o'clock did we reach the Inquisi which crosses the valley in a deep cut. We went across the river and camped on the slope of the opposite bank.[11] After we had crossed the Zambezi this river was, apart from the Luenge, the most interesting one we encountered on our journey north of the Zambezi. It had there the character of a broad mountain river with crystal-clear water; it formed numerous little waterfalls and rapids from which thousands of little rock islands protruded, either bare or overgrown with tropical vegetation. Elsewhere its waves foamed over huge blocks of rock, some of which might have travelled a long distance before they found there a kind of resting place.

In that respect the Inquisi reminded me very much of our wild rivers in the Alps. Yet the wildlife along the river everywhere indicated the tropics. Innumerable fish were playing in the clear water, but there were just as many of their enemies—the fish eagle in the air and even more the water leguans in the water. Instead of our deer there were zebra, gnus, antelope, buffalo and lion coming to drink. And what about the river banks as such? The banks as well as the rocky islands were literally overgrown with subtropical and tropical vegetation.

My dear reader, I would have loved to revel for days in this ideal landscape which was as beautiful as it was interesting and instructive. What a delight would this flora be for the observer and natural scientist when it begins to sprout with all its splendour in early summer and everything is laden with a rich display of colourful blossoms.

The river was over 100 m wide from one bank to the other. Each of us fell badly several times before we made it across the slippery blocks of rock, the washed-out rocky banks and the rough boulders. Finally we were across the river. In the solid rock as well as in loose rock we found formations of mica slate and diorite, as well as gneiss and quartz blocks. After the camp site was chosen my servants began to make a fence of thorn bushes around the camp. Before they had finished this job Mapani and Simundaj came to report that they had killed a fat buffalo cow. Mapani was the lucky hunter. I gave him all the men I could spare and they went off immediately. During the night four of my servants returned with the skin for curing and with fresh meat. Mapani himself did not come with them, but had them report that he had killed en route a magnificent male zebra and that I should send the men back to him early in the morning as he needed them to transport the carcass. Boy had wounded four buffalo bulls, they reported, but he had killed none. He, as well as Mapani, had encountered a pride of lions, but they had not dared to attack so many carnivores with the few cartridges they had had at their disposal.

About noon all the venison and the second skin had arrived and that evening we were able to enjoy a hearty although unfortunately unsalted meat broth. On that 15 August all of us Europeans suffered from the fever. Yet Fekete's and my fever attacks were nothing in comparison to the terrible relapses my wife and Leeb suffered. Their attacks lasted over eight hours. The accompanying asthmatic symptoms as well as the general exhaustion of their strength in the evening made us fear the worst.

I considered ourselves lucky that we had not stayed in Mala and thus were 28 km closer to the Zambezi where one could get medicine. That day of rest I gave Boy twenty cartridges and my Werndl carbine so that he could follow the lions and attack them. But he was less lucky that day than the day before and did not see a lion.

I was collecting seeds and fruits along the river and regretted that we had no paper on which to preserve some of the most interesting plant species and no hammer to knock off some samples of the rock formations.

At the end of this chapter I still want to mention that the buffalo cow which Mapani had killed must at some point have recovered from a fierce fight with a lion. At the back of its head I found a small wound in the process of healing. It penetrated deep into the thick skull. It was the hole of a canine tooth of a huge lion. The right half of its lower jaw showed a complete fracture. Yet for the most part it had healed, but had developed into a mis-shapen jaw. Only at one spot did I still find an abscess, but even this was in the process of healing. One would have thought that this buffalo cow would have been completely unable to chew. Yet her grazing had not been harmed by this great damage, because one could even call her rather fat.

In the afternoon the inhabitants of Mala passed us with their herd. Lions had not only penetrated into their yard but again into one of the huts and had carried away a fat sheep. They had hardly disappeared towards the valley and water when the Matoka had hurriedly left their palisade villages with the rest of their herd. They were on their way to their chief who was living only a few kilometres further away to the west of our camp. My renewed attempt to buy the skin of the lioness, this time for ten empty cartridges, was no more successful than the attempt of the previous day. There was no hope that I could buy the skin from the chief for what I would have been able to pay. For the chief sold such skins to Sakasipa's people for one sheep. They in turn exchanged it in Panda-ma-Tenka for a woollen blanket. There one cannot buy it for less than 18–20 guilders and further south it has an even greater value.

I was sorry that the Matoka had to leave Mala because their little village was the tidiest and cleanest and their huts the best I had seen throughout the Matoka lands. In addition, its inhabitants were diligent, true-hearted and kind.

Return trip through the Matoka areas

From the Makalaka-Inquisi to the mouth of the Tschobe

ON 16 AUGUST WE CLIMBED UP A VALLEY which entered the actual Inquisi valley at a right angle. In our fourth kilometre when we had reached the top, we came to a little fortified Matoka kraal. Its maize fields were still full of dry maize stalks with the watch scaffolds overlooking them. The valley reminded me of the scenery in a large English park.

It was a crisp and cool morning and since my sick people had eaten some hearty meat broth before our departure we progressed fairly well. I was leading my wife by her arm all the way. What was incredibly bothersome on these long marches was the dry sharp grass. The path trampled by the feet of the blacks was so narrow that only one person could walk on it. When I was leading my wife by her arm I did not exactly have to 'bite the grass' but to walk in it and that caused incredible pain because of our poor footwear and our pussy wounds. Only with great efforts was I able to conceal these pains from my wife. Otherwise she would not have tolerated my supporting her. Yet she was not able to get onwards on her own.

From the fourth kilometre to the eighth the path suddenly followed an eastern direction. In the eighth kilometre we reached a village called Sikiwinda where chief Siatschongwa, to whom Mala too belonged, was residing. I realised at first sight that there could not be any lions in the immediate vicinity since Sikiwinda was in a rather desolate state. The wood of the palisade fence had been used to a large extent as firewood, the huts were in ruins. Their insides as well as their inhabitants were begrimed with filth. Yet here, too, the kernel was better than its shell. The people were warm and kind. They gave my people a pot full of beer and a calabash full of groundnut oil. For two cartridge shells I bought from them a water-pipe with which they smoke hemp, called 'dagga'. Each day I was glad and praised myself that I had again taken the deserters whom I had found at Mo-Panza's into my service. Apart from the meat which we carried with us regularly every day brought some new objects for our collection. I could never have taken them along without these porters.

The news that Sakasipa could be reached in two days was very much appreciated, yet a second report that Mr G. Westbech had left Gazungula for a hunting expedition put us somewhat out of humour. This meant that only his representative, Mr Wa, who was not very much liked by any of us, would be present at the trading post at the mouth of the Tschobe. On the chance that the next fever attack of my wife's might be as violent as the last one, which had in fact endangered her life, I decided to send two people ahead in order to buy a container with tea and some quinine from Mr Wa.

Sikiwinda is situated on the watershed between the Makala and the Maschupia-Inquisi. After we had left the village our way led through several valleys and we crossed seven streams, the third one of which was called Manjanganga. All these streams flowed to the east or south-east. Our way went on across wooded chains of hills which were full of rocky cliffs and gorges. In short, they showed very interesting rock structures and were populated by much game. Mica slate and granite were the formations which I found.

That day we covered almost twenty-four kilometres. We encountered, among others, a family which was emigrating from Sakasipa to the east. Yet they were not familiar with this area and could not inform me about the names of the mountains, rivers and streams. The head of the household was walking leisurely in front, armed only with two light spears and an axe. The younger of the two

12   *The Matoka (Tonga) village of Sikiwinda*

women was burdened with a huge basket so full of grain and other supplies that at home a strong man would not be able to carry it for a long period of time. The second, older woman was gasping under a load of cooking utensils, wooden bowls, spoons, hoes, and so on. This was a load of at least fifty kilogrammes. A girl of about ten years was carrying the clothing of the whole family which was superfluous at that time as well as the bedding. The grand old man was wearing a leather strap, the two women little skirts made out of skin reaching to their knees and the girl was dressed in an apron made out of narrow thongs. The spare clothing which the girl carried rolled up consisted of two small and dirty leather coats and the bedding consisted of two reed mats and a cured kakatombe skin.

We pitched our camp for the night by a little stream which was surrounded by wooded hills.[1] It forced its way through a picturesque rock gate in the north-west. Unexpectedly we had all been gripped that day by a fever relapse. Even though it was not a severe one it was unpleasant enough and made it impossible to try our hunting luck in the thick bush nearby. On 17 August we started early. We were tired from the fever and the march was doubly exhausting for our sore abscess-covered feet, since we had to traverse valleys and then climb up steep hills again. We crossed six streams worthy of mention. They flowed in an easterly and east-south-easterly direction. During the rainy season, when the hills are green and the valleys are in full bloom, this area must be a magnificent sight with its rocky heights and the streams which are then full of water.

Because of our sore feet and a fever attack suffered by my wife we were forced to take a more lengthy rest by a stream in our tenth kilometre. In our fourteenth kilometre we reached a plateau which was a watershed. Our eyes roved far over a completely uninhabited plain descending somewhat towards the west. Without coming across a single hut we marched on for 10 km. According to our experience of the morning we expected that we would find at least some water in the many streams which we had to cross that day. Acting on this assumption we only took two calabashes of water along. In the afternoon we found not even a single little pool of water in all the streams we crossed. Thus, we had to suffer badly from the lack of water on our exhausting march in the great heat. A few cups of water poured over our feet would have felt wonderful. My reader will comprehend how slowly the march was proceeding when I report that we had started out at 5 o'clock in the morning and that it took us until 9 o'clock in the evening, i.e. sixteen full hours, before we completed the 24 km journey.[2] I would not have marched that far if we had not been driven by our thirst. We only stopped to rest when night had already set in and the roaring of lions close to us on our right forced us categorically to halt. I had the camp set up on a partially suitable site. When three of my blacks, Mapani, Marumo and Kabrniak, realised how much we were suffering from thirst they decided secretly to go and hunt for water. I never would have allowed them to do this because of the lions. The other servants —and I did not realise that three were missing—chopped down the nearest trees around us and in spite of the darkness they constructed in an hour's time an enclosure. By tree trunks placed in the middle they even divided it into two rooms, one for us and one for them.

It was a sad rest. We had thrown ourselves hungry on the grass. Because of our great thirst we were unable to get meat which had been roasted over charcoal past our lips. Nobody said a word so we soon put out the fire. Then a sudden rustling in the dry branches made us grab our arms quickly. But who could describe my astonishment when we saw through our protective fence the three dark figures of our returning servants. I was alarmed about their rash deed and yet I was grateful for the water in their calabashes. We quickly lit the fires again. The pot we had received as a present from Mo-Panza was put on it and a meat broth was prepared for us. Our blacks cooked their meal after us in two parts and when the last had finally eaten the morning was already dawning in the east. Later than usual, i.e. only about 8 o'clock, we left our camp site on 18 August. When we awoke we were again greeted by the roar of a lion which gave us company for several more kilometres. The aim of this day's journey was Mo-Sinkobo, Sakasipa's residence. In order to reach it we had to make the longest march which we ever made on the whole expedition north of the Zambezi and this with incredible efforts. In our twelfth kilometre we reached about noon the village, Ki-a-Njama after we had crossed quite a number of streams belonging to the Inquisi system.

We took a rest in Ki-a-Njama and there I was struck by the inhabitants' shields made out of gnu and eland skins. They were hanging in the trees which shaded the huts. Unfortunately I was not able to buy one of these defence weapons. At our question, how far was it still to Mo-Sinkobo, the blacks pointed towards the setting sun which meant still five to six hours.

Thus we soon got on our way again to get to Mo-Sinkobo. But in our joy about this news we forgot that a trip which the blacks make in five hours could hardly be accomplished by us in nine or ten hours. It was a terrible march. My wife and I felt particularly exhausted that day. And when I remember today the tortures we had to go through that day I must call it a miracle that we reached Mo-Sinkobo at all, even though only late at night. The wounds of our feet had never been as painful as on that 18 August. My wife was unable to drag herself along and was leaning on me so heavily that I had to half carry her. More and more often we had to rest. We had food yet we were too tired to eat it. Thus it became evening and soon the dark night set in. My wife's voice failed. For the last two hours she had staggered on sobbing continuously and sweating like myself with an attack of fever. Yet suddenly I realised that the hands of my wife had turned cold and that she was about to fall down. The most obvious thought—to have her carried—was impossible to realise. My people themselves were all too exhausted. And all Matoka whom we met on the way and whom I asked for help laughed or shook their heads when they heard that they were supposed to support or to carry my wife since I had nothing to pay them for this 'work'. I forced myself to walk as fast as possible in order to make my wife warm and I asked her to put forth once again all her remaining strength. For in Mo-Sinkobo we could get some milk which was truly a remedy for her since she was suffering from the fever more than any of us. 'My beloved, only half-an-hour still, only a quarter of an hour still, we must be in

Mo-Sinkobo right now.' She only shook her head and I heard the aspiration of her hardly audible voice 'Is the cup of sorrows not yet full to the brim? How long will it take still?' '*Muci, Muci*', we heard some of our black servants calling from far ahead of us through the quiet of the night. I felt the effect of this call in her trembling hands resting on me and I felt it by a jerk of her exhausted body which was leaning against me while she walked. We came to the village—yet it was not the desired kraal but only a settlement located 2 km before it and there was no milk to be had. I wanted to send some of the villagers to Mo-Sinkobo yet they refused to go claiming that they would be beaten up by Sakasipa's wives if they dared to wake them up that late. If Sakasipa were at home his people would be still awake until after midnight, but since he was away they went to bed early.

Since all my servants had walked ahead and since Fekete and Leeb were just as tired as we were we had no choice but to make a last attempt to reach Sakasipa's kraal. How should I describe to you, my dear reader, the sufferings of this last march of 18 August? These two kilometres took us two full hours. Yet finally we stood before that miserable kraal, to which we had been looking forward all day long, as if it comprised bliss and salvation. My blacks had roused the whole village into an uproar with their noise.

Here in Mo-Sinkobo these chaps felt at home. Here we had reached the route again from where before we had started north to the Luenge. Immediately my blacks moved to their old camp site which still existed from our departure to the north. They had begun to clean it. Some of them even came running towards us to support my wife and me for the last 600 paces.

Yet to us, too, Mo-Sinkobo appeared like the hospitable house of an old friend. Already there were waiting for us a little pot with milk, a container with beer, and a plucked chicken. These treasures Sakasipa's head wife had sent us. Even though it was so late at night she herself came to our camp and reported that her husband had gone to Luanika—firstly, to congratulate the king upon his recent re-accession to the throne; secondly, to bring him tribute; and thirdly, to report the death of his relative Matakala, the Matoka chief who is already known to the reader. Sakasipa suggested as his successor our good servant Jonas, whom I have reported earlier was the closest relative of Matakala. Later we heard that Jonas had indeed taken over the chieftainly heritage.

In Mo-Sinkobo where we were so well taken care of we took a day of rest on 19 August. If only we had been able to enjoy it. We were all deadly exhausted and my wife especially was suffering so much from the fever that early in the morning of the 19th I sent the healthiest of my black servants to Gazungula to Mr Wa to ask him to give me some quinine and some coffee. The servants were supposed to describe our situation accurately, especially the condition of my wife in order to move this man, whom I knew to be not very good hearted, to fulfill my request.

I intended to leave on 20 August and hoped to meet my servant half way with the desired medication, that is if Mr Wa would give it to him immediately, which we assumed would be the natural thing to do. It was the first time that I had so much faith in this man, yet this time, too, I had hoped for too much.

Thus we stayed on 19 August in Mo-Sinkobo and continued our trip on 20 August. We took the shortest path which was pointed out to us—the path from which the perfidious porters had led us astray on our way north as is known to the reader. On this more direct route via the Silamba valley we reached the mouth of the Tschobe in three and a half days, whereas before we had needed six days for the same distance via Mo-Rukumi, not including our stay there. The fever of my wife no longer dropped at all. Since the sore feet of some of my blacks had improved just as much as ours had become worse, they were willing to carry my seriously-ill wife half of the distance we travelled on 20 August. This was 14·5 km. Of course, we took a longish rest several times, yet we marched on until deep into the night. Finally we pitched our camp after we had covered 29 km.

In our fifth kilometre we crossed the Namatere stream as well as two other streams further on which flowed towards the east and south-east into the Ki-Sinde river which was flowing parallel to our path in a south-westerly direction. At our first rest in the tenth kilometre near a village we got some refreshments from the blacks. Even the inhabitants of the kraals in the fourteenth and fifteenth kilometres which belonged to a village called Pasila, as well as the inhabitants of the Mo-Tschara[3] village 3 km further west, gave us millet, beer and chickens. In fact they even offered their help in carrying my wife which, however, my servants did not allow. In the twentieth kilometre we passed through a partly wooded and partly swampy valley. It was a wide valley broken up by many side valleys lined by rocky hills. At that spot we started along the second laterite ridge of that day. It was over seven kilometres long, whereas the first one measured 9 km.

The Matoka living there were all very diligent farmers. They were working only with hoes, without using any irrigation. They took millet and beans, then maize and tobacco, wild fruits and goats to sell in Gazungula, the Letschumo valley, and Panda-ma-Tenka. Their fields were located along the thickest part of the laterite ridge. Their kraals were lying next to them and were quite well built and enclosed by palisades. They inhabit these kraals only during the growing season. They had cut down trees and bushes and left only those trees in the fields which bore tasty wild fruit. The grass on the laterite ridge through which we passed in the afternoon had been burnt over by a violent bushfire that very day. The fire was still raging in the Katubia valley where we camped for the night.

On 21 August we left at dawn. We marched across an eight kilometre-long laterite ridge and traversed a broad wooded valley already covered again with fresh grass. Through this valley a broad stream flowed and when we descended into the valley we came to a deserted village which could clearly have boasted of one of the most beautiful locations in the Matoka lands. The village ruins were situated on a flat wooded overhang of the laterite ridge which dominated the whole valley. The site was shaded by huge blue mimosa trees and a few fan palms. In this valley Boy succeeded in killing a kakatombe hartebeest.

After we had taken a short rest in this valley we went on along the second wooded laterite ridge. There I collected interesting species of mushrooms. Already in the fourth kilometre a view opened up on our right to the north-west and the west. We went on for 6 km, always towards a valley in the west, which was—as I realised later—the Silamba valley. We climbed through a narrow side valley down to the bottom of the main valley where we pitched our camp in a small basin of the slope under a baobab tree.[4] The next morning we continued our march. We crossed many little streams which were tributaries of the Silamba stream on its left side. In the fourteenth kilometre we entered the path which we had followed on our trip north to Mo-Kanda's village. On this march I realised that the upper and the middle stretches of the valley of the Silamba stream were more than one kilometre wide and thus three to four times as wide as its lower stretch. Twice we took a rest, once on the Silamba stream and the second time on the Ki-Mona lagoon where we camped for the night. On 23 August we continued our march to Gazungula.

The morning was crisp, which was extremely good for my wife. Every hour on this march from Mo-Sinkobo she had looked forward to the return of the blacks whom I had sent to Mr Wa, but always in vain. This morning we were hoping to meet these men for sure; we encountered many a black and many a dark woman who stopped and looked after us with stupefaction. These people who lived at the mouth of the Tschobe and sold their products to Gazungula to the Leschumo and Panda-ma-Tenka of course dealt with Europeans occasionally. Yet they had never seen whites in a condition like ours. Our emaciated bodies, the ugly ashy-grey colour of our faces caused by the swamp fever, the rags on our bodies which were no longer able to cover our nakedness, the state of our feet—all this did not leave much of the prestige of the white man visible in us. We might have made a similar impression on the blacks as the Frenchmen returning from Russia in 1812 made on the Germans through whose villages they limped, begging their way home. In our case, too, the slogan was 'Onwards. In the south is our salvation.'

While we were passing through the thick bush along the Ki-Mona lagoon I spotted a fish eagle soaring slowly above me. At the very instant when he was shooting upward my bullet hit him. I was glad to have such a valuable object for my collection. Unfortunately we were not able to cure his skin properly. Not far from this place my blacks, who were only armed with spears, encountered a leopard still devouring his prey. When he heard the noise of approaching people the carnivore rose and fled into the bushes along the bank before any of the spears thrown at him found their mark. My servants wasted several hours in the completely useless pursuit of the animal. Only in the afternoon did they return to Gazungula dragging along the rest of the kill which they had taken away from the leopard. The remainder of the kill turned out to be the head of a kabunda gazelle and was very welcome since this was still absent from my collection.

In the meantime we had marched on as well as we could. It might have been 11 o'clock in the morning when we reached the ferry crossing of Gazungula opposite of the trading station of the same name founded by Mr Westbech and Mr Wa. With beating hearts and quickened steps we walked up to that spot. For us Gazungula meant salvation. Here Europeans were living. Once we had crossed the Zambezi we stepped on to ground where the blessings of civilisation and law and order surrounded man and his activities. The kingdoms of the barbarians were lying behind us. Any sensitive reader will comprehend how doubly painful for us was the cold welcome of the first European, i.e. Mr Wa—especially since we were in such an elated mood that we would have forgiven even a mortal enemy.

On the opposite bank we saw some busy blacks and shouted across to them. Since the wind happened to be blowing across to them we were able to make ourselves understood. In spite of this no arrangements were made at the opposite bank to come across with a boat. And thus I had no choice but to sacrifice again a couple of cartridges since my shots perhaps might move Mr Wa to lend us for the crossing the boat which we had sold to his firm. No matter how deep his hatred was he could not avoid helping us this time—and, indeed, so it was.

Half an hour later Mr Wa was standing in front of us. My messengers in fact had reported to him all about our unfortunate situation; however, this report was not able to move this 'soft hearted' man to send us 3 gr of quinine and 0·5 kg of coffee. Our actual condition, however, disconcerted him and he offered immediately to take us to the south bank. The boat which I had sold to the firm had been painted green in the meantime—of course, only in order to paint over the name Holub which Captain Glass had given it. I asked Mr Wa where Westbech was and he answered, 'Three days' journey further west in the swamps between the Tschobe and the Zambezi.' 'Then', I said while we were climbing into the boat, 'I have to send to him immediately for help. We need medication, clothing, underwear, and cartridges. A few more days like the last ones and we will die of fever and deprivation. I must also send messengers to Schescheke to the missionary Coillard in order to ask for a dress for my wife and writing material.' Before we arrived on the opposite bank I knew from Mr Wa's words that his firm had none of these items in stock.

He said he could not spare anything from his own clothing and medication. And about those things belonging to him and Mr Westbech jointly he could by no means decide on his own until Westbech agreed to it, i.e. until an order to this respect had been given by Westbech. Upon these words my wife began to sob loudly. We had hoped to find help and support for certain from the whites and Christians on the Zambezi—and now once again this dreadful disappointment! If it had not been for the extremely critical state of my wife and the condition of my companions I would never again have exchanged a word with Mr Wa after that statement. I was convinced that he had, in fact, most of the things we needed but refused to give them to us or at most he would sell them to us only for exorbitant prices if I pressed him again and again.

It cost me a terrible struggle with my pride, yet the condition of my companions forced me to ask this selfish man after our landing to sell me and my people four miserable woollen blankets, an iron pot, two sets of eating utensils, two tin cups and four plates, a needle and thread, 2 kg of coarse gunpowder and 4 lb of shot.

My blacks immediately began to bring grass and reeds from the nearby Zambezi and to build for us a temporary rondavel since my wife was suffering tremendously from the beating sun with her incessant fever. In vain, however, I asked Mr Wa to sell me a dwarf goat or a sheep so that I could cook some soup for my wife. I believe no other Englishman would have been guilty of refusing such a request for a mortally ill lady. Even many Matoka had not only fulfilled the requests of my servants when they were trying to beg for some food for us in the villages, but had occasionally even offered it without being asked and completely on their own.

After a lot of effort I finally succeeded in persuading Mr Wa to sell me 75 kg of millet on credit for £2 sterling (24 guilders). He himself had probably paid the blacks 1 kg of small glass beads for it. How completely different would our arrival on the Zambezi have been if our friend George Westbech, the founder of the firm, had welcomed us on the bank of the Zambezi instead of Mr Wa.

XV

*Three months
at the mouth of
the Tschobe*

MANY A KIND READER WILL PROBABLY ASK HIMSELF with surprise when reading the title of this chapter: Well, why did Holub stay there that long, why did he not hurry as fast as possible to Cape Town? The next lines will explain this 'why'.

At the end of August 1886 we four Europeans stood as ragged and sick beggars on the banks of the Zambezi. And now the main thing was to make the colossal journey to Europe. Yet I as a man of science still had to secure my honour as a scientist. Even though I had to admit that the losses I had suffered from the Maschukulumbe were irreplaceable I still intended to collect as much as possible. The achievement of these two tasks, i.e. the journey home and the completion of my collection, henceforth took all my time and energy. First of all, I realised that we had to collect ourselves here at the mouth of the Tschobe both mentally and materially in order to get on at all. In addition, there was still another practical reason. It was only three months after our arrival that I got a wagon from Westbech for the trip south.

Without medicine, with our clothing and underwear lost, and with only native millet as food, there was not much hope that we would recover very soon from our diseased condition. Therefore I decided on the very day of our arrival to send two servants to Panda-ma-Tenka to Mr Blockley and four to Schescheke to the missionary, H. Coillard, to ask them kindly to send me the necessities of life on credit for the time being. By the fifth day the messengers had already returned from Mr Blockley and brought half the things I had asked for. The rest of the things he did not have himself. Except for 6 kg of sodium arsenite which I had sold to him on my trip north, as I had too much of it, he sent everything else to me as a gift with his best regards. This poor man, indeed, had a kind heart. He sent me a tea kettle, two spoons, a pencil, a pair of scissors and he promised to make me veld-shoes. His wife gave my wife her best dress as a gift. Six months later we sent her in return a completely new one from Schoschong. He acted differently from Mr Wa who only once showed some pity and gave me some medicine when one of my servants who had been bitten by a snake fell seriously ill. Mr Blockley also reported that of the three groups of porters I had sent to him with items collected on the journey into Matoka land, only one had arrived. Two weeks later, however, he informed me of the arrival of the other porters who would probably never have delivered their loads without my sudden appearance, which deterred them from their thievish intentions of keeping these things.

Since Blockley had neither salt nor flour nor medicine nor underwear for us we waited desperately for the return of the four messengers to Schescheke. Every day we went countless times to the river bank which was not even 150 m away and looked for our eagerly-awaited servants. Finally late one evening when a violent wind storm was raging we heard clearly from the opposite bank the welcome words 'Hella, batu a Njaka, itenji' (Hello, the doctor's people are here), carried rapidly across by the wind. Fekete and Leeb were sick with fever, my blacks were out hunting and my wife did not want me to cross the river in that storm and darkness with only Muschemani. The river was almost 500 m wide and was throwing up high waves. Yet my impatience to receive the needed medicine at last made me discard all my hesitations and grab the paddles. I had to cross the mouth of the Tschobe at an angle of 45 degrees and then the Zambezi itself downstream by steering for an island situated close to the opposite bank. I had to steer around the island in order to reach the landing place located behind it. This was the most dangerous crossing which I ever made on the Zambezi. I do not know today where I got so much strength considering that my physical condition was so much weakened from the fever. Yet I was able to steer the iron pontoon into the raging waves whose foam splashed over a metre high at the gunwales. In spite of the great exhaustion of the day I then did not feel tired at all. I would even have liked to go on rowing. I first shouted across from the tip of the island to make sure that these were really my people calling me, then I steered into the landing place and jumped on to the shore. I did not ask any questions, but merely looked for the loads which my people had brought. I had sent four blacks. Three came back empty handed and one was carrying half a load! Then I knew everything; I was crushed. The hope on which we had been living for days was destroyed. How would my poor sick wife take this? With these thoughts I suddenly felt the strength which had carried me across disappear. Two of the servants had to help me to row the boat back.

The opposite shore was already veiled in darkness when we approached it. In fact, we were not even able to recognise the characteristic landmark, the tree on the Gazungula river bank and we were afraid of missing the proper landing place. This would have been dangerous because of the crocodiles. Yet the loud shouting of my people served as a helpful pilot signal.

What I had feared became true. Rev. Coillard had already gone to Barotseland with the largest part of his possessions. In Schescheke he had left behind Mrs Coillard and his representative. They could not spare much for us since, as they had my people tell me, they themselves had only little at their disposal. We were very disappointed and yet grateful for what they gave us, especially for 6 gr of quinine and a cotton dress for my wife.

Blockley's present was equal to that from Schescheke and yet Blockley was only a beggar in comparison to the rich mission in Schescheke. Their help would have been substantially different if Rev. Coillard himself had been present in Schescheke. Among other things I had asked for some calico and had promised to send it back from Schoschong with the missionary's wagon which came south twice a year. Mme Coillard had not sent me the calico even though I needed it so badly to buy a few goats—for our soup.[1] How all of us regretted the fact that the good-hearted Father Boom had left the Zambezi area.

One project after another for our future had disintegrated into nothing. There was only one man left on whom we concentrated our last hopes. And he indeed proved to be a faithful friend in the worst time of my life. He was Mr George Westbech to whom I had sent a messenger. As soon as the messenger reached him he immediately called off his hunting expedition and hurried back to Gazungula. After he had welcomed all of us warmly and had visited my wife who was languishing in that miserable grass hut he immediately ended our misery.

This meant that Mr Wa had to part with 2 kg coffee and 0·5 kg tea. He had to give us half of the 30 m of calico and 6 gr of quinine. In addition, he had to part with a sheep for my wife, and to give me back 1,000 of the 3,000 cartridges which I had originally sold to the firm. Thus with our carbines we could make our own way. Mr Westbech also promised us clothing and underwear, but only when his friend the Schoschong trader Mr T. Fry,[2] from whom he was expecting a wagon-load full of goods in one or two months' time, arrived.

He was not able to give us better living quarters. Westbech himself was still living in a Betschuana hut. We knew very well that we could not stay for long in our miserable little grass hut which gave us no protection against the rain. For that reason, and also because of our limited quinine supply, I did not want to stay for long. I asked Westbech to give me a yoke of oxen and the wagon which I had given to him before as a present, for our trip to Schoschong. This he promised us immediately. Yet in view of the dryness of the area he did not promise it for then, but only for November when it would rain. I argued that the oxen were being bitten by the tsetse. The earlier they left this place the better it would be for the animals since the rainy season there would kill them soon. Westbech did not believe this, but later he had to atone painfully for his refusal by the loss of all his oxen.

The reception we received from Mr Westbech, of course, infuriated Mr Wa greatly. Although he had no influence on the good heart of my friend in his personal relationships, he had gained all the more power over him in business relationships. For years Westbech had realised only too well that his business was in decline. With his smooth tongue Mr Wa knew how to make himself appear as a messiah who would soon make him a wealthy man. And yet he was his Mephistopheles. The shift of the trading post from Panda-ma-Tenka to Gazungula instigated by Mr Wa was leading to the ruin of the business. Fortunately, Westbech did not survive his downfall for too long.

After it had become clear that I could not leave the Zambezi valley so soon I decided to make immediate arrangements for a longish stay of at least three months. The first problem was on what to live during that time. Hunting was the only possible solution. There was game all around us in the bush and thus I told Fekete about my plans. He suffered less severely from the fever than we three others. I wanted him to lead hunting expeditions. I had come to this decision after an attempt to send my blacks under Boy's leadership up the Tschobe had proved to be unsuccessful. I still remember our conversation pretty well and it went thus. I said to Fekete: 'I am convinced that you can hunt sufficient game with these sixteen blacks so that you will be able to feed yourself and them as well as to provide us with meat. I am equally sure that these hunting expeditions will provide us with valuable objects for our collection. This must now be our main goal, now that we have lost our scientific instruments, my sixteen diaries and my numerous sketches and after our attempt to penetrate into Central Africa has failed.'

Fekete agreed immediately and he was successful in every respect in executing my orders exactly. It was this involuntary three months' stay at the mouth of the Tschobe which yielded us the largest and most valuable mammals for our collection. I shall describe Fekete's most important experiences concisely in the last section of this chapter.

Fekete's 'glorious' outfit corresponded with our conditions at that time. He was sufficiently equipped only with rifles and cartridges. The rest of his outfit was something like a hat on his head, a carved wooden comb, a shirt which was a gift from Mr Westbech, a rather torn jacket which again was a gift, unmentionables which were far too short, and sandals of gnu hide. In addition, he had 2 m of calico to be used as a towel and for carrying a knife, a container of poison, a clay cooking pot, a few calabashes as water containers, and one woollen blanket.

From the moment Fekete left worries about our food vanished. He sent us more meat than we needed. After his departure I immediately began with the construction of a little house. Our grass hut was too small for us four Europeans, apart from the fact that it provided no shelter against wind and rain. Furthermore I needed a completely dry room for the preparation of the skins. I built a large and sturdy hut around our little hut. As soon as it was finished we broke the little one down and threw it out. Since we were sure that Fekete's hunting luck would be good and that we would have to dry and to keep skins frequently under our roof during the rainy season, our dwelling place had to be roomy.

I had Jonas, Muschemani, Kabrniak and one other black to help me with the construction. The fever hindered me very much in my work. We cut down trees, made boards and poles. We tied them together with the bark fibre of mimosa trees, since we had no drill and thus could not use wooden plugs, nor did we have iron nails at our disposal. Our tools consisted merely of a borrowed saw and an axe which I had bought from Mr Westbech. We gathered giant grass and covered the walls and the gabled roof with it by making bundles out of it and then by tying them to the poles of the walls and the boards of the roof with bark fibre.

On 9 September our 'Robinson Crusoe cottage' was finished. It had cost me many a drop of sweat. I had to work even while shivering with fever. The days became hotter and my wife and Leeb suffered dreadfully from fever attacks in their stuffy and stiflingly hot grass hut. Every fourth day the ground had to be watered so that the sandy clay did not become too dusty.

Before our departure to the north I had left Mr Wa in Gazungula a beautiful big chest in which the large skins which we intended to send him from our trip to the north were to be shipped home. This chest now served as our table. In our 'Robinson Crusoe cottage', which consisted of a large, airy room 8 m high, it was somewhat cooler. Inside we set it up as comfortably as possible. And soon everything was filled with rare curios, for the collector's passion which necessarily was suppressed during our trip north of the Zambezi, then could be active again.

Our condition of health improved slightly so that Leeb soon was able to go out again. Since Mr Westbech gave me back all the buckshot (20 kg) which I had sold him months ago Leeb could devote his time to bird hunting. He alone gathered half of the collection of 500 birds which we made during our three months stay in Gazungula. Whenever it was possible we took turns every other day on such excursions. The one of us who stayed at home was busy, together with my wife, in preparing and stuffing our catches, preserving our other collections of fruits and insects, pressing plants and making baskets for the items collected. In spite of the fever which tortured us almost daily we were again fully immersed in work. This work, however, was good for us in another respect; it kept our minds occupied and made us feel less the desperate situation in which we were. In fact, in a very short time a kind of daily work schedule crystallised by itself. During Fekete's two-month hunting expedition with his sixteen servants, this schedule was generally the following.

At dawn I got up and worked until sunrise in front of our hut, writing notes from my memory about our trans-Zambezi expedition in order to replace the lost general diary. I wanted to write up our experiences while the impressions were still fresh in my mind. Then I recorded the research results from the day before. At 8 o'clock I sent Leeb out with two blacks to hunt and collect plants. If I went myself I left our camp by dawn in order to be back again around 10 o'clock. I was less able than the others to stand the heat of the noonday sun ever since our return to the Zambezi. We made our most fruitful studies and richest collections during our stay in ornithology and in botany. I was successful in discovering many species which had never been observed before and I got more information about other species which were already known to me. Yet in other fields as well our three months' stay (from 23 August to 20 November) brought quite remarkable results.

During that long rest at the mouth of the Tschobe I was trying too to complete as much as possible my studies of the neighbouring tribes, some of whom I had visited myself and some of whom I knew only by hearsay. Since the thread of my travelogue is anyway interrupted here I should like in a kaleidoscopic fashion, so to speak, to introduce to my reader some of my interesting data. It cannot be done otherwise.

I was told that the funeral celebrations for the Mankoja chief Momba,[3] who had died in 1885 and who was venerated far and wide, were still not yet over in 1886. I was also able to find out with certainty that the Batowana-Makuba build huge rafts out of papyrus which are 1 m thick, 4 m wide and 5 m long. With these rafts they transport their cattle herds across the tributaries of the N'game to whatever pasture is needed. These Makuba have the same relationship with the Batowana as the Maschupia have with the Marutse. The neighbours of these Batowana especially in the west, are the Masarwa who call themselves Ma-Kouka and Andari-Andarisa.[4] As weapons they use only bows and arrows, the tips of which are made of poisoned ivory. The bows are short and undistinguished like those of the bushmen in former times. At the time of his visit Mr Fry always exchanged twenty of these weapons (one bow plus arrows) for one knife (worth 30 kreuzer) and he sold them again in Schoschong for 12 guilders each. The arrows are poisoned. Shortly before our arrival two coloureds from Schoschong, Gert Batji and Tom Damara,[5] had been elephant and ostrich hunting in the Makouka territory where they were killed by these Masarwa. One cannot hunt in this area without a guide because of the few waterholes. The coloured hunters had two Makouka as guides, but they betrayed them to their friends who did not want to allow the strangers to hunt for the most precious game of their country. While they were sleeping at night both coloureds woke up at the same time with a burning pain which one of them had in his chest, the other one in his leg. Both had been hit by poisoned arrows and both died with most dreadful asthmatic pains, but fully conscious, about twelve hours later.

When the Makouka hunt game with these arrows they find it as a rule dead six hours after they wound the animal. Then they cut out the injured and swollen part, throw out the heart and the big blood vessels and eat the rest of the meat without any harm to their health.

As for the scientific results of our three months' stay on the Zambezi I would mention the following. In terms of mammals this stay, together with the trip north of the Zambezi (i.e. the joint hunting expedition, as well as Fekete's separate one), yielded almost as much as our stay on the Limpopo. It included species which were either not yet at all or only scarcely represented in our collection. We added to our collection as new animals one spotted hyena, one pair of lions, one mongoose and a number of winged mammals (all of them being new species), one black rhino, three buffaloes, six kakatombe hartebeests, one puku, a family of duikers (the small kind), and numerous rodents. Welcome were several specimens of the Zambezi variety of the kudu and the impala as well as five zebras and the mother and her young of the striped gnu. We got several specimens of a new type of long-tailed yellow brown Zambezi baboon, one roan antelope, a beautiful bush buck family, some reedbuck antelopes, six warthogs, some honey badgers, vervet monkeys and other species.

Since I am very interested in the mental abilities of the baboons and since many a reader might have the same interest, I take the liberty of adding here the experiences with them which I had on the Zambezi. I learned from the blacks that baboons, as I had already observed in the south, repeatedly keep completely quiet in order not to give themselves away when they raid the fields of the blacks. Often people who work at the other end of a maize field of 5,000–10,000 m² have not the slightest idea that baboons are raiding the field at the other end.

If it so happens that the babies misbehave and begin to bark they are immediately thrashed by their mothers and forced to be quiet. As a rule, however, the whole clan then takes to flight. Usually if a herd of baboons is pursued their guards, sitting high in the trees, inform their companions, who are hidden on the ground, in the grass, in bushes or behind rocks, by screaming loudly and thus indicating the moves of the enemy. Yet the guards of a baboon herd which is raiding a field as described above keep completely quiet. If they see a human being approaching they slide calmly down from their post and this is enough warning to their fellow raiders to get away quietly. On one of his many excursions Leeb once wounded a half-grown baboon. He barked and dragged himself along with extreme effort. Suddenly a strong female came up to him, grabbed the wounded baboon by his mane and pulled him right into the middle of the fleeing pack which took him off into safety. In vain Leeb searched for hours, but he never saw his prize again.

The little wood which surrounded our camp closely in the south-west and in the west was usually visited at noon by the baboons. At the north side of our camp a *mabele* (millet) field was situated and this was their target. The animals had gradually found out that around noon-time a human being was hardly ever to be seen outside and on this they had based their plan. Our Daisy was the first one to find them and we soon put a stop to their thievish activities.

The packs of these animals, which in this area are 150–200 strong, usually divide themselves up into two or three groups before their outing in the morning. In the evening they then return to their common place of rest. I shall come back to these baboons later in connection with some hunting experiences.

A yellow brownish rat was very interesting, too. It lived in the wooded laterite ridges along the Zambezi valley. The ground was so dug up and undermined by its burrowing that we sank ankle-deep into the sand. There must be thousands of these animals and yet we did not see a single one during daytime. Like so many rodents, they are animals of the evening and night.

One day Leeb came across a strange find. He found a family of bats in the nest of a hyphantornis. This catch led us to investigate all nests and hollow trees. Our efforts were rewarded by a collection of almost fifty winged mammals (four different species). We were especially lucky with a baobab tree. Thus I have made a model of this baobab tree in bloom, on a smaller scale, i.e. of one third of its height and diameter. I shall display it for the visitors of my exhibition with a small inner opening and with some of the bats inside.

My slowly recovering wife assisted me diligently with the preparation of these animals. And with each successful piece of work our confidence increased that at some point we would return after all from this bottomless pit to our dear home country. At that time we realised what a blessing work can be.

I made mats out of reeds with four of my blacks to pack these items. In these we rolled, for instance, the mammal skins after we had put a similar mat made out of dense dry grass on the inner side of the skins to absorb any possible secreted fat.

As I said, birds offered very rich material for my collection and studies. It would take pages to describe our hunts for osprey, desert eagles, crowned eagles, hawks, falcons, kites and eagle owls. The banks of the Zambezi, its swamps, the basin-shaped valleys and their high grass, the thorn thickets at the mouth of the Leschumo valley, the high mimosa trees in the valleys and the laterite slopes overgrown with dense bush—each of these sharply different habitats has its own characteristic bird life and serves as a resting place of only certain migrating species.

It was a great delight to study the birds during this stay in Gazungula and often they were for hours and even deep into the night the subject of conversation in our little grass house. We obtained species which were not yet represented in the collection which then already consisted of 1,300. Among them were one type of falcon, two types of sunbird, two types of swallow, one type of roller, one type of hoopoe, one type of kingfisher, one type of drymoica, one type of warbler, one type of flycatcher, several shrikes, among them two samples of a telephorus which later in a collection from the east coast (collected later than mine) was labelled as a new species. There were also a number of hornbills, two cuckoos, live crested guinea-fowls, etc.

The observations of the habits of the Jacobin cuckoo, a bird of the cuculidae family, and the nest building technique of the carmine bee-eater, the red-billed hoopoe, and others offered rich material for my diaries. The black and white chat which Oates brought home often amused us for hours with his cautious behaviour on the hollow tree trunks which he inhabited and into the holes of which he fled, as the *myrmocichla formicivora* flee into holes in the ground. Equally interesting was the cackling of the red-billed hoopoes when they were sitting close together in parties of three to six. They began to squawk when they felt that they were unobserved—ducking down continuously and behaving most amusingly.

The quarrelsomeness of the sunbirds was greatest when they were swarming in large numbers around the blossoms of the mimosa trees and the giant dark carmine-coloured calyxes of the Gazungula tree. Many birds were busy building their nests. So, for instance, were the carmine bee-eaters which dig holes up to one metre deep into the sloping loess banks. At the dead end of these horizontal holes, so to speak, they then go about their breeding activities and hatch their beautiful white eggs. The annual flood must harm their nest-holes yet the birds return to them faithfully. In some of their deserted nests we found some river swallows breeding.

We tried to keep many birds alive yet we were not successful. For preserving the stuffed birds I had to make reed baskets and put the birds as well as bats and small rodents between several grass layers. We felt the lack of any preservative bitterly. For that reason I was unable to do much in the field of reptile and fish collection as I had no alcohol at all at my disposal. Instead my collection of insects grew all the more as well as that of a few other animal species, especially of a type of *bulimus* which I observed for the first time alive. It only leaves its underground habitat at the beginning of the rainy season.

Our herbarium, too, grew at an equally pleasing rate. Particularly valuable were the spring plants of the deciduous forest zone. Among them were some species which just had been washed down in the water from the upper Zambezi. Nobody was more upset about our growing collections than Mr Wa. The fact that after a few weeks we beggars already were in possession of such remarkable collections rankled in his soul. Yet he comforted himself and asked me smilingly and gloatingly how I intended to transport such a large quantity of objects south. I did not answer a word, yet I brought them south after all.

I still want to mention the solar eclipse which we had the opportunity to observe on 29 August. In a completely clear sky the solar eclipse began at 4 o'clock in the afternoon at the lower edge of the sun. Then it moved gradually upwards and covered the north edge of the sun and darkened the northern sky and the northern horizon almost completely. The uncovered part of the sun gave only a weak light from the south-east over the south to the south-west. The light conditions were those of a strongly cloudy evening sky, i.e. as if the clouds were covering the evening sky and made the setting sun invisible.

For the blacks on the Zambezi this solar eclipse was a frightening event which caused them to make various, always negative, conjectures. In one village people claimed that 'it meant that Luanika had ordered more chiefs to be killed'. From another village the frightening news was propagated that an army of the much feared Matabele was approaching. 'The sun, favouring us, cannot bear to witness our enemies sharpening their spears to immerse them into our blood.' These and similar things the Maschupia and Matoka were saying. I was very curious to learn what the Marutse were thinking since they believe in an invisible god living 'in the blue' of the skies who has power over moon and stars and the lives of men. The Marutse said that the eclipse signified Njambe's (their god's) just furor about what the Maschukulumbe had done to the *makao*, i.e. to us whites. Inevitably his punishment would be inflicted on them in the form of a raid by their king Luanika-Lebosche.[6]

It was a feast each time when Fekete's servants came with new trophies and occasionally with fresh meat as well. If Mr Wa had sold us salt our menu at times would even have been opulent. As it was, however, we had to eat all our food unsalted for weeks which we each day deplored. We got the greatest of service out of our pontoon which I had sold to Mr Westbech before and which this good man had placed to our disposal. My blacks hunted north of the Zambezi and I would not have been able to pay the crossing fees for them. As it was, however, whenever I heard their calls across the river all of us rushed to the boat which was a piece of our good old motherland. We brought them across even when the wind was blowing and when the small canoes of the natives were unable to venture out.

Our joy was greatest when Fekete himself finally returned to our headquarters. He and his blacks were laden with many a beautiful trophy. Our questions and their reports did not cease until late into the night. In what follows my kind reader will get acquainted with the main results of Fekete's hunting expedition.

His expedition took place during the time between 1 September and 26 October. I had given him three rifles, sufficient ammunition, and some blacks as his companions. The hunting party went north. They passed the village of the subchief Mangwato, one of our former guides to Matakala. He gave them a generous present of maize.

Barely half a day's journey from the Zambezi two Maschupia whom they happened to meet drew their attention to the fresh tracks of a black rhino. A rhino? The idea of getting such an animal for my collection if possible excited the whole group. Boy, together with some companions, immediately followed the track. It did not take long for Fekete to follow him with the whole group since four quick shots, one after another, indicated Boy's success. And indeed, this was the case. Boy had surprised a sleeping rhino on a laterite ridge. Cautious a hero as he was he had climbed a tree from where he fired those four shots at the animal. Fekete found it at its last gasp and a few additional bullets ended its suffering quickly. Thus the most valuable mammal was gained for our collection.

After the huge animal had been dissected and skin, meat, and skull had been sent back to us, the hunting party marched on for three and a half days up the Inquisi valley, encountering eland and kakatombe hartebeest yet unable to kill any of them. They crossed the area between the Inquisi and the lower part of its tributary at the right hand side, the Lu-Rungu stream. Then they moved upstream along its narrow valley until they reached a deep waterhole in the stream bed. One kilometre further on they pitched their camp in the bush. That same day the hunters encountered zebras, buffaloes, kakatombe hartebeests and a herd of twenty-five gnus. Boy was able to get close only to this herd, yet he failed again. When Siroko and Braggart were fetching water in the evening they encountered a second herd of buffaloes. Quickly they reported their discovery and Boy and Mapani, together with four servants, immediately took up the pursuit of these buffaloes. Yet it was only the next day that they encountered the fleeing herd. Mapani wounded a cow who then attacked him while all his companions quickly fled up trees, without helping him. The enraged animal chased Mapani several times around the tree behind which he had escaped. Finally he managed to gain one moment in which he brought her dead to the ground with a shot in her neck. Mapani even killed a second buffalo cow that same day. In the meantime Fekete and Marumo had gone out hunting early that same morning. Fekete was only armed with a Winchester. Three kilometres further on the two encountered some warthogs. Fekete wounded one of them from a distance of 60 m. Marumo caught up with it quickly when it was running away and speared it to death. On their way back Marumo killed a big young boar. This hunting day thus had been very successful for my collection. In addition to the above mentioned trophies it even provided me with a trans-Zambezi genet cat or cypha. Simundaj, 'the long one', who was assigned to Boy and Mapani, had gone out hunting for two hours on his own. He soon detected a cypha which immediately ran up a seven-metre-high tree with sparse foliage. The black made a good fire around the trunk of the tree in order to cut off all retreat. Then he threw his stave (*kiri*) so often at the animal that it fell to the ground badly wounded.

The day after this success Boy killed a buffalo cow whose skin was preserved for our collection. Then he sent part of the booty south to us. He himself moved westwards to an eastern tributary of the Inquisi and pitched camp 10 km away from it.

The following day Boy killed a young buffalo bull 18 km further on. He covered him with branches and then sent for Fekete to go there in order to prepare the animal as early as possible the next morning. When Fekete got there in the morning he found the carcass half eaten up by lions. Only the skull could be used for the collection. The next morning Fekete again crossed the Lu-Rungu and returned to the old camp. One and a half kilometres from the camp the hunters spotted a large herd of kakatombe hartebeest and with only two small Winchester bullets Fekete killed a magnificent buck and thus secured a magnificent sample for our collection. After a short rest in the camp Fekete sent out Boy and Mapani with five servants in order to obtain, if possible, a buffalo bull for our collection. None of the skins obtained up to that point had turned out to be really beautiful and perfect.

The black hunters, indeed, soon encountered a herd of thirty-six buffaloes, of which Boy killed two bulls, one of them being good enough to be prepared for our collection. During the night two hyenas, attracted by the smell of the meat, tried to invade the camp which was protected by branches. But they had to atone for their boldness with their own lives. Mapani was not to be trifled with in such matters. Yet the laurels of the god of the hunters, for which thousands of passionate European hunters would have envied him, were waiting for Mapani. Far from the camp he shot a buffalo whose pursuit he had to abandon with the onset of darkness. When he took up the tracks again the following morning he found the animal dead and around it eight fully grown lions who were just about to begin their breakfast. Mapani's shock was all the greater, because he only saw these obviously angry 'kings of the desert' when they rose very close to him out of the high grass. In a split second he pulled his rifle from his shoulder and without aiming at any particular lion he fired point blank straight into the pride. Paralysed with fright Mapani saw how the eight lions took flight, but soon one was lagging behind and collapsed. The bullet had hit him, it had penetrated through his back into his lungs and this had killed the animal quickly. Great was the joy when this beautiful skin was brought to my headquarters.

Soon after this adventure Fekete left the Lu-Rungu stream and the Inquisi area and moved on with his group to the Mudschila in order to hunt near the large pan there which I had called Blockley kraal on my first trip. Here his efforts, too, were successful in every respect. He and his blacks shot a lot of game. Worthy of mention would be a female striped gnu, a magnificent male roan antelope, and three zebras which were the gems of my collection. The porters who were bringing the dried meat, skins, and skulls to my camp unfortunately had to go through Mambowa, the residence of the induna Makumba. The result was that the Maschupia, who envied us our success in hunting, easily persuaded the induna to forbid Fekete and his companions from hunting further in those rich hunting grounds. Since he was such a good shot Mapani, however, still succeeded at the very end in securing an animal which did not yet exist in our collection. Even later it remained the only specimen and now when I am writing this it is already stuffed and waiting for the exhibition. It was a puku buck belonging to the water antelope group.

When my people under Fekete's leadership came back again to our headquarters in Gazungula they were very pleased with their results and would have been ready to leave again immediately for another hunting expedition if I had sent them. My blacks had the abundance of fresh meat for which they had longed so much and they were even able to buy beer for the surplus meat. Their physical well-being made them forget the considerable exhaustion of the hunting expedition and the porterage of the trophies to the headquarters from which they were often two and a half days' journey away.

As I have mentioned already several times, I owe this hunting expedition a good deal of my collection. Thus I regretted at that time, and I still do regret today, that, because of my desperate financial situation I could not reward more generously these good black chaps who secured the trophies for me. Fekete was quite amazed at all that we had collected and worked on during his absence. Our new country house, too, was greatly approved by all. And with jollity and seriousness our work proceeded quickly. Indeed, we had to be diligent since the time for our departure to the south was drawing closer.

Thus our stay at the Tschobe was almost of a satisfactory and pleasant nature. In comparison to the hardships which lay behind us we could have been almost happy if it had not been for the many illnesses. Most seriously ill were my wife and Leeb. Both had become very emaciated. Leeb, in addition, was depressed whereas my wife was cheerful and in good spirits, as soon as the fever attacks vanished. Shortly after our arrival she suffered very much from an abscess in her mouth, in addition to which she got erysipelas which was quite dangerous for her. About two weeks later both of us came down with dysentery which lasted quite a long time since we were lacking the proper medicine. I suffered as well from a renewed attack of my chronic rheumatism which I had contracted originally from a visit to Victoria Falls. All this, however, was still tolerable except for the symptoms of our malaria—especially those dreadful headaches which almost drove me out of my mind during one attack. Equally unbearable was my extreme exhaustion and fatigue. On 20 October the fever of my wife rose towards the peril point and my reader can imagine my feeling when I realised that she might have been denied the sight of the south and her home country ever again. Yet even in this gravest emergency our good star was watching over us. Her strong constitution carried her through this dangerous state. I myself suffered constantly from the fever. Often it happened that I was overcome by an attack in the middle of an excursion and that I had to return immediately. How hard such a return trip was. My back, especially the small of it, ached violently with every step. My head ached, I had a burning pain in my neck, and my eyelids were heavy. My feet and in particular my thighs were heavy as lead—as if a hundred weights were hanging at them.

During such attacks one's strength vanishes extremely rapidly. More and more often one has to take a rest. It becomes increasingly difficult to get up and to drag oneself on until finally the comforting sweat breaks out which brings relief after about half an hour. In addition to my fever I suffered from still another evil. When we had been building our hut I had often cut my hands while getting mimosa fibre. Because of the blood change through the typhoid fever these wounds quickly began to suppurate which again caused abscesses all over my body and especially a very painful sore on my tongue. But enough of these depressing pictures.

I have talked about the collections I obtained during that three months' long stay in Gazungula and about some observations made of mammals. I now shall report some further hunting successes and some more observations related to them.

On our excursions we often had the opportunity to encounter those yellow-brownish baboons who have chosen the mimosa trees at the entrance to the Leschumo valley as their sleeping places. These apes suffered a great deal from the numerous leopards. We found many skulls of baboons killed by leopards. Leeb several times encountered a leopard near those baboons and once he just happened to see how one of these bold robbers grabbed a fat female baboon on a high mimosa tree right in the middle of a herd of baboons. It was strange that Leeb, who had concentrated his hatred in particular on the leopards and was especially eager to stalk them together with the blacks, only got to know these carnivores more closely at the end of our stay. I should say fortune spared him for a long time, for the first encounter was very dangerous for Leeb.

It was at the end of our stay on 19 November, around noon. I, my wife and Fekete were just stuffing birds when we heard loud shouts and somebody yelled Leeb's name. We rushed outside the hut. Leeb came walking up to me covered with blood and then he collapsed in exhaustion. While I was busy cleaning his wounds his companion Maruma reported the following: 'Up there along the Tschobe, you know, Bass, under those dense trees along the river banks, we were chasing a bushbuck. It escaped into a clearing where from the right a leopard appeared. I drew the baas' attention to it and he fired and wounded the animal, yet we did not know how badly. Since it fled towards the river we thought it was seriously wounded. The baas followed his track. I wanted to hold him back since the animal had already reached the high grass but no, he went on. "Our master", he said to me, "has three leopards yet no *namakari* [female] and you say that this one is a female. This is very good, and we have to get it so that our master has a full leopard family. Also the leopards have infuriated me so much and this one shall not get away." Thus we came to the high grass, but did not find anything. Finally we stood on the shore where only a narrow strip of reeds was between us and the water. Suddenly my baas began to scream. The leopard had been lying in the reeds and had jumped at Baas Leeb from behind before he was able to shoot. With his hands he tried to tear the animal from his body yet the leopard bit his fingers. I rushed up and drove my spear several times into the back of the animal but the leopard snapped again and again at Baas Leeb's head. That is the cause of those dreadful wounds on his head. Finally the Baas was able to shake off the animal and we rushed away out of the reeds. The animal is still alive. Hurry there, master, before it can hide itself.'

My blacks wanted to go there immediately together with Fekete, yet I did not allow it since Fekete was suffering from the fever and I intended to go myself. First, however, I had to dress Leeb's wounds. I examined his head first and found that the leopard had bitten Leeb's skull three times, but without puncturing it. Fortunately his teeth had glanced off each time and the fangs had only caused deep cuts on the sides as if the head had received six big slashes. The bone was damaged but fortunately not broken. Leeb's hands were much more badly wounded. The extensor ligaments of his left middle finger were damaged and those of his little and his ring finger were bitten through into pieces. I did what I could do with my dull pair of scissors and my skinning knife. I only used cold water because of the lack of any medicine. Leeb was put into a half lying and half sitting position and two servants had to make him cold compresses day and night until his fever had decreased. Two of Leeb's fingers were crippled, yet two of his head wounds healed within twenty days. The third one developed into a fistula. The edges of the wound healed and closed themselves except at the ends. Yet underneath them the wound began to suppurate. Since I had none of the necessary instruments I was only able eight weeks later (counted from the day Leeb was wounded) finally to get this wound to heal as well. I used some solutions containing tannic acids which I got from the local plants. I pressed them into the pus channel and thus finally cured the fistula.

One day Mr Blockley came. He had been called from Panda-ma-Tenka because of the construction of the house. He was very pleased to see us yet he regretted that he could not do more for us which we, however, understood completely. He and Mr Wa made two hunting expeditions, one upstream to Mahala's village and the other one to the Impalera island. Yet they had no luck and my hope of enriching my collection through Mr Blockley's success was in vain. The first hunting expedition ended with a big beer drinking bout so that the drunken hunters almost lost the pontoon and nearly their own lives. On their second boat trip they were attacked by a hippo and only just escaped it. I regretted this very much since it was very difficult to get the skin or the skeleton of a hippo for my collection from the blacks.

During our stay in Gazungula the Maschupia on the opposite river bank killed a hippo twice—once on the day after our arrival and again five weeks later. According to the law the hunter, however, had to deliver the entire cut-up animal—except for its intestines—to the induna of Mambowa. I was trying to buy part of the meat from the fishermen passing by. Yet they told me about the law and I was unable to get any meat, the hide or the skull of the animal. Mahala's people still had to fire twenty shots at the last hippo which had been wounded by spears, before the coward finally was killed.

With lions I did not have any luck either. There were still lions in the

Gazungula area. In fact, even in Panda-ma-Tenka a lion got himself a dog at that time. And the king of the beasts, together with the queen who accompanied him, enjoyed the flower and manure beds in the garden of the station. They did not even despise a good portion of lettuce for desert.

After Fekete's return from the hunting expedition north of the Zambezi my people still obtained in Gazungula proper many a valuable animal for our collection. My people, especially Boy, Mapani and Maruma in the end were such good shots that, even though we lacked small shot, they were able to shoot birds the size of guinea-fowls with their carbines.

On one of my excursions to a small hill in the south I had the misfortune to fall into a kudu trap which was very deceptively covered with grass. Instantly I realised the situation and spread my arms wide apart; thus I kept myself suspended at the edge of the pit. By this action alone I saved myself from falling all the way to the bottom and impaling myself there on one of the three sharp mimosa-wood spikes.

Of the other noteworthy events during our three months' stay, of which I have rich material in the new diary which I started there, I shall only report the following items. One day we got the news that our friend Mr Westbech had been driven out of the hunting area which had been assigned to him by Luanika. He had been hunting there with his elephant hunters, those coloureds who are already known to my readers. We could not believe this, yet when Mr Westbech returned he himself confirmed this matter. After his ascension to the throne Luanika had left Mr Westbech the same hunting territory which Sepopo had already granted him. Yet he realised, as all the other rulers residing south of the Zambezi had years before (if elephants were still to be found at all in their territories), that the Europeans were carrying his best and most certain revenue, i.e. the ivory, out of the country. Thus he changed his policy. With an ambivalent feeling I listened to Mr Westbech who was fighting for his trade interests and thus lashed out fairly harshly against Luanika and his councillors.[7] For the conservation of the elephants Luanika's recent decision was the best I could have heard. I must confess that this feeling prevailed over the sympathy I had for Mr Westbech whose income had been reduced considerably.

For years past every hunter has had to give to the chief in whose territory he is hunting—so to speak, to his hunting lord—a present in advance of £5–£100 sterling, depending upon the game population of the territory. Luanika now wanted to introduce the same taxation along the Zambezi. Even though I have to confess that it was Luanika's right to do so he should have considered that those few Europeans who come into his country—because of the long cross-country journey—have far greater expenditures for such an expedition than the people who are hunting further south. Therefore he should have asked for lower prices; yet on the other hand he should have prevented an absolute annihilation of the animals by law.

Westbech who had given the king very generous presents in the beginning was treated with much consideration which, indeed, he could claim. Luanika allowed

no other European except for Mr George Westbech to hunt elephants in his territory. He had given him the monopoly to hunt in the area between the confluence
of the Zambezi and the Tschobe and the Nambwe Falls in the west. To that extent
Westbech was very content. But soon the cowardly cunning of the black mani-
fested itself in all kinds of attempts to get around the promise. Since there were
many elephants living in this area he had his blacks drive them off. (At the time of
our departure they were driving them northwards.) Then he sent to Westbech to
tell him that he wanted to hunt together with him and to divide the trophies between the two of them. Westbech had waited in vain for weeks and finally he
went into the hunting territory alone. The king used this default of their agreement as an excuse to forbid the European completely any further hunting, and to
push him and his hunters out of his country. He even gave orders to the people of
Schescheke to take all his ivory away from him. But they did not dare to do so and
let Westbech and his people move on unmolested to Gazungula.

To these developments we owed a supply of coffee and tea which Mr Westbech
had intended to give to Luanika and which then was left to us. This indeed was a
feast when the tin mug which was the only container we had saved from our trip
to the north was again filled with coffee.

Deep in his heart Mr Westbech was furious at the king's action. Day and night
this was on his mind. I noticed that he brought up a delicate topic, asserting that
La-Bengula had been planning a raid against the Marutse for a long time, but
Westbech talked him out of it and had prevented it because of his position in
Panda-ma-Tenka.

Westbech had good reason to be in bad spirits. His business, once flourishing,
had declined substantially and he himself realised this. Since the Marutse now
offered Mr Westbech only very little ivory for sale and since the king once again
was toying with the idea of getting elephant hunters from Walfish Bay and Mossamedes Mr Westbech was entirely dependent on the trophies of his own hunters.
The moment when Luanika forbade him to hunt for elephants his main source of
income dried up. He could no longer fulfill his obligations to the traders from
Schoschong and elsewhere. How important his hunting was for him the following list of kills may illustrate—and one must consider that Westbech was only
able to hunt for a short time in 1887. His best hunters showed the following results: August: ten elephants; April: eight elephants; Henry Wall:[8] four elephants.
The Dutchman Weyers did not himself kill any elephants yet his servant shot one
with tusks weighing 32 kg. Of the other hunters some killed two and others only
one animal. Only three hunters did not kill any elephant at all.

The hunting tales told by the returning hunters were very interesting. I could
fill pages with them, yet I am afraid that I have anyway talked too much already
about hunting in this book. The most important fact to report might be that the
elephant population has decreased surprisingly over the last two years in that tri-
angle between the lower Tschobe and the western part of the central Zambezi as
well as in the area between the Maschila and the large western bend of the Zambezi. Furthermore, they have become so shy and fierce that instead of running away

after the first shot like they used to do even before they were wounded, they now charge the hunter directly and thus have already killed many a hunter. August himself barely escaped one of the animals. The wounded animal followed him for so long so that finally he had to creep into the bushes of the otherwise fearsome hawthorn mimosa. Elephants usually avoid these thornbushes, but this one drove the hunter out of them. August then hid himself in more dense bush nearby. Here the elephant besieged him for hours before he finally left the place in response to the trumpeting of his distant companions. Afrika (who is already known to my readers) had as his best hunter a Masarwa called Skral. He did not escape so luckily from a similar dangerous situation. He had wounded an elephant and had fol-lowed him for two days. When he did not come back to the camp people fol-lowed his trail across the sandy terrain interspersed with waterholes, but they only found his body. He had found the elephant again but apparently he had been im-mediately attacked by him since they found his trampled body already partly eaten by small carnivores. His rifle, still charged, was lying not far from him. This hunting expedition claimed a second victim at a different location. A servant of Mr Westbech was thrown up into the air by a badly wounded buffalo when he was trying to track him down in the reeds. Then the buffalo mauled him so bru-tally with his horns and hooves that the man died a most painful death eight hours after he had been brought into the camp. Mr Westbech had already seen many wounds caused by wild animals, yet as he reported 'I have never before seen a man so mutilated. To this day I cannot understand how a man with such wounds was still able to live for so long'. The buffalo had pierced one of his huge horns into the chest of the man and then when he pulled his horn out again its bent tip had torn out part of the man's thorax. This part of his chest cavity was sticking out like a wing so that one could clearly see the movements of his lungs. The poor chap was fully conscious until he died and he screamed to the very last gasp. Apart from these two accidents this last hunting expedition of Mr Westbech had claimed yet a third human life. This was a black in April's service who was killed by an elephant. These elephant hunts are organised so that the entrepreneur, in this case Mr Westbech, has a headquarters (a central camp) from which he remains in con-stant contact with his hunters who are posted in a wide semicircle around the camp but change their position quite often. Of special importance were lists of kills which were sent to the headquarters. One of the poorest lists was sent in by Van der Berg[8] junior and senior and by Jantje. They had not killed a single elephant. Niklas (Afrika's son) killed only three and Adons only one elephant. Perhaps the reader might be interested to learn about an elephant hunt which went on very close to our camp.

Adons, one of the coloureds employed by Westbech, had returned to his kraal (near Gazungula on the north bank of the Zambezi) after he came back from a completely unsuccessful elephant hunt. One day he went antelope hunting in the nearby woods. Here he found fresh elephant tracks. The animals were going in the direction of nearby Mambowa. Close to the river the herd had divided and the bigger group moved downstream along the Zambezi. Adons followed that group; yet the elephants had made a sharp turn and had moved again towards a laterite ridge on the top of which the track of one, and obviously the biggest, elephant separated and again went in the direction of Mambowa. Adons followed that elephant until he was so exhausted from the heat of the day that he stretched out tired near the track and fell asleep. The elephant, who was the leader of the herd, went up to the gardens of the village Mambowa. Then, however, he smelled human beings, his worst enemies, and he doubled back on his own track to find his female again. Adons suddenly woke at a loud rustling and he saw the elephant approaching him. The next moment the animal received two big bullets in his chest and fell down dead with the second shot. A quarter of an hour later many Maschupia gathered around the hunter. They had heard the shots and had assumed that buffaloes were in the vicinity. The reader can imagine how angry they were when they saw that instead of a buffalo a big elephant had been killed, and by a hunter of the white men at that.

Speaking of the coloureds I might as well mention two episodes which at that time made us even forget our tribulations on the Zambezi and made us laugh a good deal. The well-known elephant and lion hunter Afrika, whom I had introduced earlier to my reader as the Don Juan of the coloured group, always remained true to his character in this respect. He was married to a good Masarwa woman, yet this did not hinder him from knocking at one or another door when his colleagues were away. Thus he also knocked at the hut of a man whom he thought he had to fear least of all. This was little unpretentious Jantje, yet this false step cost Afrika dear. Jantje heard about the matter but he was not satisfied with soundly beating his better half. He demanded satisfaction through a duel and possible compensations for the disgrace which had been done to his marriage. A double duel with cudgels between the two resulted—one in Gazungula and a later one in the Leschumo valley. The giant Afrika got the worst of it in comparison to the nimble Jantje. The coloureds declared him defeated and sentenced him to pay compensation in the form of a blanket, some metres of calico and some glass beads. The blows these two heroes gave each other on their heads would undoubtedly have knocked out the brains of ten Europeans.

The second episode concerns the marriage of the young Van der Berg. The promising 18-year-old son of the old Van der Berg, called Gert, decided to start his own family. Therefore he asked Makumba, the induna of Mambowa, for a wife. The induna fulfilled his wish and gave Gert his most beautiful slave as his wife. Being a Maschupia she was brownish-black, which upset all of Gert's brown relatives who, like all coloureds, were very conceited because of their lighter skin colour. His father was so angry that he forbade his son to enter his hut. The induna Makumba left for Barotseland to see his king. Just at the same time all the coloureds who were hunting for Westbech joined him to go on the big elephant hunt. Among them was also Gert, who had no idea at his departure for what high honours he was to be chosen. Their march went first to Mambowa where Makumba's family lived, consisting of his wives, his mother and his sister Wakumela. The latter was a stately and, by Marutse standards, even a beautiful woman. As the induna's sister she was called princess—except in the presence of a member of the royal family. Quite some time before, she had decided that she did not want to be buried a virgin—the only question was to whom this proud heart should yield. In this frame of mind she saw Gert. He was neither a hero nor was he rich, but his skin colour was lighter than hers. This virtue alone outweighed all possible advantages of any black rivals. Her decision was quickly made; she was not a woman of devious ways or many hesitations.

When the coloureds had gathered in Mambowa for the hunt the young princess had Gert Van der Berg called before her. 'Gert, I want you as my husband', she said. 'You—me?' 'Yes, you, I like you. My brother married you to a slave. Shame on you, she is a Matlanga [slave]. Have you degraded yourself so much?' 'Yes, she is a Matlanga'. 'Let her go, you must become my husband. Go and think about it.' Gert did not think long. He went home, gave his wife two blankets along with some glass beads and other trinkets of the same value and told her to go back where she had before served as a slave. He would not need her any longer since Wakumela had chosen him as her husband.

After Gert had thus become an available bachelor again the princess immediately prepared a drinking feast as the beginning of their wedding festivities. Gert drank bravely yet the entire affair did not seem quite proper. To take Wakumela as his wife just like this in Makumba's absence and without having asked him for his sister made him feel uneasy. He tried to cover himself and intended to ask the advice of Lytia, the loose-living son of the king whom my reader knows already from Panda-ma-Tenka. All were invited into a hut for the discussion. The shrewd princess tried to make the business somewhat easier for the council. She sent several containers of butschuala, each containing 10 l, to Lytia and his hunting companions in the improvised council chamber. The honourable council soon was in high spirits and approved Wakumela's decision in every respect. In fact, when she appeared in the hut as if by chance with a fresh supply, they immediately married them. Gert and Wakumela were called by name and when both of them declared that they had rightly chosen each other, Lytia gave his approval as the king's representative.

Situba, Makumba's wife, attempted to declare this marriage invalid since Wakumela was not allowed to get married without the consent of her brother. This was suppressed by the whole council. The newly wed couple left smiling. Situba later took revenge since she was in the right. In the Marutse kingdom the king and his indunas are represented by their legal wives in their absence.

Thus fortune smiled upon the two only very briefly; soon clouds drew near. The hunters left with their employer Mr Westbech for the hunting grounds. Gert left his young wife behind in Mambowa. Her brother Makumba returned from Barotseland. He declared this civil marriage in complete contradiction to the laws valid in the Marutse kingdom. He dissolved the marriage immediately and sent a compensation present to Gert in Gazungula. He punished Wakumela, who had scoffed at his wife, Situba, in a rather barbarian fashion which is peculiar to the blacks on the central Zambezi. He gave her as a slave to the new Marancian of

Schescheke—the induna and a relative of the king, a son of Wana-Wena.[9] He was only a young lad of sixteen.

Gert, who was head over heels in love with his brown wife, was completely unsuccessful on his hunting expedition. The thought of his wife troubled him so much that he returned early. Yet already on his way home he heard the bad news of what had happened. He went directly to Schescheke and by a present he persuaded the young induna to send 'the slave' back to Makumba as one who had not found favour in his eyes. This, of course, was yet another disgrace for Makumba. In the end Gert was welcomed as her husband. He got his Wakumela back and this time he immediately took her to his home. On the occasion of this honeymoon trip we, too, had the honour of receiving these 'high visitors' in our grass house in Gazungula. Wakumela was clad in a little skin skirt reaching to her knees and then had wrapped 4 m of transparent red material around her fat body. Slaves were carrying her utensils and her husband's weapons. I never heard later whether this clever Wakumela had developed into an angel or a devil for stupid Gert.

On 30 October we received the very good news for us that Mr T. Fry from Schoschong had arrived in Panda-ma-Tenka. We were hoping that he would bring us mail from home. Also that he would be able to tell me what had happened to those wagons that I had sent south. Finally, his own wagons would contain many absolutely necessary items for us such as clothing, underwear and medicine which I now could buy. Of course, we could not buy them cheaply since the load did not belong to the good-natured Fry but to the firm Westbech and Wa. Once again Mr Wa stood between me and objects we wanted so much. Since Fry's draught animals were extremely exhausted because of the great drought on the stretch between Schoschong and the Zambezi Mr Wa had to send his own draught animals to Panda-ma-Tenka in order to get the wagon through. Mr Fry was very distressed at all the misfortune which had hit us and he did everything for us that he could. His flour was used up except for two full buckets, but he gave us half of it immediately so that 'Mrs Holub can bake herself some bread'. He gave us everything he had for nothing. Even some of his clothes he gave to Leeb and Fekete because he knew how very much I had to pay Mr Wa for everything and all the more since I bought on credit.

He brought some letters of April 1886, yet only bad news about my wagons. One of them, he told us, had turned over in a stream near the Nokane springs because of the carelessness of the wagon drivers. And in Schoschong T. Meintjes had refused to obey my order to sell the wagons and to move south with rented wagons and draught animals. This would have been the most practical thing to do. Wagons in the south are not high priced and we wanted our draught animals to be driven behind until Kimberley without pulling anything in order to get to the market fat and healthy animals. This was bad news which upset all of us. What we learned later was even worse than that first news. Under the assurance of the inhabitants of Panda-ma-Tenka those of my people whom I had sent south had the firm conviction that we had been killed by the Matoka or Maschukulumbe and would never return south. Many of their actions unfortunately were based on this assumption.

After Mr Fry's arrival I was able to buy from Mr Wa some bales of material. Since I could not take sufficient food along to Schoschong for all my twenty servants, I decided to pay them and let them go except for six of the best ones. On the Zambezi the payment for two months' service is a woollen blanket, that for three months' service is a musket with ammunition. My servants had mostly served for four months and the question was whether they would be satisfied to be paid with blankets and calico. Had I had any idea that later on I was going to get such ample help from my home country as I did[10] I would have taken all my servants to the south with me since I had good use for them. Except for the brawler Tschimborasso all the others were content with their payment. I kept on only Boy, Mapani, Jonas, Kondongo, Kabrniak and Maruma.

On 20 November I began to load my wagon and to prepare for the trip home. Mr Westbech had not yet returned from his visit to king Luanika to complain about the withdrawal of his hunting grant and the fact that his hunters had been driven out of the hunting grounds. Right in the midst of these preparations to leave the Zambezi, perhaps for ever, two blacks came to us. They were Matoka sent to me by King Mo-Panza. They brought highly important news. One of them I recognised easily. He was Amase, the friend and spy of Marancian, who had been in my service. Their news was about Oswald and my plundered belongings. They reported about Oswald Söllner that the Maschukulumbe were even afraid of his body and only had dared to come close when the vultures were already circling over it. 'They immediately divided his clothes among themselves and cut off his head with their spears. Now it is hanging from one of the poles over Galulonga. Yet punishment soon came for these dogs—listen, master. Before a month had passed some Maschukulumbe from Bosango-Kasenga—you know them well—came to Mo-Panza. They brought your clothes and a lot of other things including even your books. They laid these things down in front of Mo-Panza and began to speak'. Holub, they said had been a great witchdoctor, which they had not believed while I had stayed in their country. I had bewitched all my belongings, so they claimed, because from the day they had plundered our camp many had become seriously ill with diseases they never had known before. Some of them were covered with boils, others had died and some were still on the verge of dying. They would not know any way out, they reported, and therefore they brought all those things which they still had found unharmed and were asking Mo-Panza as the chief who had been a good friend of mine to send everything back to me with some messengers and to beg me to have mercy upon them and send them medicines to take away the evil spell. When the old Mo-Panza heard their request he jumped up and shouted, 'You miserable creatures, you dogs, you brood of vipers, most certainly you have eaten from his medicine. They are bewitched because you have done wrong to their master. He has given us some medicine, as well, yet we have been healed by them.' Those Maschukulumbe who had undertaken to bring the objects from the people of Galulonga, Diluka-Nikoba and Njambo's village had been to ask for counter medicine. They admitted at once all they knew. 'The Maschukulumbe had hardly stormed the camp when they fell upon the medicine.' The most important medicine such as quinine and similar things were in limited supply. However, there were still large quantities of tinctures like atropa belladonna, nuxvomica, opium aconitum, digitalis, etc. as well as medicines such as morphium, opium, chlorodine santonine, etc. To emulate us they sipped and swallowed everything. In fact, people were literally fighting over it. When the bottles were empty they moved on to the sealed containers. Because one sealed zinc bottle containing sodium arsenite, used for the curing of animal skins, was sealed so tight it seemed to the chief of Galulonga that it was a very effective medicine. He immediately popped a handful of this elixir of life into his mouth and in a minute all the 6 kg were eaten up. And thus came the consequences. Mo-Panza listened to this, then he grabbed a stick and the men around him did the same. The Maschukulumbe messengers were beaten up and thrown out together with all that they had brought. Then he shouted after them 'I can see, these things now are all bewitched and cannot stay here for a single night otherwise the spell will affect me and my people as well and we will have to die just as miserably as those people north of the Luenge.'

Thus I missed an excellent opportunity to secure the stolen objects as well as some of my diaries. Mo-Panza had sent his own messengers empty-handed to bring this news. And yet I had promised him for each book (*lungalo*) a musket with ammunition as payment. After I had left Mo-Panza sent some of his men to Bosango in order to buy my books from the inhabitants of this twin village. For that purpose he sent along fourteen hoes to barter as in that area they are very saleable objects. Yet the people of Bosango were afraid to go to Galulonga and to Njambo. Previously Mo-Panza had sent a Makalaka woman as an object for barter yet fortunately she had escaped from her tyrants during the night. Mo-Panza was all the more sad about it since she had been one of his own wives.

It was a strange coincidence of fate that I got a second message concerning my diaries that very same day from the west, i.e. directly from Luanika. Luanika had his messenger assure me once again of his sympathy and tell me that he was planning in the next year, i.e. in 1887, a second raid on the Maschukulumbe. This time he was intending to use two hosts of warriors—one was supposed to invade them from the western, and the other from the northern part of Mankoya country. That meant that they could move directly against Galulonga through the Franz Josef pass. He intended, so he let me know, to kill thousands of Maschukulumbe and to send me Oswald's head along with the heads of the chiefs of Galulonga and Nikoba as well as Njambo's skull. He also let me know that he was very upset about Matakala who had caused me such difficulties in getting porters. 'This son of a bitch needs to be beaten up again.' He (Luanika) had heard too late that Matakala had tried to get rifles from me at any price, otherwise he would have had him killed by an *impi* (troop of warriors).

As great as Luanika's words sounded I don't believe that I ever will get even a single page of my diaries back through his heroic deeds. Because of Mo-Panza's fear I have probably lost them for ever. Perhaps a more fortunate traveller than me may still get his hands on individual parts of them in the future.

Often we were visited by the chiefs of the nearest settlements in the north, for instance Mambowa and Schescheke. The latter ones were the worst. Thus there also came a relative of the king, a young lad also called Marancian since all the indunas in Schescheke are called Marancian just as those of Mambowa are all called Makumba. They all have to give up their previous names.

In Marancian's company were the worst knaves of Schescheke, among others, for instance, the chiefs Talima and Rattau.[11] Rattau objected to Wa that he was sitting in Gazungula like a guard and hindered other strangers from entering the kingdom. He told Mr Wa openly how tired the Marutse were of seeing his and Westbech's faces and that they would want to have new traders. Rattau would have loved to see strangers in order to rob them as he had poor Mr Clark of Schoschong.[12] His hatred of Mr Wa, however, did not at all prevent him from going to him clandestinely during the night and selling him some ivory. This act, however, is a capital crime in the Marutse empire since all ivory is private property of the king, which he uses, in turn, to buy arms and ammunition for all his subjects.

Makumba, as I mentioned before, was not as bad as those chaps. Earlier he had even been an honest character, yet those of Schescheke had spoiled him. His good fortune was that his head wife Situba was an intelligent woman who had a certain amount of power over him so that whenever he was doing some wrong she reprimanded him in public.

As I have mentioned earlier, the wives of the king and of the chiefs are their legal representatives in the Marutse kingdom. In earlier years Sepopo had sent all his elderly wives whom he did not like any more into the various provinces as his representatives. They had to see to it that the tribute which was assigned to each tribe was properly delivered to the king.

Marancian claimed tribute from Mr Fry. 'For what?' Fry asked. 'Am I living on the Marutse territory? Did I sell anything to you? I sold things to Gorossiana but not to you. Are you intending to drive the strangers away from your borders?' Marancian had already earlier claimed and sent for certain presents from Mr Fry. And when he did not fulfill Marancian's wish he had come himself with those chiefs and a hundred companions. But he did not achieve anything. This new induna of Schescheke was clad in a woollen shirt and armed with a bayonet which I had given earlier to Makumba as a present.

Soon afterwards another visitor came from Schescheke. He was the young missionary and deputy of Rev. Coillard.[13] He came for some business and brought us as a valuable present 0·25 kg tea, 2 kg sugar and 0·5 kg cocoa. He complained much about constant thefts. 'Well,' we said, 'that is very bad indeed. If you put up with everything the blacks do they will get out of hand. One day you will be robbed and thrown out.'

The blacks do not speak respectfully of the mission. Without respect, however, a European missionary cannot live and exist in the area north of the Zambezi. A benevolent behaviour is certainly quite proper, yet the blacks cannot be managed only with kindness. One has to show them firmness as well, then the thefts will stop. The blacks are just like children and even our children need the whip.

In the middle of November Mr Westbech returned from his visit in Barotseland. He complained much about Luanika who owed him as well as the traders from Walfish Bay and Mossamedes thousands of pounds and refused to pay any of them. We had already had some rain and since Mr Westbech had promised us that we could depart immediately after his return we were all surprised that he constantly gave some evasive answers to my questions concerning this matter. I had bought from Mr Blockley an old tent which Leeb, who had more or less recovered, converted into a wagon cover. Unfortunately it was not waterproof. My collections probably did not weigh more than 1,500 kg yet they were very bulky so that we had overladen the borrowed wagon both at the sides and at the top. I had even to make a kind of net out of thin buffalo straps and to suspend it under the wagon in order to pack the buffalo heads and other skulls of big mammals into it. The calico which Fry had sold me I had traded with the blacks for three sacks of millet as well as beans and maize, exactly what we needed until Schoschong.

In our miserable state we had waited nervously for Westbech's return since we were counting the hours until we could leave the Zambezi and could finally hurry back to our home country. Westbech's hesitation to lend me the promised yoke with the wagon to take us to Linokana made me realise that very probably our 'friend' Mr Wa was again active behind the scenes. We were not in doubt about this for long. It was 27 November. Mr Fry planned to depart on the 29th and we intended to travel with him. Then Mr Westbech called me into his tent where he informed me in Wa's and Fry's presence that he could certainly lend me the wagon but not the yoke. Mr Wa had to go south with ivory and would need two yokes. 'Why', I asked, 'does he need two yokes for a small amount of not even 1,700 kg of ivory?' 'Yes, I need them', Mr Wa interrupted. 'Because', I answered, 'Mr Wa has now realised that what I said months ago is true, namely that the oxen have been bitten by the tsetse.' I could not have said harsher words to Mr Wa. Everybody had advised Westbech against going to Gazungula, mainly because of the tsetse. People had talked about it repeatedly and Mr Westbech began to believe it himself. Now Mr Wa had admitted it indirectly. Yet he still refused to hear the truth. The colour in his face changed and he trembled with rage, 'No, this is not true. There is no tsetse here', he claimed, 'Well,' I asked, 'Mr Fry, have we not caught tsetse flies here in our hut in your presence?' 'Yes, indeed. And my oxen are so emaciated, they do not seem to recover at all. I think myself that the tsetse flies have bitten them.' Mr Fry's words were very helpful. Westbech seemed to think it over. Then he said, 'How about you two [I and my wife] riding with Mr Wa in his wagon? You could sleep on the ivory and you could leave your collection and your people here until you send a yoke and wagon from the south.' 'No, never. We should go with Mr Wa? Then we would rather stay here.'

'Should I desert my people who are so ill? No, never. Should I throw away my collections here? No, not in this way, Mr Westbech. Is this Mr Wa's plan?' I talked to Westbech as if his partner were not present. 'Listen, Mr Westbech, three months ago when we came to you as a man of Khama's was hunting near here. I intended to go south with him. I did not do so since you promised me solemnly that you would lend me oxen and the wagon I had given to you for the trip to Rev. Jensen in Linokana as soon as the rains set in. I relied on your word. In my state of need I had to buy things from you for £90 pounds sterling [over 1,100 florins] which I would have obtained for 300-400 florins in Schoschong if I had gone there right away. I have had to pay here much more than if I had left with that Bamangwato. We nearly died here from disease and I only stayed because of your promise. Do you want to brush me aside today like this? No, that is impossible. Either you give me what you have promised me or I won't accept anything and I shall leave my collections in the care of Mr Blockley and we shall all go on foot to Schoschong. If any one of us dies from exhaustion it will be your responsibility and all the whites in the south will learn about it. It will not remain unknown that we have escaped from the Maschukulumbe only to die because you have broken your promise on account of that man to your right who has already done so much wrong to us. I am positive that your oxen are bitten by the tsetse fly and that anyway I won't get far with them, yet you have to keep your promise. For two weeks you have seen how much effort we put into packing the wagon and you have not objected to it. And now suddenly two days before the scheduled departure, you change your mind.' 'What should I do then?' interjected Mr Westbech. 'I do not need a whole yoke, only ten oxen. If I find on the way to Panda-ma-Tenka that they are ill I shall leave half of my collections behind there and shall send for them later from Schoschong.' 'Well, but then you will have to be financially responsible for every ox you harness to the wagon', our good friend Mr Wa allowed. 'Oh no, we will not play that game—never. Should I pay for oxen which have been bitten by the tsetse? Did I bring the animals here or did Mr Wa by moving the trading post here from Panda-ma-Tenka? Do you think I am mad?'

This, indeed, was truly like Mr Wa. This was the last trump of this character and his greediness. Westbech, an absolutely honest man, was not hurt by my frankness; indeed, he was converted. He was a gentleman by nature and he did what a gentleman had to do in his situation. He gave me the wagon and the yoke. He only allowed Mr Wa to choose the oxen for his trip and, of course, I got the worst ones. Yet Mr Wa paid a price for his actions. On the trip to Schoschong nearly all the oxen died from the effect of the tsetse bites. Yet the first to die were those pulling Wa's wagon which caught up with us and Mr Fry.

On 29 November we left Gazungula and the confluence of the two big rivers after a stay of thirteen weeks. This stay had enabled us to obtain for our collection the biggest and rarest mammals and the most valuable birds as well as other objects belonging to different disciplines of natural science. Yet what a price we had had to pay for these trophies.

For three months we had all fought off death more than once in the form of malaria and dysentery. In addition, there was Leeb's accident with the leopard.

We had lacked any medicine and all salt. Often we had nothing but dried venison. In terms of clothing and underwear we had had hardly enough to cover our
nakedness and on top of it there had been the dreadful memories of our misfortune
in Maschukulumbe country. There was only one thought which made us bear all
this. And that was that we were not returning to our home country empty-
handed, as merely 'unsuccessful travellers in Africa'. That was the reason why we
stretched our nerves to the limit to make all possible efforts to wrest from the
black continent all the information for science that we could possibly wrest from
it. And the results we gained encouraged us even when disease and privation had
reduced us almost literally to skeletons. When one or the other was spared from
the fever for just one day we were filled again with new hopes even in our misery.

We thanked our creator when we left the Zambezi valley that we had been allowed to see this day after all. But already the first twenty-four hours of our trip
south were full of grievances, suffering and disappointment. On the following
seventy days' journey to Schoschong we were to drink the cup of sorrow still to
the very last drop.

NOTES

INTRODUCTION

¹ I am using the term Toka for those Tonga-speaking peoples in the south-west of the Tonga territory who were living within the sphere of influence of the Lozi kings, while referring to those Tonga-speaking peoples living outside this sphere of influence as Tonga. It is interesting to note here that Holub's book is the first written source clearly delineating the ultimate borders of the Lozi influence in the east and south-east.

Following Gluckman, I use the term Lozi for the ruling people of Barotseland, referring collectively to those Lozi-speaking inhabitants of the Lozi kingdom (Barotseland), many of whom may be of other ethnic origin, as Barotse.

² Holub's first stay in Africa is described in his book *Seven Years in South Africa*, published in 1881.

³ See Chapter I, notes 2 and 4.

⁴ The most important of Holub's scholarly writings are: *Eine Culturskizze des Marutse-Mambunda-Reiches in Süd-Central-Afrika*, Wien, 1879; 'On the central South-African tribes from the south coast to the Zambezi', *Journal of the Royal Anthropological Institute*, 1880; 'Über das Marutse-Mambunda Reich in südlichen Inner-Afrika', *Verhandlungen der Gesellschaft für Erdkunde zu Berlin*, 1880; 'Über einige Fossilien aus der Uithage-Formation in Süd-Afrika', *Denkschriften der mathematisch-naturwissenschaftlichen Classe der Kaiserl. Akademie der Wissenschaften in Wien*, 1881; 'Über die Vogelwelt Süd-Afrikas', *Mitteilungen des ornithologischen Vereines in Wien*, 1882; *Beiträge zur Ornithologie Süd-Afrikas*, Wien, 1882; 'Die Ma-Atabele', *Zeitschrift für Ethnologie*, 1893.

⁵ Holub's journey from Cape Town to the final departure from Panda-ma-Tenga to the north is described in the first volume of his book *Von der Capstadt ins Land der Maschukulumbe*.

⁶ Selous, F. C., pp. 221–35.

⁷ Rawson, O. C., pp. 538–40.

⁸ Smith, E. W. and Dale, A. M., vol. 1, p. 54.

⁹ *Ibid.*, p. 52.

¹⁰ In compiling the notes referring to the Ila country, I relied considerably on comments on Holub's book written by Robin J. Fielder. I wish to express my gratitude to him for having made his comments available to me.

CHAPTER I

¹ A Jesuit mission station was initiated at Panda-ma-Tenga in June 1880. After the mission had failed to establish itself in the Zambezi Valley and after some missionaries had died and others had been seriously ill, the station was abandoned in November 1885. Holub counted Father Booms of the Jesuit mission at Panda-ma-Tenga among his best friends in Africa. See Depelchin, H. and Croonenberghs, C.; Coillard, F., pp. 187–88, 198; Holub, E., 1890, pp. 356–63, 442–4.

² George Westbeech emigrated from England to Natal in 1862. In 1863 he made a trading journey to Matabeleland and soon afterwards settled there as a hunter and trader. In 1871 he arrived at Chobe–Zambezi confluence and became the first European from the south to trade successfully with the Lozi. From 1871 he had a store at Panda-ma-Tenga and

later on he opened other stores near the Chobe-Zambezi junction and at Sesheke. He spoke Sotho, Ndebele and Tswana and was recognised by both the Ndebele and the Lozi as headman of Panda-ma-Tenga. He was extremely skilful at playing the local politics and managed to exercise an extraordinary influence on the Lozi kings, while remaining a great friend of the Ndebele king Lobengula. He opened the Zambezi Valley to the European penetration from the south by continually improving and shortening the wagon road to the Zambezi from Shoshong and by establishing a postal service of African runners between Shoshong and Panda-ma-Tenga. All missionaries, hunters, traders and travellers coming to the Zambezi were helped by Westbeech and his staff, and it seems that no European received permission from the Lozi to cross the Zambezi unless he was recommended to them by Westbeech. He died at Kalfontein, Transvaal, in July 1888. See Tabler, E. C. (ed.), 1963.

[3] Wankie (Hwange) is a dynastic name of a Kalanga chief whose capital was originally in the Deka valley south of the Zambezi. After the Ndebele raid in 1862 he moved his capital to the northern bank of the Zambezi some 65 miles beneath the Victoria Falls. For the earlier reference to Wankie see Holub, E., 1890, p. 348.

[4] George Blockley went together with G. Westbeech to the Chobe mouth in 1871 to open the Zambezi trade and remained later in his service. He was the best known of Westbeech's storekeepers, traders and hunters. Except for occasional journeys to the Transvaal, he lived continuously either in Panda-ma-Tenga or in the Zambezi Valley from 1871 until his death in 1887.

[5] Lesuma Valley is eleven miles south of the Chobe mouth and about fifty miles north of Panda-ma-Tenga. Westbeech's road from Panda-ma-Tenga to the Zambezi passed through Lesuma which was used as a watering and camping place by all early travellers. In 1878 Westbeech built a few huts there which he used as his storehouses and living quarters.

[6] See Introduction, p. xiii.

[7] Mambova is a fairly large village on the northern bank of the Zambezi about 8 miles upstream from the Chobe mouth. In 1886 it was inhabited mainly by the Subiya people and had a population of about five or six hundred.

[8] Rev. François Coillard was the founder of the Barotse mission of the Paris Evangelical Missionary Society. He started as a missionary among the Sotho people. After his attempt to establish a mission in 1877 among the Nyai north of Limpopo had failed, he decided to establish a mission among the Lozi, mainly because the language they speak is similar to the Sotho language in which he was fluent. He visited Barotseland for the first time in 1878-9. In 1884 he started his second journey to Barotseland, and being helped by Westbeech, succeeded in establishing a mission at Sefula. In 1892 he moved to Lealui.

[9] Later on in 1892, on Lozi King Lewanika's order, a village called Kazungula was founded on the northern bank of the Zambezi opposite Chobe mouth to serve as a gateway to Barotseland. The tree Holub refers to is *kigelia pinnata*, called *mzungula* in Kalanga.

[10] G. Westbeech started building his store at Kazungula in September 1886. See Tabler, E. C. (ed), 1963, pp. 82, 89.

[11] Coillard, F., chapters X-XIII.

[12] Khama (1828?-1923), chief of the Ngwato tribe. His residence was at Shoshong and he ruled 1872-3 and 1875-1923. For Holub's meeting with Khama see Holub, E., 1881, vol. II, pp. 42-44 and Holub, E., 1890, pp. 239-47.

[13] See Introduction, pp. xii-xiii.

[14] Thomas Baines was engaged by David Livingstone to paint the pictorial record of his 1858 Zambezi expedition. He returned from England to South Africa to prospect for gold. After visiting Matabeleland in 1868 he obtained a concession from Lobengula in 1871 to prospect in the Shona country between the Gwelo and Hunyani rivers. He died in South Africa in 1873.

[15] Captain Frederick C. Selous (1851–1917) came to South Africa in 1871. He was South Africa's most renowned big game hunter who travelled widely in Matabeleland and in the Zambezi area. He played an active part in bringing Matabeleland under the British control.

[16] Probably Jan Weyers, who was together with many others employed by Westbeech as an elephant hunter.

[17] Litia, at that time, the fourteen-year-old son of Lewanika who succeeded his father in 1916 as Yeta III.

[18] See Tabler, E. C. (ed.), 1963, pp. 54–5 for fuller description of this episode.

[19] See Tabler, E. C. (ed.), 1963, p. 54.

[20] Lozi King Lewanika, ruled 1878–84 and 1885–1916.

[21] It seems that Holub here misunderstood Liomba's position. Liomba was one of Lewanika's indunas, probably not a prominent one, whom, as Coillard confirms, Lewanika used to send to Kanzungula to trade ivory. Liomba's visit to Khama is also confirmed by Coillard. See Coillard F., pp. 280, 332–3, 349; Clay, G., 60.

[22] Frank Watson, since 1884 a trading partner of George Westbeech (Tabler E. C. (ed.), 1963, pp. 54–5).

[23] A Subiya headman of Mambova, Lewanika's representative at the southern frontier of the Lozi empire. The present Makumba village is about 5 miles west of Livingstone.

[24] John MacDonald operated as a trader in Lewanika's capital Lealui and in October 1885 helped Lewanika to regain his throne by actively fighting on his side against Mataa, and against Sikufule, the chief of Lukwakwa who aspired for the Lozi throne himself. See Clay G., pp. 44–5.

[25] See Coillard, F., pp. 231–2.

CHAPTER II

[1] Mulasiane was the title of the chief of Sesheke. Mulasiane Siakabenga was related to Mataa, the leader of the rebellion against Lewanika in 1884. After Lewanika regained his throne Siakabenga was attacked by Lewanika's forces in December 1885. He escaped and took refuge with the Tonga chief Siachitema (See note 12). Mackintosh, C. W., 1907, p. 324; Coillard, F., p. 206; Tabler, E. C. (ed.), 1963, p. 33; Clay, G., p. 46.

[2] Leswane is probably a dynastic name of a chief or headman who was responsible for the ford in Kazungula as a representative of the Lozi king. Leswane supported Mataa during the rebellion against Lewanika. After Lewanika regained the throne, Leswane took refuge in Panda-ma-Tenga but was killed there in March 1886 by a group of Subiya loyal to Lewanika. Holub E., 1890, pp. 468–9, 504–8; Schapera, I. (ed.), pp. 325, 328; Worthington, F., pp. 4, 7.

[3] Sipopa ruled as a Lozi king from 1864 to 1876. He moved his court permanently to Sesheke in July 1875. After paying a brief visit to him there in August 1875 (Holub, E., 1881, pp. 134–75), Holub spent three months from October 1875 to January 1876 at Sipopa's court in Sesheke. Holub, E., 1881, chapters IX–XII; Holub, E., 1879.

[4] This is a Lozi view which does not correspond with the Ila view. According to the

latter, Sipopa fought the Ila in 1871. Smith, E. W. and Dale, A. M., vol. I, p. 41.

⁵ In 1882. Clay G., p. 29; Arnot, F. S., 1883, p. 48; Smith, E. W. and Dale, A. M., vol. I, p. 42.

⁶ Lobengula (1836?–93), king of the Ndebele. His residence was at Bulawayo and he ruled from 1870 to 1893. Holub never met him.

⁷ Toka chief Mudukula (died 1886) of the dynastic name Musokotwane. Chief Musokotwane was subject to Lozi kings and paid tribute to them.

⁸ Czech for 'brick'.

⁹ Probably Sing'andu, a Toka name. See also Coillard, F., p. 143.

¹⁰ Jan Afrika, a coloured elephant hunter in Westbeech's employ. See Holub, E., 1890, pp. 448–54.

¹¹ Reference to killing of Leswane described in Holub, E., 1890, pp. 504–8.

¹² See Introduction, p. xii.

¹³ Bovu stream, tributary of Zambezi just under Kazungula, about 40 miles upstream from Victoria Falls. The upper tributary of Bovu is called Kalamba and Holub refers to both Bovu and Kalamba as Silamba.

¹⁴ Siachitema is a recognised chief in Kalomo district of Zambia, his present residence being about 17 miles north-east of Kalomo and about 6 miles north-west of the railway at Tara Halt. In 1886 Siachitema was living about 40 miles north-west of his present village, probably in the tsetse-infested area around the head waters of the Idiamala (Kasangu) river about 50 miles north-west of Choma.

¹⁵ Probably Siamakanda village, whose present location is on the Zambezi river 27 miles west of Livingstone.

¹⁶ A former Toka chief Siyakasipa. He was recognised by the early British administration as a subchief under Musokotwane. In the 1940s his chiefdom, which consisted of about forty villages, became part of Musokotwane's area and Siyakasipa himself was recognised only as a headman. At present Siyakasipa's village is situated about 5 miles north of Senkobo siding and about 21 miles north of Livingstone. In 1886 Siyakasipa's residence was about 1½ miles south-east of its present location in a place called Cinkobo (Senkobo; Holub's Mo-Sinkobo) and probably Siyacidunga was then chief Siyakasipa.

¹⁷ Kooma village whose present location is on Bovu stream about 23 miles north-west of Livingstone, north of its site in 1886.

¹⁸ Siluela village, which does not exist any more, was situated 16 miles west of Livingstone along the modern Livingstone–Mambova road.

¹⁹ Lukuni, Musokotwane's residence, was situated on the left bank of the Sinde stream about 7 miles north-west of Livingstone. When this territory was later declared an Intensive Conservation Area, it moved to its present location at the upper course of the Sinde stream about 15 miles north of Livingstone.

²⁰ Katubiya stream which flows into the Sinde stream 7½ miles west-north-west of Livingstone. Holub camped on the lower course of the Katubiya stream on his return journey (p. 253), not realising that it was the same stream which he had crossed on his journey north.

²¹ The area between the Victoria Falls and Panda-ma-Tenga.

²² See note 13, chapter IV.

²³ Holub, E., 1890, pp. 418–19.

CHAPTER III

[1] Villages and hamlets along the waterhead of the tributaries of the Maramba stream in the area from about 6 to 11 miles north of Livingstone approximately between the present Natebe and Kananga sidings on the line of rail. This territory is nowadays Intensive Conservation Area and is uninhabited, but archaeological evidence indicates a fairly intensive occupation in the nineteenth century.

[2] See note 15, chapter II.

[3] It seems that Holub misunderstood the meaning of the ceremony. Death anniversaries are not observed among the Toka. According to Holub's description, it seems that a libation was performed at the grave of the chief's father, as is still nowadays customary in case of illness or any other misfortune, if the rains delay or if new inhabitants move into the village who should be presented to the ancestors and put under their protection.

[4] Luenge (*lwenje* in Ila) simply means a big river. In Holub's time the Kafue was generally known as Luenge, the name Kafue being used only for the lower course of this river.

[5] Shindu was a Toka chief who was recognised by the early British administration as a subchief under Siachitema. Later he became headman under chief Nyawa. His present village is near Kauwe school 24 miles west of Kalomo. In 1886 his capital was near Sichifulo river about 15 miles north-west of the present village, about 33 miles west-north-west of Kalomo.

CHAPTER IV

[1] Bankombwe Hill about 18 miles south-west of Zimba. Holub considerably overestimated the distance; he could not have been camping more than 4 miles (some 6·5 km) east of it. Dambos south of Nampongo stream where Holub camped contain numerous pans and waterholes; it is not possible to identify Njama.

[2] Of all these streams only Nampongo, Ngwezi (Inquisi) and Chinkozia (Tschi-N'kosia) appear on present maps. Sinjika is probably Nasiakonga on the present maps.

[3] None of these streams exist on present maps. As Holub points out, they are all probably small tributaries of Chinkozia and Ngwezi.

[4] Probably Toka chief Nyawa, whose capital at that time was near Sichifulo river some 45 miles north-west of Zimba and some 27 miles west-north-west of Holub's camp on 24 June 1886.

[5] There is a village Siakabale about 24 miles north west of Zimba, a mile south of the tsetse fly control camp on Mabwa (Wuamba) stream and some 6 miles north of Mwemba (Muembwa) stream. As Holub passed through this area on 25 June 1886, it is very probable that his Amare village is actually Siakabale. If this assumption is correct, Siakabale was then located about 4 miles south of its present site. Holub crossed Mabwa stream somewhere near the present Mabwa tsetse fly control camp.

[6] This assumption is correct only for Mabwa. It is a tributary of Sichifulo which itself flows into Machili. Mwemba is a tributary of Ngwezi.

[7] Probably Katanda village located at present on Nguba stream 29 miles west-north-west of Kalomo and about 4½ miles south of Sichifulo river.

[8] See note 5, chapter III.

[9] African, coloured and possibly even Portuguese traders from the west coast.

[10] David Thomas, son of Thomas Morgan Thomas, one of the first missionaries in Mata-

beleland. Probably some time in 1885 David Thomas established a trading post on an island in the Zambezi near the mouth of the Lufua river where he was later (in 1888?) killed by the Tonga. See Selous, F. C., p. 207.

[11] At present there is a village called Siankwembo at Nanzhila river about 12 miles south-west of Siachitema's capital in 1886. It is probable that Holub's Mo-Monquembo is actually Siankwembo.

[12] Siachitema was the northernmost traditional Toka chief recognising at least at times the sovereignty of Lozi kings over his territory and paying tribute to them. Tonga who were not in the sphere of influence of the authority of the Lozi had no traditional chiefs (Colson, E., pp. 1–2) and all chiefs who nowadays have their territories north and east of Siachitema (Mbila, Chikanta, Muchila, Macha Chilala) were only appointed by the British administration. None of the smaller 'independent chiefs' whom Holub visited on his way north from Siachitema are among the official chiefs of the same areas these days. The only exceptions were Mapanza and Shezongo (see notes 13 and 14) to whom Holub refers as 'great princes'.

[13] Mapanza is still one of the most important chiefs in the Southern Province of Zambia, his capital being near Mapanza Mission, 39 miles north of Choma. In 1886 his village was near Ngonga stream some 5 miles south of its present site. Although Colson suggests that the Tonga did not have chiefs traditionally, it is clear that Mapanza did wield political power and had a reputation derived from his control over trade and his ability to attract followers and offer them protection. His Toka neighbour Siachitema, his Lumbu neighbour Shezongo (see note 14, chapter II and note 12, chapter IV) and probably also Monze of the Tonga were all chiefs of a similar importance. The relations of these chiefs with Lozi kings were uneasy; sometimes it was to their advantage to co-operate with them and to recognise their sovereignty, at other times they offered refuge to Lozi political exiles (e.g. Siachitema).

[14] Chief Shezongo, whose present capital is near Nanzhila Mission some 35 miles south-west of Namwala. Shezongo's relations with Lozi kings varied from hostile (Shezongo I, Kauka, was killed in the 1850–60s) to conciliatory. Lewanika recruited Shezongo's people in his raid against the Ila and Tonga in 1882 (Smith, E. W. and Dale, A. M., vol. I, p. 42). Shezongo's people call themselves Lumbu, an Ila word which simply means 'foreigner'. They speak Ila and are of very diverse ethnic origin: Tonga, Ila, Nkoya, Totela, Lozi and others (Smith, E. W. and Dale, A. M., vol. I, pp. 34–8).

[15] In suggesting that the Ila had pushed the Nkoya north across the Kafue, either Holub or his informant was speculating. Almost certainly ancestors of some present Ila were settled on the southern bank of the river long before Nkoya-speaking peoples came from the north and north-west. The 'northern Mankoya' who traded with the Ila are Ila of Mumbwa. They are not accepted as Ila by the people of Namwala but as Bambala, people of the north. The 'southern Mankoya' mentioned as being subjects of the Lozi, are presumably the western Nkoya, such as Mwene Kahale of Kaoma District, and perhaps Kabulwebulwe, then in the Kafue Hook.

[16] In August 1888 Ndebele warriors crossed the Zambezi intending to raid the Ila. With Toka assistance they attacked Siachitema's village where Mulasiane was in refuge. He was killed during this attack together with many of his supporters (Selous, F. C., pp. 242–3; Tabler, E. C. (ed.), 1963, p. 99; Clay G., p. 56).

CHAPTER V

[1] Present Mwebo (Mwema) school is situated near Lungunya stream 37 miles north-west of Choma. In 1886 Mwebo's village was probably situated several miles south-west of the present school.

[2] Salt was made in several areas along the south side of Kafue flats, the most important and well known being Basanga (the present Chief Musungwa's area) in the west, some 10 miles south of the point where the Kafue flows through the Itezhi Tezhi gap. The salty earth is dug from pits rather than 'salt lakes' as Holub surmised, dissolved in water, filtered and evaporated, and then placed in the 'tube-like' reed baskets about twelve inches long and 2–3 inches in diameter, smeared with cattle dung in the cracks.

[3] Munyeke stream and its tributary Lungunya. None of the villages mentioned by Holub appear on present maps, but this area is and probably always has been densely populated.

[4] Probably Bambazi or Mulundika hills about 27 miles north of Choma.

CHAPTER VI

[1] Akufuna Tatila, who usurped the Lozi throne from Lewanika in 1884 and ruled until 1885 when the throne was again regained by Lewanika. See note 24, chapter 1.

CHAPTER VII

[1] Kasenga is a name of a slightly elevated part of the plain five miles west of Busangu and 17 miles east of Namwala where Rev. Edwin Smith opened a mission station of the same name in 1909. It is possible that the whole area was collectively called Kasenga (meaning a 'sandy place'), although it is not nowadays.

[2] Holub is obviously speculating here. Mulambwa, Lozi king at the end of the eighteenth and beginning of the nineteenth century, raided the Ila, and the Ila were raided at least five times by the Kololo when the Lozi were under Kololo rule. See Smith, E. W. and Dale, A. M., pp. 32–41.

[3] Chief Nalubamba, who rules over an area called Mbeza. His present capital is near Munyeke stream about 45 miles south-east of Namwala and 34 miles north-west of Monze; in 1886 his village was generally in the same area as it is nowadays. Holub's attribution of the name Bamaala (Bamala) to the Mbeza people is puzzling; Bamaala are the people of Maala, the very important densely populated community three to four miles south-east of Busangu. It may be possible that Maala people had temporarily scattered at this time, some finding their way to Mbeza, but more likely Holub's information came second-hand from his servants and porters, who had less local knowledge that they cared to admit.

[4] The famous Ila tall hair arrangement (*isusu*) was the prerogative of young warriors.

[5] Mukaluenje, (i.e. wife of the Kafue), probably one of a number of ponds where the Chitongo river seeps away in the dry season.

[6] Bweengwa is an area about ten miles east of Mbeza, and Shamusonde is nowadays the official chief there. Namaanda Sholoshula (?)—Holub's Namadschoroschula —may be an ancestor of Shamusonde. Although Bweengwa is nowadays counted as Tonga and is part of Mazabuka District, its inhabitants have more in common with

the people of Mbeza than with the Tonga proper. Smith and Dale (vol. 1, p. 314) consider them as mixed Ila and 'Lundwe'.

⁷ Kabulamwaanda is an area about 17 miles north-west of Mbeza. There are five independent villages still at Kabulamwaanda and currently also the headquarters of the Namwəla Marketing Co-operative.

⁸ This palm forest, about 4–5 miles south of Kabulamwaanda, is one of the most attractive sections of the modern Choma–Namwala road. The ponds where Holub rested are the lower end of the Makotolo stream which he crossed on the return journey (pp. 230).

CHAPTER VIII

¹ Kabulamwaanda is a place name (see note 7, chapter VII) and there was never a chief of the same name. Smith and Dale (vol. 1, p. 314) mention Kabulamwaanda as being under chief Chikoti, but soon afterwards it became part of Chiinda's chiefdom until his chieftaincy was merged with that of Mungaila in the 1940s.

² This part of the journey is very accurately described. Holub clearly took the direct path from Kabulamwaanda to Kantengwa which is a mile beyond the first sandy ridge. There do not appear to have been any villages there in 1886. The first one he mentions (at 12 km) is in Shamakunci area about where the present Chibiabe is situated and the second (at 14 km) is where Shimunungu is now. From there Holub reached the open plain and, realising he had been misled, turned west along the edge of the plain until he reached the path coming from Shimukupola in the south-east. The place reached by Holub was Busangu, some 22 miles east of Namwala. He never reached Kasenga, which is a similar sandy elevation five miles west of Busangu (see note 1, chapter VII).

³ Chief Shambamba, whom Smith and Dale (vol. 1, p. 54) mention as residing at Maala, two to three miles south-west of Busangu.

⁴ Lubosi was the personal name of the Lozi king Lewanika, and he was usually known as Lubosi until some time after he had become the king.

⁵ See note 1, chapter IX.

⁶ See note 7, chapter X.

⁷ See note 2, chapter X.

⁸ See note 9.

⁹ The lagoon described by Holub as a 'sac-shaped bay' is easily identifiable at Chibenda, 31 miles east of Namwala. Nikoba and Diluka villages are not remembered by the present inhabitants of this area.

CHAPTER IX

¹ Nyambo is a place situated 3½ miles from the lagoon at Chibenda. In 1886 the chief at Nyambo was Muwezwa Mobola (died 1919). The chief's village has never moved more than half a mile from its present site.

² Deliberately distorting the face to make it look as ferocious as possible is a feature of Ila war dancing.

³ Holub had the information that there was a Portuguese living with chief Masaka (see note 2, chapter X), constantly enquired about him and desperately tried to reach him. He does not mention anywhere from whom he obtained this information, but it seems that it was not completely inaccurate. According to chief Muwezwa's notebook, during the

time of Muwezwa's reign the Mapupusi (Portuguese) settled down at Masome-Mafwele beyond the Cholobete Hill, some 15 miles north of Nyambo. They were attacked by Muwezwa's people and driven away. As Holub came to Nyambo during Muwezwa's reign, it is very likely that some Portuguese traders might have been temporarily living near the Cholobete Hill shortly before his arrival; it seems that they had already left during Holub's visit (see p. 204 and 205 of Holub's narrative).

CHAPTER X

[1] The men met by Holub could have been Nkoya from the north-west, 50–100 miles away, but most probably they were the Ila-speaking peoples from the north called Bambala (meaning northerners) by the Ila proper. Bambala live only from twenty to thirty miles north of Nyambo. Smith and Dale's pictures of various northern hair-styles (vol. I, pp. 78–9; vol. II, frontispiece) fit Holub's description. Bambala of chief Chibuluma, living some 25 miles north of Nyambo, still trade 30–40 lb cakes of tobacco with Maala people across the river in exchange for a heifer.

[2] Chief Masaka lived in Mwako (Smith and Dale, vol. I, p. 314), immediately south of the pass between Bulala and Mwako hills (see note 8). Masaka's people moved in the 1930s into Musulwe's area at Makunku 9 miles north of Nyambo. Musulwe's chieftainship itself was merged with that of Muwezwa at Nyambo in 1952.

[3] Lulonga, 7 miles north of Nyambo, is no longer inhabited. It suffered severely from Lewanika's raid in 1888 from which it was never restored (Smith, E. W. and Dale, A. M. vol. I, p. 52). It was completely abandoned some time in the 1940s.

[4] According to Smith and Dale (vol. I, p. 315) the population of Nyambo was 586 in 1915. At that time it certainly was not the largest of the Ila areas.

[5] The swamp is in fact the Nansenga stream spreading out as it reaches the flats. The swamp is 5–6 miles long, until it reaches the Kafue flood waters on the plain during the rains, but it varies enormously in extent with the season.

[6] The pass between Bulala and Mwako hills which Holub tried to reach is 16 miles (some 26 km) north-west of Nyambo.

[7] Zumbwa Shimata was a headman in Lulonga which was then in Chief Musulwe's area. Some time after the Lozi raid in 1888 (see note 3) Mwanashimabula was installed as headman. In 1952, Musulwe's chieftainship was abolished and Lulonga became part of Muwezwa's chieftaincy.

[8] The Franz-Josef Mountains are in fact two separate ranges. Beginning in the west 15 miles north-west of Lulonga and 30 miles north-east of Namwala are the Bulala Hills; the range is then cut by the Nansenga stream in the deep narrow gorge which Holub was aiming at, and which is a conspicuous feature from as far away as Busangu. The range east of the gorge is known as the Mwako Hills, the highest point being 3,838 ft, little more than 500 ft above the surrounding land. For its last 6 miles the range, known here as Cholobete Hills, sinks to a mere 200 ft until it finally runs into the ground. Holub's north-north-eastern 'saddle-shaped depression' is a wooded plain over 10 miles wide through which flow the Lutale and Chibila streams. Beyond these, 20 miles north-east of Lulonga, rising almost sheer from the ground for 1,100 feet is the cone-shaped Sonkwe Hill (4,473 ft in height) which is the beginning of the Nambala mountain range running northwards for 10 miles.

CHAPTER XI

¹ Holub's six-hour dawn journey through the swamp from Lulonga seems to have been totally unnecessary as there is permanent dry land to the east of the swamp, running north-north-west from Lulonga. The returning tobacco traders who met Holub at Nzovu came from Lulonga obviously on the dry land (see p. 204 of Holub's narrative). Holub's claim that the swamp extended 30–40 km from the north-east to the south-west would have been an exaggeration at the height of the flood in March; in August, when Holub's party had already walked from the river across dry flats, it was a complete delusion. The swamp could not have extended more than a mile on either side.

² As they had only just emerged from the swamp, they must have reached Nzovu village, recorded by Smith and Dale (vol. I, p. 315) as being under chief Lutangu in 1915. Masaka's village was 5½ miles further on to the north-west.

³ Holub was actually only 5½ miles (slightly over 7 km) from Masaka's village.

⁴ Smith and Dale rightly point out the fact that Holub is rather vague in describing what actually happened at Lulonga beyond saying that his wife seized a gun and enabled him to escape. Smith and Dale received the information from the Ila themselves that Mrs Holub fired and killed a man and with her second shot killed a man and a woman. According to the Ila, Dr Holub did not shoot (Smith, E. W. and Dale, A. M. vol I, p. 51). In a letter written to Westbeech informing him of their return to Kazungula (p. 259 of Holub's narrative), Holub evidently mentioned that he had shot three Ila, for Westbeech recorded this fact in his diary on receiving the letter (Tabler, E. C., (ed), 1963, p. 76). Holub's reticence in his narrative about killing three Ila may have been in deference to liberal opinion in Europe, but as even Westbeech seems to have been given the impression that it was Holub himself who did the shooting, it is more likely that he was protecting his wife from the reputation of having committed an action so unbecoming to a nineteenth-century woman.

CHAPTER XII

¹ They seem to have slept somewhere near Shimukopola, or perhaps even eastern Maala.

² There are palms about three miles north-west of Kabulamwaanda around Njili on the present Kabulamwaanda–Maala road.

³ They had evidently entered the small tributary valley where these days the main Choma–Namwala road crosses it 1½ miles west of Kabulamwaanda. They walked down the small valley until it entered the main valley near Katantila, a mile above the present Kabulamwaanda dam. The huts that surprised them on their left could not have been more than two kilometres from Kabulamwaanda. They were much nearer to Kabulamwaanda than they had guessed.

⁴ Makotolo village near the present Choma–Namwala road 5½ miles south of Kabulamwaanda.

⁵ Chitongo or Masompe stream some 11 or 12 miles south of Kabulamwaanda.

CHAPTER XIII

¹ The Ngonga valley south of Mapanza is densely inhabited but none of the villages mentioned by Holub appear on present maps.

² Mulundika Hills, 27 miles north of Choma.

³ This village does not appear on maps but must have been located in the vicinity of the present Mandala school, 22 miles north of Choma.

⁴ See note 2.

⁵ Probably one of the tributaries of Silukuya stream, itself a southern tributary of Munyeke.

⁶ Most probably Chifusa, 17½ miles north-west of Choma.

⁷ Possibly Nakabanga, 17½ miles west-north-west of Choma and 27 miles north-east of Kalomo.

⁸ A densely populated area round the present Siachitema mission 18 miles west of Choma.

⁹ One of the tributaries of Sichikwenkwe river, itself a tributary of Kalomo.

¹⁰ Kalomo river.

¹¹ They camped on the western bank of the Kalomo river no more than 4 miles north of the present Kalomo township.

CHAPTER XIV

¹ The camp was most probably near Bowwood, 16 miles north-east-north of Zimba and 13 miles west-south-west of Kalomo.

² Holub's party camped somewhere in the vicinity of Lily Pond, 2 miles north-east of Zimba.

³ Mujala village, 16 miles north of Livingstone, visited in 1855 by David Livingstone. See Schapera, I., (ed.), pp. 333–4.

⁴ The camp must have been somewhere near the present Sekute village, 20 miles north-west of Livingstone. From there the march proceeded through Bovu dambo.

CHAPTER XV

¹ Compare Coillard, F., pp. 245–6.

² Tom Fry. See Tabler, E. C. (ed.), 1963, pp. 89–90.

³ Momba is a recognised chief in the Southern Province of Zambia residing currently at Kabozu, 97 miles north of Livingstone.

⁴ Tawana (Batawana) are a branch of Tswana peoples together with Koba (Makuba) inhabiting Okavango swamps and the area of Lake Ngami in Botswana. Sarwa (Masarwa) bushmen living in this area are mostly subject to neighbouring Bantu tribes.

⁵ Elephant hunters employed by Westbeech. Tabler, E. C. (ed.), 1963, pp. 59, 62, 65.

⁶ The raid at Lulonga in 1888 was often interpreted as Lewanika's reprisal for the Ila attack on Holub's party, travelling with his consent.

⁷ See Tabler, E. C. (ed.), 1963, pp. 67–82.

⁸ August, April, Skraal, Jantje, Adonis, Jan Afrika's son Nicolas, Gert van der Bergh and his father, Henry Wall and John Weyers were elephant hunters employed by Westbeech. Tabler, E. C. (ed.), 1963, pp. 59–63, 65, 71, 72, 100.

⁹ The new Mulasiane of Sesheke was Kabuku, a son of the Mulena Mukwae. He was installed in August 1886. Mwanawina II (Wana-Wena) was the Lozi king preceding Lewanika.

¹⁰ See Introduction, p. xiv.

¹¹ Ratau and Tahalima were headmen of Sesheke.

¹² Richard Clarke, a trading partner of William C. Francis in Shoshong. Tabler, E. C. (ed.), 1960, p. 22.

¹³ D. Jeanmairet, a Swiss missionary who came with Coillard to Barotseland.

GLOSSARY

Adons *elephant hunter:* Adonis; note 8, ch. xv
Akuruba *chief:* unidentified
Albertsland: Albertsland; note 21, ch. II
Amare *village:* Siakabale; note 5, ch. IV
April *elephant hunter:* April; note 8, ch. xv
August *elephant hunter:* August; note 8, ch. xv

Bains *traveller:* Baines, T.; note 14, ch. I
Bakwena *tribe:* Kwena, a tribe of the Tswana group in Botswana
Balila *village:* unidentified
Bamala *Ila tribe:* Bamaala; note 3, ch. VII
Bamangwato *tribe:* Ngwato, a tribe of the Tswana group in Botswana
Bamaschi *tribe:* Mashi, a Bantu tribe in eastern Angola and south-western Zambia
Bangweolo *lake:* Lake Bangweulu
Batowana *tribe:* Tawana; note 4, ch. xv
Betschuana *tribe:* Tswana branch of the Sotho peoples in Botswana and South Africa
Blockley *trader:* Blockley, G.; note 4, ch. I
Bosengo *or* **Bosango** *area:* Busangu; note 2, ch. VIII
Buerva *village:* unidentified

Clark *trader:* Clarke, R.; note 12, ch. xv
Coillard *missionary:* Coillard, F.; note 8, ch. I

Damara *tribe:* Herero
Derefe *stream:* Derevu stream about 12 miles north-west of Livingstone
Diabora *village:* unidentified
Diluka *village:* unidentified; note 9, ch. VIII
Djesa *stream and village:* Chifusa; note 6, ch. XIII
Dongafa *stream:* unidentified; note 2, ch. IV

Franz-Josef Mountains: note 8, ch. x
Fry, T., *trader:* Fry, T.; note 2, ch. xv

Galulonga *village:* Lulonga; note 3, ch. x
Gaschuma *ridge:* Gazuma, between Panda-ma-Tenga and the Zambezi
Gazungula *village:* Kazungula; note 9, ch. I
Gorossiana *chief:* unidentified
Go-Tschoma *stream:* Choma
Gu-Njati *stream:* Sichifulo river

Impalera *island:* the land at the mouth of the Chobe between the Chobe and the Zambezi rivers
Inquisi *or* **Inguisi** *river:* See Makalaka-Inquisi and Maschupia-Inquisi

Jankuba *village:* unidentified
Jantje *elephant hunter:* Jantje; note 8, ch. xv
Jensen, Rev.: missionary in Zeerust

Kabanzi *village:* unidentified
Kabonda *stream:* Kabondo, tributary of Sinde, about 12 miles north of Livingstone
Kaboramanda *or* **Kaboramonda** *chief and village:* Kabulamwaanda; note 7, ch. vii and note 1, ch. viii
Kakalemba *chief and village:* Kalembwe village, now about 35 miles north-west of Livingstone
Ka-Kumamba *chief:* Nalubamba; note 3, ch. vii
Kalata *rapids:* Nkalata rapids on the Zambezi at Mambova
Kamakuni *stream:* unidentified
Kandatzowa *or* **Kandatzora** *valley:* Nanzhila valley
Kapani *stream:* unidentified; note 2, ch. iv
Karanda *or* **Ki-Randa** *village:* Katanda; note 7, ch. iv
Karsibabatunja *stream:* note 3; ch. iv
Kasenga *or* **Kasenge** *chief and village:* Kasenga; note 1, ch. vii
Katubia *stream:* Katubiya stream north-west of Livingstone; note 20, ch. ii
Katumba *stream:* See Katubia
Katwe *village:* unidentified
Kaunga *village and chief:* Nakabanga (?); note 7, ch. xiii
Ketschwe *stream:* unidentified; modern spelling would be Kejwe
Khama *chief:* Khama; note 12, ch. i
Ki-Akuruba *village:* unidentified
Ki-Angamargua *stream:* probably Nankulu
Ki-a-Njama *village:* unidentified
Ki-Assa *village:* unidentified
Ki-Atschika *village:* unidentified
Ki-Atschowa *stream:* unidentified; modern spelling would be probably Shachoba
Ki-Bondo *village:* unidentified
Ki-Bukura *stream:* unidentified western tributary of Muṅyeke
Ki-Gomatje *river:* unidentified
Ki-Indabile *villages:* note 1, ch. iii
Ki-Kabura *village:* unidentified
Ki-Kambo *village:* unidentified
Kikinde *stream:* Sinde
Ki-Mona *pool:* unidentified pool in Bovu stream
Ki-Monjeke *or* **Ki-Monjeko** *stream:* Munyeke river; note 3, ch. v
Ki-Namadschoroschula *chief:* Namaanda Sholoshula; note 6, ch. vii
Ki-N'onga *stream:* Ngonga stream
Ki-Randa *village:* Katanda; note 7, ch. iv
Ki-Rungunja *stream:* Lungunya; note 3, ch. v
Ki-Shindu *village:* Shindu, note 5, ch. iii
Ki-Sinde *stream:* Sinde
Ki-Sombo *range:* probably Bambanzi or Mulundika hills; note 4, ch. v
Ki-Vuata *stream:* unidentified

Kobo *village:* unidentified; one of the present tsetse fly barriers in this area is called Chubo
Kosara hills: Mulundika Hills; note 2, ch. XIII
Kosora *village:* unidentified

La-Bengula *chief:* Lobengula; note 6, ch. II
Lebosche: Lubosi; note 4, ch. VIII
Leschumo *valley:* Lesuma; note 5, ch. I
Linokana: Linokana, locality near Zeerust in South Africa
Liomba *chief:* Liomba, Lewanika's induna; note 21, ch. I
Lo-Bengula *chief:* Lobengula; note 6, ch. II
Lo-Lente *stream:* unidentified; note 3, ch. IV
Lorenz *trader:* unidentified
Luanika *chief:* Lewanika; note 20, ch. I
Luenge *river:* Kafue river; note 4, ch. III
Lu-Rungu *stream:* Lunungu, northern tributary of Ngwezi
Luschuane: Leswane; note 2, ch. II
Lytia: Litia; note 17, ch. I

Mabunda *tribe:* Mbunda of the Western Province of Zambia
MacDonald *trader:* MacDonald, J.; note 24, ch. I
Madenassana *tribe:* Galikwe bushmen of the northern Botswana and Western Province of Zambia
Madschila *stream:* Machili; note 6, ch. IV
Mahala *village and chief:* unidentified
Makalaka *tribe:* Kalanga tribe of the Shona group in Rhodesia
Makalaka-Inquisi *river:* Kalomo river, tributary of Zambezi
Makuba *tribe:* Koba; note 4, ch. XV
Makuluani *palm forest:* note 8, ch. VII
Makumba *chief:* Makumba; note 23, ch. I
Makumba *rapids:* Nkalata rapids on the Zambezi at Mambova
Mala *village:* unidentified
Mambari: note 9, ch. IV
Mambowa *or* **Mamboa** *village:* Mambova; note 7, ch. I
Mangete *tribe:* Nyeti of the Western Province of Zambia
Mangwato *chief:* unidentified
Manjanganga *stream:* unidentified
Mankoja *or* **Mankoya** *or* **Mankoë** *tribe:* Nkoya of the Western Province of Zambia
Manscha *stream:* unidentified; note 2, ch. IV
Marancian: Mulasiane; note 1, ch. II
Marico *river:* Marico, tributary of Limpopo
Marutse *tribe:* Lozi of the Western Province of Zambia
Massangu *chief:* Masaka; note 2, ch. X
Masarwa *tribe:* Sarwa Bushmen; note 4, ch. XV
Maschukulumbe *tribe:* Ila of the Southern Province of Zambia
Maschupia *tribe:* Subiya of southern Zambia
Maschupia-Inquisi *river:* Ngwezi river, tributary of Zambezi
Masosa *village:* unidentified
Matabele *tribe:* Ndebele of Rhodesia

Matakala *chief:* Mudukula; note 7, ch. II
Matetse *river:* Matetsi, tributary of Zambezi
Matoka *tribe:* Toka or Tonga of the Southern Province of Zambia
Matotele *tribe:* Totela of the Southern Province of Zambia
Matschila *river:* Machili; note 6, ch. IV
Matso *stream:* unidentified
M'beza *village and chief:* Mbeza; note 3, ch. VII
Moëba *chief and village:* Mwebo; note 1, ch. V
Mo-Goma *village:* Kooma, note 17, ch. II
Mo-Kalubanda *village:* See Mo-Monquembo
Mo-Kanda *village and chief:* Siamakanda; note 15, ch. II
Moka-Ruange *pool:* Mukaluenje; note 5, ch. VII
Mokau *stream:* note 3, ch. IV
Moko-mo-Prosi *or* **Moko-mo-Rosi** *stream:* unidentified
Mo-Kongo *stream:* unidentified
Mokuni *or* **Mokuri** *chief:* unidentified; *not* chief Mukuni
Mo-Kuruani *stream:* unidentified; note 2, ch. IV
Mo-Longa *village:* Katanda; note 7, ch. IV
Momba *chief:* Momba; note 3, ch. XV
Mo-Monquembo *or* **Mo-Monguembo** *village:* Siankwembo; note 11, ch. IV
Monjeko *river:* Munyeke river
Monkoja *tribe:* Nkoya of the Western Province of Zambia
Mo-Panza *chief:* Mapanza; note 13, ch. IV
Mopiti *chief:* unidentified
Mo-Romenonghe *stream:* unidentified
Morube *stream:* unidentified
Mo-Rukumi *village:* Lukuni; note 19, ch. II
Mo-Schabati *stream:* note 3, ch. IV
Mo-Sinkobo *village:* Cinkobo; note 16, ch. II
Mossamedes: Moçâmedes in Angola
Motande *village:* probably Mandondo
Motokoro *village:* Makotolo; note 4, ch. XII
Mo-Tschara *village:* Mujala; note 3, ch. XIV
Mudschila *river:* Machili; note 6, ch. IV
Muembwa *stream:* Mwemba; note 5, ch. IV
Mukuluani *palm forest:* See Makuluani
Muschongo *stream:* unidentified
Musosa *village:* unidentified

Namasumbi *stream:* Namazumbi, tributary of Ngwezi
Namatere *stream:* Nakamulwa
Nambwe Falls: Ngambwe rapids on the Zambezi 14 miles upstream from Katima Mulilo
Nampe *rapids:* Nampene rapids on the Zambezi at Katambora 31 miles west of Livingstone
Namponga *hills:* Bankombwe hill; note 1, ch. IV
Nampongo *stream:* Nampongo; note 2, ch. IV
Naviëti *river:* Malombwe river; flows in the northern direction 4 miles east of

Ndundumwense gate (southern entrance to the Kafue National Park) and 59 miles west of Choma

N'game *stream:* Ngami

Niklas *elephant hunter:* Klaas (Nicolas) Afrika; note 8, ch. xv

Nikoba *village:* unidentified; note 9, ch. VIII

Njama *waterhole:* unidentified; note 1, ch. IV

Njambo *chief:* Nyambo; note 1, ch. IX

Njunjani *stream:* note 3, ch. IV

N'Onga *river:* Ngonga, tributary of Munyeke

Panda-ma-Tenka: Panda-ma-Tenga in northern Botswana

Pasila *village:* unidentified

Rattau *chief:* Ratau; note 11, ch. xv

Sakasipa *chief:* Siyakasipa; note 16, ch. II

Samokakatwe *chief:* unidentified

Sanza *rapids:* unidentified

Schambalaka *village:* unidentified

Schescheke: Seskeke

Schindu *chief:* Shindu; note 5, ch. III

Schoschong: Shoshong in Botswana

Sebelebel *chief:* unidentified

Selouts *hunter and traveller:* Selous, F.; note 15, ch. I

Sepopo *chief:* Sipopa; note 3, ch. II

Seruera *village:* Siluela; note 18, ch. II

Siambamba *chief:* Shambamba; note 3, ch. VIII

Sianquimbi *valley:* Idiamala (Kasangu); note 14, ch. II

Siasonga *chief:* Shezongo; note 14, ch. IV

Siatschongwa *chief:* unidentified

Sietsetema *chief:* Siachitema; note 14, ch. II

Siketa *village:* note 3, ch. XIII

Sikiwinda *village:* unidentified

Silamba *stream:* note 13, ch. II

Simutili *chief:* Simukale, headman under Siyakasipa, now under Musokotwane

Si-Namandschoroschula *chief:* Namaanda Sholoshula; note 6, ch. VII

Sinde *stream:* Sinde, tributary of the Zambezi

Sinjandu *ferryman:* Sing'andu; note 9, ch. II

Sinjika *stream:* Nasiakonga (?); note 2, ch. IV

Sipanga *chief:* unidentified

Situba: Makumba's wife; See Makumba

Skral *elephant hunter:* Skraal; note 8, ch. xv

Talima *chief:* Tahalima; note 11, ch. xv

Thomas *hunter:* Thomas, D.; note 10, ch. XIV

Tschambiqua *village:* unidentified

Tschanci *chief:* unidentified

Tschi-Akuruba *village:* unidentified

Tschinganja *chief:* unidentified; modern spelling would be probably Chinganya
Tschi-N'Kosia *stream:* Chinkozia; note 2, ch. IV
Tschi-Rufumpe *stream:* unidentified
Tschobe *river:* Chobe, tributary of the Zambezi

Usanga *stream:* note 3, ch. IV
Uschumata-Zumbo *chief:* Zumbwa Shimata; note 7, ch. X

Van der Berg *elephant hunter:* Van der Bergh, G.; note 8, ch. XV

Wa *trader:* Watson, F.; note 22, ch. I
Waga-Funa *chief:* Akufuna Tatila; note 1, ch. VI
Wakumba: sister of Makumba; see Makumba
Walfish Bay: Walvis Bay in South West Africa
Wall, Henry *elephant hunter:* Wall, H.; note 8, ch. XV
Wanke *chief:* Wankie; note 3, ch. I
Westbech *trader:* Westbeech, G.; note 2, ch. I
Weyer *trader:* Weyers, J.; note 16, ch. I
Wuamba *stream:* Mabwa; note 5, ch. IV
Wuenga *Ila tribe:* Bweengwa area; note 6, ch. VII

Zulu *tribe:* Zulu of South Africa
Zumbo *chief:* Zumbwa; note 7, ch. X

BIBLIOGRAPHY

ARNOT, F. S. (1883), *From Natal to the Upper Zambezi*. Glasgow: The Publishing Office.

CLAY, G. (1968), *Your Friend, Lewanika. The Life and Times of Lubosi Lewanika, Litunga of Barotseland, 1842 to 1916*. Robins Series 7. London: Chatto & Windus.

COILLARD, F. (1971), *On the Threshold of Central Africa. A Record of Twenty Years' Pioneering Among the Barotse of the Upper Zambezi*, 3rd ed. London: Frank Cass & Co., Ltd.

COLSON, E. (1962), *The Plateau Tonga of Northern Rhodesia. Social and Religious Studies*. Manchester University Press.

DEPELCHIN, H. and CROONENBERGHS, C. (1883), *Trois ans dans l'Afrique australe, au pays d'Umzime; chez les Batongas; la Vallée des Barotses. Débuts de la Mission du Zambèze; Lettres des Pères H. Depelchin et Ch. Croonenberghs, S. J., 1879, 1880, 1881*. Brussels: Pollemius, Ceuterick & Lefebure.

GLUCKMAN, M. (1955), *The Judicial Process among the Barotse of Northern Rhodesia*. Manchester University Press.

HOLUB, E. (1879), *Eine Culturskizze des Marutse-Mambunda-Reiches in Süd-Central-Afrika*. Wien: Gerold & Comp.

HOLUB, E. (1881), *Seven Years in South Africa. Travels, Researches, and Hunting Adventures, Between the Diamond-Fields and the Zambezi (1872–9)*. London: Sampson Low, Marston, Searle & Rivington.

HOLUB, E. (1890), *Von der Capstadt ins Land der Maschukulumbe. Reisen im südlichen Afrika in den Jahren 1883–7*, vol. I. Wien: Alfred Hölder.

MACKINTOSH, C. W. (1907), *Coillard of the Zambezi*. London: T. Fisher Unwin.

RAWSON, O. C. (1961), 'Cattle buying on the Kafue, 1903', *The Northern Rhodesia Journal*, vol. IV, 536–45.

SCHAPERA, I. (ed.) (1963), *Livingstone's African Journal, 1853–6*. London: Chatto & Windus.

SCHULZ, A. and HAMMAR, A. (1897), *The New Africa*. London: William Heinemann.

SELOUS, F. C. (1893), *Travel and Adventure in South-East Africa*. London: Rowland Ward.

SMITH, E. W. and DALE, A. M. (1920), *The Ila-speaking Peoples of Northern Rhodesia*. London: Macmillan & Co.

TABLER, E. C. (ed.) (1960), *Zambezia and Matabeleland in the Seventies. The Narrative of Frederick Hugh Barber (1875 and 1877–8) and the Journal of Richard Frewen (1877–8)*. Robins Series I. London: Chatto & Windus.

TABLER, E. C. (ed.) (1963), *The Trade and Travel in Early Barotseland. The Diaries of George Westbeech, 1885–8, and Captain Norman MacLeod, 1875–6*. Robins Series 2. London: Chatto & Windus.

WORTHINGTON, F. (1902), 'Note on the Mampukushu'. MS in the Livingstone Museum.

INDEX